# Marcia's Life Application
# BIBLE

## A Living Translation

By

*Marcia Zubradt-Cheevers*

Shapato Publishing, LLC
Everly, Iowa

Published by: Shapato Publishing, LLC
PO Box 476
Everly, Iowa 51338

ISBN 13: 978-0615597911
ISBN 10: 0615597912
Library of Congress Control Number: 2012934122

Copyright © 2012 Marcia Zubradt-Cheevers

All rights reserved. No part of this book may be reproduced or transmitted in any form or by any means, electronic or mechanical, including photocopying, recording, or by an information storage and retrieval system, without permission in writing from the publisher.

Source material: *New Living Translation Bible* (NLT)

First Printing April 2012

This is dedicated to my Lord and Savior Jesus Christ, for going to the cross for me, for my sins. This book is all for HIS GLORY!

*So the Word became human and made His home among us. He was full of unfailing love and faithfulness. And we have seen His glory, the glory of the Father's one and only Son.*

John 1:14

**ACKNOWLEDGEMENTS:**

Thank you, Lord, for your Living Breathing Word; without it there would be no *Marcia's Life Application Bible*!

*All Scripture is inspired by God and is useful to teach us what is true and to make us realize what is wrong in our lives. It corrects us when we are wrong and teaches us to do what is right. God uses it to prepare and equip His people to do every good work.* 2 Timothy 3:16-17.

Thank you to my husband Digger, who always tells me, "You can do anything!"

Next, to my dear friend Vennetta, who told me, "Before you speak to the masses, you will write a book!"

Last, to all my Facebook Friends (you know who you are) who have encouraged me for more than a year to write a book!

## INTRODUCTION

The Lord's ways are mysterious and writing a book was not something I felt qualified to do! I am a perfect example that He alone is in control, for the Lord does not call the qualified—He qualifies the called!

I was born again September 20th, 1992, and it was not long after that, at a Christmas service, my Pastor shared of the Mary Miracle that some of us would be birthing, a Miracle—yes, something we could not do on our own. In fact He said some would birth twins. At the altar that day, the Lord said I would do mission work in Mexico, and I have, but He also said I would write.

My reaction was one of disbelief. Not me, Lord, I can't spell! Only He knew that I would someday have a computer with spell check!

I knew at age 42 if I was going to grow spiritually, I needed to read God's word, and I soon found if I was going to comprehend what I was reading I must take what was going on in my life and apply God's word to it! The word became my owner's manual on how to live my life, and it is so exciting for me to see the living, breathing word of God apply to me.

Falling short daily, but still applying.

My daily practice of apply God's word to my life became so much more while my husband was going through cancer treatment at the Mayo Clinic. I was doing a lot of sitting and waiting, with access to a computer and Internet. That was the start of my daily posts, my status, in less than 500 characters, on Facebook!

It was August of 2010. I had no idea why the Lord would have me copy and then print the Facebook posts for the next year and a half, and unfortunately for Jean, my publisher, not in any particular order!

*1 Timothy 4:5—For we know it is made acceptable by the word of God & prayer.* My posts are the word of God, and what a relief, acceptable in any order!

My posts (short stories) are of what is going on in my life! They are stories that include my husband, Digger; my stepson, Kurt; his wife Sheli; and our grandchildren (who call me James)—Summer, 14; Xander, 9; and Audra, 6. I also write of my extended family, my sisters, Pam (Lou); Sue (Randy); my brother, Buddy (Teri). Along with my nieces, nephews, and many friends! My church family at DaySpring Assembly of God. Ministries, like Say Yes To A Dress, at the Spencer Dream Center; a women's retreat, VdC, that is a yearly blessing to me; and of my life long mission field as a hairdresser! Along with the J.O.Y. Seminars that I am so privileged to do!

So as the Lord directs, I post each day on Facebook of what is happening in my life, as applied to God's Word. What started as therapy became a God-directed ministry! One of which is now going from Internet to paperback!

I pray you will enjoy my book and will take a look at your own life as it is lined up to the living word of God!

I have heard it said many times that as Christians we may be the only Bible some may ever read . . . and I pray to be a Living Translation.

*Marcia Zubradt-Cheevers*

# TABLE OF CONTENTS

| | |
|---|---|
| ACKNOWLEDGEMENTS | iv |
| INTRODUCTION | v |
| JANUARY | 1 |
| FEBRUARY | 13 |
| MARCH | 23 |
| APRIL | 35 |
| MAY | 49 |
| JUNE | 61 |
| JULY | 77 |
| AUGUST | 87 |
| SEPTEMBER | 99 |
| OCTOBER | 111 |
| NOVEMBER | 127 |
| THE TWELVE DAYS OF CHRISTMAS | 141 |
| DECEMBER | 145 |
| ABOUT THE AUTHOR | 167 |

# *Marcia's Life Application*
# BIBLE

*A Living Translation*

# January

*For everything there is a season, a time for every activity under heaven.* Ecclesiastes 3:1

A s a teenager, I never fit in, did my own thing, the wilder the better! Always looking for the next high!
*Psalm 119:9—How does a young person stay pure? By obeying your word!* So blessed to have spent this weekend with Godly women that are helping to guide & mold our next generation. These women are Leaders, through them, young people see that Christianity ROCKS, because they do! Go . . . Give 'em Jesus!

≈

Many women plan what their grandkids will call them nana, mema, grammie! My grandkids call me James, a name I got when Xander went through his Thomas the train phase, we all had train names mine stuck, James is Thomas/Xander's bff! *Proverbs 19:21—You can make many plans but the Lord's purpose will prevail!* Plans change, all for your glory, Lord & when the kids say . . . I Love you James, not planned but perfect!

≈

I only park in row 5 at WalMart, makes it easier to find my car. I have walked from one side of lot to the other to looking for my car that I parked! LOL! *Hebrews 11:1—What is Faith? The confident assurance that what we hope for is going to happen, evidence of things we cannot see.* My faith walk is much like finding my car! My confident assurance is found in His Word! My car & Jesus, my driver, are found in row 5!

≈

January 1st–I kick it in gear, I exercise every morning, but not this year. *1 Timothy 4:8—Physical exercise has some value, but spiritual exercise is much more important. Promises rewards in this life & next.* You see my mornings I have spent in His word as I prepared for the day & to speak at VdC/women's retreat. My reward blessed by my sisters in Christ & the scale/weight stayed the same! His promises Yes & Amen!!

≈

I remember my baptism, it was a day that forever changed my life . . . It was 1993 & I asked Digger to marry me after church before the Baptism service at Scharnberg Park & after living together for over 20+ years he said yes! To publicly *DELIGHT YOURSELF IN THE LORD, HE WILL GIVE YOU THE DESIRES OF YOUR HEART—Psalm 37:4.*

≈

Baptism yesterday, reminds me of mine! The Pastor said if there was sin in my life, get rid of it. I came home from church before the baptism and asked Digger to marry me? He said yes! That is when you know someone loves you, when you live with them for 20+ years and still say yes! Thank you Jesus for your life changing GRACE! *Jeremiah 29:11— God has a plan for my life!!* Yahoo!!

≈

Dig said yes & off to the printer to make wedding invitations! I found just what I wanted, it described just what I felt! I asked the owner of the shop if she knew who wrote this? Nope, she didn't! All I knew is it spoke to me . . . *Delight yourself in the Lord & He will give you the desires of your heart!* Much later, I started to study the Bible & found it, *Psalm 37:4!* You see, it was from His living word, wrote just for me, & alive in my life!

≈

Tuesday I was in a hurry, preoccupied, driving too fast for the conditions & at a corner, a truck! I am out of control, turn to the left so not to get hit & now stuck in a snow bank. *James 4:17—Remember it is a sin to know what to do & not do it.* Sometimes in life I am preoccupied take my eyes off Jesus & I get hung up, my wheels spin but I go nowhere. Thank you Lord for your Grace (like my neighbor that pulled me out). Amazing!

≈

Thursday, by the Lord's direction, I knew I was to stop to see my friend Marlys! *Proverbs 3:6—Seek His will in all you do, & He will direct you paths.* Thursday night I realized, it was Chuck, her son's birthday, he was killed in an accident 8 years ago. God sent me, to be Jesus with skin to her, much huggen & kissen. As much as I love Marlys, God loves her more! He comforts the brokenhearted! Used by Him . . . a privilege!

≈

1/29 - Day 1 of Jillian 30 day shred . . . here I go again. *I can do all things through Christ who is my strength—Philippians 4:13.* Yes, the best 20 minutes of physical exercise I have ever done! They sell the DVD @ WalMart anyone... join me???? Plus a night with family & just dance!! Thank you Jesus, a great day!!

≈

To whom this may concern . . . I thank you for the beautiful clothes that scream my name, & fit, that you gave me! But most of all thank you for your note, I cherish your words! You see, He sees what you do also. *Matthew 6:4—Give your gifts in secret & your Father who knows all secrets will reward you publicly.* As for my new dinosaur, it will fit perfectly in a Nativity?!?!

≈

1/30 - Day 2 of Jillian's 30 day Shred . . . yes on day 2 I do have abs muscles, only because I can feel them ouch. *I Will never leave you or forsake you—Hebrews 13:5.* In remodeling this temple, I will need His help, & I have His promise!

≈

Dear God, I pray for the cure of cancer. Amen. (93% WONT Copy and Paste this, will YOU?) Maybe easier to copy & paste than to pray. *James 5:16—Confess your sins to each other & pray that you may be healed!* Many people with cancer, OK Lord I copied and pasted now time to pray! Who are you praying for? Add my husband to stay cancer free we go to Mayo next week, pray for my friend Jody! Who are you praying for?

≈

This week we have celebrated birthdays of 2 young women that follow after Jesus, in all they do, both are beautiful inside & out! *1 Timothy 4:12—Don't let anyone think less of you because you are young. Be an example to all believers in the way you live, love, your faith & your purity!* Blessed by the wonderful young people, God has put in my life. A mentor is not always older than you! Happy Birthday Beth & Shaunna!

≈

I had placed an ad in today's Shopper for Say Yes To A Dress, with the help of my friend Tom at the Reporter. The paper came I could not find the ad, I looked once, twice, right away emailed Tom, can't find my ad where is it . . . ya, sooo embarrassed, found it. I am a work in progress! Dig will tell ya, I am always very short on patience! *1 Corinthians 13:4—Love is patient and kind.* Me not so much! So sorry Tom, the ad is great!!

≈

*The prayers of the righteous accomplish so much!—James 5:16.* So I am counting on all of you! My friend Jody is having her second round with chemo, and she needs our prayers. So please pray in agreement with me, for the Jesus we serve is still in the healing business!

≈

Today a reality check . . . ya, I realize I am replaceable! A dinosaur hairdresser! As I have aged so has my clientele, times change & so does the business. Not so with the body of Christ! *Romans 8:1—There is no condemnation for those who belong to Christ Jesus!* We are all important part of the Kingdom! You see, with Christ's help there is no end to the maturing process! We are all valuable, all respected, all matter!

≈

Today is the birthday of my friend Susan! In our lives many people cross our paths, but friends that are brought to you by Jesus, are eternal. Susan being in my life, has enriched it, brought to me much humor, & deepened it spiritually. Never ever take your friendships for granted! Tell them how you feel! *Matthew 18:20—Where 2 or 3 are gathered because they are mine, I am there!* Jesus & I cherish & celebrate you, Susan!

≈

So gooood to know that God's word is true!! *Acts 20:35—It is more blessed to give than to receive!* I was blessed! But I gotta believe the 10 girls that took home prom dresses yesterday were also. Hard for some to understand that this is a GIVE AWAY TO EVERYONE, all are deserving of the love of Jesus, & yesterday that love was through a dress, amazing!! So much fun doing it again next Saturday 1-3! I am still smiling!!!

≈

Fusion tonight! It is final week of the study . . . God speaks, 6:30 at DaySpring! When you make or receive a call on your cell phone you need all those little bars to get reception. Not so with God, bars/prison/sin are what sometimes keep you from hearing from God! *1 John 1:9—Confess our sins to Him, God is faithful and just to forgive.* Can you hear me now? God speaks!

≈

I watch *The Biggest Loser*, amazed in the transformation in a Temple in a few months, after years of abuse. Last week 1 team considered themselves the Davids against the Goliaths. I smile when a very worldly show acknowledges the Bible! *2 Timothy 3:16—All scripture inspired by God & is useful to teach us & make us realize what is wrong in our lives, & to do what's right!* Maybe a Mission statement for *Biggest Loser*??

≈

Blessed by our couples Bible study, 4 couples ages 40-60, handpicked by God to study His word & encourage each other. Many different ministries, bikes, prison, Pastor, worship, children, women's, intercessory, all touching lives in our own unique way! Going forward knowing we cover each other in prayer! *Matthew 7:12—Do unto other as you would have them do unto you!* We all Pray! Thanks, love you guys!

≈

1/31 - Day 3 of Jillian's 30 day Shred . . . my armpits hurt, who says everyone could use a good chest fly? Oh ya, that would be Jillian. *Isaiah 40:31—Those that wait on the Lord will find new strength, they will fly high on wings like eagles . . .* ! Am waiting on you Lord, my wings are sore!

≈

Just Dance . . . Audie's favorite & can she dance. Different than the rest of us she does ALL the moves, not just move the hand controller. *Joshua 22:5—Love the Lord your God, walk in ALL His ways, obey His commands . . . serve Him with ALL your heart.* That is how she plays Just Dance, the way we should serve the Lord, with Enthusiasm, she gives it her ALL! She is a dancen & still tellen papa "shake your booty!"

≈

Years ago, when we were at a Super Bowl party, Xander was first learning to walk! At half time with a big grin, he stood up took a few steps & down he went! Everyone in the room applauded, that is the kind of support every kid should get. *1 Thessalonians5:11—So encourage each other & build each other up* . . . An encourager will help you to take your first steps, be there to cheer you on & pick you up! Everyone needs an encourager . . . a good friend, your Pastor, your spouse? You don't have one? Then be one, you will be encouraged!

≈

Going through old pictures and found one taken in 1970, yes I did have BIG TEXAS HAIR just like all the other girls in Beauty School! To get it like that I would back comb & then measure it had to be at least 6 inches above my head that was the style! *Romans 12:2—Don't copy the behavior & customs of the world but let God transform you into a new person* . . . Praising God for my transformation in behavior & lifestyle, & my hair well when you have hair that high you are "Closer to God!"

≈

I jogged over it, so weird I had to go back to picked it up, it was a magnet. *James 4:8—Come close to God & God will come close to you!* Many times before I was saved I would feel that magnetic/pull of the Lord & I would run! Major crisis in my life, I would run to Him & then away from Him! I remember running out of a church in tears, hoping that no one would think I was one of those BORN AGAIN BELIEVERS, that I am now proud to say I am! Just like a magnet . . . I came close to Him & He came close to me! He's got allot of pull!

≈

Blessed to join a new Bible Study, we are studying, Henry Blackaby Experiencing God! Not my first time doing this study & I am sure it will not be my last! *1 Peter 1:23—Your new life will last forever because it comes from the eternal, LIVING WORD OF GOD!* You see each time I have done this study, I am at a different place in my life & yet the Word of God remains the same, always able to minister to me right where I am at. You see, the word is alive & eternal! I can see my Bible cover breath! It's exciting to . . . Experience God!

≈

Today is the Grand Opening of Say Yes To A Dress! Our God uses many different ways to share the love of Jesus with others. As I collected the dresses, I could see the blessing of giving on the face of each girl! *Matthew 10:42—If you give even a cup of cold water in my name you will surely be rewarded!* Shaunna, Tiffiny, & Ashley all donated & today will give away, not cold water, but a dress! His plan, that we all be blessed!

≈

Say Yes To A Dress is OPEN! *Colossians 3:14—The most important piece of clothing you must wear is love.* I tell ya this ministry has been so much fun, & what a privilege to experience the excitement of getting/giving a dress! 36 beautiful young women have Said Yes To A Dress, in doing so they put on LOVE, & it looks real good on each one of them!! Hope to see YOU today!!

≈

We had a real great Grand Opening last Saturday at the recently opened Spencer Dream Center, giving away dresses but have soooooooo many left, so come see us if you are looking for a Prom Dress! Every Saturday in January from 1:00 to 3:00 and 1st and 3rd Saturday in February and March!! This is a giveaway for everyone, Come be blessed & Say Yes To A DRESS! *Genesis 12:3—I will bless those who bless you.*

## FEBRUARY

*My heart has heard you say, "Come and talk with me," & my heart responds, "LORD, I am coming."* Psalm 27:8

**2**/1 - Day 4 of Jillian's 30 day Shred . . . so why do we work big muscles with little muscles, because Jill says so! *Proverbs 12:15—Fools think they need no advice but the wise listen to others.* Marcia is a hairdresser Jillian my personal trainer, just do it . . . enough said!

≈

I got stood up Tuesday for lunch! It was time for reflection, how many times does Jesus want to spend time with me & He waits, I get busy with the things of life, things that are overwhelming, He waits! *Matthew 11:28—Jesus said, Come to me all you who are weary & carry heavy burdens. I'll give you rest.* If you saw me yesterday at Sports Page, I was not eating alone, I left full & RESTED! Thank you Jesus!

≈

My prayer every day before I post on FB is that someone will be able to see "Jesus Through My Eyes." This daily post started as obedience and therapy as Dig went through treatment, but now has me constantly looking to see Jesus in all things, big and small, He's amazing! Everything that happens is not by coincidence, but by God-incidence! *1 Chronicles 28:9—If YOU seek God you WILL find Him!* I guarantee!

≈

I heard a sermon Tuesday night on what are you nourishing/feeding your soul? What are you feasting on, the life giving Word of God, or empty calories that you consumed from face book, TV, movies, newspapers, or magazines? *Jeremiah 15:16—Your words are what sustain me. Bring me great joy & delight* . . . I get it, too much junk food can make ya fat & spiritually starved!

≈

2/2 - Day 5 of Jillian Michaels 30 day Shred . . . I have heard it said that 60 is 'officially' the new 40, we don't get old till we hit 66! Have ya done a plank jack? 60 might just be 60 LOL!!! *Nehemiah 8:10—The JOY of the Lord is my strength!*

≈

2/3 - Day 6 of Jillian Michaels 30 day Shred . . . I am doing skaters, like speed skaters big explosive movements crossing over like the real deal! *Romans 12:3—Be honest in your estimate of yourselves* . . . I am sure this is really funny to watch & I am not even on skates! Gotta love the burn!

≈

My good friend Christy has been so fun to work with. I remember when she started, I was TOLD that we would NEVER get along, because I was to religious & she to wild. *Luke 6:36— You must be compassionate, just as your Father is compassionate.* Christy taught me about compassion, not wanting anyone to know all the good she does! She is opening her own salon, I will miss her! Lord Bless my BFF, Christy!!

≈

2/4 - Day 7 of Jillian Michaels 30 day Shred . . . it has been a week, & sometimes it has been very hard to stand up quickly but that's ok, I like to feel the burn. *Psalm 32:6—The Lord says "I will guide you along the best pathway for your life."* With that said . . . may I walk my talk, in all things, I can't ask the Lord to guide my footsteps if I'm not willing to move my feet! Week 2 . . . Jillian bring it on!

≈

We call it "Say Yes to A Dress" how cool to fill a need. *Matthew 7:12—Do unto others as you would have them do unto you!* Each week the girls that have Said Yes, come back & donate a dress. To share the love of Jesus is contagious. Are you looking for your mission field . . . The Spencer Dream Center could be just that for you, volunteering, contributions, prayer & the list goes on! I got involved & You can't out-give God!

≈

Dig & I had lunch at HyVee Friday, & got groceries. Not to lose the ticket for lunch I stuck it in pocket & last night I found it. *1 Timothy 1:19—Cling tightly to your faith in Christ and always keep your consciences clear.* Today I went back & paid it, the young girl looked at me with a you got to be kidden me look, she said this is really nice of you, actually up until that very moment I was a thief & now I cling to my faith, conscience clear!

≈

2/5 - Day 8 of Jillian Michaels 30 day Shred . . . how can a plié pose also be a sumo squat, that would be Jillian. I am sure sumo squat describes what I do. *Philippians 4:13—I can do all things through Christ who is my strength!* At this point in time she says your thighs should be burning . . . call the fire department!

≈

Our grandson Xander turned 8 Monday! I admit I really didn't like kids/babies, in fact I told Sheli I would scrub her kitchen floor before I would take care of a baby. *Ezekiel 36:26—I will give you a new heart with new & right desires.* I want to say thank you Jesus, for new desires or I would have missed so much! You see this Nana James, is blessed by Summer, Xander & Audra every day! Sorry Sheli, about the kitchen floor!

Saturday night we had a Seasoned Saints Valentine party! What an honor to be a part of the 55 & older group! *Ephesians 4:16—As each part does its own special work, it helps the other parts grow . . . healthy, growing, & full of love!* Thank you to all my mentors, for those who have prayed Jesus/Joy into my life. I'm blessed by excellent role models, & my prayer is that I may also enrich a life, just as they have & continue to do mine!

No one can witness to that one person the way you can, God has equipped you and only you in a certain way to do that. It is your life lessons that give you the compassion to look across the room and know what someone is feeling and help them go through it. Be sensitive to the Holy Spirit and touch a life today! Tomorrow someone might touch yours!! *Psalms 1:1—Obeying God always brings great JOY!*

≈

I love the previews before the movies, the coming attractions that peak your curiosity make you want to see the movie & then tell all your friends about it! *Mark 4:30—Jesus said, How can I describe the Kingdom of God? What story should I use to illustrate it?* Now that is a preview that excites me, a coming attraction that peaks my curiosity! Jesus a parable/story teller couldn't describe it & that makes me want to tell everyone about it . . . no mind can conceive what's in store for those of us who love Him!

≈

Today Jillian Michaels/my trainer LOL, offered an option, if, I have a knee problem. Philippians 4:6—*Don't worry about anything but pray about everything.* Praise God for options, to pray I don't have to be on my knees. Oh Lord bring me someone today that I may pray with, for healing, acceptance, or repentance . . . Worry is not of you, & prayer is not an option, pray about everything! As always, great talken to you Jesus!

≈

Happy Valentine's Day! You know someone really loves you when you live with them for 20+ years & they will still marry you! *1 Corinthians 13:4—Love is patient & kind* . . . Married to me is not always easy, I have the highest of highs & when I am low, well you get it! All relationships are hard, but with Jesus as the center of our life it works. You see Digger is patient & kind!

≈

We're getting old & we're doing it together! Yesterday Dig gave me a heart shaped box of chocolates & said Happy Birthday! LOL. I gave him a card, it said all I wanted to say plus it sang "You're Still the One" the writing inside of the card . . . to my beautiful wife, LOL. *Philippians 1:6—I am sure that God who began a good work with in you will continue until it is finished.* This scripture gives us hope! Jesus, You're Still the One!

≈

Time to start jogging again, so started on treadmill this week 5,10, & 15 minutes today, not to injure old joints. I told Dig let me know when 15 minutes were up. *Philippians 4:13—For I can do anything with the help of Christ who gives me all the strength I need.* Kidding I said don't leave me on it all day, 25 minutes later, ya he was checken bike parts on eBay . . . l can do all things! Maybe 30 minutes tomorrow, thank you Jesus!

≈

Pastors & Leaders Conference quote "If you want to be a bridge of hope, you have to let people walk over you." *1 Timothy 6:18—Give generously to those in need . . .* Ouch, spoke to me & not my reaction last Saturday. Ministry not always easy, but my only role is to share with a loving heart & that's all! I thank you Jesus for all I get that I don't deserve & your mercy & grace instead of what I do deserve!

≈

I love the game of golf, greatest game ever played! *John 8:12—Jesus says I am the Light of the world if you follow me you won't stumble through the darkness.* In my B.C. (Before Christ) life I stumbled allot, did everything at night. The temps are rising & I am so ready for the crack of the club & the clink of the cup! My life now, no stumbling in the dark! I'm liven in the LIGHT! In the sand, water, or on the green it's all good!

≈

Sunday was Xander's 1st wresting meet. We arrived he was crying, Kurt said he was messen around with some kids & hurt his back. Was he hurt or scared, he is only 7. *Philippians 4:6—*

*Don't worry about anything, pray about everything. Tell God what you need.* So we prayed, he knows the protection, & power of prayer! Ask Xander about his nana James, may he say . . . she prays! Yes a 2nd place medal around his neck!

There is snow on the ground, so, Digger should just grow his beard & we can call him Santa! *Luke 6:38—Give & you will receive!* Over the last few days Dig has given away 10 bikes & because of that he has received!!! He is smiling ear to ear blessed beyond belief!! You cannot out give GOD!!

# MARCH

*But even before I was born, God chose me & called me by His marvelous grace.* Galatians 1:15

3rd week Jillian Michaels 30 day Shred. If you want a 20 minute workout Jill says, do a 20 minute workout, YOU DONT PHONE IT IN! *James 2:17—It isn't enough just to have faith. Faith that doesn't show itself by good deeds is no faith at all—it is dead & useless.* In serving you Lord, may I NOT PHONE IT IN, may my faith walk confirm how awesome & amazing you are! 20-minute workout, no phone, building a temple!

≈

Dig & I are both hoarders, so we are in trouble. *Matthew 7:1—Don't store up treasures here on earth . . .* For that to be truth in my life, to keep everything or to hoard is not scriptural. We had a time in our life with very little & those times have made us who we are, some of it good & some not so good. It is time to acknowledge that my storehouse is in heaven. Bring me a dumpster!

≈

Do I look like the word police? Happened again, looking directly at me, a confession, if this is going to offend anyone . . . don't listen! *Romans 14:11—Every knee will bow and every tongue confess Jesus Christ is Lord.* It is all about what you confess! The tongue small but mighty & words much like toothpaste once out of the tube can't be put or taken back. Why care if I am offended, Jesus Christ is Lord!

≈

It is so heart breaking to watch what has happened in Japan! So, we all must do the most powerful thing we can PRAY!! *James 5:16—The earnest prayer of a righteous person has great POWER & wonderful results!* May our prayers like a tsunami cover & engulf them all in His healing, His comfort, His protection, & His peace!

≈

Our birthdays are coming up & we were checking expiration date on our driver's license, memories not so good. Teasing Xander, we asked him to remember 2012/me & 2013/papa. *John 3:36—& all those who BELIEVE in God's Son have eternal life!* We have eternal life! A license or memory not needed all we have to do is BELIEVE! & Xander, well he looked at me for a moment & then he asked for a post it note! LOL!

≈

My friend Jamie & I text back & forth during the *Biggest Loser*. What amazing weight loss these people have had this season! But as we know it is a daylong workout & probably no pizza delivery, LOL. *Matthew 11:28—Come to me all of you who are weary & carry heavy burdens, I will give you rest.* Yes, this would be God's ultimate WEIGHT LOSS PLAN, & also relieves stress, depression & discouragement! Come to Jesus!

≈

Friday not my best day, But Saturday I knew His mercies are new each morning! Ya, it is not all about me! *Matthew 5:6— Blessed are they that hunger & thirst for righteousness, for they shall be filled!* Great devotions, love His word, cooked for Digger & gave away prom dresses, a total of 50 given away so far.

Hungry, thirsty, no I'm filled! Righteous, only in His eyes . . . Jesus Satisfies!

≈

Today 1 of my birthdays, I have lived 2 lives! 1st wild & of the world & now, the life I live for Jesus. *2 Corinthians 5:17—Those who become Christians become NEW persons. Not the same anymore, old life gone a new one has begun.* In 1992 I was born again at age 42,I am now a child of God, a New Creation! PLEASE send me a Bday gift, & click LIKE on this if you know Jesus as YOUR Savior! Greatest Gift ever given!

≈

66 people clicked LIKE to confess Jesus as their Savior on my Bday post yesterday. 6 of them were not even officially friends of mine on FB!! *John 14:2—Jesus said "There are many rooms in my Father's home & I am going to prepare a place for you!"* These 66 people are spending eternity with me, in heaven . . . where reservations ARE required! You can only get to the Father through the SON!

≈

I received a gift box recently, in it beautiful clothes that screamed my name! *1 Corinthians 9:11—When we take your gifts to those who need them, they will break out in thanksgiving to God.* I want to thank God again for you, WHO EVER YOU ARE, for the wonderful gift & your kind words! Blessed by the love of Jesus through you & yesterday I found shoes ON SALE that match the gold jacket!! God-incidence . . . YES!

≈

Spencer Dream Center is a-buzz today, so much going on. This is our last scheduled day to be open for Say Yes To A Dress (1:00-3:00) to GIVE away prom dresses, we have many more to give/call me! *Psalm 60:12—With God's help we will do mighty things.* So is giving of a prom dress a mighty thing, if you need one it is, & as of now over 50 dresses were needed! Thank you God, for your help! I've been Blessed by a Dress!

≈

Grandson Xander has had some problems at school, basically a good & very smart boy, but recently struggling. He now calls me each night at 8:00 so we can pray . . . our prayer is for Jesus to sit beside him every day at school! He says that is why he is now having good days. *Philippians 4:6—Pray about everything.* Xander doesn't have orange hair LOL! But like me, He knows the power of prayer, & we pray about everything!

≈

My brother Buddy, went to the Dr. last week, because he was dizzy, sick to stomach, no balance. Diagnosed with inner ear problem, Dr. prescribed medication. *John 10:14—I am the good shepherd, I know my sheep & they know me!* We must listen with our inner ear to hear His voice, when we don't . . . ya, dizzy, sick to stomach, no balance! Medication a big dose of Jesus! To know Jesus, is to know balance!

≈

I love the family of God & last night we attended a benefit fund raiser for the Spencer Dream Center. We had great food, fellowship, & received information on what ministry is happening & what is planned for the future. *Joshua 24:15—But as for me & my family we will serve the LORD.* The choice is always ours, do I volunteer, donate time, talent, money! Just wanted to thank God's/my family, together we will serve the LORD!

≈

I love the sisterhood! Just spent the last 2 days with the women of DaySpring, eating, shopping, laughing, crying, talking! But most important we spent time in EXTRAVAGANT WORSHIP as we attended Embrace our Iowa women's conference! *James 1:18—In His goodness He chose to make us His own children* . . . We are united as sisters, all worshiping Our Father! I am so blessed by all of YOU!!!

≈

We got new phones, I had not set an alarm & yet there was a clock icon on! Dig doing a benefit for Dream Team, had to be up 4:00 a.m. so to bed at 10:30. *Proverbs 15:28—The Godly think before speaking* . . . 12:01 a.m. my phone rang & I tried to answer & tried to answer! It was the alarm, a calendar reminder of the benefit. Half asleep couldn't think, Hello hello! LOL! Oh Lord find me faithful & may I think before I speak!

≈

Yesterday I was about done with my 2 mile jog when I saw 2 pennies on the street. I picked them up! *1 Peter 1:8—Though you do not see Him you trust Him!* So . . . "In God we Trust" It says so in the word & on the penny! To really know Jesus personally is to trust & obey! Yup . . . that's my 2 cents worth for today!

≈

A week from today What's Stealing your JOY will be over! I love sharing what God has given me! He has given me a boldness in my faith & a desire in my heart to share what He has for us all, a inward JOY that can't be stolen. *1 Timothy 4:16—Stay true to what is right & God will save you & those who hear you!* Praying for all of you that plan to attend, come expecting He has something special just for you!

≈

Digger loves to ride & fix bikes! We have a backyard full that he will fix & give away! *Corinthians 8:12—God wants you to give what you have, not what you don't have.* Digger rides Ragbrai with The Dream Team & so right now he has grown a beard, so when he camps, no need to shave, so he looks like Santa Claus! Just last week he gave away 5 bikes! It's so cool he does what Jesus would do & looks like Santa!

≈

For my 60th B-day Jody gave me golf balls. *Matthew 25:29— To those who use well what they are given, even more will be given, & they will have an abundance.* The gift freely given, but I don't know if I can play the golf balls? Bible says to use what you have been given & be blessed & I can hear Jody say that's stupid Marsh hit those golf balls, right down the ole gutter uuu! Jody, you will forever bless me . . . I love & miss you!

≈

Many jog/run with a partner, that was always difficult for me! My pace was either too fast to slow, my stride too long to short! *Jude 1:24—All glory to God, who is able to keep you from stumbling & who will bring you into His glorious presence . . . with great JOY!* I don't jog alone, Jesus, my partner, keeps me from stumbling & brings me great JOY! Our pace & stride perfect . . . I try to stay within His will, so not to get in His way!

≈

Exhausted yet exhilarated at the end of the J.O.Y. seminar! I was so blessed by the women as they listened intently to what I had to share. *Psalm 21:6—You have given them the JOY of being in your presence.* Thank you Jesus for we were filled with Joy overflowing to be in your presence. *Psalm 26:8—I love your sanctuary, Lord, the place where your glory shines.* Father, humbled to be used, I pray I brought you glory!

≈

I'm excited planning my families Thanksgiving vacation, we have rented the Lodge @ Basswood Resort, north of K.C. it sleeps 16! I love the anticipation! Part of the fun is the preparation as all the plans come together. *John 14:2—Jesus said . . . There are many rooms in my Father's home & I go to prepare a place for you.* This scripture always excites me, like the Basswood Lodge many rooms, all being prepared for you & me!

≈

Judy Taylor called, she just got home, & the doorbell rang! Jim got the door, they asked for Judy & gave her a beautiful bouquet of roses. The sun was glaring & she could not see who made the delivery! Judy went to the door & asked why me, they said because you are wonderful! *Psalm 84:11—The Lord will withhold no good thing from those who do what's right!* That's Judy! But she would love to know who sent them?

≈

My dear friend Jody, is courageously battling cancer & today is her benefit. *James 5:15—& a prayer offered in faith will heal the sick.* So today I would ask that you would not just reach deep into your pockets, but also pray for Jody, pray with faith that God will heal her, He is still in the healing business. The book of James also says the prayers of the righteous can accomplish much. Privileged to pray for Jody, with you!!

≈

The weather was yucky but we all came together to help our dear friend Jody. There were all the girls from the Luke as well as the SMGolf & all the Knights. *Matthew 7:12—Do for others as you would like them to do for you!* That pretty much says it all, you get what you give, & by the size of the crowd & all the bake goods to sell, Jody has touched many lives, she has touched mine. Dig & I Blessed to be included. So Keep Praying!

≈

Our paths crossed & I am so humbled that she would share from her heart with me. We found that our addictions were similar but we both know the words says, *Matthew 6:24—You can not serve two masters!* So, along with Jesus, we have joined forces. My TEST through my 59 years has equipped me, given me compassion, a ministry, a passion!! So hang on Girlfriend, this is the start of Our Great Adventure!

≈

My friend Vicki shared this quote . . . Live in a way that those who KNOW YOU, but don't KNOW GOD, will come to KNOW HIM, because they KNOW YOU! *1 Peter 2:12—Be careful how you live among your unbelieving neighbors . . . they will see your honorable behavior & they will believe!* Ya, that would be for me to walk my talk! In other words I am to WITNESS to my neighbor, using words only if NECESSARY!

≈

Thank you all for your encouraging comments about SYTAD piece on KCAU Channel 9! But I know what I saw! *Philippians 2:3—Don't be selfish, don't live to make a great impression on others. Be HUMBLE!* Let me tell ya to see yourself on TV as a bobble-head doll is very HUMBLING. I really don't think I could talk if I could not move my head. Who knew I was that animated? It just affirms, God can use anybody!!

≈

Spent last night with my VdC Sisters. *Matthew:18:20—Jesus said "For where two or three gathered together because they are mine, I am there among them!"* We did what the sisterhood does best, laugh, cry, eat, love & pray for each other. When friendships are based on Jesus there is something remarkable, yes supernatural, that happens when we get together. You see we were in His presence, we had SUPER CHURCH!!

≈

They call it Talk of The Town, it is a SMU cable show that interviewed me about Say Yes To A Dress! *Colossians 3:17—And whatever you do or say, let it be as a representative of Jesus.* Think about it, how cool would that be if the Talk of Spencer would be all about Jesus! Ya, just good news people helping people, young as well as old, food, clothing, all good things, that would be the Talk of the Town.

≈

Have you been outside today, if you haven't you need to go out & feel the warmth of the sun? *Romans 8:39—Nothing in all creation will ever be able to separate us from the love of God.* What an awesome reminder of how much He loves us for us to be able to feel the warmth of the SON!

≈

To renew my cosmetology license I HAD to attend an 8 hour class on Sunday, as styles & laws continue to change. *Philippians 3:12—I keep working toward that day when I will finally be all Jesus saved me for & wants me to be.* My spiritual journey is one that I also keep striving for the prize, learning just what He wants for & from me, all to bring Him Glory . . . It is just too bad all con ed classes are on Sundays!

≈

Had supper last night with our very good, forever friends Brenda & Allan. *Romans: 12—I'm eager to encourage you in your faith, but I also want to be encouraged by yours. In this way, each of us will be a blessing to the other.* Friends like this are priceless, as we shared stories of the Faithful God we served . . . we took turns breathing & talking! Thank you Lord for our Brothers and Sisters in Christ, they are priceless!!

≈

Yesterday I asked & got a great day of prayer. *Philippians 4:6—Worry about nothing pray about everything.* Digger & I in the morning prayed for the Miraculous in a situation in our family, & for our Fusion Group healing, protection, comfort. Prayed with Jody, healing & Dr. agree to her plan. Last but not least, prayer with my 96-year-old friend, V.! She prays in the King James version, O how I love Thee Lord!

# APRIL

*When he prayed again, the sky sent down rain & the earth began to yield its crops.* James 5:18

G*aiatians 5:24 says . . . Those who belong to Christ Jesus have nailed the passions & desires of their sinful nature to His Cross!* I am forever humbled to know my sin put Him there! Not just on Good Friday, but every day I try to do just that, nail my sinful desires to His cross! You see He loves me from one nail scarred hand to the other! When He was on the cross that day...I was on His mind! Oh how I love & thank you Jesus!

≈

"I was There!" The Easter Musical Drama at DaySpring, is an awesome portrayal of the life of Christ, through the eyes of a Roman guard. *Colossians 1:15—Christ the visible image of the invisible God!* What a reality to watch Jesus as He, laughed, ate, & just had fun with his buddies/disciples & then went to the cross for you & me. You won't want to miss it! You will want to say "I Was There!"

≈

Xander was the boy with the fishes in the Easter program, rehearsals got long when you just stand on stage and wait. Terry Klien and I just kept talking to him to keep him entertained. I said Xander, Terry sang the king for papa and my wedding. Xander looked and Terry and said you sang about Jesus? I said no, the king of Rock and Roll, oh Elvis he says. *Proverbs 22:6— Teach your children!* It's all about King Jesus!

≈

 Easter is my favorite Holiday! You see it is all about the Gift, The Greatest Gift ever given, it is all about Jesus, *John 3:16—For GOD so loved the world He GAVE His son, that whoever believes in Him will not perish but have everlasting life!* You see the stone was rolled away so we could see in, not for Him to get out! He did it all for us, He is our RISEN SAVIOR, don't leave Him on the cross, He is alive, & COMING BACKl

≈

 Xander's good friend Josh was in the Easter drama this year, & Xander was telling me, that Josh was a little hesitant about being involved! *Matthew 25:21—Well done my good & faithful servant!* Josh did great as a healed leaper, & when he came off the stage Xander was sitting right there giving Him the big thumbs up! Stepping out requires just that faith, knowing, it is what God can do through me! May He find me faithful!!

≈

Every year I ask Dig what if I have forgot how to swing a golf club, lot. What if I don't remember how? *Hebrews 11:1—Faith is the confidence that what we hope for will happen it gives us assurance about the things we cannot see.* Played yesterday, yes I do remember how, but I used muscles I have not used for a while! FAITH is like a muscle . . . you have to use it to strengthen & increase it! Tee Time Today 11:32

≈

 Dig & I played golf yesterday, he hits from the blue & I from the red, it's the female yardage advantage! Dig says the way I have been driving, I am going to have to move back to the white or he is moving up! *Galatians 3:28—There is no longer Jew or Gentile, slave or free, male or female, you are all Christians.*

Thank you Jesus, for at the foot of the cross no one has the advantage, we're all the same, no red, white, or blue!

≈

I was a greeter for the DaySpring Easter production, what a fun job! *Hebrews 11:1—Faith is the confidence that what we hope for will happen it gives us assurance about the things we cannot see.* Most everyone that came knew the Easter story, but they walked through the door excited, in anticipation to see the drama, ya, Faith! So today a greeter at DaySpring who knows maybe tomorrow WalMart! LOL!

≈

The Women's Tuesday morning golf league meet yesterday to prepare for the season to come. We come from many different walks & seasons of life! *Romans 15:7—So accept each other as God has accepted you, & He will be glorified.* We come together to do something we all love the game of golf & sure we will have some food & fellowship! I pray that it will bring Him Glory! Golf . . . Greatest game ever played!!

≈

My friend Vennetta is blind & very hard of hearing, so when you visit you have to get in her space! Today, I walked into her room & as usual she yells HELP! *Psalm 23—For you are with me!* I said it's me Marcia, I am here, you are not alone. She says "I am never alone!" I know because of her faith, Jesus is always there! But she said "I'm glad you came!" I am so blessed, She loves Jesus & me!

≈

I believe the telephone was invented for prayer, so I can pray with my grandkids before bed, with my girlfriend concerned about her son, my friend Jody while she goes through treatment. *Matthew 18:20—For where two or more are gathered together because they are mine, I am there among them.* The best part, I never have to worry if He CAN HEAR ME NOW!!! He is always there . . . He's among us!!

≈

I looked at my alarm clock & it was 4:49! Wow it was so quiet . . . the rattling of the windows & the sounds of a January blizzard on the last day in April had stopped! *Psalm 46:10—Be still, and know that I am God!* You see, whatever is going on in your life today a blizzard or just a good old windstorm . . . be still, He is God!! May you experience His peace today!!!

≈

Our neighbors have a new puppy, it barks! Why does it seem that I hear it & they don't? *Ephesians 4:2—Be humble and gentle. Be patient with each other making allowance for each other's faults because of your love.* Faults, I got em, annoying things that I do that drive others crazy, things that I don't always see, much like a barking puppy! Praising God today, for His love & the unconditional love of others!

≈

The dress beautiful brand new & had been altered to be a perfect fit for someone! This dress had been tried on by many the response . . . it's pretty, but not YES TO A DRESS, today I know why! *Colossians 3:14—Most important piece of clothes to wear is Love!* My VdC sister, Connie will wear this dress for her son's wedding, she put on love & she looks good on her! As usual, I'm blessed by a dress!

≈

I have been jogging outside for the last week, when weather permits, the wind makes it very difficult! *James 1:3—When your faith is tested, your endurance has a chance to grow.* Jogging will be easy the day the winds stop, as my endurance is better because of the wind gusts! So I thank you Jesus for the gusts that test my faith, to build up my endurance, as I am older now but still running against the wind!

≈

I am going to be doing my very first Women's J.O.Y. seminar next Saturday at the Light of the lakes church in Arnolds Park! The paper said to RSVP to Brenda! *Hebrews 11:1—What is faith? It is the confident assurance that what we hope for is going to happen.* The phone number listed in the paper 250 200 not even a phone number, let alone Brenda's. LOL! Ya, you just gotta have FAITH!

≈

I gave away a very cute black sequin dress yesterday, to one of my favorite young women, & her husband came along! His mother-in-law asked him to describe the dress, he said it had buttons all over it! *Samuel 6:7—People judge the outward appearance, but the Lord looks at the person's thoughts and intentions.* Buttons? No, very big palette sequins LOL! Thank you Lord, no matter our appearance, you check our hearts!

≈

For the last 3 days I have been out of coffee filters! I have went to the store 3 times just to get the filters & all 3 times purchase allot of other stuff but forgot the filters! *Nehemiah 8:10—The Joy of the Lord is my strength!* Getting old & forgetful takes strength & it is hilarious, plus I do it so well! Joyfully I went to the store today, hmmmm I can smell the coffee!

≈

I love how the Lord speaks through His word, circumstance, & His people! PK shared Sunday there is no need for a title only a testimony! *Romans 8:28—We know that God causes everything to work together for the good of those who love God & are called according to His purpose for them.* I step out on Saturday, in faith & confidence, my qualifications a testimony & to love & obey, all to bring Him Glory!

≈

We attended the surprise going away party for the Meier family Tuesday night. *John 15:5—I am the vine you are the branches. Those who remain in me & I in them, will produce much fruit.* What a blessing Pastor Scott, Kim & their family have been at DaySpring & the Spencer Dream Center, the proof much fruit!! God Bless them & their new church family! We will miss them!!

≈

What a privilege it is to have Shaunna lead worship on Saturday for J.O.Y. seminar? *Matthew 25:29—To those who use well what they are given, even more will be given, & they will have an abundance!* That is Shaunna, she uses what God has gifted her with so well, she could take you into the Lords presence singing . . . "row, row, row, your boat!" She has a special anointing in leading worship!! I can't wait!!

≈

Good Morning FB friends, what peace there is in knowing I have a God that goes before me! *Psalms 37:4-5—Take delight in the Lord & He will give you your heart's desires. Commit everything you do to the Lord. Trust Him he will help you!* I am delighted, humbled, blessed, & excited to speak for Him today!

May I trust & obey, have His thoughts, speak His words . . . & touch lives for Jesus, that's my heart's desire!

≈

Yesterday a great day, I stepped out in faith, armed with God's word & the love of Jesus, & JOY filled the room! *Nehemiah 8:10—The JOY of the Lord is my strength!* As I looked at the beautiful faces of the women in attendance, I drew strength from the Joy each of them shared as I saw Jesus on every face! I pray each were blessed because, I am! I'm ready to do it again there is JOY to be shared, who knew I could touch lives!

≈

Digger is 62 & retired & I'm 60 & semi-retired! *Philippians 1:6—I am certain that God, who began the good work within you, will continue His work until it is finally finished on the day when Christ Jesus returns!* There is no retirement age when you are working for the Lord, you are never too old! God still has work for all of US to do . . . we are so blessed by new ministry opportunities, all for His Glory!!

≈

I journal . . . do you? A year ago an oilrig exploded, I ran outside, played golf, & Dig rode bike! *Hebrews 13:8—Jesus Christ the same yesterday, today, forever!* So I write daily of our ever-changing lives, but no matter the circumstance, Jesus . . . He remains the same & He is still on the throne! Because HE lives I can face tomorrow & write of His JOY & Perfect Peace!!

≈

Today is my husband, Digger's Birthday! *1 Corinthians 13:4—Love is patient & kind!* Dig will tell you that over the years I have worn out his ears as he does not hear very well any more.

He says he forgets some of the things I tell him because no one can listen 24 hours a day, & no matter how hard I try to be, I am not funny! That said . . . Digger is patient & kind!!

≈

I am a multi-tasker, comes from 40+ years of being a hairdresser! I can text, talk, watch TV, & repeat to Digger what he can't hear! *Jeremiah 29:11—"I know the plans I have for you," says the Lord. "They are plans for good & not for disaster to give you a future & a hope."* That is allot of things that we are ALL promised, ALL at the same time! You see our Jesus is the Ultimate, Master, Multi-tasker!!!

≈

I lost one of my favorite orange & gold earrings many many months ago & I found it today!! Yahoo!! *Luke 15:24—He was lost but now he is found* . . . I was so excited to find this earring! I can't even imagine what our heavenly Father feels when the Lost are Foundl! His Grace Ya, Amazing! For I once was lost but now I'm found!!!

≈

I was gone for a couple days, so when I went to the nursing home to see Vennetta she was so glad to see me. We held hands & both fell asleep. *Hebrews 10:33—Let us hold tightly without wavering to the hope we affirm, for God can be trusted to keep His promise.* Every time I would try to pull my hand away she held on tighter . . . like her faith never wavering, knowing that Jesus is her hope & He keeps His promises!

≈

Papa, Xander, & I went to the *Diary of a Wimpy Kid* matinee! We were the only ones in the theater & even then according to OUR plan, we sat in the same row! LOL! *Romans— 8:38 . . . nothing can ever separate us from God's love.* OUR plan. If we get separated from each other in theater, we always know where to look. GOD'S plan . . . no separation!

≈

59 dresses have been given away from the Spencer Dream Center's "Say Yes To A Dress." Wednesday I gave a dress away that will be worn in Botswana, Africa! *Colossians 3:14—the most important piece of clothing you must wear is love!* As each girl puts on her dress, it was as if she was doing just that, putting on the Love of Jesus & now we have gone INTERNATIONAL! As always, Blessed by a Dress! Open today 1-3

≈

Birthright Benefit last night, the table settings were beautiful & dessert was the menu! We came together as the family of God, to Celebrate Life! *Matthew 25:23—Well done my good & faithful servant . . .* Whether you donate time, money, or are faithful in prayer, we took a stand for the unborn child! Every child has the right to be born . . . the gospel of life!! Well done Family, may He always find us faithful!!

≈

I am an old rocker, on weekends you would have found me in a pasture, on a fair ground, or auditorium, rocken out to what is now called Classic Rock! *Psalms 37:4—Delight yourself in the Lord & He will give you the desires of your heart!* I love my Savior & DaySpring, my church where I am free to run & I am free to dance, all the while delighting myself In Jesus, I am free to live for Him I am free, yes I'm free!!

≈

Sunday Night Live was awesome! Our youth performed what they will be doing at the Fine Arts Festival, this coming weekend! We have preachers, actors, composers, writers, singers, pianist & guitarist! *1 Corinthians 10:31—You must do all for the Glory of God!* Amazed, by the all the talent, in that room, I was moved to tears! SNL . . . Our God was glorified, the evidence all were COMPELLED by LOVE!

≈

Last Thursday not a good day for Xander at school & his dad said he had to go to bed earlier, instead of our 8:00 prayer time he called at 7:00 & I was at Peebles shopping. *Matthew 6:6— When you pray go to your closet, shut the door, & pray to your Father in secret.* You're right, I went into the dressing room & prayed! A lady was waiting & looked amused, as if I had been talking to myself! No matter, a closet is a closet, Amen!

≈

My exercise, I run but not fast! I love the runner's high & the way my old muscles feel when running & when it is over, it's kinda hard to explain! *Hebrews 12:1—Let us run with endurance the race that God has set before us.* My spiritual exercise, I am steadfast, running after the things of God, excited to what He has for me each day, exhilarated to what He does through me! His ways mysterious, ya it's kinda hard to explain!!

≈

My friend Jody is continuing her cancer treatment, & this week the Drs are changing it all, AGAIN! A very scary, emotional, & confusing time. *Hebrews 13:8—Jesus Christ is the same yesterday, today, & forever!* That is a promise we can stand on, Jesus OUR great physician is never changing!! Please continue to pray, that the Drs. have supernatural wisdom, & peace & healing for Jody! Love you Jody!!

≈

Today, is the last scheduled day for Say Yes To A Dress & 62 dresses have been given away! I thank you Kim, Ashley, & Tiffiny, for making this ministry a priority & a success, many young girls were blessed by each of YOU! *Philippians 2:3—Let nothing be done through selfish ambition or conceit, but in lowliness of mind let each esteem others better than herself . . .* Jesus sees what each of YOU do & He likes what He sees!

# *May*

*He gives the childless woman a family, making her a happy Mother.* Psalm 113:9

Yesterday beautiful, as I jogged the smell of lilacs & cut grass filled the air. The warmth of the sun made me lift my face to the heavenlies & smile. *Psalm 19:1—The heavens declare the glory of God!* Later 18 holes of golf with Digger, so I really got to enjoy the day! We must remember to worship the Creator not the creation! So I thank you Jesus, for the creation of this day, yes even for the sand!

≈

Yesterday I heard coffee is good for you! New test say a hardboiled egg is a daily requirement & cereal can make your heart healthy! But wait tomorrow this will all change! *1 Corinthians 10:31—Whatever you eat or drink or whatever you do, you must do all for the glory of God.* So I thank You Lord for your provision, even when eating the brown food group "DARK CHOCOLATE" a vegetable I think, it comes from a bean!!!

≈

Digger lent our Garmin to a friend so she won't get lost in Omaha. It tells you turn by turn how to get to your destination! *Romans 1:5—Through Christ, God has given us the privilege & authority to tell people everywhere what God has done for them so they will believe.* We had the privilege to share "God's Plan . . . Salvation," to be a GPS to the lost of the world, to tell, turn by turn how to get to The Eternal Destination!

≈

Yes it's May 22nd! *Mark 13:32—No one knows the day or hour, not even the angels in heaven, nor the Son, but only the Father.* When interviewed I heard Harold Camping compare himself to Edison saying he did not get the light bulb right the first time, either??!! Today & every day I praise God, He alone is in control, I am not swayed by the ideas of man! I know where I am going & my God knows the date & time!

≈

Audra Xander & I went to get ice cream, love having conversations with the two of them! *Proverbs 22:6—Teach your children to choose the right path* . . . I asked what they had learned in Kidmo this morning & when one of them spoke the other breathed & vice versa! Both excited about what they had learned from the Bible & what it meant in their lives at 5 & 8, wow! Thanks Pastor Dave & teachers for showing the right path!

≈

I can still see the face of a lady being interviewed, she quit her job, left home, all to get the word out about *May 21st! John 16:33—Jesus said, Here on earth you will have many trials & sorrows. But take heart, I have overcome the world.* So today please pray with me for her & the many like her, may she realize, Christ is still Christ, still on the throne, still her Savior & He will return, He promised!

≈

Praying for the people that were & are in the path of the deadly storms. *Psalm 147:3—He heals the broken hearted, binding up their wounds.* Faith is the only way you get through something like this, even in the midst of it all, Jesus is our hope, our peace, our comfort! We are to pray for our brothers & sisters in Christ, to lift up tired arms just as Aaron & Hur did for Moses! We are called to hold each other up . . . to pray!

≈

I really like shoes . . . sparkly, glittery, glow in the dark kind of shoes! *Romans 10:15—And how will anyone go & tell them without being sent? That is what the Scriptures mean when they say "How beautiful are the feet of those who bring good news."* My plan today & every day is to share the good news found in His word, applied to my life & my feet . . . beautiful yes a gift, thanks Suz Q, new sparkly sandals, to bring Good News!

≈

Scotty McCreery won American Idol this season, what a talent a God given gift of a voice. *Psalm 34:1-21—Will praise the Lord at all times I will constantly speak His praises, I will boast only in the Lord* . . . That is what Scotty did, he won & thanked the Lord, & when interviewed he would always acknowledge His faith, & God's faithfulness. Like David in this Psalm had God's Favor, I believe the same favor was there for Scotty!

≈

My friend Barb Van Wyk is a missionary in Africa, when she was here she told me about a girl named Neo (NEO means gift) that she carried a gift bag for a purse, so when Barb went back I sent a gold purse for Neo! *Colossians 1:8—He is the one who told us about the great love for others that the Holy Spirit has given you!* I do not know Neo personally, but I love her! We love because He first loved us . . . what a Neo/gift!

≈

All you Jesus Freaks, my run today ended with this song an OLDIE but GOODIE! When I was born again, that is what many thought, a JESUS FREAK & that's what I thought when someone got saved! *Romans 12:14—If people persecute you because you are a Christian, don't curse them, pray God will bless them.* Today if you don't identify with my life style, I pray God's richest blessings on you & your family! Yes I'm a freak!

≈

One of the beautiful faces of our future, Miss Kearsten! The picture that is painted of this generation is many times gloom & doom, not the young people the Lord has put in my life! *Jeremiah 29:11—For I know the plans I have for you, says the Lord, plans for good & not disaster to give you a future & a hope!* Praising God for young people that chase after HIM as we head into the future with Jesus, our hope!

≈

Yesterday was one of those very strange days, & we all have em! *Corinthians 10:31—Whatever you eat drink or do you must do all for the Glory of God!* I was tired I ate, frustrated I ate, alone I ate. So it comes down to this, I either read what I believe, or BELIEVE WHAT I READ. Bring Him Glory not so much! Today a new day, believing what I am reading!

≈

I journal, so I can tell you about the weather, my golf game, grandkids, & the miracles God has done in my life. *Hebrews 13:8—Jesus Christ is the same yesterday, today, forever.* Thanks PK! From yesterday's sermon . . . If you lose your memories of what God has done, you will forget what He can do. God incidences write them down never forget . . . I have courage to face tomorrow because of what God did yesterday!

≈

My friends Suz & Darla promised that if I don't show up for lunch on Wednesday, they will talk about me! *Ephesians 4:2—Be humble & gentle. Be patient with each other, making allowances for each other's faults because of your love.* This is unity in the Body of Christ! They love me unconditionally even with all my faults, so what could be said! LOL! El Parian Wednesday at noon . . . I wouldn't miss!

≈

I have noticed that the profiles of SINGLES on FB often change their relationship status! So today I have put that I am in a relationship . . . a relationship with Jesus Christ. *Luke 10:27— You must love the Lord your God with all your heart, soul, strength and mind & your neighbor as yourself.* Because of that relationship I have better relationships with friends/neighbors & my FB marriage status. It's secure!

≈

Tuesday I received this phone call . . . did I ever wonder about peace, did I ever think about perfect peace? *John 14:27— Jesus said I'm leaving you a gift, peace of mind & heart. The peace I give isn't like the peace the world gives. So don't be troubled or afraid.* My answer to the caller yes, I do understand perfect peace, it is not the absence of war, but the presence of God, & hey thanks for calling, so I could share with you!

≈

Early this morning, I was praying, my list is long, then I heard it the beautiful ringing of my wind chimes! *Acts 2:2— Suddenly there was a sound from heaven like the roaring of a mighty wind and it filled the house* . . . Today I pray for healing for Jody, for my friend Elizabeth, for my grandson, for direction in my life, & the list goes on an on an on. With every chime it was like He was saying I hear your prayers! He's in the wind!

≈

I love summer but spring not so much. It has to do with mud! *Isaiah 1:18—No matter how deep the stain of your sins I can remove it. I can make you as clean as freshly fallen snow.* I see mud like sin, I have slipped & even fell in it. But Jesus, went to the cross for me, when I accepted Him as Savior I experienced His mercy & grace ya, forgiveness for all the mud/sin that's in my life. My New Life . . . hello summer!

≈

Sunday morning in prayer at the altar during worship. Awesome to be in His presence, when a felt a hand on my shoulder & then a head on my other shoulder. *1 Timothy 4:12—Don't let anyone think less of you because you are young. Be an example to all believers in the way you live, love, your faith & your purity!* I was being prayed for 2 girls, 17 & 18 years old, an example to me & all believers! Humbled, loved, & blessed!

≈

It is so heart breaking to watch what has happened in Japan! So, we all must do the most powerful thing we can PRAY!! *James 5:16—The earnest prayer of a righteous person has great POWER & wonderful results!* May our prayers like a tsunami cover & engulf them all in His healing, His comfort, His protection, & His peace!

≈

Devotionals books, are to inspire with God's word & life application! *1 Corinthians 2:9—No eye has seen, no ear has heard, & no mind can imagine what God has prepared for those who love Him.* So today I encourage you don't read your devotional spend that time in devotion, tell Him how you feel! I have a great imagination, & yet the word says, I can't imagine what He has prepared for me & all I have to do is to love Him!

≈

*Psalm 143:10—Teach me to do your will for you are my God!* Lord I want to do YOUR will, not to get in YOUR way! I know that to have more of you, there must be less of me!

≈

We can become addicted to a long list of masters. Gossip, greed, food, all undesirable habits. Each day we should review, have I adopted a new master? Am I addicted to it? *2 Peter 2:19— For you are a slave to whatever controls you!* Are you in chains? Cry out to Jesus, the only master that leads to goodness and healing!

≈

I wonder some times, Lord what is your will for my life? *James 4:17—It is a sin to know what to do and not do it!* So, when in doubt, I pray Lord, use me till you use me up! I know He will show up at the perfect time to show me my next step, until then I worship and adore Him and share the love of Jesus with others. It EXCITES me, to let go and let God!!!

≈

Jesus came into my life, and changed me. I struggled with overeating! I was never REALLY HUNGRY, an emotional eater, that found comfort in food! Jesus Christ set me free! The Word my guide, whatever I go through or feel, He promises to comfort and sustain me. I fall short many times, but His saving grace has set me free, His sustaining grace that keeps me free. *Ezekiel 36:26—God will give us new desires.*

≈

Today I am going to run outside, my body needs physical exercise to stay fit, but more than that I need to stay spiritually well. *1 Timothy 4:8—Physical exercise has value but spiritual exercise is more important.* I must always be working towards being a better Christian, to be spiritually fit. Yahoo, I have Jesus as my Personal Trainer

≈

Prayer Changed my life! Prayer is not a blank check from God. Prayer, as Jesus explained, means that anything is possible with faith, because nothing is impossible for God! *Mark 11:22, 23—Have faith in God . . . all that is required is that you really believe and do not doubt in your heart!* And when I just don't know how . . . to pray I call on the name of Jesus, the name above all names, there is power in His name!

≈

Prayer changed my life! Prayer is definitely the proof of our faith, it is constant, and persistent, including confession, adoration, requests, as well as listening part, to be still and know that He is God! Prayer is often spontaneous, not enough to say I will pray for you, do it now! *Exodus 14—Prayer must be accompanied by a willingness to obey with our actions.* What are you praying for?

≈

Proms are over, as well as the reenactments of what can happen when drugs, alcohol, & speeding are involved! *John 5:14—we can be confident that He will listen to us whenever we ask Him for anything in line with His will!* A few years ago, Jamie called a terrible accident at high school ambulance &

police everywhere, so WE PRAYED & PRAYED! Found out much later, yes reenactment . . . Jamie & I, we call it preventive prayer!

≈

To build relationships, communication is required! Prayer changed my life! To be in constant communication with my Heavenly Father, builds a strong, loving relationship talking and listening! I want to be more like you Jesus!! *Mark 1:35—Jesus awoke and went out alone to pray!*

≈

42 years ago I graduated from Everly high school & I knew everything! Today, I have so much to learn, but this is God's promise to me . . . *Come here & listen to me! I will pour out my spirit of wisdom upon you & make you wise.—Proverbs 1:23.* Yup, 42 years later I am still learning, you see some wisdom comes with age, & life lessons, but Spiritual wisdom, comes only from the Lord!

≈

I was blessed to be invited to many graduations! It was like going from one family reunion to another, hugs, laughter, & gooood food! *Joshua 24:15—As for me & my family we will serve the Lord!* So what now . . . well, I (& I hope you will to) will continue to pray for the graduate, they are the future, they are my family, a family that serves the Lord!

≈

Thank you all for your prayers for the prayers of the righteous have accomplished much! A good report from the Dr. at Mayo. Health is a treasured gift from God. *Psalm 103:1-3—He forgives all our sins and HEALS all our diseases!* Thank you Jesus for still being in the healing business

≈

Because it was Memorial Day many tributes were posted on FB, honoring veterans past & present! *Romans 12:10—Love each other with genuine affection & take delight in honoring each other.* My prayer is that we don't honor the vet on designated days, but all days! Lifting them & their families up honoring & loving them for the sacrifice that they make for us, not just on Memorial Day but everyday!!

# JUNE

*Honor your father & mother. Love your neighbor as yourself.* Matthew 19:19

Thor sits by us at church & Digger & he had an immediate friendship, who is the kid Thor or Dig I don't know! Last night we went with Thor & his mom Kristie to the midnight showing of THOR! *Psalm 127:3—Children are a gift from the Lord!* It was 2:00 am when we got home, but so worth it! Thor the movie was good, Thor the kid a gift! Yes there will be a Thor 3 . . . for we saw Thor 2 & sat with Thor, he is the number 1!

≈

Friday it was my privilege & pleasure to take a meal to a young couple that just had a baby a week ago! *Ephesians 2:10— We are God's masterpiece. He has created us anew in Christ Jesus, so we can do the good things HE PLANNED for us long ago.* He is a God detail, all knowing, yes even down to the pizza I delivered! Success in life . . . we are called to be His Hand & Feet & I got to hold baby Annabelle!

≈

I'm part of a blended family . . . I am the STEP MOM! I have always said I knew how to marry because I got Kurt as a son! *2 Corinthians 3:5—It is not that we think we are qualified to do anything on our own. Our qualification comes from God.* So, my qualifications to be a mom, I love Kurt! You don't have to give birth to love em & he promises to bring me depends when I go to the home! LOL! Happy Mother's Day FB friends!!

≈

I saw my SHADOW as I jog/ran outside today! *Romans 6:12—God has given each of us abilities to do certain things well.* We are all made in His image, just like my SHADOW is a mirrored image of me & the abilities He has given me, may I use them well. As for my running not one of my God given abilities & my SHADOW confirms it! But with my God given abilities, I am equipped to finish the race!

≈

My mom did not have the easiest life, she was 37 when my dad died, & then raised her family alone! *Proverbs 31—A woman that fears the Lord will be greatly praised.* She & I alike & yet so different! Important things to my mom, not to me & vice versa, except for Jesus! Today I PRAISE & thank my mom this little lady that carried a big old family Bible almost as big as her, she understood the fear of the Lord!

≈

I received another beautiful gift on Saturday & I THINK I know who has been blessing me! *2 Corinthians 9:7—God loves a cheerful giver!* So you see she had to be cheerful, filled with the JOY of JESUS, the kind of joy that spills on to others! Being around her is time to be cherished! To know her is to love her & Jesus & I, we love HER & because she & I know Jesus as our Savior, our friendship is eternal!

≈

In my before Christ life . . . Friday the 13th you stay home, black cat back up, never walk under ladder! Yes I was superstitious! *Jeremiah 29:11—"I know the plans I have for you," says the Lord, "they are plans for good & not disaster, to give you a future & a hope."* There is no need to knock on wood, for you see I might not know what the future holds, but I know who holds my future! Thank you Jesus!!

≈

*Genesis 1:27 God created people in His own image* . . . The word IMAGE according to Webster . . . "is a sculptured likeness." I know that God is always working on me chiseling away at all the sin in my life, & sometimes like today, it hurts! So I strive be His masterpiece, that Jesus would be seen in me! So go ahead Lord there is allot to chip away! You see He is the POTTER & I'm clay!

≈

Xander's 1st. game was last night! He, Kurt, & Audie rode bikes to the ball park. X. crashed as they got there, nose first! *Philippians 4:131—can do everything with the help of Christ my strength.* Many times we crash, even nose first, but with Christ as our strength we can get up & keep on going! X. scraped up but played his game. Xander says, Thanks Pastor Kevin & Kim, for your help last night, you're the best!

≈

If you know me you know I can talk, I am a hairdresser! *Luke 19:40—If they kept quiet, the stones along the road would cry out.* I will not keep quiet for I have a story to tell about what Jesus has done & is doing in my life, I gotta praise Him! Girlfriend I hope you can join us . . . come expecting He has something just for YOU!

≈

During Praise & Worship Sunday I was in the midst of our Jesus seeking youth, standing with them my arms high & heart abandoned! WOW! *Romans 6:13—Give yourselves completely to God since you have been given new life. Use your whole body as a tool to do what is right for the Glory of God.* My arms were high, batwings flappen, my heart abandoned, surrendered to the one who gave it all! Thank you Jesus!

≈

Today is the women's golf tournament at the Muni course, it is called the "TRIPLE TREAT!" 6 holes you just play your own ball, 6 holes best ball, & 6 holes alternate shot. *Matthew 7:12—Do for others as you would like them to do for you.* Defiantly words to live by, even playing golf, my plan today, stay out of the sand, water, & trees, & pray my partners do the same for me! GOLF greatest game ever played!

≈

My dad died when I was 17, he was a great man, even tempered, & loved his family. They say that many times you marry a man just like your dad, that would be Digger even tempered loves his family, just like my dad! *Psalms 103:8—The Lord is merciful & gracious. He is slow to get angry & full of unfailing love.* Happy Father's Day to My dad (who I miss) & Digger for they are just like their Heavenly Father!

≈

God's gift of Jesus for my salvation is more than just for my ETERNAL LIFE, I was saved/born again to work for Him in THIS LIFE! *James 2:20—Fool! When will you ever learn that faith that does not result in good deeds, is useless.* Some might say how foolish to share your faith & God's word in a FB status every day, it's the good deed I'm called to do. Results. If only one reader is inspired by what I write, it is useful!

≈

Ok so I am not the typical grandma whatever that is? My grandkids call me James, that should tell ya something. Yesterday Xander & I were talking & I said that I wasn't very good at making anything . . . baking, sewing, crafts, grandma kinda fun stuff! Xander says but you are MY James & you make the best kind of love! *1 Corinthians 13:4—Love is patient & kind* . . . Thank you Jesus for supplying me the recipe!

≈

As I ran by the neighbor's house, the smell of cake baking floated out their kitchen window! *Romans 15:16—I bring you the Good News & offer up a fragrant sacrifice to God so that you might be pleasing to Him* . . . We are to be sweet sacrifice lifted up to my Father, to smell like cake, mmm that would be good, to share the Good News & please Him! Home from my run & neighbor girls offered up warm cupcakes, can you smell em?

≈

The filtering system for our little above ground pool moves the water around & around making the leaves, bugs, dirt, settle in the center. Even when you shut the filter off the crud is still there. It's like unconfessed sin! *1 John 1:9—If we confess our sins to Him He is faithful & just to forgive us and cleanse us* . . . so we vacuum the center of the pool removes the crud, now clean. Just like confession, we have to do it EVERYDAY!

≈

On mission trip to garbage dumps of Mexico, my Spanish is hand language. A mom wanted, by motioning, all of her child's hair clipper-cut off. It was matted to the head, could not get clipper through, the child cried, I cried, mom motioned off! off! Oh help me Lord, as I started to sing JESUS LOVES ME, the child fell asleep, I cut his hair! *John 15:5—I am the vine you the branch . . . without you Jesus, I can do nothing.*

≈

My friend V. is 96, blind, deaf, lives in nursing home! I knew that someday she might not know me. Well it happened, at first I was upset trying to get her to understand who I was, and then it hit me. I said, V., do you know who Jesus is? She said, He is my Lord and Savior! At that moment it did not matter if she knew me, only that she knows who holds her future! *John 3:16—Believing in Jesus brings eternal life.*

≈

My sister's Pastor talked about what identifies/defines us, how do people describe me? I have been the fat chick, a druggie, a hairdresser, a redhead, wears gold, James/nana, Digger's wife, and yes, religious. Not all bad descriptions, but my ideal, to be known as a follower of Christ! *2 Corinthians 3:18—As the Holy*

*Spirit works within us we become more like HIM.* What a promise!! May Jesus be seen in me!!

≈

Dig & I always pray for safety when on the road, yesterday left my sisters, a car came right into our lane, semi drifted over into our lane. Stopped for gas, car just started to steam, broken reservoir, took a few minutes as Dig fixed. Down the road 3 vehicles had crashed, not bad, but crashed. Coincidence that we had a little delay, I don't think so, God-incidence. *Psalm 91:11— Angels ordered to protect!*

≈

It is my privilege and responsibility to help my grandchildren know of God's faithfulness, not just in my words, but in my actions. Many times Xander has called for me to pray with Him! *Isaiah 39:19—Each generation can make known of God's faithfulness.* Praising God that my grandchildren will never know the old me, the B.C. (before Christ) me. I am a new creation!

≈

May my belief and my behaviors be consistent, always to bring you glory! *When people do not accept divine guidance they run wild. Whoever obeys God knows the Joy of Jesus—Proverbs 29:18.*

≈

What do I believe? How big is my God? Lord may my actions always be guided by my beliefs. *Hebrews 11:1—Faith the confident assurance that what I hope for is going to happen!* WOW!

≈

When good behavior speaks for itself . . . Don't interrupt! *Blessings come when I apply God's word— Luke 11:28.* Our God is Faithful!! May you find me faithful, Lord!

≈

To know that I am a part of the family of God brings peace and assurance, of what is to come, that is faith! *James 1:18—In His goodness He chose to make us His children!* Sooooooo blessed by my Brothers and Sisters in Christ, we are never alone, our family is HUGE!!!

≈

Xander is spending the night, we just got done with prayers and I was leaving the bedroom when he asked, James, will you sing me "Amazing Grace?" Wow, as I sang that sweet 7 year old boy to sleep, I was reminded of the Grace I received. Praise the Lord Xander will never know the old me!! *1 Corinthians 5:17—I am "a new creation!"* His Grace Amazing!!

≈

A mission field is where ever God has you! It wasn't until I went on the mission field that I understood that I did mission work every day at my job. How about YOU!! The missionary @ DaySpring this morning said, "You are either on the mission field or you are one!" Wow, that will make ya think! *Isaiah 6:8—Here I am Lord send/use me!*

≈

I pray, Lord break my heart for what breaks yours! Yesterday got a call while playing golf of a homeless person needing a place to stay. Broke my heart!! We need the Spencer Dream Center!! God's will/heart is that we love each other. Lord you know my heart! *1 Corinthians 14:1—Let love be the highest goal!*

≈

All I have to do is to love HIM! One of my favorite scriptures, *1 Corinthians 2:9—No eye has seen, no ear has heard, and no mind has imagined what God has prepared for those who love HIM!* I have a good imagination, so this really excites me to know that HE, the one that hung the stars, has a plan for my life!!! Oh how I love HIM!

≈

*Nehemiah 8:10—The Joy of the Lord is our Strength.* Plus all of you!! Digger has treatment today! So, we Celebrate the Healing Hand of Jesus, and the prayers of the righteous. Humbled by your love, concern, and prayers! You cannot out give God or His People! Please join us and give Praise and Thanksgiving to the one who still Heals!! Thank You Jesus!!

≈

*Nahum 1:7—The Lord is good. When trouble comes, He is a strong refuge!* When I need . . . medicine, a pharmacy, hair cut a beauty salon, gas the gas station. Comfort, Jesus! He knows my needs even before I come to Him, and He loves me back, different than macaroni n cheese or ice cream. Today Jesus is my Comfort!

≈

*Jesus Christ is the visible image of the invisible God . . . Colossians 1:15.* He alone is the ultimate role model in all of our lives! Oh Father may Jesus be seen in me today!

≈

*Matthew 5:8—God blesses those whose hearts are pure for, for they will see God.* When we have intimacy with God, in other words we learn to understand the very heart of Him, then all other relationships take on a new meaning. God created us for intimacy heart to heart, mind to mind, or soul to soul. He made us relational beings, thank you Jesus, so blessed by my husband, family and friends.

≈

There are no spectators, bench warmers or "gift impaired" in God's army!! We are all through the power of the Holy Spirit given gifts . . . it is our responsibility to use them!! In *Romans 12:15* it says *We are all part of His body, all gifts are important, we need each other!!!*

≈

We are to be open and bold for the gospel of our Lord and Savior, Jesus Christ. Not ashamed to put a Bible on your desk at work, not ashamed to pray before you eat, not ashamed of the One who died for us? We are not called to be in the Secret Service! *Luke 12:8—Acknowledge God on earth, He will acknowledge us in heaven!* A week from today Digger done with treatment!! Yahoo!

≈

We are never more like God than when we do our best to encouraging people! So today may we find a needy person & then enrich her, a lonely person & include her, a misunderstood person & affirm her! *James 4:10—Bow before Him and He will lift you up!* God is the Greatest encourager, because He alone knows your future! Wow!

≈

In every human heart there is a hunger for significance, we want our lives to count, to make a difference, worth something, but most carry feelings of insignificance. Others are more successful, more gifted, all of us have potential. It is not what we can do in this life, it is what God can do through us!!! *2 Corinthians 12:9—My power works best in you weakness . . .* Wow, so good to know!

≈

Obedience to God should not be motivated by fear but by love! To really know Him is to love Him and to love Him is to obey, that is FREEDOM (found in His word), blessing and JOY! *Hebrews 8:10—God will give you the desire to obey His Word!*

≈

*Proverbs 18:21—The tongue can bring life & death.* Speech is like toothpaste once it is out of the tube you cannot put it back. So if I am smart I will speak less and only with peace in my heart, and when I do speak I will try to keep my words warm and sweet because I may have to eat them later

≈

Through the power of the Holy Spirit God promises to be with us always! When we were born again He forgives and purifies us on the inside that He may reside in us. We are the temple. *1 Corinthians 10:31—Whatever I eat or drink or do, Father may it glorify YOU!* NO other Idols!

≈

Faith is like a muscle you have to use to see it grow! God can't move a parked car, we have to take that first step into whatever sea we need to cross, He will provide the dry land! *Psalm 23:6—Where ever we go God is there!*

≈

My dear friend Jody that has been battling cancer has had a very tough week, & yesterday she had a stroke. She was sent to Sioux City where Dr. will evaluate. *Philippians 4:6—Says don't worry about anything instead pray about everything!* It is really hard not to worry, I cherish her, as do many others. But I will do what the scriptures say . . . please please join me & PRAY FOR JODY!!!

≈

Jody is now in hospice, not how I saw this play out. 2 weeks ago I went out to play in a ladies golf tournament, I text her & said how much I was going to miss her that day, & next year, ya her & I would swing the club till our arms fall off. She texts back. I'm in! That was my hope! *Psalm 42:11—Why is my heart so sad? I will put my hope in God!* The only way you get through things like this? With Jesus, our only HOPE!

≈

Yesterday as I stood quietly in worship praying for my friend Jody, a young boy named Thor that was sitting in front of me reached out & grabbed my arm. He pulled me to him & asked are you ok? I said yes, & he said oh, with a look of compassion, I thought you were crying. *Psalm 34:18—The Lord comforts the broken hearted!* And yesterday the Lord used Thor to do that, as he could see my heart was breaking!

≈

*Psalm 33:4—For the word of the Lord holds true & we can trust everything He does.* When the Word of the Lord and the Lord of the Word become your authority, you are supernaturally empowered! Thank you Jesus, humbled by your Grace!

≈

*John 14:27—I am leaving you with a gift* . . . Jesus called the Holy Spirit the Comforter. So, whenever peace enters your heart in the midst of grief, or joy enters your heart in the midst of a trial, or you see evidence of His life in yours, you can be sure the Holy Spirit is flowing through your life. Thank you Jesus!

≈

My heart is broken my friend Jody died. I have cut her hair since she was a little girl! She was loved by many, a wonderful mom & my friend, that I can never replace, never! *John 11:35 Jesus wept.* I also weep! When Jody was diagnosed with cancer I either told her in person or in a text everyday that I loved her! So today tell that someone you love them, tomorrow may be to late! Heartache ya, but no regrets I Love ya Jody!

≈

*God will fight for us!* Yes the word says so. *Joshua 23:10.* Like my bumper sticker says Jesus is the answer, no matter the question!

≈

We can become addicted to a long list of masters. Gossip, greed, food, all undesirable habits. Each day should review have I adopted a new master? Am I addicted to it? *2 Peter 2:19—For you are a slave to whatever controls you!* Are you in chains? Cry out to Jesus, the only master that leads to goodness and healing!

# *July*

*So Christ has truly set us free. Now make sure that you stay free, & don't get tied up again in slavery to the law.* Galatians 5:1

Today is my friend Jody's funeral, I had the privilege of making her beautiful yesterday, as a hairdresser I think of it as the last greatest gift I can give. *John 3:16—For God so loved the world He GAVE us Jesus . . . believe in Jesus & you will be saved!* If there is to be any peace on a day like today it is because of the promise we have in Jesus, that we will see each other again . . . JESUS the Greatest Gift!! I love & will miss you Jody!!

≈

When I was born again, I was fortunate to be surrounded by Godly people, that discipled/mentored me & I'm forever grateful! *Hebrews 5:12—You have been a Christian along time now (19 years) & you ought to be teaching others.* I was at the alter Sunday, praying for my dear friend Jody & her family, with two of my mentors & realized I too have the God given ability to teach others! Not to be a Leta or Judy . . . but a Marcia!

≈

Joy seminar Saturday, at DaySpring! *Jeremiah 29:11—For I know the plan I have for you, says the Lord. They are plans for good & not disaster, to give you a future & hope.* As I have prepared, I have prayed that all the women that attend would be able to see Jesus through my eyes! So, if you are planning to attend, I encourage you come with an expecting heart, for He has a plan for YOU one of hope & filled with JOY!

≈

Tuesday night as Xander watched, I sat at the computer & read FB posts of how my friend Jody had touched lives & I cried! *2 Thessalonians 2:16—May Jesus who loved us & in His special favor gave us everlasting comfort & good hope, comfort your hearts.* Enter Xander with 2 "Jesus is Lord" pins for us to wear & says . . . Here James, put on Jesus it will make you feel better! I Love that boy . . . Jesus my comfort & hope!

≈

The church was packed, Jody touched lives young & old. The priest shared of visiting the Vietnam wall & watched people trace the name of their loved one & remember! I looked around the sanctuary & knew that like me, all were remembering Jody. *1 John 3:1—See how much our Heavenly Father loves us, for He calls us His Children!* And ya, He gave us a memory, so I trace her name, gone but not forgotten!

≈

Couldn't hit anything @ golf this morning thinking of Jody & all the golf we have played! So I asked the girls if we could stop & pray! I prayed. *1 Corinthians 2:9—No eye has seen no ear has heard, & no mind has imagined what God has prepared for those who love HIM.* Jody does not have to use her imagination as Jesus took her by the hand & took her home. She'd be tellen me hit it Marsh, straight down the ole gutter-uuuu!

≈

This Sunday there is a benefit for my friend Jody's family! It is being held at the Spencer Municipal Golf course, Brunch is from 9:00 -1:00, there is a silent auction & of course some are playing golf. *Matthew 5:4—God blesses those who mourn* . . .

Jody has 3 children who miss her terribly, so please, please come out & Bless them!

≈

My Aunt & Uncle will celebrate, with family & friends 60 years of marriage today! *Ephesians 2:19—You are members of God's family.* So today we will call little boys & girls by their dads & moms, names because they resemble them. My prayer may our lives resemble the life of Christ, each of us serving Him in the way He has planned! As for me & my house . . . serving the LORD! Happy Anniversary U. Bob & A. Eunice!!

≈

Today is the 4th of July, a day we celebrate Freedom, the day we thank our forefathers for the Freedom of speech, religion, to write. But maybe you feel like a slave, a slave to money, food, drugs, & the list goes on! This could be your day for freedom, come to Jesus for He alone can set you free! *John 8:36—So if the Son Sets you free, you will be indeed free.* Today I celebrate & thank you Jesus for setting me FREE!!!

≈

4th of July morning so what's for breakfast? Xander had ice-cream, I always figure it's no different than sugar, cereal, & milk & he thinks it is sweet, good, & gives him energy, the way to start his day! *Hebrews 6:5—Taste the goodness of the word of God.* Yes the way I start my day the Word of God, it is sweet, good, & energizes me for the day! Love the Word, & like ice-cream it's not just for breakfast!

≈

Yesterday Dig & I had lunch Taco House & then a 12:56 tee time! He had already biked to Gillette Grove, & I had jogged 2.25

miles. Not bad for two over 60 year olds, on a beautiful summer day! *Luke 1:37—Nothing is impossible with God!* It was about a year ago that Dig was diagnosed & healed of lymphoma! Today & every day we thank the healer, Jesus, for good health, family, friends, & ministering opportunities!

≈

Privileged yesterday to meet a FB friend for the first time, we were introduced by a mutual friend on this "Social Network." They are both young enough to be my daughters, so what do we have in common . . . JESUS! *Romans 12:10—Love each other with genuine affection & delight in honoring each other!* I love you Darla & Jennifer! I'm honored our paths have crossed . . . I delight in seeing God's plan unfold in our lives!

≈

What a privilege to speak at the Bethlehem Lutheran church in Royal, last week on "What's Stealing your JOY?" *Nehemiah 8:10—The JOY of the Lord is my strength.* In my grief there was still great JOY & it gave me the strength to share what He wanted to be heard! So we ate, we laughed, & we cried, the things women do best! Thank you Jesus. He always works best in my weakness!!

≈

I jog on the bike path. *Psalm 37:23—The steps of the Godly are directed by the Lord He delights in every detail of their lives.* It's 9:00 pm, 85 degrees. I'm loven the warm summer nights. There is the smell of something sweet like clover right off the bike path, my Christian music playing, fireflies are flickering . . . ah perfect! A car stops my sister in Christ Suzie gets out just to hug me . . . yup God of Detail!

≈

Logged on FB, got a message of the impact the JOY seminar had on a life. Got in car, phone rang, someone wanting to drop off clothes at SDC. At subway to get lunch to eat on golf course, stopped by a lady wanting to bring me prom dresses. *1 Corinthians 15:58—Always work enthusiastically for the Lord. Nothing you do for the Lord is ever useless.* This all before lunch . . . blessed to be a blessing!

≈

Digger & I were relaxing on the deck after playing a round of golf, when he laughs & says don't fall asleep . . . I looked up & there were some kind of scavenger type birds circling over top of us, I fell asleep anyway! *Psalm 4:8—I will lie down in peace & sleep, for you alone, O Lord, will keep me safe!* Thank you Lord I love peaceful naps in the sun! But this bird thing, does make me wonder . . . how old do we really look?

≈

Ragbrai Day, praying for Dig/Dream Team safety & success they are committed! Dig is prepared he trained rode to Royal, Greenville & Gillette. Raised funds, mentored young people, all to accomplish his plan, what he has been working for. *Proverbs 16:3—Commit your work to the Lord & then your plans will succeed.* What are your plans, what are you committed to? What on earth are you doing for Heaven's Sake?

≈

Digger is ready for Ragbrai & leaving today! I told him I would copy the daily maps for him that show mileage, elevation, destination, & the towns along the way. Now the writing on the maps is pretty small but I read that they were having service times! *Matthew 18:20—Where 2 or 3 gathered together because they are mine I am there among them!* OK, so the "service times" is for fixing bikes! For me, I was haven church!

≈

My sisters are here for the week & my brother lives here, soooo we have had the days of reminiscing! *Psalm 60:12—With God's help we can do mighty things.* OK so we have no wealth, beauty, or fame . . . but we have His help His guarantee to be bold in our faith, equipped to do the mighty things that each of us to do. Plus He gave us a sense of humor & great memories! Thanks Jesus for in your eyes, we have done mighty things

≈

Yesterday was Audra's 6th Birthday, we came together as a blended family to celebrate . . . to open GIFTS, to sing, eat homemade ice-cream cake (wonderful Sheli) & play a fun game of Apples to Apples. *Psalms 127:3—Children are GIFT from the Lord, they are a reward from Him.* So we thank you Jesus for the GIFT of Audra, Xander & Summer, you see. Mom & Dad, nanas, papas, aunts & uncles we all reap the reward!

≈

I went out to jog & Xander joined me riding his bike! As we started out he told me immediately he did not think he could go as slow as I jog. Soooo he would ride ahead & then ride back. *Proverbs 22:6—Teach your children to choose the right path & when they are older they will remain upon it.* Like X. riding his bike he would get way ahead of me but always came back. Standing on your promises Lord, teaching the right path!

≈

Yesterday's jog started out pretty cloudy & a few sprinkles, a tap now & them to tell me He loves me! This song comes on . . . Your Love! That is all that really matters, is His love! *1 John 4:19—We love because He first loved us!* So today FB friends & family I need to tell you . . . His love is all I have to give! I turned the comer on the homeward stretch down pour . . . yup drenched soaked in His Love! All that really matters is HIS LOVE!

≈

Priceless . . . time spent with family, we have ate, shopped, laughed, & cried for the last 6 days! Our mission on our day at the lake was to purchase something special to remember our time together, getting old memory not what it used to be. *Hebrews 10:23—For God can be trusted to keep His promise.* We found cross bracelets yes perfect, a keepsake of our week & a reminder of the grace received at the cross!

≈

Sisters shopping Spencer & we stopped at Bogenrief Studios! Great time, Jesse made a vase just for me! It is gold & beautiful, one of a kind! *Romans 12:5—We are all parts of His one body, and each of us has different work to do!* My God given gifts are different than my sisters, yet all part of His body, only comparing myself to the old me, the me I was yesterday! Tomorrow I get my vase like me, yup a one of a kind!!

≈

It was a great week, with my family. We made memories to cherish . . . Grotto, The Anchor (purchased cross bracelets), Okoboji, Terrazzo, Minerva's, Goodies, Bogenrief, & 910 E. 7th! *Psalms 84:11—The Lord will withhold no good things from those who do what is right!* Sooo do we always do what is right? We try & knowing at the cross we received His Grace! So we may not have it all together but with Jesus we have it all!!!

≈

Digger came to the door to say he was leaving, Ragbrai bus had to be unpacked & I was sitting on the deck! *Isaiah 40:31—*

*Those that wait on the Lord will find new strength.* Faith is confident assurance, He will never leave or forsake, He has a plan, Christ the visible image of invisible God! Love it when powerful strength building scripture runs through my mind as I wait . . . Dig had locked the door, so I wait on the deck!

≈

What's on your Bucket list? I have checked off some easy/singing happy birthday & rolled out a candle lit cake & some tough/ran 5k. The ones I strive the hardest to accomplish I must be Jesus powered to achieve. *Philippians 1:6—I am sure the God who began a good work in you, will continue until finished . . . that's when Jesus comes back.* I am His work in progress! Jesus perfector of my faith, He knows my bucket list!

# AUGUST

*Such a prayer offered in faith will heal the sick, & the Lord will make you well.* James 5:15

My cousin Chass lives in Dakota Dunes, where they are sandbagging to protect their homes. Chass said as a community, they are united, that surrounding towns are busing in people to help, all working together. He said "it makes you feels good." *Psalm 3:3—But you, O Lord are a shield around me my glory & the one who lifts my head high.* I pray Lord be their sandbag, their shield, for their heads are lifted high!

≈

I Refuse is a song I have heard every morning this week as I jog! God defiantly speaks through music. To sit around and wait for someone else. To do what God has called me to do myself. Oh, I could choose, not to move . . . BUT I REFUSE!" *Ephesians 1:11—For He choose us from the beginning & all things happen just as He decided long ago!* Yes, I know what I am called to do & I DON'T REFUSE! How about you?

≈

I played 18 holes of golf on Wednesday & by the power of the SUN my skin changed color, from white to pink to a shade of tan! *2 Corinthians 5:17—Those who become Christians become new persons. They are not the same anymore. Old life gone. A NEW LIFE begun!* This also happens by the power of the SON! Just like getting a tan He does the work in me, no oil or lotion needed, it's what He does through me!

≈

Friday evening I was the Lobby Lady at the Spencer Dream Center. *Proverbs 22:6—Teach your children to choose the right path, & when they are older they will remain upon it.* So I watch the young people as they are choosing to come to the UNDERGROUND, the right path! As the next & the next generation are there to guide them, still on the right path! I am privileged to hang out ABOVE the UNDERGROUND.

≈

This is the day the Lord has made I will rejoice & be glad in it! Today my head is killing me & my throat is scratchy, sinus or allergy, I don't know! *Psalm 145:3—Great is the Lord! He is most worthy of praise.* So today is not one of my best days, but I will rejoice, because He alone is WORTHY, it is not for what He does it is just because He IS!

≈

Are you called to pray for neighbors, city, nation? If so I have a privilege for you! *2 Chronicles 7:14—If my people will humble themselves & pray, seek my face, I will forgive their sins & heal their land.* Spencer Dream Center has a "Prayer Room" if you are a prayer warrior have an intercessors heart contact Amy for info! You see, greater things are yet to come! Word says seek His Face & He will heal our land!

≈

Bible study last night was awesome, it was wrote just for me! It affirmed my thoughts . . . God speaks. *Joshua 1:8—Study this book of law, MEDITATE on it day & night, sure to obey all that is written. Only then will you succeed.* When you know you are doing what God calls you to do, others will always try to destroy, you need to MEDITATE to be empowered by His word! I can do all things through Christ . . . yes success!

≈

I love hot weather, now I am not saying that I want to go without air-conditioning, but I complain in the winter months. *Psalm 139:14—Thank you for making me so wonderfully complex! Your workmanship is marvelous.* Yesterday as our women's golf league finished & came in out of the heat it was very evident how different yet complex, God has made each of us! Yet we are all His & marvelously made!!! Loven Summer!!

≈

I have pins & screws in my ankle from a break many years ago, yet if I see someone with a injury it hurts in my ankle. *John 20:20—As Jesus spoke He held out hands for them to see & He showed them His side.* Xander fell off bike & scraped his knee today, yup I love him. It hurt in my ankle! I believe that when we are hurt or in any kind of pain, Jesus feels it in His hands, His feet, His side, that's how much He loves us!!!

≈

Today is the Grand Opening of The Terrazzo Coffeehouse in the Spencer Dream Center!! *Hebrews 10:25—Let us not neglect our meeting together, as some people do.* Coffee brings people together, we have tea & smoothies too! You see the coffee at Terrazzo doesn't just taste good it feels good to, as all the monies go back to support the Dream Center! I hope to see you there!

≈

At the wedding I attended last night they did what they called the "Unity of Sand." *Matthew 19:6—Since they are no longer two but one, let no one separate them, for God has joined them together.* You see the brides sand was pink the grooms was black & the priest poured white, symbolizing God. What a great visual as pink, black, & white were all poured together! Congratulations Beau & Alyssa God has joined you together!!

≈

I believe the way you play the game of golf, is also the way you live your life! Golf is a game that you play against yourself, except when playing league/tournaments. I don't understand the handicaps, but I do know you must play with honesty & integrity, a stroke is a point & close enough is not in the cup! *Psalm 25:21—Integrity & honesty protect me for my hope is in the Lord!* So, I will swing the club playing as if Jesus is my partner!

≈

I love this season of my life, I'm 60 & loven it! *Ecclesiastes 3:2—There is a time for everything. A season for every activity under heaven.* WOW, was this true yesterday morning, as I opened the door to go jog, the temperature said I was in a different season. Oh how I hate to see summer & the heat end! So, I wore a sweatshirt, you see there was the smell of Clay County Fair in the air!

≈

Prayers appreciated, today is Digger's check up at Mayo, a year ago he was diagnosed & healed of lymphoma. Thank you Jesus! *Luke 2:14—Glory to God in the highest & peace on earth to all whom God favors!* It's ALL for your glory Lord, as we are all your favorite! Praising the Banner God, that goes before us. Because He does we have His peace . . . not the absence of war but the presence of HIM!

≈

Can the Holy Spirit ever forget you? Never, you are His child. Whenever you pass through a room or walk through a crowd, may His oil of gladness send a sweet aroma of Christ through the air! I am His temple . . . may Jesus be seen in me today and every day!!! *Ephesian 5:2—Live a life filled with love. The example of Christ* . . . A pleasing aroma to God. Off to Mayo.

≈

Digger was told he was in remission, exactly what we have prayed for, for the last year. But whatever the outcome was to be we knew that going through anything & everything with Jesus is do able! *Hebrews 13:8—Jesus is the same yesterday, today, & forever!* Our Jesus is still in the healing business! Word says so! Thank you. YA YOU. *The prayers of the righteous have accomplished much— James 5:16.* Word says so!!

≈

We left Friday at 2 am for Mayo, so when I got up Saturday & looked at the clock in bathroom & it said 12:00 noon, wow, was I rested! I said to Dig, we really slept in! But the living room clock, the actual time, 8:00 am! *Matthew 11:28—Jesus says Come to me all of you who are weary & carry heavy burdens & I will give you rest!* True to His word our burden lifted & we are rested! The bathroom clock must be on God's time!

≈

Sunday we participated in the Special Olympians golf outing at the Spencer Muni Course, we were the Partners to the Athletes playing best ball format! *Ecclesiastes 9:11—The fastest runner doesn't always win the race & the strongest warrior doesn't always win the battle.* My Special Athlete Alex & I won a Silver medal! We went to do the blessing & you know how that works out yup, we got blessed! All involved WINNERS!

≈

Monday, another trip to Mayo & Digger doesn't need knee surgery! Yahoo! Xander went with us & he hates to travel, so this was a big deal. He wanted to see where papa has been going, plus he knows that his papa is cancer free! *Psalm 119:93—I will never forget your commandments, for you have used them to restore my joy & health!* So we say thank you Jesus, to God go the Glory & goodbye Mayo for another 6 months!

≈

Praying today for the Wells family as this is the day of their baby Natalie's funeral. I am coping a part of what is on the back of the Obituary brochure that I got last night at the visitation . . . So when a little child departs, we who are left behind. Must realize God loves children . . . angels are hard to find. *Psalm 34:18—God is close to the brokenhearted.* This family is brokenhearted . . . please join me & pray for them God's Peace.

≈

Everybody needs an encourager, someone that is on your team, that has your back! It might be your spouse, a friend, co-worker, or maybe your Pastor! We need each other the word says so. *Romans 12:5—Since we are all one body in Christ, we belong to each other & each of us needs all the others!* So today I thank YOU, for making me a better me, because of you I step out in faith, all for His Glory . . . you see I need you!

≈

Wednesday night someone broke down our fence & stole the bikes that Dig spends his time & money fixing up to give away. My husband is a better person than me, or maybe because it was done to him, that it upsets me! I would have called the police! *Psalm 103:8—The Lord is companionate & merciful slow to anger & full of love.* That's my husband, so please if you need a bike KNOCK, Dig is merciful & still has bikes!

≈

Thursday while we were playing golf same thing happened! I called the police. *Jeremiah 29:11—I have plans for you, says the Lord, plans for good, not disaster!*

≈

Thursday night I got up to go to bathroom, then to kitchen to look out into back yard to see if I could see the bike thief or if the gate was open! As I walked into the kitchen & toward the sliding glass door, it was like someone was coming right at me! *Joshua 1:9—Be strong & courageous do not be afraid, the Lord is with us wherever we go.* The someone, it was me, my reflection in the glass door. So glad I'd went to bathroom first!

≈

Thank you to all who have donated bikes this week since so many were stolen, it has been awesome to see that Digger's ministry will continue. *Galatians 6:9—Don't get tired of doing what is good. Don't get discouraged & give up, for we will reap a harvest of blessings at the appropriate time.* Digger has been blessed in the giving & receiving.

≈

Digger says cancer puts everyone on the same playing field, none richer, or smarter, etc. Just like the people God uses to build the Kingdom, plain, simple people, like me, and the exact opposite! Look at the disciples, they turned the world upside down. Not beauty, fame, wealth, or knowledge are necessary to be used by God. *1 Peter 4:10—God has given gifts/talents to each of us!* It is our choice to use them!!

≈

I pray with a friend every Monday morning, for an upcoming event in both of our lives & today was the 2nd Monday in a row I have forgot to call her! I text her that I pray in agreement with her, for the upcoming week & our upcoming event! You see we are united in Christ! He knows both of our needs, even before we do! *Isaiah 65:24—While they are still talking about their needs, I will go ahead & answer their prayers.*

≈

This week I've questioned myself as I prayed, Lord am I advancing the Kingdom in the things I do? Things like the status that I put on FB everyday, so I stopped! If it brings Him Glory, it would be missed! Yesterday I received messages, about missing my posts! *Zechariah 8:16—Tell the truth to each other.* My prayers, answered! May YOU see Jesus through my eyes as I continue to share from "Marcia's LIFE Application Bible!"

≈

Day 2 of putting in a new sliding glass door in our kitchen, what a mess! As I looked at the hole where the door used to be, it reminded me of the hole that was in my life before Jesus, how I tried to fill it with food, drugs, money, & shopping! Jesus was a perfect fit, no need to shim or caulk. *Jude 1:20—Continue to build your lives on the foundation of your Holy Faith.* Thank you Jesus, my mess . . . became my message!

≈

*Ephesians 6:11—Put on all of God's armor that you will be able to stand firm.* Xander came into church by himself yesterday, I said what's up? He said Audie's dress broke! (when he was a little he called shorts, broke pants) Sure enough a little later Kurt & Audie arrived, Kurt said it was a "Superbowl" wardrobe malfunction! Moral to story . . . wherever we go, to church or football game, we all need the full armor of God!

≈

Went to "The Help." Living in Iowa in the 60s I never saw that kind of racial discrimination, but I have seen discrimination of the old, young, poor, female. *Galatians 3:28—There is no longer Jew or Gentile, slave or free, male or female, we are all Christian.* In the movie they were just reading the WRONG BOOK on how to interact with people! Thank you Lord for your word, but we must read it! Can't do better till you know better!

≈

Took my friend V. outside for a walk. When you live in a nursing home it is so cool to have a change of all of your senses different temperatures, sounds, smells! Going outside will do just that! V.'s favorite, *Genesis 2:15—God placed man in the Garden of Eden to tend & care for it.* She says wouldn't that be wonderful to walk with God in the garden. Sunglasses on, V. tilted her face to the heavenlies, as we both felt the warmth of HIS SON!

≈

*Psalm 26:8—I love your sanctuary, Lord, the place where your glory shines.* It has been almost a week since we put in the new sliding glass door in the kitchen & I love it, the window, not the kitchen. My dream kitchen would be a living room! LOL But new glass is always so bright & shiny! Every morning I am so blessed as the sun comes up, my kitchen becomes a sanctuary, a place where HIS GLORY really shines!

≈

My golf partner dumped/spit me out of the cart, she said "I just did a u-turn!" (FAST) & I still came in 3rd in the 1st flight of the ladies morning league tournament! Sue & Deb could defiantly give me lessons but I did have a good day, you could say my stick was hot! God says in *Revelation 3:15-16—You are neither hot or cold . . . since you are like lukewarm water, I will spit you out of my mouth!* Not me Lord I'm hot & now hangen on!

≈

Digger's dad Dutch always sang, "Good Night Irene" . . . at last call! In the song it says I'll see you in my dreams. Not so right now on the east coast, it sounds more like a nightmare as Irene is no lady! *Psalm 4:8—In peace I lay down to sleep, for you alone. Oh Lord, will keep me safe!* The news continues to say they are without power, but NOT SO . . . thank you JESUS! Praying for east coast! Last call . . . "Good Bye Irene!"

≈

While jogging down the street I heard this song, by Sidewalk Prophets! It's really not about the college bound, but that is how it spoke to me! Ephesians *2:10—You His masterpiece . . . you will do good things He planned long ago!* You see, God's Got His Hand on you Sydney, Keartsen, Derek, Jordon, Jenna, Gabrielle, Meaghan, Luke, you're going to do great things God already knows & I WILL take some time to pray, for you today!

≈

Morning jogs verses night jogs? *Lamentations 3:23—His mercies begin afresh each day!* That's morning, everything fresh & waking up! *Psalm 46:10—Be still & know that I am God!* This is night, just Him & me! How awesome is He, that He alone would know what I need & when I need it! Sometimes I must be very still to appreciate His tender mercies!

## September

*For all who have entered into God's rest have rested from their labors, just as God did after creating the world.* Hebrews 4:10

My sister-in-law Teri & I went to our 3rd Zumba class. Does not matter, if you are old or young the statistics say you burn 800 to 1,000 calories an hour & I know it is true because I drip as if melting! *Nehemiah 8:10—The Joy of the Lord is my strength!* Good thing . . . As we dance in front of big/huge mirrors! LOL! A salsa dancer I will never be, I have a hard time walking & chewing gum . . . ZUMBA!!!!

≈

The perils of publicity . . . parties announced on FB to everyone & then invitees are shocked by the number that show up! So today I am inviting you to a Come to Jesus party! *Romans 10:9—If you confess with your mouth that Jesus is Lord & believe in your heart that God raised Him from the dead, you will be saved!* Party will be held in your recliner, at your kitchen table, your bedroom, He wants to spend time with you, no need to RSVP. He's always there!

≈

I have heard perseverance defined as "courage stretched out." Sometimes God delivers us from difficult painful circumstances, but more often it requires courageous enduring faithfulness. We are not just to endure, but to overcome. That takes obedience, hope, and joy. *James 1:3—Perseverance is what turns suffering into maturity.* Oh Lord, find me courageous & faithful while at Mayo!

≈

We call it Kidmo/children's church at DaySpring, Xander & Audra love it! 2 times Sunday we had review of what was learned, right after church, & at supper time! Xander says it in the back of my mind, the word . . . apostasy, as he grins at his sister, Audie says to abandon your belief! *Proverbs 22:6—Train a child.* Thanks to the "bus driver" Clint Nielson & all the rest that help to train my grandchildren.

≈

My fair purchase was a new belt, as I always buy accessories 1st! I was looking at the racks of belts & I hear "Marcia, when I saw this belt I thought of you!" Thanks salesgirl, Callie, as she knew me & could see me wearing it! *Ephesians 6:14—Stand your ground, putting on the belt of truth* . . . No matter the color, the belt of TRUTH is what I need to put on everyday! My new belt is gold & sparkly, ya it's my sense of style or lack there of & like TRUTH, it goes with everything!!

≈

Dig went to "Grab 'n Go" to get parts to fix a car. You bring your own tools & remove what you need to fix what needs fixen. GREAT CONCEPT! *Romans 8:39—Nothing will ever be able to separate us from the love of God that is revealed through Christ Jesus!* GREAT CONCEPT, no need for tools He will fix what needs fixen! Once He Grabs ya, He will never let you Go!

≈

Praising the Healer . . . Digger has treatment today! *A sincere prayer brings wonderful results—James 5:16*

≈

I have noticed over the last few weeks, as I have sat in the cafeteria at Mayo, that heads do bow before they eat. Many times it is head because of treatment, has no hair, how encouraged I am by the body of Christ. That our faith stays strong in the midst of trials. *Jesus is our Blessed Hope—Romans 1:16.* I am not ashamed of the good news about Christ. Not ashamed to communicate to Him, are you?

≈

The trip to Mayo yesterday was beautiful, the paintbrush of the creator was very busy this week, as the trees have really started to turn gorgeous colors. *Nehemiah 9:6—You alone are the Lord, you made the & skies & the heavens & stars.* Again we praise and worship the creator/healer not creation! He alone holds the world in His hands . . . that is you and me!! Thanks for your prayers!!!

≈

One of my life lessons! A reality check, happened a few years ago, MANY people did not like or want to be around ME! Oh, I pity partied, I wallered in it, pointing, blaming, angry, yup BITTERNESS! *Ephesians 4:31—Get rid of all bitterness, rage anger, harsh words & slander . . .* Definition of bitterness, I was drinking poison & expecting the MANY to die & the MANY didn't even give me a 2nd thought. Bitterness is a root that if not cut off can kill ya! My advice . . . stop drinking the poison!

≈

There was a clap of thunder & I sat straight up in bed . . . oh no, my car was parked in the drive, under a tree, with the top down! I ran out through the rain & the already standing puddles in the drive! *Job 1:10—You God have always put a wall of protection around him & his home & property.* Got in the car & the seats were dry! Thank you Jesus, for walls of protection & a ceiling too!

≈

The no-see-ems are out in full force! It is just a speck & you have to look real hard to see. *Matthew 7:2—Why worry about a speck in your friend's eye when you have a log in your own?* I get it Lord it's not my place to judge or be critical of others. To point out their faults, especially when I have to look real hard to-see-em & a big ole mosquito is biting me!

≈

Thank you to . . . iSHOPspencer.com this site is not a virus! I know because I have visited it, registered, & WON the iPad 2! Until I won it I had no idea what it was. *Matthew 25:29—To those who use well what they are given even more will be given.* Soon to have the Bible on my iPad! *1 Thessalonians 5:16-18—Always be joyful. Keep on praying . . . always be thankful!* So I pray filled with joy & thanksgiving, do I believe this was luck? No I'm humbled by His favor! Thank you Jesus!

≈

Today we are going to the 2nd annual grape stomp'n @ InnSpiration Bed and Breakfast owned by our friends Paul & Shelia. So what happens at a grape stomp'n? Well I see Lucy stomp'n in a big barrel & "Pretty Woman"—Julia laughing hysterically as she watches Lucy on TV. *Deuteronomy 16:13-15—After the grapes have been pressed . . . this will be a happy time of celebrating . . . all to honor the Lord!* My hair, a Lucy sorta red & I am ready to stomp'n!

≈

A problem is really an opportunity in disguise. God wants us to see problems as potentialities and adversaries as opportunities. As a Christian we should not see a difficulty in every opportunity, but an opportunity in every difficulty! Thank you Jesus for a good trip to Mayo today, and Lord may I see the opportunity hidden in this struggle. *Galatians 1:5—All glory to God forever & ever amen.*

≈

Happy 17th Anniversary, Digger, I love you! For 20+ years Dig & I lived together & then according to God's plan we were Born Again & needed/wanted to be married! *2 Corinthians 5:17—Those who become Christians become new persons. They are not the same, old life gone.* New Life, begun! Sept. 4 1994 was a very foggy day, but we were not in a fog! In fact things had never been so clear! You see because of Jesus in our lives . . . the fog was lifted!

≈

@ At WalMart buying screen protector & cleaning cloth for my new iPad! Thanks iSHOPspencer.com Found protectors, no cloth! *Matthew 7:12—Jesus said "Do to others whatever you would like them to do to you."* @ checkout line WalMart employee came over & said to me, remember a month ago you let me go ahead of you in checkout line, as I only had one item? Well, I would like to give you this, yup a microfiber cloth used to clean glasses & iPad! God knows what I need when I need it! Keep paying it forward!

≈

I read that according to the worlds standards "The one who dies with the most shoes wins." *John 13:35—Jesus says "Your love for one another will prove to the world that you are mine!"* Yup we are relational beings He made us that way, & yes I do love gold sparkly shoes, but it is our relationships that we live for & when you have personal relationship with Jesus it makes all the others golden! Thank you to all who extended to us the MANY Anniversary Wishes, we win, you are HIS!

≈

The town of Spencer was without POWER in the middle of the night! At our house it was so dark it was our house WITHOUT CHRIST. *Acts 16:31—Believe in the Lord Jesus & you will be saved, along with your whole household.* As for the post I wrote last night for today, yup I forgot to save, computer shut down all LOST! Different than man-made power the power of Jesus never shuts down but it is our choice to receive Him & be SAVED! My future post, lesson learned I will choose to save!

≈

Dig & I had lunch at Taco House yesterday, I love their red hot sauce, apply it to anything & it makes PERFECTION out of any dish! There is only one sauce better if you are looking for PERFECTION, it's the hot sauce, found in the word & printed in red . . . Yup, the words that Jesus spoke to teach, words to live by, just open the word . . . Jesus said, Jesus replied . . . all printed in RED! Today & everyday I will APPLY my favorite hot sauce to my life!

≈

The change of seasons, especially Fall, make me cry, it is a cry from deep within, to be moved by the Holy Spirit to tears. It is a happy, sad bittersweet, emotional cry, one of remembering the good & bad times! "Precious Memories." *Psalms 34:18—The Lord is close to the brokenhearted.* He is so close to me today I am sitting on His lap. I remember & miss my friends . . . Kathy Somers, Lori Odor, Jody Mowery! Who are you missing today? To acknowledge them in death, is to say they really lived!

≈

While Dig & I golf we listen to the Refuge or Kinship Christian radio! Kinship says that it is a station that fits your life style, fits like a pair of your favorite jeans! So we try to witness through our life style, as we play the radio & golf! (greatest game ever played) *Colossians 1:15—Christ the visible image of the invisible God!* So if you play golf @ Spencer's Municipal course I have prayed over all 18 holes & you are playing . . . on HOLY GROUND! He's everywhere!

≈

After 9/11 all agreed that life as we knew it was forever changed! I remember a friend's daughter did not want to go to the C.C. fair after the attack, as she had heard, we were to stay away from crowds! When things like this happen, people immediately call on Jesus, churches were full, attendance was up! *Matthew 11:28—Jesus said "Come to me, all of you who are weary & carry heavy burdens & I will give you rest!"* 10 years later I pray . . . that lives were changed, & our churches still full!

≈

Our church was FULL yesterday & PK had a great sermon & some very poignant film clips, put to patriotic music, of what happened 10 years ago! A time in our history that will always draw us together as a nation! A nation that I believe is under God! So we mourn our losses, even if you knew no one that died we still mourn! *John 11:35—Jesus wept.* Jesus, in this scripture gave us permission! You see when Jesus squeezes my heart it comes out my eyes! Marcia Weeps!

≈

I jog faster than the street sweeper, sweeps! What's on the streets of Spencer? Same stuff I did before I was SAVED, sex, drugs, alcohol. *2 Chronicles 7:14—If my people humble themselves & pray . . . I will heal their land.* The word says MY people that's me, not those who don't know Him! So I PRAY, ya for boldness to share, that Jesus saves, doesn't matter what you have picked up on the street! Jesus is the ultimate street sweeper! To be honest, the street sweeper didn't know we were racing! LOL

≈

I do love driving my convertible this time of year, even if I have to turn on the heat. It is funny when the top is down I can't & don't wave like normal. My arm flies up & over the windshield to wave, so you will notice it's me, Marcia. *Romans 8:39— Nothing in all creation can separate us from the love of God.* No need for arm waving, God knows me! So if you see a gold Sebring coming down the street, with "bat wings" waven, over the top of the car . . . yup it's me!

≈

Teenagers sometimes get a bad rap, I did back in '02! LOL It's all about RESPECT, 1st a fear of the one who hung the stars, that's a good thing! Next respect yourself, others, & authority! *1 Peter 2:17—Respect everyone . . . Fear God, respect the King.* I was jogging & young man going to school, was walking towards me, I didn't know him. I could see he was enjoying his music on his iPod, & then he pulled out the earbud to say good morning! You might say, so what? I say RESPECT, good job mom & dad!

≈

"The place James will not go!" is what Xander calls the midway! Kids never forget, they are sponges, they take it all in. Where we go, what we do, or say! *Proverbs 3:6—Seek His will in all you do, & He will show you which path to take.* This is the path that we want stay on, to show especially to our grandkids, the importance of being in God's will. As far as the X. & me at the fair . . . exhibits & livestock & "The place James will not go" nothing wrong with it! I believe it is a dad & mom expense . . . I mean enjoyment!

≈

My brother-in-law loves to fish, he & my sister are here this weekend to do just that at Okoboji! I have never really understood fishing, to just sit in a boat when it is cold, hot, windy, calm, or just right! *Matthew 4:19—Jesus called out to them, Come, follow me & I will make you fishers of men!* Thank you Lord for YOUR calling . . . Blessed to be a "Fisher of Men" not a fishermen!

≈

"Hope Floats" one of my very favorite chick flicks, was on cable & of course I watched it, again! The movie is one of infidelity & the domino effect that happens in a family, with many life lessons! Beginnings are scary, endings are sad, it's what goes on in the middle that counts. I do feel like the mom/grandma (Gena Rowland) in the movie, as my cup runneth over! *Psalm 39:7—Lord . . . my only hope is in you!* In the movie . . . Hope Floats & My Hope . . . He Walks on Water!

≈

I never see women scavengers hunt for golf balls! A man gets close to water or out of bounds, they gotta look! Why? Because they might find the one that they lost! *Luke 15:4—Jesus said "If a man has a hundred sheep & one gets lost, what will he do? . . .*

*go search for the one that is lost until He finds it."* Jesus is the Good Shepherd, always ready to seek & save the lost! My husband well, he has a cart full of someone else's golf balls & looking for the one/many he has lost!

≈

Happy Birthday to ME, 19 years ago, I was Born Again, this is my spiritual BDate, when I celebrate, the start of my 2nd life! 1st life I lived in the world, 2nd life I live for Jesus! *2 Timothy 1:8— So never be ashamed to tell others about our Lord!* Everyday I try to do just that, as JESUS Is the greatest gift ever received! Are you Born again, if not, message me, I would love to share 9/20 with you! At 19 I might not have it all together, but with the living breathing Word of God, I got it all!

≈

I recently attended a prophetic ministry service, wonderful worship, teaching from the word, & prayer! *Galatians 6:9—Let's not get tired of doing what is good. At just the right time we will reap a harvest . . . if we don't give up.* Like many of you, I have a heart for those who don't know Jesus. I try to plant seeds & pray that Jesus will be seen in me! I'll never give up, as I was told I would witness the in gathering & be a Harvester! The farm girl in me doesn't care, John Deere or International, it's about Souls, I'm a Harvester!

# OCTOBER

*The harvesters are paid good wages, & the fruit they harvest is people brought to eternal life. What joy awaits both the planter & the harvester alike!*
John 4:36

I stepped on a very small pebble, I stumbled, lost my balance, it almost took me to my knees! *1 John 2:2—Jesus himself is the sacrifice that atones for ALL our sins.* You see sin is sin, no one sin bigger then another & much like that very small pebble, when I sin, I stumble lose my balance & it definitely takes me to my knees! I thank you Jesus for your atoning power, yes forgiveness for all my sins!

≈

I am humbled & blessed when someone reposts what I have written! *Hebrews 4:12—For the word of God is alive & powerful . . . It exposes our innermost thoughts & desires.* We all go through similar life situations, we all have similar thoughts & desires. It's good to know that we all struggle with the same things! What happens in my life is often similar to yours so what I post, speaks to you. What I write is also a repost, as I share from the living, powerful, word of God! It speaks to all of US!

≈

10/3 Experiencing God Reflection . . . Out jogging & there was a big pile of leaves & as I stepped forward a gust of wind blew through the center of the pile, very "Red Sea like." You could see the street & leaves like walls on each side! *Isaiah 30:21—Your OWN ears will hear Him . . . "This is the way you should go."* According to Blackaby, I cannot stay the way I am & go with God! So I step out in Faith on a cleared street listening for His voice, knowing God is always at work & wants ME to join HIM!

≈

Golfing & I have noticed around the greens that we have gone from smoking cigarettes to munchen on sunflower seeds. That's the story of my life I have swapped one addiction for another. *1 John 2:16—For the world offers only a craving for physical pleasure, a craving for everything we see . . . These are not from the Father, but are from this world.* Thank you Jesus as I'm a work in progress, I have craved cigarettes, drugs, food, shopping & the list goes on! Good thing I didn't leave them all around the green!

≈

Today V.'s Birthday, Dr. Hunziker asked her how old she was, she said she was "old enough!" V. is "old enough" to have 2 Doctorates, be the 1st women private investigator in Iowa, airplane pilot, artist, farmer's wife, a mom, my very good friend & the list goes on! *Psalm 91:16—I will reward them with a long life & give them my salvation.* V. always told me, she really didn't do so many things, she had just lived a "long life," her wonderful reward! Happy Bday V. thanking Jesus for You & our gift of Salvation!

≈

My hand mirror cracked, so my reflection is really strange, as my face is also cracked with lines, of my age, my cigarette smoking, the sun plus baby oil & iodine. I am sure I am not alone when I say what I see on the outside does not reflect how young I feel on the inside. *Psalm 119:5—Oh that my actions would consistently reflect your decrees!* You see, more important than the cracks & lines or if I feel young & look old, is that MY LIFE REFLECT JESUS, who is within me!

≈

To verify who I am for banking, credit cards, medical records, even FB . . . I need my social security #, birth date, mom's maiden name, driver's license #, & PASSWORDS! *2 Corinthians 1:22—He has identified us as His own, by placing the Holy Spirit in our hearts as the 1st installment that guarantees everything He has promised.* Thank you Jesus my identity is in you & I only had to pray the PASSWORDS once . . . Lord I am a sinner forgive me & come into my heart Lord Jesus, I want to live for you! He keeps His promises!

≈

*Whether you turn to the right or to the left, your ears will hear a voice behind you, saying, This is the way; walk in it!— Isaiah 30:21.* This appears IMMEDIATELY on the screen when the movie "7 DAYS IN UTOPIA" starts. I love the game of golf, greatest game ever played & I recommend this G-rated movie based on the book "Golfs Sacred Journey." It is a story about burying your lies & moving past your failures, to find the sweet spot in life & in golf! SEE it, FEEL it, TRUST it! As always . . . For God's Glory!

≈

Good Morning, *"I LOVE YOU LORD, you are my strength!"* May this great weather never end, but just in case I played hard this week! 78 holes of golf, jogged 8 miles, 2 hours of Zumba, 3 Bible Studies, 1 movie, a bridal shower, V.'s Bday, gave away 4 dresses, worked a day & half & WON "The Price is Right" at Pastor appreciation party! Cooking & cleaning not so much! *Philippians 4:13—I can do all things through Christ, who is my strength!* THANK YOU, JESUS!

≈

Dig & I played golf in the 45-mile an hours winds on Friday, we are committed golfers! *Psalm 37:5—Commit everything you do to the Lord. Trust Him & He will help you.* When I was hitting into the wind much like going against God, disastrous! But just like going with God, when I hit with the wind, it flew & soared, better than I could ever do on my own! I parred #18 thank you Jesus, as I commit everything to you! As far as playing golf in the wind, well maybe we should be committed! LOL

≈

For our Pastor Appreciation party our sanctuary became our fellowship hall & we played "The Price is Right" & I WON! We had a great time guessing what you would have to pay for things, from a garage door opener to lipstick. *1 Corinthians 7:23—God paid a high price for you . . .* In the pictures of that night is the CROSS, the constant reminder of the high price that was paid for me. Humbled, God knew "The Price was Right!" He gave His Son & I WON!

≈

Did you know that when you capture a lightning bug/firefly that in captivity, their light will soon go out. (7 Days in Utopia info) *Galatians 5:13—For you have been called to live in freedom . . . use your freedom to serve one another in love.* Much like the firefly I was not called to live a life in a prison/jar of sin & bondage. I am called to Freedom through Christ who died for the forgiveness of my sins, I am called to love you & to let My Light Shine!

≈

I love music, if you listen almost all music can & will minister to you. I just heard this country song & the words really spoke to me . . . "Never let your praying knees get lazy, & love like crazy!" I used to think prayer was for old ladies, ya, now I am old, & I even journal my prayer requests & praises! Would the lack of prayer in my life be a sin . . . Oh I know so! *Thessalonians 5:17—Never stop praying!* Call me crazy but praying is one of the most exciting things I do each & everyday & my knees . . . old but not lazy!

≈

Late last night I could hear the neighbors calling their dog! This morning I saw that stay out all night dog, still out! *Jeremiah 3:22—My wayward children, says the LORD, come back to me, and I will heal your wayward hearts. Yes, we're coming, the people reply.* The neighbor was in his car, when his dog heard & saw him! The dog was soooo excited, just like I will be the day I meet my Master, my heavenly Father, even though I am sometimes wayward, like I've been out all night, for He has Healed my Heart!

≈

My friend S. JOY asked me if I would do her hair for her wedding? I said "No!!! I don't do wedding hair any more, too stressful!" *Isaiah 62:4—For the Lord delights in you & will claim you as His Bride.* Saturday morning, as we prayed together at the Salon On Grand, (before I did Stephanie's hair) I was reminded of just that we are the Bride of Christ! Jesus is coming back for us, the church, His Bride! Thanks Mrs. Carl Napp, for the Honor & Delight! FYI future reference, I don't do Wedding Hair!

≈

10/17 Experiencing God Reflection . . . this week we were to take a 30-minute walk with God, something I do every day! *Leviticus 26:12—I will walk* (jog) *among you; I will be your God, and you will be my people.* HE always takes the initiative in our love relationship. HE pursues me! HE is faithful as we spend special time together, HE writes, in my head, while we jog, what I am to share on FB each day! I am HIS people HE is my God! Oh how I love to EXPERIENCE HIM!

≈

Sunday before church started Digger as usual, had the young boy sitting by him wound tight, yup 2 rowdy boys & one is 62! *1 Timothy 2:8—In every place of worship, I want men to pray with holy hands lifted up to God, free from anger and controversy.* As worship started & my husband began to sing, for the first time I also heard this young boy sing, with hands lifted high! You see Dig by his actions & interactions had given this young boy permission to worship, as he was doing what he was seeing Digger do, ya . . . FREEDOM

≈

One size fits all, what does that mean? Look around that's impossible! Doesn't matter dress, pants, shirts, I have found the more you pay the smaller the size. I suppose that could make you feel smaller/poorer! We need a chart that all can understand, so a 12 is a 12 no guess work! *Ephesians 3:18—May you have the power to understand, as all God's people should, how wide, how long, how high, & how deep His love is!* Everything is possible with God & His Love, it's big & one size fits all!

≈

Joggen through the leaves & I KICKED up a pack of Pall Mall cigarettes, yes, my former brand the ones with no filters, so no one would mooch off me, ha! *1 Corinthians 10:13—The temptations in your life are no different from what others experience.* God is FAITHFUL *He will not allow the temptation to be more than you can stand.* 26 years ago I KICKED that habit & I know that I am not alone when I say it is a tuff one to kick! Temptations I got em & I'm still work in progress, but wonderful to know He alone is FAITHFUL!

≈

Say Yes To A Dress is in transition, we have moved up a floor & have been trying to figure out how to keep the dress racks upright! *Psalm 75:3—When the earth quakes & its people live in turmoil, I am the one who keeps its foundations firm.* The racks can hold the weight of the dresses, but the foundation/wheels are too small. Shut the door & like an earthquake the racks tip over, yes turmoil! Moral to story, In all things God I need YOU to stay upright! YOU are my firm foundation!

≈

My FB profile picture on my iPad went to a ? mark. I'm not good with technology, so how did that happen, what did that mean? My identity was a ? mark, my face was now a ? mark! *Matthew 7:20—Yes, just as you can identify a tree by its fruit, so you can identify people by their actions.* So if my profile picture had stayed a ? mark, could I still be identified by what I post? I pray that my actions in words would identify me! I finally figure it out! Signed, Yours Truly ? Mark, I mean Marcia!

≈

Xander called he had a great, no, perfect day! He has had some behavioral struggles in the past so I am encouraged when he has a day that will cost me a frozen hot chocolate! *Psalm 103:8—The LORD is slow to get angry & filled with love.* I recite this scripture to X. all the time, there is power of the spoken word & the Lord the best role model. X. told me the only way he could have had this good a day last year, was if there had been an early out!

≈

10/24 Experiencing God Unit 4 . . . *Exodus 3:14—God replied to Moses, I AM WHO I AM . . .* Wow! God shows me who He is this week through my circumstances! Sick granddaughter-my Healer! Fusion leader-my confidence! Dieting-my Bread of Life! A step of faith-my Guide! A business associate-my Mediator!

Death in family-my Comfort! He is all I need & more, my Strength my JOY! He says to me "I will be what I will be!" Who will He be for you & me today?

≈

I was ready to head out for my jog, Dig said he was a going along! He was a going to ride his bike & as he said "pace me!" *1 Corinthians 12:4—There are different kinds of spiritual gifts, but the same Spirit is the source of them all.* So I am not a bike rider & Dig is not a jogger, yet we have same source just different gifts & as far as pace, you run your own race, all for the same prize . . . His Glory!

≈

Wedding dress boxes are BIG, I've been opening them for Say Yes To A Dress! *Psalm 66:5—Come & see what our God has done, what miracles He performs for people.* When I 1st heard the statement "Never put God in a box" I pictured a small carry in my hands kinda box not a wedding dress box & really there is no box the size of God! I realized soon after I was saved, that I tried to keep Him IN a box, for fear of what He wanted me to do! OUT of the box, He is able to perform the miraculous for His people by His people!

≈

Digger bought a new golf club & God has blessed us with wonderful October days to play! I love my woods, so I don't buy new clubs & I never use an iron, not on the golf course or on wrinkled clothes! (air fluff in dryer) *Proverbs 27:17—As iron sharpens iron, so a friend sharpens a friend.* I am so blessed to be challenged, held accountable, yes sharpened by my husband my best friend! We are iron!

≈

Digger's brother in law died & the funeral brought the family together. It seems when your parents are gone the only time you see extended family, is at funerals, or weddings. *Romans 1:12— When we get together, I want to ENCOURAGE you in your faith & be encouraged by yours.* We are going to do better, we have a PLAN to get together each month. If we sound like your family I ENCOURAGE you make a plan to get together it's all about Faith & Family!

≈

I don't just HEAR music I SEE it! "I'm a Believer," Shrek & Fiona in SHREK! "I Will Survive," Keanu Reeves in the REPLACEMENTS! *John 9:25—I know this: I was blind, and now I can see!* "I'm Going To Worship YOU Forever," Kim leading worship, Pastor Dave to my left & Kristin to my right, in DAYSPRING last Sunday! Blind not me, I can hardly wait to SEE what I will HEAR tomorrow 10:00 at DaySpring! Come join us!

≈

I love the family of God! Sunday night we were invited & attended a Harvest Party, with Xander, Audra, & Kurt, there was a maze & all kinds of fun carnival games! *Romans 15:7— Therefore, accept each other just as Christ has accepted you so that God will be given glory.* We were so blessed, when we got there Brenda asked to help, we became carnies, so much fun! Thanks Light of the Lakes for accepting & using us . . . all for HIS GLORY!

≈

The ABS light (automatic brake system) is lit in my dash, Digger fixed the brakes, but the light is still on! *Titus 1:9—He must have a strong BELIEF in the trustworthy message he was taught; then he will be able to encourage others . . .* I know the brakes are fixed, because I trust in Digger's mechanical ability & my BELIEF is that the light is staying on as a constant reminder, to me, to tell others about my ABS . . . AMAZING BEAUTIFUL SAVIOR!

≈

I have a friend that is from Germany, & she is a real joy to me, & many others. She shared with me that her priests tells her she does not have to go into the confessional, because he always recognizes her voice. I Love it! *John 10:14—I am the good shepherd, I know my own sheep, and they know me!* Awesome, my God knows me! Like the priest & Mary, God recognizes my voice!!

≈

The letter was dated October 28, it told us that Digger would have to come back to Mayo in January for his check up! In October, January seems so far away. We continue to praise the Healer & pray that He, over the last 3 months, has found us faithful, for we know He is! *Hebrews 11:1—What is faith? The confident assurance that what we hope for is going to happen!* Enough said!

≈

We are prepared!! Our women's retreat is this weekend I am blessed by the sisterhood, from the more mature women that are so grounded in their faith, to the young women raising children in a Bible reading home. We all come together with expectant hearts to seek His face! *Psalm 23:6—Your goodness & unfailing love will pursue me ALL the days of my life!* No need for ticket refund, He's never a no show . . . He pursues us!

≈

The cruise control in our car stopped working. Much like us cruisen & then Digger's diagnoses of lymphoma slow down &

speed up. Did we pray more yes! Did we read the word more & stand on it yes! *Proverbs 3:6—Seek His will in all you do, & He will direct your path.* The Dr. told us today, lymphoma is GONE! Thank you Jesus! May our path directed by Him, bring Him Glory! We are cruisen & Dig fixing the cruise control!

≈

It started last night a flash like an arch in the corner of my eye, now this morning black dots seem to float across my vision. Googled it & sure enough, another aliment attributed to old age. Not life threatening or even vision loss, but a reminder that time marches on & my witnessing to the lost becomes more urgent, for it says in *John 9:25—For I once was blind but now I see!* For Life in Christ gave me sight!

≈

10/31 Experiencing God Unit 5 . . . *Isaiah 55:8—For my thoughts are not your thoughts, neither are your ways my ways.* God speaks through His Word, NEVER EVER would I have THOUGHT that I could write. But if I love Him & I want to accomplish His WAYS, I must listen & obey. Each day I write, I take God's word & apply it to my life to share on FB! For His thoughts & ways are not mine & for me to accomplish it takes GODfidence!

≈

October 31st & we're still playing golf. I did trade my golf shoes/gold flip flops for sparkly shoes! *Isaiah 52:7—How beautiful on the mountains are the feet of the messenger who brings good news, of peace & salvation, the news that our God reigns!* It doesn't matter if my feet are beautiful, in flip flops, or shoes, or if I am, on mountains or greens, I'm called to share the Salvation Message! The Good News . . . Our God Reigns!

≈

41 degrees, warm jogging pants, gloves, ear muffs, starter jacket, ready for my jog . . . zipper in jacket just broke! *Ecclesiastes 4:12—A person standing alone can be attacked & defeated, but two can stand back-to-back & conquer* . . . Digger & I together fixed the zipper, you see our God is a God of DETAIL! If it matters to me it matters to Him. The sun was shining brightly when I hit the street. More DETAILS . . . I felt the warmth of His SON!

≈

Recently I was accused of being SELF-SERVING, by what I had posted on FB. Definition . . . Self-serving describes a person/action done only for one's own benefit, sometimes at the expense of others. *2 Corinthians 11:30—If I must boast, I would rather boast about the things that show how weak I am.* I pray that in all I post that JESUS is seen as my only strength, that I am a work in progress, weak & nothing without Him! I want to be accused of being JESUS-SERVING!

≈

I was humbled & empowered by all the encouraging comments I received on my post of being self-serving! *Revelation 14:12—God's people must endure persecution patiently, obeying His commands & maintaining their faith in Jesus.* Patience is not one of my strengths, but if I love Him I will obey, *James 2:20—How foolish! Can't you see that faith without good deeds is useless?* I'm JESUS-SERVING with YOU!

≈

My car automatically goes to certain places. Turn down a street & it is on auto pilot it goes to work, golf course, SDC/Terrazzo . . . *Psalm 32:8—The LORD says, I will guide you along the best pathway for your life. I will advise you & watch over you.* Good thing! I was on my way to my friend Kay's off W. 18th & ended up at DaySpring! I love the path the Lord has me on, that He watches over me! Today I'm going to DaySpring, my car knows the way!

# November

*And give thanks for everything to God the Father in the name of our Lord Jesus Christ.* Ephesians 5:20

Experiencing God Unit 6, 11/7 . . . NO LORD, the 2 words you NEVER say, if He is truly the Lord of your life! He speaks through the Bible, prayer, church, circumstance & Holy Spirit! *Matthew 19:26—Jesus looked at them intently & said, Humanly speaking, it is impossible. But with God everything is possible.* He speaks to me & I feel like Noah, building an ark! But I trust & obey, because all things are possible with God! ALL THINGS!

≈

11/10 Experiencing God Reflection . . . God speaks through the Bible, prayer, circumstances, people, or in my life He just speaks! The moment God speaks to me is when He wants me to respond! So I get it, when I am called to pray for YOU, I will not say I will pray & walk away, oh no, it is right now. This week I prayed at work, restaurant, store, & phone! Because I love Him, it was a great week of obedience, prayer, & praise! He says if am faithful in the little tasks, He will give me the big ones & He keeps His promises!

≈

Judy is one of my mentors & has been told that she is loosing her eyesight! As we sang "My Faith Will Be My Sight." on Sunday, the Lord said this is for Judy, you go pray for her! *2 Corinthians 5:7—For we live by faith, not by sight.* As I crossed the aisle to pray with her I realized she was praying selflessly with the man in front of her, for his eyesight! That is why I want to be like Judy, Her Faith Continues to Give Her Sight!

≈

RIP Andy Rooney. He said it is a WRITER'S job to tell the TRUTH! *John 14:6—Jesus said, I am the way, the TRUTH & the life. No one can come to the Father except through me.* Soooo here's the TRUTH . . . There is only one way I could get to my Father in heaven! I had to admit to being a sinner, believe Jesus died & rose, asks Him into my heart & try to live for Him . . . JESUS SAID THIS! My job . . . to WRITE the TRUTH!

≈

Tuesday morning I met no one as I went for my jog! *Luke 3:5—Crooked roads shall become straight, rough ways smooth.* I looked down my street as I headed towards home, it is kinda crooked & defiantly not smooth. But I never jog alone, Jesus, is always with me, He makes my crooked roads a little straighter & my rough ways smoother, all the way to my Heavenly Home!

≈

Happy National CORDUROY Appreciation Day! 11/11/11 looks like corduroy, use your imagination! LOL! *Colossians 3:14—Above all, clothe yourselves with love, it binds us all together in perfect harmony.* Today I am wearing corduroy 1 of my favorite fabrics, but I also put on love, as everyday should be NATIONAL PUT ON LOVE DAY, to be clothed in harmony & bound together in love. LOVE looks sooooo good on YOU!

≈

My client Mary & I were talking, "What we're known for?" I said, "I PRAY to be known as a person that PRAYS, not just for wearing gold!" LOL. *Philippians 1:4—Whenever I pray, I make my requests for all of you with joy!* That day there was a Pedicure Party at Salon, as I left the salon that evening, so humbled as each woman requested my prayers. My PRAYER that my idenity as one who PRAYS was answered & Joyfully I PRAYED!

≈

Royal Rangers camped out, last Saturday. Digger, Kurt, & Xander built a primitive shelter/home to sleep in. *Matthew 7:14—But small is the gate & narrow the road that leads to life, only a few find it.* Xander was afraid that the door/gate to their shelter was to small, papa might not get in. LOL! No problem, because of the grace of the Father & the love of Jesus we are on the narrow road & able to enter the small gate, to our eternal shelter/home!

≈

Wow, we have had great golf weather! Usually by November, my golf game is only a SPECTATOR SPORT, as I watch on TV! *Ephesians 6:13—Therefore, put on every piece of Gods armor.* So to play, I put on 2 sweatshirts, ear-muffs, gloves, socks n SHOES. It was like serving the Lord & putting on His armor. But different than the game of golf, you can't just watch & still serve the Lord, there are NO SPECTATORS!

≈

11/14 Experiencing God unit 7 . . . According to Blackaby the opposite of FAITH is SIGHT! *Luke 18:42—Jesus said to him, "Receive your sight; your faith has healed you."* Faith heals & not just physical healings! My eyesight is bad, in fact without glasses I have double vision. So without my glasses my problems look twice as big, but as I see it, I also have twice as much JESUS POWER! That's FAITH & I'm THANKFUL!

≈

Today I am SO Thankful for . . . THE BIBLE, God's Word, my owners manual, my road map! *Psalm 119:105—Your word is a lamp to guide my feet & a light for my path.* God's word is alive & it breaths life into mine, without it *I* would have NOTHING to POST! Randy shared a statement at Fusion, that made me take a long hard look at my life & my witness . . . "We are the only BIBLE some people will ever read!" I pray to be a LIVING translation!

≈

Today I am thankful for . . . My New life, I'm a JESUS FREAK! *2 Corinthians 5:17—Anyone who belongs to Christ has become a new person . . . old life is gone; a new life has begun.* I have been told that I was a good person, before I was Born Again. But being good does not get me into heaven! The only way to the Father is to accept the Son, plus I could have never been good enough, as I always fall short. So thankful for HIS GRACE & my Freaky New Life!

≈

Today I'm Thankful for . . . Having Jody as my friend, today is her Birthday & a celebration in her honor is planned! *Ecclesiastes 3:4—A time to cry & a time to laugh. A time to grieve & a time to dance.* This scripture says it all . . . I have cried many tears because I miss her, yet I laugh because I remember her. Jody was a gift to me & many others & I still grieve, but I can hear her say Marsh, it's time to dance! Happy Birthday Jody, I love & miss you my friend!

≈

Today I am Thankful for . . . It's TGIF . . . Thank God It's Friday! *Psalm 136:2—Give thanks to the God of gods. His love endures forever.* TGIF . . . Thank God I'm Forgiven! Thank God I'm Free! More than that, it is just . . . THANK GOD! Not for the things He does for me, it is that HE is worthy to be PRAISED, in the GOOD & BAD times. TGIF . . . Thank God I'm FAVORED! HE said, He will LOVE ME FOREVER!

≈

Today I am Thankful for . . . My husband's faith & witness. *James 2:22—His faith & his ACTIONS worked together. His actions made his faith complete.* I have learned so much by Digger's faith ACTIONS. Times when our world seemed to be falling apart physically/cancer, emotionally/death, or spirituality/a church split, I learned from him, you JUST STAND! Because no matter the outcome, Christ will still be Christ, our Savior & still on the throne! I love you Dig!

≈

Today I am Thankful for . . . The many people that get/understand our vision/ministry & want to be involved! *Hebrews 7:7—Without question, the person who has the POWER to give a blessing is greater than the one who is blessed.* EMPOWERED . . . is the look on the faces of the young & old alike as they drop off a bike or wedding/prom dress! It is true, "To be blessed you must 1st be a blessing!" It's POWERFULL STUFF!

≈

11/21 Experiencing God Unit 8 . . . EVERY DAY I'm thankful GOD wants a love relationship with ME! *John 15:5—Yes, I am the vine; you are the branches . . . apart from me you can do nothing.* To follow someone else's method or program, is to forget my dependency on God. It is Spiritual Adultery! It never works! HE WORKS! Only God can tell me what to do . . . without Him I can do nothing!

≈

Today I am Thankful for . . . My job & that God knew the wax room at the Salon on Grand would be a prayer room! *Psalm 17:6—I am praying to you because I know you will answer, O God. Bend down & listen as I pray.* What a privilege for Mary & I to enter the prayer/wax room, knowing He would bend down, listen, & answer. No need to call in advance, He is always available. It's a DIVINE APPOINTMENT!

≈

Today I am Thankful for . . . My sisters Pam & Sue, my brother Buddy & their families as later today we will all be together on VACATION! Matthew *18:20—For where two or three gather together as my followers, I am there among them.* Thank you in advance Lord, for safe travel, time together, food, coffee, games, love, & laughter. But most of all for YOUR presence! Destination . . . The Lodge @ Basswood Resort, Platte City, Missouri here we come!!!

≈

Thanksgiving the Present! For 23 days I have LOVED reading YOUR heart felt posts of gratitude! *1 Thessalonians 5:18—Be thankful in all circumstances, for this is God's will for you who belong to Christ!* Not just in November am I to be grateful, BUT in all GOOD & BAD circumstances. Today I come to Praise Him for the life of my friend V. Grateful for our 20-year friendship, honored to officiate her funeral service! Thankful . . . I will see her again, because we both belong to HIM!

≈

Thanksgiving the Past! Kurt & family would spend one year with his mom & one with us, as sharing is a part of being a blended family, at holidays! On the year that it would be just Dig & me we would go to the MOVIES! *Psalm 20:4—May He grant your heart's desires & make all your plans succeed.* I would plan what we wanted to see, 1 year we got in 3 matinees & 1 night show, yes success!

≈

Thankful for . . . THANKSGIVING DINNER, loved it popcorn, raisenets & junior mints! Thanksgiving Past Present & Future! Day after Thanksgiving is called Black Friday! Retailers sometimes call it A GOOD FRIDAY! *John 3:16—For God loved the world so much that he gave His one & only Son, so that everyone who believes in Him will not perish but have eternal life.* Now that was a GOOD FRIDAY! God did not sell, HE gave! I did not have to get up early & it cost me nothing! Thankful for . . . The real, GOOD FRIDAY for it effects MY past, present, & FUTURE!

≈

Thanksgiving the Present! Time with family, we ate, hiked, paddle-boated, played games, pool, Just Dance, shopped, movies, or you could take a NAP! *Galatians 5:13—For you have been called to live in freedom, my brothers & sisters.* Freedom, yes to do what you want to do or do nothing at all, with my brothers & sisters! Thankful for . . . the LODGE, only in a furniture store have I seen 8 recliners in a row & here, there all for napping!

≈

Thanksgiving the Present! 11/28 Experiencing God unit 9 . . . My dear friend V. died Monday & we were to leave for vacation Wednesday morning, her funeral Wednesday afternoon. *John 14:15—If you love me, you will obey what I command.* Obedience & a love relationship with my heavenly Father enabled me, no matter the circumstances that preceded her passing, to officiate her funeral! If I love Him, I will obey Him. Thankful for . . . without Him I can do nothing!

≈

Thanksgiving the Past! On vacation in Salina, Kansas, looking for a place to eat Thanksgiving dinner, the ONLY place open Applebee's! *Matthew 6:11—Give us today the food we need.* After being seated we realized we were being fed by the Salvation Army as Applebee's had opened their doors to the less fortunate! We tried to leave, but we were told just donate! The meal was awesome & the memory made by my family priceless! Thankful for . . . supplying ALL of our needs Lord!

≈

Thanksgiving Past! My sister was moving over the Thanksgiving Holiday, we were young, never thought ahead & it was time to eat. *Psalm 62:5—Let all that I am wait quietly before God, for my hope is in Him.* What to eat, a holiday, in a small town, gas not turned on so no stove, & before microwaves. Yup Campbell's soup in a crock pot. We waited & waited, maybe not so quietly, our hope back then, in electricity! Thankful for . . . maturity & to really know Hope, yes Jesus!

≈

Don't know why I noticed how many friends I had on FB, maybe because it was an even number & the next time I looked it was odd, I had lost a friend! Someone unfriended me! *James 2:23—Abraham believed God, & God counted him as righteous because of his faith. He was even called the friend of God!* I am righteous only in God's eyes, that is by my faith, & God will never unfriend me. I am a friend of God & YOU!!!

≈

I bought Xander & Audra gifts while on vacation. X. a snake & A. what I THOUGHT was a really cool, shiny, purple hat! *Ephesians 4:11,12—Now these are the gifts Christ gave to the church . . . to equip Gods people to do His work . . .* Audie informed me, next time I bought her something make it about puppies or blue . . . that made me think! Forgive me Father for the times I wanted a different gift! Only by your grace can I lead a study, write, speak, give away a dress, or take out the garbage. YOUR gifts equip!

≈

I spent Sunday afternoon with Christian Sisters that I do not see very often, and I was so blessed! I am always encouraged by others walks and to recognize that we do serve a very personal God! The way He has worked in my life is often the opposite to my sister. So if you have served Him all your life and think you have no testimony, YOU have the best testimony! *1 Thessalonians 4:12—ALL people will respect the way you live!*

≈

We went to my Aunts for Thanksgiving, Xander had just started praying for our meals, so I THOUGHT/my plan, it would be wonderful if he prayed! Aunt E instead asked Digger, he blessed the food, afterwards I said Xander would you also like to pray? He said Papa just did! Didn't you listen? No I didn't, but God did! *1 John 5:14—He hears all prayers that are in line with His Will.* Ya, not my will be done!

≈

Have you seen the Santa movie where whoever picks up empty suit is Santa? My Aunt E had an air blown Santa in her yard and it was shut off so looked just like empty suit. Xander said, oh James, as I got close, don't touch it. He did not want his nana to be Santa. Ya gotta love child like faith? That is how we are to come to Jesus! *Luke 18:17—Anyone who doesn't have childlike faith will never enter the Kingdom of Heaven!*

≈

Over the years I bought many diet books, low carbs, calories counters, and many others, thinking they would have the magic formula! I now know the only formula I needed was found in the book that breaths, is alive, of freedom, The Bible, It changed my life. *Psalm 63:5—My soul satisfied as with the richest of food!* Feelings, not hunger is what I was feeding! My Jesus, is better than bread and butter!

≈

My sister called me on her way home. I could hear the fire trucks in back ground. The barn had burned and flames were heading for the house, please pray she says. Pray we did! It burnt right to the edge of the house, down the side walks, even burnt the dirt in the flower beds. The local paper acknowledged that there was divine intervention. Thank you Jesus! *James 5:16—A sincere prayer great power and wonderful results!*

≈

2 of my nieces ran 5ks Thanksgiving morning, so proud of them both! Marathon runners say there is something emotional about crossing the finish line. From experience I believe that is true for those of us who have run a 5k. My age I know entered into way I felt, Bucket List check! *For I can do all things through Christ who is my strength—Philippians 4:13.* So I keep reaching for the Highest Goal, ya, The Ultimate Finish Line!

≈

Thanksgiving the Future! It is the last day of November & I am THANKFUL that I have a whole year to make plans for Thanksgiving 2012 & even if all MY families' plans don't materialize, I sure love to plan! *Jeremiah 29:11—For I know the plans I have for you, says the LORD. They are plans for good &*

*not for disaster, to give you a future & a hope.* You see I do not know what My FUTURE HOLDS, but so Thankful . . . I know who HOLDS My FUTURE

# The Twelve Days Of Christmas

*Contrary to popular belief, these are not the twelve days before Christmas, but are the twelve days from Christmas until the beginning of Epiphany January 6th; the 12 days count from December 25th until January 5th.*

≈

On the 1st day of Christmas, My true love . . . MY HEAVENLY FATHER, He loved me before I loved Him, He loved me even when I was unloveable! Gave to me . . . HIS SON JESUS, He came to earth knowing He would die for my sins, so that I would receive GOD'S GRACE! *2 Corinthians 9:15—Thank God for this gift too wonderful for words!* I Thank you God, for JESUS, THE GREATEST GIFT I HAVE EVER RECEIVED! Merry CHRISTmas to YOU my FB family & friends!

≈

On the 2nd day of Christmas . . . I received a Snuggie last year, keeps me warm & I love it! The idea is to put it on & then sit down as the opening is in the back! *Ephesians 6:13—Therefore, put on every piece of God's armor so you will be able to resist the enemy in the time of evil. Then after the battle you will still be standing firm.* God's armor like the Snuggie covers you completely in the front, but different than God's armor, you don't have to sit down, as God always has your back, so stand firm!

≈

On the 3rd day of Christmas . . . We got a new TV, our old eyes now have better sight! *James 1:27—Pure & genuine religion in the sight of God the Father means caring for orphans & widows*

. . . Our new TV is seeing things as they really are, the colors are so pure & genuine the same way our religion should be seen by God. RELIGEON is not to be a program, law, or denomination, but an intimate RELATIONSHIP with Jesus! To see where He is a work & join Him, caring for ALL people.

≈

On the 4th day of Christmas . . . I do the shopping for the stocking stuffers, is that a word . . . stuffers? I buy stuff like frosting, cherry pie filling, kaleidoscopes, prisms, movie passes & everybody needs a flashlight! These are things that my family members like! *Joshua 24:15— But as for me & my family, we will serve the LORD.* Because they are MY FAMILY, I know their likes & WHO THEY SERVE!

≈

On the 5th day of Christmas . . . Papa always takes the grandkids shopping or their Christmas presents, something that he started doing a few years ago & now a tradition that is more about being in presence than the present. *Proverbs 15:20— Sensible children bring joy to their father*; Dig was real surprised this year as the G-kids knew exactly what they wanted & it was all very reasonably priced! Grandkids, sensible & brought to papa great JOY!

≈

On the 6th day of Christmas . . . My 1st piece of jewelry Digger ever gave me many many years ago, was a diamond heart necklace. We went together, a week before Christmas to shop & even had it gift-wrapped! (Digger thought that was really stupid!) *Proverbs 15:13—A glad heart makes a happy face.* For the next week every day I would come home from work, unwrap & rewrap this gift, yes that little heart made me so happy & still does!

≈

On the 7th day of Christmas . . . Digger bought me 2 dresses for Christmas, this back in the day when we wore dresses for everything! I had looked for that special dress for New Year's Eve, no luck, & he found me 2! *Colossians 3:14—Above all, clothe yourselves with love, which binds us all together in perfect harmony.* His advantage he didn't even look or care about the price tag, he bought what he liked. He dressed me in love, the right color, style, & size . . . that makes for perfect harmony!

≈

On the 8th day of Christmas . . . We had decided as an outreach to give away turkeys right before Christmas. We had a list of some people we wanted to give too, but it was so fun to pray, drive down the street & just knock on a door to share the love of Jesus! *Matthew 10:42—If you give even a cup of cold water to one of the east of my followers, you will surely be rewarded.* Our reward? No words to describe the awesome feeling, the gift not cold . . . It was frozen!

≈

On the 9th day of Christmas . . . This year for Christmas I gave my grandchildren an IOU! I wrote a note saying I owed them 1 movie a month for the next year, they were not at all impressed! *Romans 13:8—Owe nothing to anyone except to love one another.* As I see it an IOU of a gift of time/movie is a way to love my grandchildren & who knows they might even end up liking the IOU/gift & love me back.

≈

On the 10th day of Christmas . . . In the garbage dumps of Mexico for Christmas, we had wrapped the love of Jesus into gifts that we were going to give to the kids, then loaded into the bus & now ready to deliver! *Luke 2:12—You will recognize Him by this sign: You will find a baby wrapped snugly in strips of cloth, lying in a manger.* The baby Jesus was recognized by the way He was wrapped & so were the soccer balls! You see the love of God cannot be disguised!

≈

On the 11th day of Christmas . . . As our families grew, my siblings & I found it harder to buy Christmas gifts & so expensive to send, so we decided on a new plan! *Psalms 20:4—May He grant your heart's desires & make all your plans succeed.* Now instead of getting each other gifts we plan a get-together every Thanksgiving & Easter! It is all about the time we plan to spend together, better than any gift money could buy, yes it is our heart's desire . . . we call it success!

≈

On the 12th day of Christmas . . . No money for Christmas gifts, Digger was laid off! *1 Peter 4:10—God has given each of you a gift from His great variety of spiritual gifts. Use them well to serve one another.* Digger had spent allot of time in the garage & to my surprise he made me a gift! It was a bell necklace, I collected bells! He whittled a mold of a bell out of wood, melted all his silver coins from Germany (army) & attached a chain! Digger has many gifts & he uses them very well. Right after JESUS, this is my FAVORITE Christmas gift!

# DECEMBER

*For God loved the world so much that he gave His one & only Son, so that everyone who believes in him will not perish but have eternal life.* John 3:16

Xander spent the night & I could hear him coughing, I got up to make sure he was OK. As he coughed his arm came up as he was taught in school, he was coughing into his armpit! He was obeying the rules to cough into his cough pocket & yet he was sound asleep! *Psalm 119:55—I reflect at night on who you are, O LORD; therefore, I obey your instructions.* Oh Lord to know you is to love you & I do love you, so I will obey . . . awake or asleep!

≈

I LOVE God's plan! We had lunch to celebrate the Birthday of my very young friend Susan! *Ephesians 2:10—For we are God's masterpiece. He has created us anew in Christ Jesus, so we can do the good things He planned for us* . . . I don't always understand His plan as a 60 year old with a table of 40 year olds, but there is a plan for us as sisters in Christ. Each of us brings something different to the table & as I looked around that table I saw . . . GOD'S MASTERPIECE, created anew through Jesus, all to accomplish good/great things!

≈

Digger & I went to the action packed movie, Mission Impossible! As usual the missions were offered & then there was the option to accept! *Mark 13:10—For the Good News MUST be preached to all nations.* The word says that this is my mission, if I should accept it, to share the Good News, at work, my neighborhood, WalMart, or FB . . . So I accept my action packed MISSION knowing with God, nothing is IMPOSSIBLE!

≈

Excitement is in the air as Friday is opening night for ONE BETHLEHEM NIGHT at DaySpring. This is when all the writing, acting, & musical talent come together, to share the GOOD NEWS! *Romans 1:3,4—The Good News is about His Son. In His earthly life He was born into King David's family line, & He was shown to be the Son of God when He was raised from the dead by the power of the Holy Spirit. He is Jesus Christ our Lord!* I'm a greeter & hoping to see YOU! The Reason for this Season all started . . . ONE BETHLEHEM NIGHT!

≈

This time of year many lawns have a pile of fabric on them, that when turned on, fill with air to become a Santa, Grinch, or Snowman! *Job 34:14,15—If God were to take back His spirit & withdraw His breath, all life would cease & humanity would turn again to dust.* You see without Him I would be like the pile of fabric/dust as HE ALONE is my power source! He fills my life with His Spirit! He breathes life into mine!

≈

To be a checker at a store at this time of year has to be a difficult job, people are in hurry, tired, frustrated, they just want to get home! A few years ago I started to carry and give away, what I lovingly call "crabby clerk candy." Not that they are all crabby, but you would be surprised what a piece of chocolate can do! *Luke 6:38—Blessings come from giving!* To be blessed I MUST first be a BLESSING!

≈

December 24th & IT'S A WONDERFUL LIFE & my favorite Christmas movie! The movie is a story of what life would be like without ONE person, how lives would be so different! It's so important to know & believe that ONE person like YOU or me, we really do make a difference! *Colossians 1:15—Christ is the visible image of the invisible God . . .* Now that is THE LIFE that made the ULTIMATE difference! Because of JESUS CHRIST. It is a WONDERFUL LIFE!!!

≈

I had self-checked myself out at WalMart. I did not think of myself as crabby . . . but I had the "Crabby Clerk Candy" so yes, I think I will . . . yum, peppermint dark chocolate! *1 Timothy 1:14—Oh, how generous & gracious our Lord was! He FILLED me with the faith & love that come from Christ Jesus.* You don't have to qualify to receive the love of Jesus, it is available to all to be FILLED with faith, love, & sometimes chocolate!

≈

Don't you wonder some times, Lord what is your will for my life? *James 4:17—It is a sin to know what to do and not do it!* So when in doubt, I pray Lord, use me till you use me up! I know He will show up at the perfect time to show me my next step, until then I worship and adore Him and share the love of Jesus with others. It excites me, to let go and let God!!!

≈

Yesterday I had the privilege to hear a young man eulogize his 58 year old dad, He told of being 4, excited, running to his dad, and oh how much he loved him. He went on to say that he looks forward to doing it again, when they meet in heaven. What a visual, for all of us, as we run excited to the arms of our Heavenly Father. What peace for Cory to know of his Dad's Salvation! If you died today where would you spend eternity? *Romans 10:9—Believing in Jesus as Lord brings eternal life!*

≈

We are to be open and bold for the gospel of our Lord and Savior, Jesus Christ. Not ashamed to put a Bible on your desk at work, not ashamed to pray before you eat, not ashamed of the One who died for us? We are not called to be in the Secret Service! *Luke 12:8—Acknowledge God on earth, He will acknowledge us in heaven!* Yahoo!

≈

Do you hang on to the bars of your own prison cell? I did! I swapped one addicting sin/habit for another, always coming back to FOOD! I was held captive by my own sinful nature. Jesus and the Bible, freed me from the bondage of guilt, released me from death row I was able to changed my behaviors! *Romans 6:23—God saves, us from the consequences of sin!* I am still a work in progress, praising Him for Grace!

≈

Friday night we attended a beautiful wedding! Before the Bride entered, Pastor Mark quizzed the groom of his intentions, and then announced "Jaimes behold your Bride!" It was awesome! Christ loves the church and He calls us His Bride! Our Heavenly Father will someday behold us with the same look of love, that Jaimes had for Krista! Wow! *Romans 8:39—Nothing separates us from God's Love!*

≈

My niece Courteney is so sick, something Dr. just can't seem to diagnose. She lives in Texas and it is so hard not to be with her and take care of her. Peace, at this time comes only because I know Jesus knows the diagnoses! He has her in His loving arms and as much as I love her, God loves her more. *Hebrews 13:5—*

*He will never leave us or forsake us.* Prayers sooooooo appreciated!!

≈

The Lord told me to pray with a client, she had a MRI done, and was waiting the outcome. She was in the back room, as I entered to offer up prayer, she took the Lords name in vain and not just once. I just wanted to walk away. My Lord said no you pray with her! He extended grace that I was not so willing to give! Always enough and amazing. *Psalm 103:8—Our God is gracious!*

≈

Ya know, following a snowplow is allot like following God! Both make a path, to see the way I should go, even sanded so I don't slip and yet I will still try to pass! *Psalm 32:8—God guides us along the right path.* Only difference, God does not want me to keep my distance, He wants me to stay very close! *Romans 8:39—Nothing can separate us from the Love of Jesus!!*

≈

I love lights, Christmas light are up and on all year long at our house. Dig says planes try to land outside and he has gotten a tan from the ones inside. I believe because of living in the dark, that would be without Jesus for the first part of my life, that the lights are a living knowledge of Matthew 26:55—*Jesus is coming back!* Ya, I want to be ready!

≈

My grandson Xander listened intently as Pastor Kevin spoke after one of our previous years Christmas performances, P.K. talked of the reason for this season & how we get it all mixed up sometimes! *John 10:14—I am the good shepherd; I know my own sheep, and they know me!* After the service Xander said to me . . . "James, Did you know that Santa calls me little boy! But JESUS, HE KNOWS MY NAME!"

≈

I have loved being a greeter for the Christmas performances of ONE BETHLEHEM NIGHT! *John 15:17—This is my command: Love each other.* It is so much fun to welcome old & many new friends to something that you know is going to bless them! I told Suzanne last night I would like to be an usher in a theater or maybe a WalMart greeter! Well until then & for 2 more performances I get to put on something sparkly & as we say at DaySpring because, it is commanded by JESUS, Come As You Are . . . You'll Be Loved!

≈

Experiencing God Unit 10 . . . God builds His body to match the assignment! *Ephesians 4:12—Their responsibility is to equip God's people to do His work & build up the church, the body of Christ.* A perfect example, of an ASSIGNMENT, One Bethlehem Night at DaySpring! God equipped the writer, singers, actors, set constructors, sound, lights, costumes . . . We were God equipped as a body, to accomplish the assignment! My assignment & I accepted it! A greeter, I was God equipped to share & receive the love of JESUS!

≈

I thank you Lord, for yesterday, for the balmy weather that I could have a December JOG! Psalm *18:36—You have made a wide path for my feet to keep them from slipping.* I jogged by many homes all decorated for Christmas, through slush, some patches of ice & then by the bin that they keep the sand for de-icing! Reminding me that when I stay on the wide path He has made for me, I will not slip! Thank you JESUS!

≈

It's almost a month since my dear friend V. died. Strange after all these years of a daily trip to St. Luke, not to go anymore. The family gave me a Christmas cactus in her memory, it is beautiful filled with new blooms everyday! *Psalm 34:18—The LORD is close to the brokenhearted; He rescues those whose spirits are crushed.* My friend Barb always talks about getting unexpected, kisses from God! So yes, the beautiful flowers in a Marcia's lipstick shade of red, are KISSES from God & V.!

≈

I am a power napper, every day I look forward to my 15 minutes! *Ecclesiastes 3:1—For everything there is a season, a time for EVERY activity under heaven.* I Love God's Word! It says there is a time for EVERY activity that would include my prayer time, jogs, Zumba, FB, my Bible Studies, & naps! You name it, there is a time for it! Love that I serve a God of detail! If it is important to me, then there is time for it, if only 15 minutes!

≈

My favorite Dove Promises is Peppermint Bark silky smooth dark chocolate & it is only available at Christmas time! Inside each wrapper is a very politically correct promise, so I contacted the company, to make a suggestion! *John 3:16—For God loved the world so much that He gave His only Son, so that everyone who believes in Him will not perish but have eternal life.* If making promises to go with their CHRISTmas candy, why not go with the "Reason for the Season?" Now that's a Promise!

≈

I love the crowds, the hustle bustle while I shop! But I know that being a clerk at a store can be very stressful, as the customer is ALWAYS RIGHT! *Mark 9:41—If anyone gives you even a cup of water because you belong to the Messiah . . . that person will be rewarded.* This time of year I hand out, what I affectionately call "Crabby Clerk Candy." This is the Love of Jesus in a piece of candy & I give it to store clerks! It's Better than cup of water & my reward . . . a smile & a thank you . . . may you be to Blessed to be Stressed!

≈

Dig & I went to Steel Magnolias at SCT, last night, great job done by all the women in the cast! I have spent 42 years behind a chair in a beauty salon, so this story was very real to me. All about the sisterhood, the strength, love, & courage of women, the bond, laughter, & the tears! *1 Thessalonians 5:17 SAYS . . . Never stop praying!* Yes, call me Annelle, a crazy, Born Again, pray about everything, kind of hair dresser & proud of it! Thank you ladies for a very enjoyable night, I laughed, I cried . . . GREAT JOB!

≈

We attended the Seasoned Saints Christmas Party, good food & a great fellowship! *Romans 12:6—God has given us different gifts for doing certain things well.* We each brought a gift for a game of exchange. You pick a gift & once unwrapped someone can take your gift, funny we always seem to want what we don't have! God gives each of us our own, special, unique, gifting, so don't try to be someone else, as there is no exchange! Unwrap your gift & use it well!

≈

I changed profile picture because the dresses we were holding were given away at Say Yes To A Dress! So what is my profile? A client came in the Salon one day & announced, have you seen it, there is gold car with a JESUS bumper sticker on it in your parking lot? *Romans 1:16—For I am not ashamed of the Gospel of Jesus Christ!* So my profile? May I be seen as His, as my sticker says, & I know "Jesus is the Answer."

≈

Luke 10:41 is the story of Mary & Martha, it is a wonderful parable for this busy season! *Jesus says "Martha you are so upset over all the details. The only thing worth being concerned about Mary has discovered!"* as she sat worshiping at His feet. It's Christmas Eve, what are you doing? Stressing or worshiping at His feet? There is only ONE Reason for the Season! May yours be a MARY Christmas!

≈

Xander & I did our "Christmas Walking" (Grand Meander) our yearly tradition! As usual X. can immediately see what is being sculptured out of ice & Me . . . well he told me it might be my glasses/OLD EYES! LOL! *Matthew 19:14—Jesus said, Let the children come to me . . . the Kingdom of Heaven belongs to those who are like these children.* There is nothing better than seeing the wonders of the Season through the EYES of a child & I agree with Pastor Kevin, as he said Sunday "When I grow up I want to be a kid!"

≈

Minerva's for Pasta Night! We range in ages, 20s to us in our 60s . . . oh how I LOVE the body of Christ! *Luke 14:15—A man sitting at the table with Jesus exclaimed, What a BLESSING it will be to ATTEND a banquet in the Kingdom of God! Matthew 18:20—For where two or three gather together as my followers, I am there among them.* Like a banquet in the Kingdom, HE was in our midst & I was blessed to attend! The pasta & Chocolate Bombe Dessert YES HEAVENLY!

≈

Tonight, Grand Meander & the toy giveaway at the SPENCER DREAM CENTER! Digger has refurbished 20 bikes to GIVE away. He takes a broken, dirty bike, fixes and cleans it till it shines! *2 Corinthians 5:17—Anyone who belongs to Christ has become a new person, old life is gone; new life begun.* That's me, refurbished by Jesus, as my old life was broken & dirty. I'm still a work in progress, but I have been told I shine! Thank you Jesus!

≈

It was a great night Grand Meander & doors were open at the Spencer Dream Center. How much coffee, hot chocolate, popcorn, bikes or toys did we give away, no idea! What I do know is the look on each face as we were cleaning up, smiles that could not be contained, filled with Jesus to overflowing! *Matthew 10:35—If you give even a cup of cold water . . . you will be blessed!* You see, you cannot out-give Our God!

≈

*Acts 20:35—The words of Jesus, "It is more blessed to give than to receive."* It's Christmas & we gave away turkeys! Just knocked on doors some people we knew some just picked a house & handed a frozen turkey to who ever answered! I cannot describe the look on faces, yes priceless! We were blessed . . . for giving in it purest form, requires nothing in return! Thank you Jesus!!!

≈

Every Christmas mom made the same dress for my sisters & me, she wanted us to look alike, but even then we had different gifts. Pam is a teacher & Suzie a physical therapist. Both important jobs & very different from mine! *Romans 12:6—God has given each of us the ability to do certain things well!* Always a work in progress, I know the only one I should ever compare myself to is the OLD ME! The me I was yesterday!

≈

Christmas in the garbage dumps of Mexico! My mission to cut hair! Mark shared in Spanish the Christmas story & the salvation message with the people that live there, many accepted Christ! I love to live out scripture as it says in *Colossians 1:6— The same Good News . . . it's changing lives everywhere!* In the work place, streets of Spencer, church, or dump, we are to share the Good News! It changed my life the day I first believed!

≈

Last Christmas a mom & dad in checkout line in front of me counted out coins to pay for the PJs & coloring books. The children, no shoes, just socks. It tugged at my heart? I ran through the parking lot to find & share the love of Jesus/$ with her. Did they really need it? I don't know. What I do know is *Hebrews 13:2—Show hospitality to strangers for some who have done this have entertained angels, without even knowing it!*

≈

I love & have many Nativities. I was putting them out & noticed that Joseph was without a staff in one, so I took a golf club off one of my trophies & used it. Audra had spent the night & was getting ready for school she looked at this nativity & said oh look James, Mary & Joseph are taking care of baby Jesus on a golf course. *Mark 10:16—Jesus blessed the children!* And Audra, oh she blessed Me!

≈

Xander asked, where is the big tree James? I said in basement, don't ya like the little one? You see since Dig was healed of lymphoma, he has nested in the comer where we have always put the big tree. Today I Praise the Lord for His healing hand & that He has given me new priorities! *Proverbs 3:6—Seek His will in all you do & he will direct your paths.* 2011 . . . new priorities, not the rut, a brand new path!

≈

Xander called me excited & happy about the gifts he had purchased for Christmas, just like me he had to tell someone. He went through the whole list down to the dog & then said do you want to know what I got the cat? I said sure. He said just a minute I have to go in other room, the cat is sitting right by me! LOL! *2 Corinthians 9:7—God loves a cheerful giver!* Xander was just that & God & I we both smiled!

≈

At Christmas Papa takes time to take each grandkid shopping. This year papa, found Xander's gifts, without him. Christmas Eve papa called to see if Summer was ready to shop, Xander answered, what about me, when do I get to go? *Matthew 2:2—We (Wise Men) have come to worship Him!* Lesson learned, like the Wise Men with Jesus, the grandkids want to be in papa's presence before the presents.

≈

The Christmas Shoes was DaySpring's spectacular this year! Maggie, my daughter in the play, was explaining to her son that God does not take us to heaven when we die, He receives us. The choice is ours, we must be born again!! *Peter 1:5—God in his power will protect you, until you receive your salvation!* "Away in the Manger" would go like this & receive us to heaven To live with Thee there!

≈

I am Joyful noise yet, a part of The DaySpring Choir this Christmas. You see Fearless Leader Randy, encouraged me to be involved! I believe Fearless is preparing me for the heavenly choir, because my ability, along with many talented gifted singers, is living out scripture. *Romans 8:28—God causes everything to work together for good, for those who love Him & are called according to His purpose! For God's Glory!*

≈

My Dad said that Santa delivered gifts Z-A. Ya, because our last name was to Zubradt. After the Christmas Eve service, we sang Christmas carols, on what seemed the longest ride from Hartley to our house by Everly! As Kids we knew our Santa gifts had already delivered, that is faith! *Hebrews 11:1—The confidence to know what we hope for is going to happen.* May you share your faith & make memories this season!

≈

Dad was carrying in the Santa gifts after we got home from church that Christmas eve. As he put down the package it rolled over & the baby doll inside cried. It only added to the excited anticipation of what was to come. The Bible is an exciting read of what is to come, but just like a present, I must open it! *John 14:2—Jesus says I go to prepare a place for you!* Make time this year, open & read the greatest story ever told.

≈

Mom always hid our Christmas gifts in the same closet, then said, stay out of it. Did I listen, yes, but as a teenager it was the first place I went when she was not in the house! *Deuteronomy 6:3—Listen closely to everything I say. Be careful to obey!* God like mom knows me, my freewill & choices are still mine, but I pray, Oh Lord may I listen & then obey!

≈

We always got to open one gift before we left for Church on Christmas Eve, mom's choice of course! It was always something to unwrap and then immediately wear. *Romans 12:6—God has given us gifts/talents/abilities to do certain things well!!* Have you unwrapped your God given gift? I am sure it will look good on you!

≈

It was the year our Dad died, no celebration of Christmas for us. Then it hits ya, in the midst of the hurt and sorrow, that life as we knew it had changed but would go on. We went downtown Everly found a branch of a tree that we stuck in coffee can that would tip over every time you open or closed the door! We said we did it for Buddy, he was 5! *Psalms 34:18—God comforts the brokenhearted!* He does it for all of us!

≈

Kurt and Sheli went shopping on Christmas Eve so Xander spent the day with us, it was his 1st Christmas! We let him unwrap & play with his toys, & then we rewrapped, so he could open again later for his mom & dad. We had a Dress Rehearsal! How we live our lives, it is the real deal, not a rehearsal! Thank you Jesus for your mercy and grace! *Joshua 24:15 says . . . But as for me and my family we will serve the Lord!*

≈

Christmas get-togethers have started, Tuesday, was pasta night at Minerva's & fellowship with the family of God! As I looked around the table at the couples, age 20 to 60, I saw Jesus in each face. *Matthew 18:20—When believers get together God is among them!!* I am so blessed & encouraged by testimonies of others! You see gender, age, or location did not matter, Jesus is the reason! We had church!

≈

Courteney was 5 we went to the Santa movie, leaving the theater she had some questions, in her little Texan accent, how does Santa get in your house if you don't have a fireplace? Her mom said well if you don't believe . . . oh I believe I believe, she said! She was confessing her hope! *Hebrews 11:1—Faith/Hope, evidence of the things we cannot see.* Like a child at Christmas, I am excited to walk by Faith!

≈

Oh how I miss my friend Kathy, she LOVED Christmas! *More blessed to give than to receive—Acts 20:35.* That was her! She was a God given gift to me, always had my back, she showed me how to live & how to die. She walked her talk! I would eat the chocolate off the nutty bar, & she would eat the ice cream, one of the many ways we were opposites, but we both love Jesus! Our eternal friendship was built on Him!

≈

Christmas carols love them, could sing them all year, why don't we? Courteney as a child would sing along with her own interpretation, & sometimes a good idea! Hark the herald Angels sing . . . Glory to the newborn King! / Peace on earth and mercy mild / God and SANTA reconciled. *Jeremiah 3:22—God wants to restore relationships!* Tiz the season, today is the day, of reconciliation & restoration, love His Word, & Courts!

≈

The Seniors from Church Christmas party today! Hard not to over eat, as conversation starts & food so good, but I have a song in my head Amazing Grace/My Chains are gone. "The Lord has promised good to me, His word my hope secures, He will my shield and PORTION be, As long as life endures My chains are gone, I've been set free!" He is my PORTION, always the right amount! *Psalms 107:9—God satisfies!*

≈

What a blessing to be a part of the Spencer's Christmas Festival of Lessons and Carols Sunday, & I believe that God was pleased! To see His family come together all to bring Him Glory! The platform was filled, as all of the choirs united to sing the The Hallelujah Chorus! It was not denominational but inspirational! *John 10:16—One flock, one Shepherd!* Serving Him together!

≈

My grandma because she loved me she called me fleshy, not fat! But, I am a teenager her biggest granddaughter! Every year at Christmas she gave each of her granddaughters the same gift, that year slippers. I will never forget, mine a size 10, biggest girl, biggest feet! *Romans 8:1—There is no condemnation for those who belong to Christ!* Just as my grandma loved me unconditionally, Jesus also loves us, just as we are!

≈

Funny what you remember as a child, my mom only sat down to eat, she never just sat and relaxed, she was a worker! Only on Christmas Eve, do I remember her sitting down for any length of time! *Mark 6:31—Jesus says, Let's get away from the crowds for a while and rest.* May your children see you take time this season to rest, to celebrate, and to worship Jesus, the Reason for Every Season!

≈

My Dad had a fabulous voice, once the Pastor had him lead the carols at our Christmas Eve services. I can still hear his voice after all these years, the smell of pine, and oranges, and the paper bags filled with candy and nuts! *Philippians 4:11—I have learned how to get along happily with much or little.* Praising God, for great memories, even in the times that there was little!

≈

Our neighbor has Christmas decorations surrounding his house, snow melts from the heat of the lights, People come by the van loads just to check it out. *John 8:12—Jesus says, I am the light of the world follow me & you won't stumble in dark, because you will have the light that leads to life!* Thank you Marv, for a bright spot, on a dark street, the Nativity that brings God Glory, & kids of all ages love it!

≈

Peer pressure, no toys everyone wanted a transistor radio for Christmas! Christmas Eve the ONLY thing that would come in on radio was the Christmas story. With earphones I listen, & the story came alive! *Matthew 2:11—They entered & fell down before Him & worshiped bringing gifts!* Today as then, the Wise Still Seek Him! Jesus, unlike any other person, sent for a very special purpose. Thank You for the Cross!

≈

No Baby, no Cross . . . Jesus the Greatest Gift I was ever given! So blessed to know people that loved me enough to pray me into the Kingdom. My list is long, who are you praying for?

*1 Timothy 1:15—This is true, Christ came to earth to save the sinner!* He hung on a cross for you & me! Humbled to know that my life nailed Him there! Eternal life is only through Him, He loves us from one nailed hand to the other!

≈

When we went to Fusion last night it was a beautiful evening, the perfect ending to a gorgeous day! We came out of church an hour & a half later, the ground was covered, yes white! I don't know who was praying for snow, but how quickly the weather can change! *Malachi 3:6—I am the LORD & I do not change.* The one & only constant, never changing, in my life . . . the LORD! So, if you don't like the weather just wait a minute it will change as this is Iowa!

≈

The Dollar Tree is one of my grandkids favorite place to Christmas shop. No need to call for a price check, everything is a dollar! *1 Corinthians 7:23—God paid a HIGH PRICE for you* . . . When Jesus went to the cross, for me, He did not call for a price check. There was no checklist to qualify me like . . . a Pastor no, a Teacher no, an Evangelist no! He paid the same HIGH PRICE for me as He did for everyone else! To Him WE are PRICELESS, as He gave it all!

≈

Experiencing God Unit 12 . . . The last chapter so . . . Read the word! Stay involved with the body! Pray! Keep your vows to God! Process what God has said or done during this course! *Mark 8:18—You have eyes, can't you see? You have ears, can't you hear? Don't you remember anything at all? Follow through with everything you promised God you would do.* Good intentions are not the same as obedience! There are NO SUBSTITUTES FOR OBEDIENCE! Experiencing God THE END . . . NO, THE BEGINNING!

≈

I've been called a Reacher not a Preacher! LOL. I write about the love of my life, Jesus! He has made me a much better person than I could have ever been on my own. He equips me with His living word that I apply to my life, so I can share my stories, of His mercy, grace, love, & great sense of humor. *Luke 2:10—I bring you good news of great joy for all people!* He is the ink in my pen! Happy New Year Face Book Friends!

GOOD NEWS!   GREAT JOY!

*The Faithful Love of the LORD NEVER ENDS!*
Lamentations 3:22

## ABOUT THE AUTHOR

Marcia Zubradt-Cheevers was born and raised in Northwest Iowa. She didn't come to know Jesus until 1992 and since then has had a heart for God's people to understand HIS WORD and experience victorious living through Him. She writes from her daily experiences, beautifully interweaving the ordinary things of life with extraordinary revelations from God. Marcia considers it a privilege to share the love of Jesus through her J.O.Y. Seminars and would rather be on the golf course than in a kitchen. Marcia has worked as a hairdresser for 42 years and lives in Spencer, Iowa, with her husband Digger. She has one son, a daughter-in-law, and three amazing grandchildren!

Made in the USA
San Bernardino, CA
19 September 2014

# Where's the Next Shelter?

Gary Sizer

Copyright © 2015 Gary Sizer

All rights reserved. No part of this book may be reproduced, stored in a retrieval system, or transmitted in any form, or by any means, electronic, mechanical, photocopying, recording or otherwise, except for the use of brief quotations in a book review, without prior permission of the author.

Cover Illustration and Design by Jon Penn.
Chapter Illustrations by Mark Calcagni
Editing by Mark Houser

ISBN-13: 978-1517083946
ISBN-10: 151708394X

# Where's the
# Next Shelter?

*This book is for Katie. She keeps the wheels on the bus.*

# CONTENTS

| | | |
|---|---|---|
| 1 | Bear Hunt: Episode One | 1 |
| 2 | Flat Feet | 14 |
| 3 | Bear Hunt: Episode Two | 26 |
| 4 | She Who Shall Not Be Named | 35 |
| 5 | Land of the Noonday Sun | 43 |
| 6 | Happy Ghost | 59 |
| 7 | Pantry | 72 |
| 8 | Disco | 85 |
| 9 | Zero Town | 96 |
| 10 | Trail Legs | 108 |
| 11 | Salad Days | 118 |
| 12 | Up, Up and Away | 130 |
| 13 | Break | 144 |
| 14 | New Rules | 155 |
| 15 | Everyday | 168 |
| 16 | Thrown | 176 |
| 17 | Lode | 189 |
| 18 | A Hostile Environment | 203 |
| 19 | A Friendly Exchange | 216 |
| 20 | Pinky Swear | 228 |
| 21 | Enter the Ninja | 242 |
| 22 | One of Us | 256 |
| 23 | Launch | 271 |
| 24 | Orbit | 285 |
| 25 | Landing | 300 |
| | Epilogue | 314 |

# BEAR HUNT: EPISODE ONE

I WAS LICKING the last bit of meat sauce from my spoon when the black rock started walking.

The sun had just set on Flower Gap, in North Carolina's Shining Rock Wilderness. With just three days left until I started the Appalachian Trail, this was my final "shakedown" hike, a quick overnighter to practice with all my gear. I had set up my small tent behind some trees near the white quartz cliff that gave Shining Rock its name. Having hiked six miles already, I still felt the need for an evening stroll in the warm air of the early May evening, so I headed for Flower Gap.

I have wanted to walk the Appalachian Trail from the moment an old girlfriend told me it existed. "Wait, wait, wait," I'd said. "You're telling me that there's a trail that goes all the way from Georgia to *Maine*? No fucking way. Has anyone ever done it all at once?" Like most of our conversations from that time, I have either forgotten or buried most of the details, but I'm convinced that she told me it would take five years and cost a billion dollars. I must have believed her because otherwise I'm sure I would have tried to do it right then.

Flower Gap is especially beautiful on any clear day, but if you're lucky enough to catch a springtime sunset there, you'll see an already beautiful spot become something spectacular. As the last bright slice of light vanished below the horizon I turned my face upward. The dome of the sky was a perfect gradient, fading from crimson to salmon to twilight. It was against this purple twilight backdrop that the silhouette of a rock became an actual black bear.

Experienced outdoorsmen will tell you to make a triangle at dinnertime. Three points: one is your camp, two is where you cook and eat, and three is where you hang your food bag. Maximize these distances to minimize your chances of a bear encounter. I had done two of those three things, and now the rock moved. I looked down at the remains of my dinner, rehydrated spaghetti in a foil pouch. Black bears can smell a raisin from miles away; I was waving a beacon: Eat at Gary's, open all night. A swift black shadow headed for my pack, leaning against a tree where I had cooked my dinner, about a hundred yards away.

Experienced outdoorsmen will also tell you that black bears are timid, skittish creatures who will scamper away at the slightest noise. Just wave your arms and yell, they say. That bear will be gone so fast you'll wonder if he was ever really there. I walked deliberately straight toward my kitchen with as much body language as I could muster. *Bear, you are in my house now.*

"GIT!" I yelled. "G'won now, git!" I clapped and stomped for extra effect. The bear gave me just the slightest glance, cocking his head as if to say, "I don't speak English." He continued, quickly and soundlessly, towards my food. "NO!" I shouted. "Bad bear! That is *my* food! You get the hell away from it right now! YAAAAAHHHH!!!!" Banging my aluminum trekking poles together over my head hoping he might mistake them for extra scary antlers, I arrived at my pack just before he did.

Suddenly the bear stopped his advance. Instead of retreating, he moved sideways, still in an eerily silent way, making a lazy counterclockwise arc and watching as I hurriedly shoved food and pots into my bag. The stove slipped from my hands, making a dull thunk against a rock, and I glanced away from the beast long enough to locate it. The sun had been down a few minutes now, and here in the trees, twilight had given way to dark. I found the stove, bent to pick it up, and when I stood, the bear was gone.

I don't know if bears can smell fear as well as they can smell food. If they can, I'm sure my own jittery stank put him off. Outwardly I showed no visible signs of fear, but on the inside it was pure terror. My heart was racing. I took several deep breaths, bent at the waist and wiped my palms on my thighs. That thing was the size of my couch, I thought.

With the stove stuffed into my pack, I was fumbling in an outside compartment for my headlamp when I heard a twig snap. Then a branch, followed by the entire rhododendron bush just to my right, which bent completely to the ground as a humongous black shadow stomped and snorted over it.

I spun toward the sound, not thinking. "Goddamn it, bear, NO!" I yelled. "RAAAAAARRRGH!" I flicked my headlamp on flash mode and banged my poles again. *Flash.* There's the bear. *Flash.* Where's the bear? *Flash.* Oh shit, there's the bear. *Flash.* Where the fuck is he now?!

They say that running from a bear may trigger a predatory instinct, causing it to chase you. So I censored every message my brain was sending my legs, and did not run. Instead I calmed my headlamp and backed away slowly, noticing the rhododendrons had bounced back to their original upright position. I cleared my throat. "Okay, bear. Party's over," I said in a loud calm voice. "This is not me running away. This is me taking my things and leaving. Bye!" With that, I stepped backwards onto the trail, a narrow rooty footpath that would carry me the half-mile back to my tent.

. . .

Katie picked up on the third ring and greeted me with cheerful surprise. "Good morning!" she said. "I thought you didn't get reception up there."

"Yeah, well, I'm not up there," I replied.

"Oh?"

"Yeah," I laughed. "No. I'm parked outside REI. I should be home around lunch. Need anything?"

My question was met with silence, and for a moment I thought the call had dropped. Then my wife answered, "I don't think so. What do *you* need from REI?"

"Oh, just new stuff sacks for food bags. Mine are shredded."

Katie sighed. "Aw geez. Was it a bear?"

"Yep. The score is now: Bear 12, Humans 0."

"Twelve?" she said. "What does that mean?"

"That means that twelve people walked out of Shining Rock this morning hungry and dejected while— You're at work. Do you have time for this?"

"I have a few minutes," she said. "You okay?"

"Oh, I'm fine. But I'm pretty sure it's the same bear that stepped on you last summer."

"Wow! No kidding?"

"No kidding. And I got a good look at him too. Got right up in his face and told him you said hi."

"What happened?" she asked. "Didn't you hang your food bag?"

The higher elevations in Shining Rock Wilderness are near or above the tree line. Much of the trail there takes you through meadows and over balds where the tallest thing for miles is you, and there is literally nothing from which to hang a bag. The areas which are wooded are mostly rhododendron bushes, some mountain laurel, and stunted pines low enough to be reached by a raccoon on its hind legs; even the tallest ones can be climbed by the laziest of bears. I had camped there numerous times, but always in the winter when all the major threats to my food supply were happily hibernating.

"You know how it is," I said. "There was a pretty big group of college kids up there too. We all used the same tree. And when I went to make breakfast this morning, all I found was a pile of ripped-up bags and empty packages covered with drool and teeth marks. My food, their food, all of it—gone."

Twelve people, each carrying five days' worth of food, and all of it now in the belly of a single creature. I have a friend who weighs over 300 pounds—roughly bear-sized, in other words—and I cannot imagine him putting away the equivalent to Thanksgiving dinner for 12 all by himself. Given the chance, I'm sure the ravenous bear would do the same again for lunch.

"Well, at least you weren't two days from the car," Katie added.

There was that. I told her about another couple camped near me who had lost their food too. They had heard a sound in their camp in the middle of the night, and when the guy shined his flashlight out of his tent he saw two glowing eyes looking back at him. He panicked and threw his food bag at the bear in hopes of making it go away.

"Wait," Katie interrupted. "They had their food *in their tent*?"

"Yep."

"Idiots."

"Yep."

"All right, well, I have to get back to work," she said. "I'm sorry a bear ate your stuff, but I'm glad you're coming home."

"See you tonight," I said. "I love you."

Three more days. Three more nights. I'd get to sleep in my own bed three more times and then that was it. I was going to live outside for the next few months, outside in whatever weather happened, no matter what. Outside with the bugs and bears. This was Day Negative Three and I had already had one bear encounter. At that rate I was due for an infinite number of bear encounters. The math checked out.

I should buy cheap stuff sacks while I'm here, I thought. Then, I haven't even started yet, and I'm already replacing gear. What the hell have I gotten myself into?

■   ■   ■

Saturday, May 10. My alarm started beeping at 4 a.m., but I had already been awake for at least half an hour, smashed up against Katie, naked spooning in the dark. It would be a long time before I got to do this again. That thought, along with many others, had been swirling through my mind all night. I did my best to ignore them. My body and mind were already stressed and I felt emotionally worn out, like an hour after a good cry, tired but unable to sleep.

I hugged Katie tightly while she slapped blindly at the clock. "Ready?" she mumbled, discarding her half of the quilt as she sat up.

"Nope." It was impossible to be ready. Never mind that I'd spent the past three weeks scrambling to prepare. Never mind that I'd spent the past three years saving, planning, and daydreaming. Never mind that I'd spent the past three decades feeling the pull of the horizon, wrestling with the inexplicable desire to sleep under the stars, even if it meant waking up in the dirt. The very nature of this endeavor was to step into the unknown, to take on something too big to even see. In my mind, the idea of preparedness was an illusion; at best you can only ever *feel* ready. You can have all the gear, you can have a plan, and you can study yourself crazy. But gear fails, plans crumble, and the information you study only exists because someone else figured it out first. I had a plan, a good one, but I had thrown it out the window. Instead of hiking the trail next year, I was doing it now.

Sitting on the edge of our bed, fumbling in the dark for my pants, I considered that they were one of only two pairs I would wear for the next however many months.

Katie flipped the light on. "Sounds like Mark is already up."

Mark has been a driving force behind many of our outdoor adventures. Katie and I met him during a whitewater kayaking trip in North Carolina. She and I had tried very hard to get into kayaking before ultimately realizing that we lacked any actual talent for the sport. We'd spent much of our time out of our kayaks swimming in the foam, bouncing off of rocks, and salvaging our gear from eddies.

Mark, on the other hand, was talented and patient, the veteran of several Class V descents. He would hurl himself into rapids, confident that a mere flick of his paddle would upright him instantly. He cruised backwards to have an unobstructed view of Katie and me flailing as we accumulated our fair share of paddling-related injuries: a broken thumb here, a banged-up knee there. In 2005 I had a "gnarly swim" and dislocated my right shoulder on what should have been an easy river. That was the signal we needed to sell off our gear and transition into slower-paced, land-based activities. Such as backpacking—at which, no surprise, Mark was an expert at as well.

(As if that weren't enough, he's blessed with the kind of good looks you generally associate with TV news anchors. Think of a slightly shorter Anderson Cooper.)

We three shared a common love of all things nerdy: *The Hobbit* (before it was a movie), *Monty Python*, and '80s synth-pop. Plus, on land we were all equally matched. When Mark told us about a hike he was planning to one of the more remote parts of Newfoundland—four days with no trails, all map and compass work—we volunteered to join him. It turned out to be an unforgettable trek, starting with a boat tour of the fjords, then scrambling up the base of a waterfall, and eventually losing our only map somewhere in the tundra. But for us, the best part was being overtaken by fits of giggling upon discovering we would get to drive through a town named Dildo.

I shuffled into my living room to find Mark sitting on the couch fiddling with the settings on his camera. He asked me the same one-word question Katie had.

"Ready?"

"Yeah," I lied. Mark was joining me for the first three days. "Have you changed your mind? You can call Sue from the road and tell her you'll see her in…August?"

"Dude. This is going to take a lot longer than August."

"Oh, I know," I said, walking into the kitchen and filling the coffee maker. "I figure that's about when you'll get hurt or give up."

"Man," he said. "You know I really wish I could come with you. Well, in a way at least. I think I'd get sick of it after two weeks. Or you'd get sick of me. I stink, you know? Plus, I can't exactly quit my job right now."

"Neither can I," I said. "But I did."

■ ■ ■

We drove three hours from our home in Asheville, N.C. to Woody Gap, Ga., where Mark and I would walk back to in three days. While he moved gear from his car to ours, Katie and I stood at the overlook, staring at the clouds below, an ocean of fog broken in places by the dark green tops of hills similar to the one we stood on. Meanwhile, through the clouds above, the only evidence that the sun was up at all was the slightly less gray area to the east. Might not rain just yet, I thought. Every leaf and blade of grass was wet with dew.

Mark pointed back in the direction we had been driving. "If we keep going that way," he said, "I know a few good places for us to get a burger and a beer. Depending on what time we get back here we should try to head into Dahlonega." The post-hike burger and beer has been a longstanding tradition. This would be one of the few times that Katie would not be joining us, and it made me just a little sad. Every beer and burger after this, neither Mark nor Katie would be with me, and I was glad to have Mark along, even for just a few days.

The three of us piled back into our Honda Element and I offered to drive, since I probably wouldn't have the chance again for quite some time. On the way from Woody Gap to Springer Mountain, it started to rain. And then stopped. And then started again. And so on.

Springer Mountain is the officially recognized southern terminus of the Appalachian Trail. An eight mile approach trail starts at Amicalola Falls, which is south of Springer Mountain, but a popular starting point nevertheless because it's much easier to access by car. There's an actual parking lot, a nice stone arch, and a visitor center complete with pamphlets and bathrooms. But I wasn't interested in taking it. The approach trail doesn't have any white blazes, which are the official symbols that let you know you're on the Appalachian Trail.

It wasn't just the extra miles. I was already doing over 2,000 as it was, and would probably tack on an extra hundred or two just detouring to towns and water sources. Not to mention getting lost. But those extra eight miles were challenging ones, and would add a full day to the first leg of the journey, the section where Mark would be joining me. He only had three days at most, and this would screw up the logistics, like where he parked his car and where we would have our traditional beer and burger.

The car crawled along the old Forest Service road to Springer Mountain, pebbles pinging the undercarriage as it bounced in and out of deep ruts filled with liquid clay the color of weak coffee. Katie glared at me and said through clenched teeth, "Is it too late to go back and do the approach trail?"

Fat drops fell from wet leaves and ran down the windshield. The GPS displayed "Acquiring Satellites." Katie turned to Mark, who sat quietly behind us. "Does any of this look familiar?"

He hesitated. "Last time I was here, there was a foot of snow, so no, not really." I swerved around a mud-filled pit of unknown depth, and Mark continued, "I'm pretty sure we're still on the right road."

We were still going uphill, so I figured we were probably fine. And after another 20 minutes we found a little parking lot dotted with brown puddles and saw our first white blaze. The rain had stopped again. Trees dripped. I grabbed Katie and hugged her tightly. "Oh my god, we're really here!"

I kissed her and removed a water bottle from my pack.

"Not carrying your whole pack to the plaque?" Mark asked.

The parking lot was just over a mile north of the AT trailhead at Springer Mountain, so we would have to hike south to get to the plaque designating the official start, then double back. I'd be right back where I was standing in about an hour. "I don't think I'll need my tent or sleeping bag between here and there," I said.

Mark smirked. "Damn. Already slacking!"

Katie joined him. "Slackpacker! Breaking the rules before you even start!"

There is a school of thought that if you don't carry every piece of your gear from start to finish, your hike somehow doesn't count. Hiking even a single step without your full kit is "slackpacking." Most people don't care, and I count myself among them. "Don't give me this 'slackpacker' crap. I'm still walking from A to B and that's all that really matters," I said.

"Dude, we're kidding," Katie said. "You know we don't care." We grabbed rain coats and she locked the car. Then for the final time she asked if I was ready, and for the first time I meant it when I said yes.

We crossed the dirt road and walked into the trees on the other side.

• • •

Mark and I like to wisecrack while we walk. Our jokes are terrible, but we still crack each other up so much that we often end up stooped over along the trail, giggling. Katie will come upon us and usually drop a bomb that tops it all. Most people think my wife is a grade school teacher or a librarian. They can't see that she has over a hundred tattoos. Her wit is quick, and her selective use of vulgarity usually triggers further outbursts, so that before we know it we're standing atop some breathtaking vista making dildo jokes. It was in that spirit that we walked for a half hour or so, before Mark exclaimed, "Oh shit! There it is!"

The bronze plaque which marks the official southern terminus of the Appalachian Trail was patina green, the same color as the moss on the rock, a mere hump in the woods. Spring had not fully sprung on Springer Mountain, so through the bare branches we could see the foggy hills below. In a month or so this place would be a mere wide spot in the "green tunnel," surrounded on all sides by ferns, rhododendrons, azaleas, the leaves of every kind of tree, with little or no scenic view.

Katie found a metal box containing the log book. I sat on a rock and flipped through while Mark took pictures and Katie explored. Then I wrote: *GARY STARTS TODAY! Two weeks and a few days ago, I emailed my boss and said, "How 'bout you stop paying me, and I'll go live in the woods for awhile." So here I am.*

Katie called out from behind a bush. "Ew!"

I put the book away and stood up. "What is it?"

"Someone decided to cut off their dreadlocks and just leave them here. I thought it was a dead squirrel at first. That would have been less gross."

Mark examined the dreadlocks while I kept back a safe distance. "This place changes lives," I said. "I could imagine someone doing that ceremonially to symbolize leaving a part of themselves behind. A drastic change in appearance to accompany the start of an epic journey. That sort of thing."

"What are you going to leave behind?" Mark asked.

"I'm going to go pee on that bush."

When I returned, we took some more pictures and headed back towards the car. "Dude! You're thru-hiking now!" Mark said. "How does it feel?"

"I guess I feel exactly like I did 20 minutes ago," I said. "It's weird to think that I live outside now."

"Now you're Outside Gary," Mark said.

Katie chimed in. "No! Bad Outside Gary! Not on the furniture! Out!"

It began to rain.

"Well!" I said. "Here we go!"

■ ■ ■

Back at the car, the rain had advanced from drizzle to downpour. Mark and I stood under the hatch to don our raincoats while Katie sat in the driver's seat with the heater on. I live outside now, I thought. No matter what the sky would throw at me, I had only what I could carry to help me deal with it. We were soaked despite our rain gear. As I put on my pack, water sloshed onto my neck and trickled down my spine.

Mark looked at my bare legs. "No rain pants, dude?"

"Oh. Uh, I guess not. I never really used them. Just pants. It's not cold and I have dry stuff for camp."

There were hugs and kisses and more hugs, but Katie and I had been saying goodbye all morning, so we kept this last one relatively short. And then just like that, Mark and I disappeared into the woods.

It didn't take long for us to warm up, and soon I had my coat unzipped. We crossed a bunch of streams and went up and down a bunch of small hills. At the bottom of one, in a small parking lot, we met four fraternity brothers in jeans, carrying water bottles. Seeing our packs, they asked, "Hey, are you guys hiking the whole AT?"

"I'm not, but he is," Mark answered.

"Oh man, that is so cool!" They swarmed us and asked questions, rapid fire. How much does your pack weigh? What will you do about food? Have you read that one book by that guy? How long will it take? We rattled off the standard answers and soon we were again on our way.

"People sure are friendly down around here," I said. "Around the trail, I mean. I wonder what they'll think of us in Dahlonega. All smelly, ordering that cheeseburger…"

"Dude, it is way too soon for you to start thinking about cheeseburgers," Mark said.

"And beer!"

The rain subsided again, but the moisture still hung in the air. The trail took us near an old picnic area with a graveyard and a seesaw. We took more pictures and moved on.

About a mile later, while Mark was ahead of me, I called for him to stop. Stuck in a pile of sand, blade first, was a plastic ninja sword. This was no child's toy, I thought. When I drew it from the sand I could feel it had real weight.

"It's a *bokken*," Mark said. "A practice sword." I handed it to him and he took a step back. "This'll be ugly with my pack on," he said, and began swinging. His pack did not appear to encumber him at all. He parried left before hacking at some invisible foe, then twirled with an upward slash and took out another.

"Good lord, dude. Is there anything that you're not awesome at?"

He passed me the blade. "I wonder if this belonged to Dreadlocks."

"I bet the dreadlocks were cut off in a duel at Springer Mountain, by a guy with a *real* sword!"

"Yeah!" Mark said, "and this Ninja guy is chasing him! He ditched the practice sword because it's so heavy!"

"There's one more clue here," I said, motioning to a heap of black cloth under a bush. The cloth had not fared well during the recent rain, and was a soggy dark mess. "Do you think it's a ninja suit?"

Mark nodded. "I think Dreadlocks took Ninja out, and he just...poofed. Obi-Wan style."

I planted the sword back in the sand beside the dark cloth. Just in case its owner, or its owner's ghost, came back looking for it.

Around 2 p.m. we arrived at Hawk Mountain shelter, which the spreadsheet Katie and I had put together said marked the end of Day One. We dropped our packs inside and explored our surroundings in separate directions. Dozens of fire rings littered the area between the shelter and the stream. Every branch below ten feet was snapped off, and nothing grew among the trees.

These were the first signs of "The Bubble." That great migratory herd of hikers does two things every spring: it gets bigger and it starts earlier, because everyone wants to get ahead of The Bubble. As I flipped through the shelter's log book I counted names. "Dude, back in March, on one day...17, 18, 19..." I turned the page. "Oh shit." I stopped counting. "The whole next page. There must have been 40 people here. In one day!"

Mark rubbed his bare foot and said, "Yeah, and that's just the people who bothered to sign the book. I bet there were 50 or even 60."

I rifled through the pages, looking for today's date. The number of names diminished as I got closer to May, but there were still a few each day. I wanted to get a feel for who some of these people were, maybe even catch a few of them. Then I saw that someone had drawn a two-panel color comic on one page. In the top scene, a young lad with blond spiky hair, our hero, was sitting in this very shelter, chin propped on fist. "I'm bored," he told us. In the bottom panel, our hero was striding confidently along a wooded trail, a white blaze on one tree, carrying a fishing pole with a large bloody steak dangling from the hook. "This should make things more fun," he said. The comic was titled "Bear Hunt Ep. 1" and at the bottom it was signed "Lemmy" and had the message, *"To be cont at next sheltar!"*

We photographed this page and wondered if it was the same Lemmy who founded Motörhead. Then, because it was still early, we decided, damn the spreadsheet, full speed ahead. We did a bit of math and figured that if we got back to Mark's car a bit quicker, we could reclaim that time in the form of extra beer in Dahlonega, or ice cream. But by five that afternoon we found ourselves doing a bit of math again, looking for stopping points and more importantly, water.

Mark pointed at the map. "If we keep going to the next shelter, there's a stream right before it, here. That's six more miles which makes our total for the day...oh shit, like 18 miles. Never mind."

I was down to less than a liter of water. Doable; I wouldn't die, but I would have to ration. I like to have water with dinner and with breakfast, and half a liter each would suffice, barely. But after walking all day, it's a good idea to hydrate or you'll get cramps. (Or wake up thirsty—the horror.) We wanted water and a flat spot to camp, but according to the map in our guidebook, Cooper Gap, a mile away, had a little tent symbol but no little water drop.

"Let's get there and see," Mark said. "With all this rain, there's gotta be something running." We must have crossed 15 streams before lunch. But over the last three hours, zero. Even a few dry ones. It was weird. It was unsettling. I was sweaty and thirsty.

As the trail approached Cooper Gap it narrowed to a footpath. White plastic jugs arranged like bowling pins awaited us at the bottom. Several were empty but at least five remained full and sealed. One was more than enough. It was our first ever "trail magic." This flat patch of dirt with its meager fire ring was visible from a small gravel road nearby, and some kind soul, some "trail angel," had spotted it and, somehow aware of the inconvenient water situation, left us these jugs as a gesture of pure kindness. Either that or some crooked-toothed madman from back in the holler was poisoning hikers with liquid meth, and soon Mark and I would find ourselves naked in a convenience store, drinking shampoo and babbling.

I popped a cap and drank straight from the jug. It was glorious. (Actually, it was a bit warm, but it was free and we were thirsty.) We set up our tents and made no attempt at a fire. Everything was wet, and the sky didn't even start to turn red until eight. We watched the sunset as best we could from down low. Then Mark got into his tent while I stayed out to look at the sky. I'd been walking all day and still couldn't sleep without going for a little walk first. Just one more. A little one.

I stepped onto the gravel road for the second time. Mark and I had crossed it earlier to find a suitable tree to hang our food bag; they were much taller here than the ones at Shining Rock. Then the gravel gave way to dirt, and I could walk without crunching and just listen. In the night, barred owls called to each other: "Who cooks for you?"

Listening to the owls, I thought about my decision to hike the trail. It had come on so suddenly. I hadn't really had time to rest since making the decision three weeks ago. There was no question it was the right thing to do, though my timing sucked. I told Katie over the phone about five minutes after I emailed my resignation to my boss. Katie and I both had known something big was up, just not what.

I'd been staring at my resume for weeks and having "what if" conversations with Katie. What if I could find something without all the damned airports, something here in town, I would say. I had enjoyed a long, successful run consulting for a software firm that did quite well—well enough that we were swallowed up by a whale of a company. We went from just over 100 employees to the belly of a beast consisting of tens of thousands. Some people gain comfort from that kind of setting. They welcome the anonymity of the corporate herd. Me, I get restless.

When I learned that my next assignment was going to be a giant pain in the ass, the wheels started turning. Instead of booking flights and hotels, I started looking at websites about hike planning. When is the latest someone can start? Can I do it? Turns out I could. The month of May might be too late to go straight to Maine before winter, but there was something called a "flip-flop"—I could start at the southern end and hike north until sometime in the middle of summer, then go to Maine, and hike the second half of the trail southbound. People do this all the time. Within hours, I had emailed the boss and was on the phone with Katie telling her what I had done.

I drew a deep breath and listened to the owls. The sky was no longer red, so the glow of my headlamp showed me back to the tent site. I could hear Mark snoring before I even got to the tents.

# FLAT FEET

WHEN YOU'RE NOT used to hearing them every day, barred owls sound like monkeys. Not that I have a solid basis for comparison; the overwhelming majority of my mornings both on and off the trail have been relatively monkey-free. Nevertheless, their hooting confused me, and it took a moment of blinking and rubbing my face to remember where I really was. Mark was already up and taking pictures. I grunted at him, took a few steps in the opposite direction, and peed on a tree.

"I was looking at the map," he said as I walked back to the log we were using as a breakfast table. "Looks like we're in for a short, easy day today." By continuing beyond the first shelter, we had positioned ourselves much closer to his car—and cheeseburgers—than originally anticipated. "You're already ahead of schedule."

I started some coffee and reminded him that I wasn't even supposed to be here until next year, that the concept of "ahead" and "behind" schedule were no longer in my vocabulary. "I'm just glad you're here at all, man," I said. "I wish you were going all the way too."

"I do too," he said. "But I think that after two weeks my knees would hate me."

That brought me back to wondering how in my head it still made perfect sense to do this crazy thing. It was surprisingly easy, like stepping off a high dive. Or a cliff. You might stare down for a long time, working yourself up, but that first step is exactly like every other step you've ever taken. Lift foot, lean forward. Sure, this step has a fall of unknown length immediately after it, but as they say, the fall doesn't kill you. It's that sudden stop at the end.

We were at a small creek gathering water when we heard rustling branches and footsteps from the trail south of us, they way we'd come. A heavyset man with a short beard, glasses, and a bulging pack plodded down the rocks to the water and greeted us. He removed his enormous pack, sat next to me and began wiping his face with a bandanna.

"Great day for a hike, isn't it?" said Mark.

"Every day is a great day for a hike," said our visitor, who introduced himself as "Third Wind."

"Wow!" I said. "You already have a trail name? What's it mean? Have you done the trail before?" I concentrated on my water filter and gave him time to answer.

He laughed at my barrage of questions. "I got it last year. I got a sudden burst of energy, and one of my fellow hikers remarked that I was too old to be getting my second wind." Third Wind explained that he had a few weeks off and was hiking to Damascus, Va., some 400 miles north of here. "Or as far as I can, that is. Right now I don't feel like I have any wind, let alone a second or third." Patting his belly, he added, "This doesn't help either."

Black rectangles suspended from the top of his pack aroused our curiosity. They were a solar array, which weighed just under two pounds and collected enough energy as he walked to charge his phone once a day. "With all these trees and clouds though…" He trailed off and began fingering his screen.

Mark, a military brat, spent his childhood moving from base to base. So when Third Wind told us he was a civilian who worked for the military, the two of them soon were conversing entirely in acronyms. I left them to it and got busy collecting enough water to get us through the day. Then we told Third Wind we would see him later, and continued north.

Despite a late start and frequent breaks, we reached Woody Gap around three in the afternoon. Mark's car was right where he left it, only now there were a few more cars. "We were just here," I said. "Did we really just walk 21 miles?" Mark braced himself on a table and began stretching. "Feels like twice that," he said.

We were ready for a burger. But first, we decided to set up our tents before heading into town, claiming some space across the road from the parking lot and toilets, near a picnic table, but not too close. Third Wind should be here tonight, I thought. I wasn't sure what to think of him, but so far he was the only person I'd met who was headed the same way. Mark would be gone in the morning, and even though we'd just met, a familiar face was always nice.

We loaded everything into the car and drove 20 minutes down the winding road to Dahlonega, a college town of about 5,000 residents. The main square had the look and feel of recent rejuvenation. Every other car was a Lexus or a Mercedes. Retirees with full heads of thick white hair led their wives from gift shops to wine boutiques. Mark and I stood outside a restaurant with a Creole-sounding name and stared at our mud-covered shoes. I shoved my nose into my armpit, inhaled deeply and asked, "Think they'll let us in?"

"Come on," Mark said. "They have outside seating."

We were given a table on the balcony, and after a thorough scrubbing in the men's room I called Katie. When our food arrived I asked the waitress if there was some place I could charge my phone. "Ah," she smiled. "Hiking the AT? Getting kind of a late start aren't you?"

In March and April the number of hikers in Dahlonega was "ridiculous," she said, but now that it was May, it had been a couple days since she'd seen any. "You're going to have to hurry," she advised. Maine was still over 2,000 miles away, and Baxter State Park closes the first week of October or the first snowfall.

I explained my plan to jump up to Maine in August and start working my way back south, which seemed to meet her approval. Mark said nothing and sipped his beer. We devoured our burgers and had another beer. "I need some ice cream," I announced. Mark knew just the place.

When we returned to Woody Gap all the cars were gone except Mark's. Three more tents were set up, and their owners were gathered at a picnic table. "What goodies did you bring for me?" asked one of them. It was Third Wind.

"Oh, hi!" I said. "Well, we didn't get your request in time, but we do have this extra gallon of water."

Third Wind returned his attention to his phone, while Mark and I met two more hikers named Donnie and Jeff. When Mark told them I was attempting the whole trail, they said they were jealous. The four of us talked and laughed until dark, with Third Wind occasionally looking up from his phone to grunt acknowledgment of a joke or to show us some picture he'd taken.

"Well, guys," Mark said, "I know we did a short day by AT standards, but I'm beat. Good night." With that the others headed toward their tents.

I put on my windbreaker and sat on a tiny rock wall along the scenic overlook. There was still enough twilight to see the smaller mountains below. I could see the lights from Dahlonega down there too. The moon had risen, and so had Mars, a tiny red dot just above it. Tall clouds stacked in the distance and lightning jumped silently between them.

Okay, I thought. Day Two. I was restless, not tired at all. Tomorrow we would break camp, only Mark would get into his car and I would walk into the small opening by the picnic table, the one next to the tree with the white blaze. There was enough moonlight now that I could probably go on and see just fine. Some moonlit night, maybe up in Virginia, I thought, I would do that—get up on a ridge and go all night.

Those ridges seemed so far off. They weren't even on the map I was carrying. I visualized all the miles between here and there, imagining myself from above, sitting on this wall, staring at the moon. The camera zoomed out, bringing more mountains into the frame, me shrinking, now just a dot. Still further out I zoomed, now above the clouds, tiny white puffs with miles and miles of green below, my little dot of a self now gone, lost from view.

Shit, I thought. That waitress was right. I probably should hurry. I wrote a few notes into my journal and then returned to my tent, unzipped it, and crawled in just in time for the owls to start.

■　■　■

By morning, the owls were gone from Woody Gap, replaced by wood thrushes. I had gone years without knowing their proper name, though I'd heard their song more times than I'd realized. Theirs is the call Hollywood Foley artists pick first when the screenplay calls for "Pleasant Sounding Forest Bird." They don't whistle or chirp; they play scales in 64th notes, covering multiple octaves in a second. There were hundreds of them in the tree line, bleeping and blooping happily. I tried my best to latch on and be lifted up by their frantic joy, but the best I could achieve was a neutral state as I watched Mark's taillights vanish over the crest.

Everyone from the picnic table was already packed up and gone. We'd spent a good portion of last night's dinner conversation looking at the map and talking about Blood Mountain, the first climb on the trail that came with any kind of reputation. The summit is over 4,000 feet and requires climbing 1,500 feet over four miles, with much of that elevation gain in the last mile. The info board at Woody Gap warned that it would be "strenuous."

The others probably had gotten an early start, wanting to be up and over before the hottest part of the day, which left Woody Gap to just me and the birds. It was the first time I'd been alone since starting, and knowing that the guys from last night weren't hiking to Maine made me feel the solitude even more. I walked to the north side of the road, looked back at the parking lot and wondered if I'd ever see this place again. Then I wondered how many times I would have this thought. Then I walked.

It didn't take long for the cool morning mist to become warm and muggy. I followed a thin swath of dirt cut though a carpet of May apples and trilliums. Bright orange flame azalea blooms hung at eye level. After about an hour, I stopped to sit on a flat rock in the shade and eat something. After a while, the distinctive sound of trekking poles clicked up the trail behind me and I was joined by an older gentleman wearing a red bandanna.

"Good morning!" he said, grinning. "Great place for a snack!"

I swallowed and said, "It really is, isn't it?"

Lifting a pole in his huge hand, he pointed down the trail. "Going all the way?"

"I am!" I said. By the size of his pack, he was only out for the day, but I asked if he had ever done the entire trail.

His big grin stretched further. "Check this out." He turned his back, raised one thumb above his shoulder, and leaned back. As I stood up, my eyes followed his thumb to a red sash wrapped around his pack which had three round patches sewn to it.

"Oh. Oh, wow," I said. "Those are..."

He turned and nodded. "Yes sir."

Now that we were both standing, his height became more apparent. I am over six feet tall, so I can rarely look someone in the eye without having to dip my chin. Even more rare is when I have to lift my chin to talk to someone; it's a bit intimidating and I'm not used to it. The two of us were exactly the same height, but I suddenly felt like I was talking to someone who was on a step ladder.

"That's the Triple Crown," I stammered. In the world of long distance hiking—well, at least in the United States of it—there are three major long trails. The Appalachian Trail, where we were standing; the Pacific Crest Trail, roughly 500 miles longer; and the granddaddy of them all, the Continental Divide Trail, almost 1,000 miles longer than the AT.

"I know," he said with a wink. "I was there."

All I could manage was, "That's so cool!" I asked him to show me again. "When did you do your hikes?"

"Well, let's see," he said. "I did the AT when I was 47. I didn't get around to the PCT until I was in my sixties, and I just finished the CDT last year."

"Last year?" I said. "If you don't mind me asking—"

"I'm 71," he offered." And don't tell anyone, but I have to go back and do some cleanup on that last one, hopefully this year or next."

"Cleanup? What do you mean?"

"Well, there was a section I had to road walk, about 50 miles or so. I was in Wyoming and the whole damn area was impassible. Feet upon feet of snow, high winds, that whole business. But hey, that's just part of the game, right?" He asked me this as if I'd also spent decades hiking thousands of miles. "So how long have you been out?" he added. "This is day three for you? Or four?"

"Three," I said.

"Ah, skipped the approach trail then? Good call. It's a pretty walk, but if they want every thru-hiker to do it, they should just paint some white blazes and be done with it. Do you have a trail name yet?"

I told him I didn't and we spent the next few minutes talking about hiking. He told me that he lived nearby and tried to do at least ten miles every day. I told him that the longest I'd ever been out was three weeks in the Sierra Nevadas for Mountain Warfare School many years ago.

"Semper Fi, then!" he said. "I would have figured you for Air Force. You look military, just not...jarhead." Again with the winking. I didn't mind his assessment; I'd heard it before. My superiors had often reprimanded me for being too polite with the troops. "Okay," he continued. "Mind a few pointers?"

"Of course not," I answered.

"You know how to adjust your pack for uphill versus downhill?" I told him that I did: high and tight for flat or downhill, low and loose for the big climbs. "That's right," he said. "And when you breathe, every few minutes stop and take the deepest breath you can." He demonstrated by filling his lungs. "Then make a horsey sound, like this: PTHBHTHBHTHBHHH!" He then whinnied and stomped his foot for effect. "Go on, do it. It's fun."

I inhaled deeply and blew out hard, making a raspberry sound with my lips, laughing halfway through.

"Do you know why we do that?" he asked.

I thought for a second and answered, "Carbon dioxide?"

"Right," he said.

I continued, guessing, "It's heavier than air, and as you use up oxygen, the CO2 sinks to the bottom of your lungs. The horse whinny pushes it out and makes room for good air, right?"

"Ah, see, you already know this stuff. You'll be fine," he said. "One last thing: Things are going to get tough for you out there. They always do. Just remember one word and you'll get to wherever you're going: *perseverance*. You keep that one word in your head and nothing can stop you."

He looked me up and down, a quick head-to-toe inspection from an old veteran. "How do you feel?" he asked.

"I feel fantastic!" I meant it.

"Of course you do," the old man said. "You're just getting started. When you get to Neel Gap, tell 'em Flat Feet said hi. This is where I turn around if I want to be home for dinner."

I offered my hand and said, "It was very nice to meet you."

He shook my hand and said, "Likewise. Have a good hike, Green Giant!" He winked a third time, turned on his heel and returned to the woods.

Green Giant? What the hell's that mean, I thought. Did I just get my trail name? I gave myself the same head-to-toe inspection. Green shoes. Green socks. My shorts were tan, but my shirt was green too. Well, I thought. I guess it fits. I'll keep it until something better sticks. I gathered my poles and began walking north again toward Blood Mountain.

■ ■ ■

Blood Mountain had been a major topic around the picnic table the night before. Donnie and Jeff both referred to it as "an ass kicker," while Third Wind had simply said, "It is what it is." Mark and I had studied a topo map and quietly decided that it was merely a bump compared to some of the things I could expect further up the trail.

Everything is relative; Blood Mountain is the tallest thing on the AT for almost 100 miles, but it's shorter than the mountain 15 minutes from my house. But the climb starts at a lower elevation. But it's not as steep. Until the part where it is. Anyway, what was I going to do, not climb it? Go around? Go home?

I caught up with Jeff at the next stream crossing, hiking with his father. He extended a hand and said, "You're Gary? Pleasure to meet you."

"Nice to meet you," I said. "And actually, I think it's 'Green Giant' now." I told them about my encounter with Flat Feet, and Jeff said they had run into him too. He had given Jeff the trail name "Happy" because he smiled so much.

Jeff and his dad had only just rejoined each other. "We're hiking at different speeds and I camped here last night. We're just getting ready for the big climb. How 'bout you, Green Giant? You ready for this?"

"Ready as I'll ever be, I guess. Hey, is that…?" I nodded toward the campsite across the stream. A large man sat in the shade holding a boot in one hand and his phone in the other.

"Third Wind?" Jeff said. "Yeah, that's him. He's trying to decide whether to go over or around Blood Mountain." Jeff showed on his map that this stream was the last low point before the climb started. "Fifteen hundred feet over the next four miles. Or," he pointed, "that trail goes around and rejoins the AT on the other side. Only goes up 200 feet."

I looked back toward Third Wind and saw him dumping his pack, still wearing only one boot. "Looks to me like he's staying here," I said. We'd barely gone three miles since morning, and I hoped he was okay.

I filtered water and filled up an extra bottle, since this stream was the last reliable source for six miles. Leaving Jeff and his dad to have lunch by the stream, I started up Blood Mountain. Occasionally a break in the skinny oaks and poplar trees would grant me access to the horizon, a rippling line of green which receded farther the more I climbed. As I got higher, the oaks gave way to mountain laurels, just starting to bud. Their sparse branches didn't block the horizon nearly as much and soon my view reached many miles. Puffy white clouds left dark green splotches on distant mountains as they blocked the sun. When one would pass directly overhead I could feel the temperature drop, just a few degrees but enough to notice. My cheeks would relax as I stopped squinting. A cool breeze would blow, the cloud would move, and my face would involuntarily scrunch as the ensuing explosion of brightness warmed my exposed skin. Oh yeah, sunglasses, I thought. Lot of good they do me buried in my pack. I'll have to remember to dig them out next time I stop.

As I neared the summit, I could hear voices. I had already passed about a dozen day hikers, some alone, some in groups, some on their way up, some coming down. According to my map there was a shelter at the very top, and suddenly there it was. Every shelter I'd seen or read about had been a three-walled wooden structure, like a garage with the door left open. The Blood Mountain shelter was more like a small house made of stone. There was no front door, just an open doorframe, and the same went for the windows. It had a well-constructed pitched roof complete with a chimney, and a welcoming sign which had obviously been recently painted.

When I stepped inside, it was as cool as a basement. There was an empty fireplace in the center of the room and a broom leaning in one corner. Otherwise the place was empty. I looked around for a while and imagined the shelter full of hikers on a rainy night, all huddled in the center as the wind tossed water through the windows. Their smiling faces flickered in the light from their fire. One of them had a guitar. What the hell, let's give 'em a dog, too. I wondered if I would ever catch those people, if any of them were behind me, or if I was the last one this year. Better sign the log book, just in case.

When I thought about calling Katie, I remembered it was Monday and she'd be at work. Bah, no signal anyway. So I put my phone back into my pocket and left the shelter. I found a flat rock nearby, where I sat and ate a Clif bar and drank my water. A cherry tree just starting to blossom shaded me. Wave after wave of green vanished into the haze on the horizon. I felt the breeze on my face, chatted with a few more day hikers, and watched more dark green splotches march from peak to peak. Time to follow the splotches, I thought.

• • •

On my way down the north side of Blood Mountain, I caught up with Donnie, who was resting on a log. "Hell of a view up there, wasn't it?" he asked.

"Sure was," I agreed.

"You stopping at Neel Gap?"

"Neel?" I said. "I thought it was Neel's with an 's.'"

"Yeah, I did too. Third Wind corrected me. Then he showed me a picture of the sign. Did you know he speaks five languages?"

"I did, actually. Anyway, no. I'll just pick up some food there and keep going. How about you?"

"That's the end of the trail for me, my man. Wife's picking me up tomorrow around lunch." He motioned up the trail and said, "We're all gonna get showers and stay at the bunkhouse. You gonna do the gear shakedown?"

During my hurried research before leaving, I had read about Mountain Crossings about a dozen times. Right at Neel Gap, it's the only place on the AT where the trail actually goes through a building. So it only makes sense to have a full-service outfitters and a snack bar there. It's the first hot water and first bed that northbound thru-hikers encounter. They also offer a popular service in which someone with years of experience will weigh your pack and go through every piece of gear you're carrying, explain why each item will prevent you from ever reaching Maine, and then happily sell you an upgrade.

"Nope. Don't need it," I said.

"How much does your pack weigh?"

I stopped leaning on my poles and bounced on my toes. "I don't know. I've never weighed it. It feels right, though. Whole lot lighter than my winter kit, that's for sure."

"Well, shit," Donnie said, standing up. "I guess that means I won't be seeing you again. Man, I wish I was going with you."

I laughed. "You could. You really could." (I had said, "You really could" to about a dozen day hikers over the past three days. None of them had believed me.)

"What, just call the boss? 'Not comin' in, bye!' Tell my wife to bring extra sandwiches? Just like that?"

"Actually, yeah. Just like that."

"What about health insurance?"

"Dude, we have smart phones now. We live in the future. Figure that shit out while you're walking!"

"Well, it's fun to think about," he said. We shook hands and he wished me luck.

"Goodbye," I said, and continued down the hill toward Mountain Crossings.

I heard it long before I saw it. Deep, resonating wind chimes bonged in the gentle breeze, making a sound that carried to the top of the gap. Someone had slung a hammock near the chimes and was snoozing as I approached.

A sprawling oak towered directly over the trail just outside the building. Hundreds of shoes and castoff boots hung by their laces from every branch. Each year, more and more people attempt to thru-hike the trail—more than 2,000 according to recent counts. But nearly 80 percent quit somewhere along the way, and for many, Mountain Crossings is the place they stop. "Fuck this!" they yell. They won't be needing their stupid hiking boots or their goddamn trail runners anymore, so they tie them together and heave them into the branches. I assume that the outfitters cut them down every year; most of these looked new.

Leaving my pack on a bench near the door, I entered, being careful not to slam the door so as not to wake the guy in the hammock. All sorts of backpacking food lined the neatly arranged shelves: nuts, bars, tuna packets, noodles, candy, and more. Packs and sleeping bags hung from hooks on one wall while a small display of boots and shoes filled another. A smiling bearded man greeted me from behind the counter. "If you need anything, just holler," he said.

He showed me a power strip by the door to charge my phone, and I moved to the shelves with food on them. My stomach had been rumbling for the last mile, and I wanted to sit on their porch with some ice cream before I did anything else. On my way to the cold section I browsed the dehydrated food. The markup was a bit shocking at first, but when I realized the nearest town was 20 miles plus a hitchhike, I decided to get all of my stuff and the ice cream at once.

After I devoured my ice cream sandwich, I called Katie. "Guess where I am."

"Neel's Gap," she said.

"Actually, there's no 's.' Can you believe it? Thirty-one miles in," I said.

"That's awesome. You're actually ahead of schedule."

"I know. Mark and I got to the first shelter super early and didn't want to just sit and stare at each other, so we kept going. How are you? I miss you."

I told her about finally getting my trail name and meeting the guys at the picnic table the night before Mark left, and how none of them were thru-hiking and that I'd just said goodbye to the last of them. "I really feel like I'm the only one doing this right now."

"Well," she said, "you'll be happy to know I've been surfing Trail Journals, and there are plenty just ahead of you. Even a few behind you, too."

Damn, I thought. I bet there's someone at Springer Mountain right this very second, getting started. People are crazy.

"Everything still set for Saturday?" I asked.

"That's up to you," she said. "If you keep getting ahead of schedule, we might have to meet somewhere else."

Asheville, N.C., where we live, is less than a tank of gas away from the place where I had planned to be at the end of my first week of hiking, a well-known peak named Standing Indian Mountain. Before my departure, we had plotted several meetings spanning the first few weeks: Standing Indian Mountain; Hot Springs, N.C.; and Damascus, Va. were all on the calendar. Once I got into Virginia, the drive would become impractical, and we would not see each other until I flipped to Maine in August.

"Are you kidding?" I said. "I wouldn't miss it for the world." After years of traveling for work, I was used to the routine of being away from my wife for a week or two, but I was already missing her. We verified the road crossing for next Saturday and took turns coming up with excuses not to be the first to hang up. "I really do need to get going now," I said. "I've got a campsite in mind and I still have to climb a bit to get there before dark."

"Okay," she said. "I love you. I can't wait to see you."

Reluctantly, I finally disconnected, shut off my phone, and hoisted my pack. The chimes were still bonging, and the guy in the hammock sat up and ran his fingers through his hair. As I turned to leave, Donnie walked out of the clearing across the street. "Hey, Green Giant!" he said. "I thought you'd be long gone. Good to see you. Again."

"Hey," I said. "Yeah. I, um…I was just leaving. Again." I laughed.

Donnie laughed along with me. "Well, good luck. Again."

"Yep, you too. Enjoy your shower." He placed his pack where mine had been and entered the shop while I walked away for real this time. I had learned an important lesson: Never say goodbye on the trail.

## 3

## BEAR HUNT: EPISODE TWO

THE NEXT MORNING I ran into Jeff. I'd last seen him before Blood Mountain, at the first road crossing—another reminder to never say goodbye on the trail. Before I saw or heard him, I smelled the pizza. His family was there to pick him up, and they brought more than enough food for everyone. My morning packet of oatmeal had worn off, so I devoured three slices and drank a can of Coke in five swallows, then burped heartily and begged their pardon. We exchanged email addresses and wished each other happy trails and I moved on.

Still burping pizza about an hour later, I heard quick footsteps behind me. The trail was narrow so I stepped aside to let this hiker pass. A lanky, longhaired kid with bright eyes and a wide smile greeted me. "Hey brother, beautiful day! How are you?"

His smile spread to my face. "I'm great! How are you?"

"Oh man, I'm loving life, you know?" He pointed at the trail and said, "You doing the whole trail?"

"I sure am. You too?"

"Damn straight! Holy shit man, you're our first thru-hiker! What's your name?"

"I'm…" Not Gary. "Green Giant."

His eyes widened. "Whoa, no way! We heard about you! Those guys back there said you're a righteous dude!"

"That's awfully nice of them. So, who's 'we?'" I asked.

As I said this, his partner, slightly shorter and with the same hair plus a bushy mustache, joined us. "I'm Big Ups and this dude with the 'stache is Floats."

We resumed walking and took turns explaining our trail names. Big Ups got his because of his positive attitude, while Floats was alleged to ascend mountains so quickly that he seemed to float rather than walk. "Tall guy, green shirt," I said. "I wish it was more interesting than that, but the guy who gave it to me was a Triple Crowner, so I'll take it."

Before their rapid pace carried them ahead of me, we agreed to meet at Low Gap shelter for the night. It had a stream, and cables with pulleys to hang our food up away from any bears.

Most of the walk that day was in the green tunnel. Compared to Blood Mountain, the terrain was significantly less challenging, which allowed me to look down for a change and pay attention to the actual ground beneath my shoes. It was apparent that tens of thousands of boot-clad feet had been walking here for decades. The dirt was pounded into a hard-packed light brown sidewalk. This brown ribbon was surrounded by green on every side, including above, making it obvious which way to go even without the occasional white-blazed tree.

The brown ribbon was also home to a variety of brightly colored millipedes. Some looked like tiny copper springs. Others boldly announced their presence with orange or red striped armor. Slowly they would crawl across the trail, not caring one bit about predators. "Go ahead and eat me," those colors say. "I'll be the last thing you ever eat."

Recent rain had left the ground damp, and tiny orange salamanders basked on rocks. I learned that these adorable little guys are called red efts. Leaning in closer, I could see that they had small black spots like freckles. Each one a baby carrot with legs, waddling like a miniature dinosaur. They live up to 15 years, and after making their way to a water source, they double in size, and then transform into something resembling an olive drab fish with legs. I prefer them this way.

Realizing I was dawdling, I looked up, holding my hand at arm's length and measuring the sun's distance from the horizon. Four fingers meant one hour till sunset. I had a hand-and-a-half till dusk and one small hill to climb before descending into Low Gap.

Big Ups and Floats were breaking sticks when I arrived at the shelter. From the garage-sized wooden box which would be home for the night came excited chirping noises. "Dude, check it out," Floats said. "There's a nest of baby birds in here!" He leaned on the platform and peered up to the rafters. "You can see the nest right here."

Mama bird was perched outside on a cable. As she chirped, the babies responded. She dove to the ground to snatch up a bug or some bit of granola and flew inside. The babies went crazy. She did this a few more times until they were satisfied. Then when the sun hit the horizon, she squashed herself down on top of them and they all fell silent.

Big Ups said, "Holy shit man, that was way better than TV."

We had started a fire during the bird show, and the orange flame cast dancing shadows on our faces. Floats produced a joint from his pocket. What the hell, I thought. I don't have to be anywhere for...a year.

"We'd better move away from the shelter, though," I said. "If we accidentally give those birds the munchies, we'll never get to sleep."

We threw some bigger sticks onto the fire and lit the joint. After the second time around I was already feeling the effects and probably didn't need any more. But I took another puff anyway, and passed it to my left. "Thanks, man," I said. I nodded and smiled. I nodded and smiled.

We became way too engrossed in each other's stories and laughed way too hard at the stupid parts. We giggled, we ate, and we laughed some more, then passed around another joint and got out the map.

We were about to leave Georgia and enter North Carolina. The AT spans fourteen states and we were about to enter Number Two. Just saying it out loud sounded weird. We're walking into another state. We're crossing lines on the map, on foot. Plus, we were crossing into North Carolina, which to me meant home. I would continue walking, right on past home, but it still felt good to be headed toward familiar territory.

Not long after entering North Carolina we would overcome another major psychological milestone, the 100-mile mark. Big Ups had hiked about 200 miles out West the year before, but neither Floats nor I had ever gone that far on foot, and contemplating that number made us giddy. Also, our next mountain of note, Standing Indian, would be our first peak over 5,000 feet. And Katie would be there. With food!

When we ran out of sticks to burn, we hoisted our food bags. I rolled out my sleeping bag on the platform in the shelter, careful not to wake the birds. My companions had already set up hammocks by the stream. "Good luck with the mice," Floats said as he left the glow of our dying fire.

"Good luck with the mosquitoes," I said.

I crawled into my bag, tired from walking all day but feeling no pain, turned on my headlamp and sat up, reaching for the shelter's log book. Two pages before the final entry was another full-page cartoon, "Bear Hunt: Episode 2." In the first frame, which filled the top half of the page, our spiky blond hero was still walking with his steak on a hook, muttering, "Jeez, no bears yet." Two other hikers looked on from a distance, wondering "WTF is he carrying?"

The bottom half of the page was a bloodbath. A bear with funny ears and a big round butt filled the frame. Beside one cute fuzzy paw was a human foot severed at the ankle, still wearing a boot. Blood splattered on the shredded torsos of the two hikers who had only moments ago been mocking our hero. One of them reached desperately for help, his face a twisted mask of horror, as the bear gnawed on his dead friend's skull.

The caption read, *"To be continued in next sheltar…Lemmy."*

He's only a few days ahead of me, I thought. I really hoped I could catch this guy. I wondered what was up with his spelling. The spiky blond hero had a sort of anime look about him. Maybe Lemmy was Japanese.

I flipped to the last entry, which stopped near the middle of the page. Thinking back to the little orange salamanders I'd watched while stopping by a big rock for a snack earlier, I clicked my pen and wrote, *If I stopped to give each breathtaking view the full attention it deserves, I'd never get anywhere.* Then I signed it, *Green Giant.*

■ ■ ■

"So how do you…um…you know…go to the bathroom in the woods?"

This question gets asked a lot. Every time I hear it I'm amazed that it even needs to be asked. Sometimes I like to pause before I answer, to let the asker think for a second. Let's imagine that you're in the woods alone and the urge hits. What would you do?

Whatever answer you come up with is probably right. I dig a hole, I poop in the hole, I cover the hole. This of course is an oversimplification; there are several preferred methods for digging your poop hole, and you'll get a different answer from every hiker you ask. I carry a small but sturdy orange plastic trowel that weighs less than an ounce. As an added bonus, its length is precisely the prescribed depth, six inches. Other hikers will tell you that a boot heel or the end of a trekking pole will do just fine, but whatever you use, make sure you dig deep. Believe it or not, there are forest creatures who are attracted to the smell of your dung, and we don't want to encourage them.

Perhaps now is too late to mention this if you've already dug your hole, but location is important too. I assume that you are smart enough to not dig a poop hole ten feet from your tent. I like to give humanity the benefit of the doubt. (As we'll see later, this is not always justified.)

But for now, we go for a stroll, trowel in one hand, poop kit in the other. I like to use a small waterproof stuff sack for my toiletries. Toothpaste, toothbrush, some wipes, Advil, that sort of thing. I carry these items about 100 or 200 feet away from camp, and especially away from water, for what should be obvious reasons.

When the hole is dug, I place my feet on either side, pull my pants down to my knees, squat and wait. "But Green Giant!" people say. "Isn't it harder to go when you're squatting?" To them I say no, it's easier than sitting. When you squat, your "poop chute" straightens, making it faster and easier to get the job done.

Long enough though, that I was still in the full squat position when I heard Katie's car. Back home a dozen cars an hour could drive by our house unnoticed, but my ears would perk up at her specific road noise from half a mile away. Hers was the only car that morning, and I heard the engine stop and the door open and shut. Katie was early as usual. "I'm pooping!" I yelled, hoping my engine sound identification skills had not misled me this time.

"Okay! I'll be right here!" Good. It was Katie.

I pulled up my pants and walked up a small wooded incline toward the Standing Indian trailhead parking lot. First I saw Katie's car, and then I saw her. I ran to her and wrapped my arms around her.

We kissed passionately. "You don't smell as bad as I thought you would," she said. "And I can feel your ribs."

"I can't have lost that much weight," I said. "It's only been a week. Come hang out with me while I pack up."

My camp didn't take long to break down because I wasn't carrying much. My small tent was only two pounds and there wasn't much to it, just a mesh cocoon with a rain cover. That, plus an inflatable air mattress for comfort and insulation from the ground chill, and a sleeping bag which, according to the manufacturer, would prevent hypothermia in temperatures as low as 20 degrees Fahrenheit. My wardrobe consisted of what I was wearing, plus a spare shirt, spare pants, socks and underwear. These all went into waterproof stuff sacks as did my "sleep system"—I started using waterproof stuff sacks for everything a few years ago after a stream crossing gone wrong soaked my pack. Last to go was my Kindle and my cookware, a single titanium pot with a Jetboil burner.

"What's for breakfast?" Katie asked as I tightened the last of my pack straps.

"I'm still trying to figure that out," I said. I'd started my trip with dehydrated dinners and breakfasts that were delicious, packed full of calories, and quick to prepare. But at seven dollars apiece, twice a day for five or six months, they seemed too pricey. There had to be a cheaper alternative, but I hadn't found it yet.

"I just had a Clif bar and some coffee this morning because I knew you were bringing food. You did bring food, right?"

She assured me that she had, and soon we were at her car going through the loot. It was more than enough for the next few days. "I made a pizza last night, and oh boy, are you ready for this? I found a recipe online for blueberry scones! I brought extra so we could feed other hikers."

I had told her about Big Ups and Floats. "That's so cool that you're already meeting other thru-hikers," she said. "They sound fun."

"Yeah, well don't get too attached. They're ready to start doing 20-mile days and I'm not."

"Aww," she frowned.

"It's okay," I said. "I've been checking the shelter logs. There are tons of people up ahead. Behind too, I'm sure. Last night was actually the first I've camped alone so far. It was nice."

We put the pizza and scones into her day pack and started north, arriving shortly at the shelter. Big Ups and Floats were still packing when we arrived. Their eyes grew huge when Katie revealed the scones.

"No way! We couldn't possibly," Big Ups said. Katie insisted. "You have to. I made them specifically for you guys."

Floats was the first to take one. He thanked Katie and took a bite. Crumbs filled his mustache and his eyes rolled. "Oh my god! This could be my favorite thing I've ever put in my mouth!"

Katie said, "Have as many as you like, but save room. There's pizza for at the top."

Big Ups reached for a scone and said, "It's impossible to eat too much." He took a bite, smiled and added, "You're an angel."

. . .

"You didn't tell me Big Ups was *hot*," Katie said.

"I hadn't noticed." I motioned for her to pass. With her smaller pack she was quicker on the uphill.

"You guys are all so skinny," she went on. "I should have made two pizzas."

"I'm just glad you brought food. I mean, I'm just glad to see you."

As we walked on our own, she asked me to describe the highlights of my first week on the AT. I told her about the mini celebration we'd had when we crossed the North Carolina border. There wasn't much to it; we high-fived and posed for pictures beside the sign.

"That climb coming up out of Georgia—I totally get why they call this the highlands. We came up about 2,000 feet over a couple miles and haven't gone back down since. Let's see, that was yesterday. Oh, and two days ago we had hail!"

"Neat!" Katie had grown up in a household fascinated by weather. Her dad has an array of weather stations on the roof and her sister Priscilla grew up to become a meteorologist. "I saw storms on radar, but it looked like rain."

"It came out of nowhere too," I said. "It was nice and sunny, just like this, and then ten minutes later, gray and cloudy. I was up high when the thunder started and I heard little pellets hitting my hat. I thought someone was throwing sand at me. Next thing I know there's little piles of ice all over the place. It was crazy! Fifteen minutes later the sun was out, and an hour later it was melted. So that was pretty cool."

I told her about my first resupply trip I'd made into Helen, a small town in northern Georgia that looks like how Walt Disney would imagine Germany. It's supposed to be Bavaria, the locals will tell you. All of the buildings are timbered Tudor-style and there are towers and turrets everywhere, and every street has "-dorf" in its name. Also, everything was closed. No one in the town had ever heard of a Jetboil or whatever kind of weird space age fuel it took. They did make a mean strudel, though.

"Any bears yet?" she asked excitedly.

"Not since Shining Rock," I said. "I've heard owls almost every night. I saw one up close the other day. He was in a tree by the trail, just sitting there being all majestic and shit. He even let me take a picture. I'll show you when we get to the top. Did you bring a memory card?"

In a zipper pouch on my pack's hip strap, I kept a small waterproof camera. Once I filled its memory card, I would mail it home and insert a spare empty card from my pack. The next package from home would include a new empty spare. That day we executed the first move in the three-card shuffle by hand rather than by mail.

A small wooden sign announced the summit of Standing Indian. We took pictures, found a flat rock with a view, and shared cold pizza. The steady breeze sometimes gusted, bringing with each gust a chill. We scooted together. "Here, look at these pictures," I said, turning on the camera.

"Here's me and Mark. There's you." I pushed the right arrow. "Here's a pretty view. Another tree. Here's a rock. Oh, look! Here's a mama spider carrying thousands of babies on her back."

"Ew!" She looked away. When she looked back the spiders were still there. "Good lord, that's too many baby spiders."

"Aha! Check this out," I said and handed her the camera. "You might have to zoom in to read." It was a picture of Lemmy's first cartoon. Katie squinted at the screen and after a minute she giggled. "He must be carrying a whole box of colored pencils."

I showed her the second installment. Blood and guts, fur and fangs, big round fuzzy butt splattered with hiker gore. "I may have missed one. I skipped a shelter or two."

This was where she would turn around and I would keep going. Our plan was to meet again at Clingmans Dome a week later, on Memorial Day weekend, when my mom and my niece Emily would be in Asheville visiting Katie, only a two-hour drive away. At 6,643 feet, Clingmans Dome is the highest point on the Appalachian Trail, and the observation deck on its peak commands a 360-degree view of the Blue Ridge and Smoky Mountains. But it was another 100 miles past the 100-mile mark, which I hadn't reached yet.

"What happened to your feather?" Katie asked. When she'd dropped Mark and me off at Springer Mountain, my hat was sporting a hawk tail feather I'd picked up during my shakedown hike back at Shining Rock. Now a long black feather was poked in the side of my hat.

"A mouse ate it," I said.

"Oh, Gary," she said, then corrected herself. "Green Giant."

"I left it outside my tent one night and when I woke up it was chewed to a nub. Maybe the mouse needed it for his nest. Anyway, I found this one the same day. I think it might be a raven."

"Looks like vulture to me," she said.

"Whatever. It still looks cool."

"It does," she said. "I like it."

# 4

## SHE WHO SHALL NOT BE NAMED

I KNEW I WAS DREAMING, but I couldn't control my actions. I was only able to observe, detached, as hot emotion boiled up from inside, a mix of frustration and anger. I was running through an office building and screaming, but no words would come out, only guttural noises. People talking on phones squirmed in their seats while others kept typing. My brain and my mouth weren't cooperating, and my overwhelming drive to inspire them just came out as "YEAARRGH!"

My stick, I thought. That'll work. I started swinging, knocking phones away from startled faces, smashing monitors and screaming. Why aren't they revolting, I wondered. Can't they see? I tried to shout "Get up!" but it came out "Geh uhhhh!" I needed them to bolt out of their chairs, flip their desks, and run with me. Instead they just stared—or worse, ignored me.

Frustration now bubbling over into rage, I swung my stick harder, scattering paper clips and binders, sending stupid plants grown under humming fluorescent lights toppling to the floor. My shoes crunched dirt and debris into the gray carpet as I rampaged through the cubicles. "Cumm ahhh! Geh uhhhh!" I raised my smashing stick once again and it became a trekking pole, and suddenly one of the workers spoke to me. "I don't think you're using that correctly," he said.

Dropping the pole and letting my arm fall to my side, I took a deep breath and closed my eyes, then opened them to blackness. I was in my tent. The sleeping bag was twisted and I couldn't find the zipper. The cloth Buff I used as a nightcap had worked its way down over my eyes, and the stuff sack of extra clothes I used as a pillow was no longer under my head. It was raining.

Pulling the Buff from my eyes, I could see the sun was up. The rain was gentle and the sound on my tent calming. I lay still and held on to the dream as it faded. It felt good to run and smash, to incite a riot. I don't get to do that for real.

My tent has a very helpful feature that allows me to pack up in the rain without getting soaked. The inner sanctum is made mostly of mesh and hangs from the aluminum poles that support the rain fly. With a little bit of contortion, it is possible to separate the two and load everything into my pack without leaving the protection of the fly. The ground was damp, and my head and shoulders kept bumping into the fly, but it worked. I opened the final zipper and emerged like a larva that has eaten its way out of its cocoon.

Pulling all the stakes but two, I used them to secure one end of the fly, then picked up the other and shook vigorously. Water sprayed everywhere and a wet guy-line slapped my cheek. While not dry, the fly was now lighter by maybe an extra pound of water. I crammed it into a plastic grocery bag I'd picked up in Helen for just this purpose, then stuffed that into an outside pouch. Pretty slick, I congratulated myself. If it was still raining at the end of the day, I could do my packing routine in reverse order. Meanwhile, all my dry stuff was still dry, and the only wet stuff were things meant to get wet.

Then I felt a pang of hunger and remembered my food was still in a bag slung over a high branch. Leaning my pack against the tree, I untied the rope holding the bag. Suddenly it slipped loose and I instinctively grabbed it to stop my food from falling. That jerked the branch, sending gallons of rainwater splashing down on my upturned face. Fine, I thought as chilly drops found their way under my shirt and between my shoulder blades. I haven't showered in a while anyway.

∙ ∙ ∙

The rain stopped shortly after breakfast, but my glasses kept fogging, so I stowed them in a hard case with my sunglasses, which I had yet to put on. Holding the case for a second and bouncing it like a scale, I figured it weighed a couple ounces. What, maybe four? Same weight as a Clif bar or a couple packs of ramen. I really didn't need either pair of glasses or the case.

How many other little things like that could I find in my pack? Four similar discoveries would relieve me of a pound. That didn't seem like much when I was preparing, but this was my ninth consecutive day carrying that extra pound. Every backpacking trip I'd ever been on was mainly about getting to a destination and spending time there, but now the point was the walking itself. There was no "there" for another 2,000 miles. Good lord, I thought, I really am just getting started. I made a mental note to give myself another shakedown in the next three days before Clingmans Dome, so I could hand unnecessary things off to Katie there. Otherwise I would have to mail it.

I put the case into the top zipper pouch of my pack and walked over to a natural window, a small opening in the trees which offered a view. Scanning the mountains on the horizon, I wondered which one I'd come from. One had a fire tower, I remembered. Without binoculars, I squinted at each distant peak until I found one with a tiny raised bump at the tip. "That one, right there," I said aloud. "The one that looks like a nipple." My good camera was in my pack, so I took a few pictures with my phone. I tried to call Katie but there was no signal.

We take phones for granted. Back home if you think of something or see something you want to share, you just do it. One person or a hundred, you can let them know almost instantly what you think, feel, or want. If you don't get a signal you just wait a few minutes, at worst a couple hours. But now I might not be able to send this picture until tomorrow, or next week. By no means a crisis, but it was the most disconnected I'd felt since starting.

And I liked it. It was more like independence than loneliness. I made a note to remember how it felt not to get that instant gratification. It's amazing that a tiny metal box can give us the power to show distant loved ones an instant photo from where we are. The generation before mine would have expected flying cars before these Star Trek communicators. Yet here we are, yawning at pictures of cats while standing in line at the bank.

A barely visible half-moon was dropping in the west, white against the powder blue sky. The moon lately had started capturing my attention. I rose and set with the sun, but twice the moon had tricked me awake hours before dawn. A waning gibbous moonrise will illuminate your tent as much as your bedside lamp. Sometimes even the birds are fooled. The birds and I usually figured it out pretty quickly and went back to sleep in no time.

My rhythms were definitely changing. By the middle of the day, I'd walked five miles and climbed three or four small mountains, and other than being a little sweaty I felt great. This was usually nap time, but I felt well-rested and ready for more. Maybe it was my imagination, but I also thought I'd been pulling my belt a little tighter each morning when I put on my pants. I patted my belly and decided to stay a bit longer, maybe have a Snickers.

The surrounding mountains were beginning to take on a vaguely familiar shape. Before I got to Clingmans Dome, I'd go through the Nantahala National Forest, down into Nantahala Gorge past one of the most popular centers for whitewater activity in the Southeast. Katie, Mark, and I, along with thousands of other kayakers and rafters, had been down the "Nanty" River dozens of times. We had also hiked along the AT there, occasionally hauling a cooler of beer and some steaks up to the Wesser Bald fire tower. Hiking into familiar territory would be weird, seeing places I recognized.

As I lifted my pack I realized that I could mail things home from the whitewater center. But I didn't feel like dumping and sorting my pack before then. Ultimately it didn't matter. I didn't have to decide anytime soon. There weren't any deadlines—and if there were, it was me setting them, so if I didn't like them I could change them. Everything was entirely up to me. This concept had usually been accompanied by a dose of anxiety, but now it triggered a giddy sense of eagerness. I wondered if I'd see something I knew from the next peak.

■ ■ ■

It was nearing the end of a warm and humid day, and I was a little worn out from the climb as I approached Cold Spring shelter. It sits a few feet off the trail at a spot where a small stream, no more than a trickle really, runs across the path. I could hear someone moving around inside, a surprise because I hadn't seen anyone all day. My assumption had been that I'd be camping by myself again that night.

When I turned the corner I saw a young woman with dark braids sitting on the boards with her feet dangling, a turquoise pack by her side. She and the pack were surrounded by a ring of stuff sacks, garbage bags, piles of clothes, and assorted food containers, some empty but most full. She was rummaging through one of the stuff sacks, either packing or unpacking, when my arrival broke her focus and she snapped her head in my direction, dropping the sack in her lap.

"Sorry," I offered. "I didn't mean to sneak up on you." I still hadn't shared a shelter with anyone, and I wasn't quite ready to begin by spending the night with a young lady who appeared to be hiking solo. My first concern was to avoid making her uncomfortable, but we also hadn't really talked yet and there was no guarantee that I'd enjoy her company either. The guidebook had mentioned tent sites a tenth of a mile up the trail, and I was considering that option when we heard a shriek.

"Ugh," she muttered, wrinkled her nose. "Do I hear *children?*" As she threw her arms up in dismay, she knocked over her cooking pot, which rolled off the boards and into the shadows below. Maybe we'll get along after all, I thought.

"Maybe we're lucky and that's the sound of one being eaten by a bear," I said.

She didn't respond and instead began hunting for her pot under the shelter. "If something drags me under there I'm going to be so pissed. Will you hold this so I can see?" She handed me her headlamp. The top half of her vanished under the boards.

I shined her headlamp into the dark below the shelter and leaned my poles against the boards so I would have a free hand to wave off the swarm gathering around my face. From up the trail came more shrieking, punctuated by angry adult barking. After a minute she yelled, "Got it!" and wiggled out backwards, then leapt to her feet and held her cooking pot up like a trophy. I congratulated her, then nodded at her mess and asked, "Packing or unpacking?"

She shrugged so hard that her hands flew above her shoulders. "I don't know. I haven't decided. There are mosquitoes breeding in the spring *right* in front of the fucking shelter, but I don't really want to set up my tent next to whatever the hell's going on up there," she said, nodding toward the tent area up the trail, in the direction of the shrieking. "Maybe a fire will keep the bugs away. Do you know how to make a fire? I mean, I do, but I'm much better at keeping one going, right? I mean, I'm good at gathering wood and putting it on the fire, but whoever stayed here last didn't leave us shit to work with." She waved her arms like someone trying to point in all directions at once. "Oh, I'm Megan, by the way. Weren't you at the fire tower yesterday? What's your name?"

"I'm Gary. Or Green Giant if you're into the whole trail name thing. Are you thru-hiking?"

I barely got the words out before she shouted, "You're goddamn right I am!" She began jumping in place.

"Ah, cool," I said. "What's your trail name?"

"Well…" She turned her back to me and resumed moving things from one stuff sack to another. "I wanted to be called Meggly Peggly, but my first trail family told me that that was too long and that I'm not allowed to make up my own trail name and it can't be based on my real name, so that didn't stick. Snail Trail told me I should be called Fire Ass because I like to warm my butt by the fire, but I was like, no, you are not going to call me Fire Ass for the next six months, oh no no no! Do you know Snail Trail?"

I confessed that I did not.

"But then I was like, you should call me Ninja, because I always sneak up on people and no one ever hears me coming. I mean, I don't do it on purpose or to be creepy or anything like that, I'm just a quiet hiker. But anyway, Ninja Mike was like, uh, no, we already have a ninja and I don't want people to think we're a 'thing' so I was like, whatever, I guess I'm not Ninja. Have you met Ninja Mike?"

I confessed that I had not.

"So I guess I don't really have one yet but I'm taking suggestions. Do you have any?"

She swatted at the mosquitoes and moved her gear around some more, making it unclear whether she was actually waiting for my reply. "I'll have to think about that," I said, silently considering variations on Motor Mouth. "Your trail name is supposed to just happen naturally, I guess. Don't worry, you'll get one."

She grunted acknowledgment and gobbled a handful of something. As this was perhaps my only chance to utter more than one sentence, I didn't want to waste it. I looked north again and reached for my poles. "Well, the bugs here are pretty atrocious, and it sounds like things might have calmed down up at the tent sites. I might go check those out."

"Yeah, I thought about that too. I might see you up there." She began picking up sticks. "How much wood do you think I need to keep these bugs away?"

"All of it."

"What time is it?" she asked.

Time to take your Ritalin, I thought. "Five thirty."

"Aw shit," she said, and dropped her bundle of sticks. She moved to the spring and began filtering water. "The next shelter's like six more miles. I might just stay here. Have you seen Forager?" I told her I

didn't know who that was and she returned her attention to the water.
"How far are you going today?" she asked.

I just told you, I thought. I pointed up the path, where the shrieking had turned to giggling—which was better but still less than ideal. "Just far enough to get out of earshot of that. Well, hey, good luck with those mosquitoes." I took a few more steps and added, "Bye!"

"You're not supposed to do that," she said.

"Do what?"

"Say goodbye," she said. "Never say goodbye to anyone on the trail."

"Oh right," I said. "Good luck with the bugs and uh...try not to kill any children?"

"God, no kidding!" she said, and I moved on.

■ ■ ■

The tent sites weren't much farther, and when I arrived I scanned the area. The best site had already been claimed by a young mother who I presumed had been barking at the shrieking toddlers earlier, the same toddlers who now ran in frantic circles around their tiny tents. Their shrieks had resumed and the barking was sure to follow. Only six miles to the next shelter, I thought. If I hauled ass, I would be there at 8:30, right around dark. I could go back to the other shelter with the mosquitoes and the girl. No, I thought. I'll go forward. Plus something felt wrong about going backwards, even a tenth of a mile. I had plenty of water and was confident I would find a flat spot before the next shelter.

And there was. As I was setting up my tent I checked my cell phone for a signal. I hadn't heard Katie's voice four of the last five nights, but tonight I was high up in the Nantahala forest and was delighted to see one bar. She answered on the second ring.

"Holy shit, is it Green Giant?" she exclaimed. Hearing where I was, she told me that some people from our kayaking days would be at the Nantahala Outdoor Center around the same time I would. I should keep my eyes peeled for paddlers. One of them might even spring for a meal. I was on board with this plan.

"Too bad you won't be there," I said.

"Looks like you're still on track for Clingmans Dome next weekend. I'll see you there. With your mom and Emily! What should we bring? What kind of food do you miss the most?"

"This is going to sound weird, but hard vegetables. Like cauliflower, or carrots."

"Hmm. I guess your body lets you know what it's missing. When's the last time you had vegetables?"

I thought about it. I'd only just been through Franklin, right? No, that was three days ago. I think I had a salad with dinner. I can't remember; it all disappeared so fast. "I guess you're right," I said. "It's been a while and it wasn't much, at that. But I also want those scones again. And cheeseburgers! Let's not do this now. I'm getting dizzy."

"I'll surprise you," she said.

"So check this out. I just ran into someone rather interesting," I continued.

"Was it Lemmy?"

"No, not yet. And I haven't seen a cartoon in a while either. No, I just met someone who I think needs a trail name."

I told her about Megan and how she dodged the first half dozen or so monikers the other hikers had thrown at her. "I think we should call her Nope," I said.

"Not bad," Katie said, "but I was thinking Voldemort."

"How so?"

"She who shall not be named."

"Damn. Voldemort is much better than Nope. Okay, I'll tell her she's been named."

"Just like that, huh?"

"Yeah, I think that's all there is to it. And I'm not going to ask her either. She doesn't get the option to consider this one. She needs to focus on other things." I described the piles of garbage bags and stuff sacks. "I seriously couldn't tell if she was coming or going. And she may or may not walk up to these tent sites. She doesn't even know what her name is."

"Gary," Katie said.

"Yes?"

"Focus on your own problems."

"I am," I said. "It's just that I have a feeling she's about to become one of them."

# 5

# LAND OF THE NOONDAY SUN

IT WAS MORNING and I was in mid-squat when I heard familiar yelling. Shrieking and barking, actually. The lady with her kids, and none of them sounded happy. I'd walked nearly half a mile past their camp the previous night and had been up since sunrise, but they must've had an early start. They were approaching faster than I'd expected, and now these kids were about to see a "full moon" rising. I was too close to the trail.

The first kid crested the hill just as I duck-walked behind a bush, hunkered down even lower, and hushed my breathing. I'm in it now, I thought. I'm committed. Like a sniper. I can't exactly pop up from behind this bush with my pants around my ankles and introduce myself. Pepper spray really hurts.

His sister followed. "Stop bouncing!" their mother yelled from behind. She repeated herself, this time loud enough to crack her voice. "Stop bouncing! It's inefficient!"

She turned to a child behind her, barely a toddler. I couldn't tell if the miniature curly mop concealed a little boy's or girl's face. The child scurried to catch up as his/her mom scolded, "Get up there with your brother and sister! Move!" She pounded her trekking poles into the ground, punctuating each command with a puff of dirt. "And stop bouncing!"

I felt an urge to yell back at her, but it's hard to be intimidating when you're naked from the waist down. I waited for them to pass. They slowed down as the boy noticed my tent and pointed, but his mom yelled and the group marched on.

Once they were out of earshot, I finished up and returned to my tent site, where rays of sunlight had just begun to touch my makeshift clothesline. My shirts were made of a quick-drying material, but the humid night air had the opposite effect and I had to wring them out. Reluctantly I removed my dry sleeping shirt and chose the lesser of two wet tees. When my head popped through the hole, Voldemort was there. "Boo."

"Good thing you didn't get here just a few minutes ago," I said, waving my shovel at her. "And you're right. You really do sneak up on people."

She leaned on her poles. "Yeah, I really want my trail name to be Ninja. Stupid Michael."

"Ninja Mike? The one you mentioned yesterday?"

"Yeah," she sighed. "He's dreamy. He dresses like a gorgeous pirate. I think he's like a judo instructor or something. Anyway, he said I couldn't be Ninja."

My pack was ready and I hoisted it, motioning for her to lead. "Well it doesn't matter, because I have your trail name," I said. "I was talking to my wife last night—"

"Oh, where is she?" She stopped and looked back at the campsite.

"On the phone," I said. "I was telling her about you and how—"

"Did you actually get a signal up here?" she asked.

"Yes."

"Who's your carrier?"

I said, "AT&T. Anyway—"

"Do you know what that stands for?"

"I think I do, but why don't you go ahead and—"

"It stands for 'Appalachian Trail Terrible!' Ha!"

I wanted to be annoyed by her, but she was right. My coverage had sucked. "That's pretty good," I said. "Do you want to know what your trail name is?"

"Oh yeah!" She quickened her pace.

"So anyway, I was telling Katie about how you kept rejecting trail names, so she said, 'She who shall not be named...Voldemort!' Huh? What do you think?"

"What's a Voldemort?"

I stopped. "You're kidding, right?"

"No. What's a Voldemort?"
"How old are you?"
"Twenty-two. No! Twenty-three."
"And you've never read or seen Harry Potter."
"I know what Harry Potter is," she said. "I grew up sheltered from pop culture. No TV in the house, no movies. You know."

I didn't know. I had been in line to see *Star Wars* the day it came out. When I was seven, I had *Mork and Mindy*, *That's Incredible*, and eventually Hall and Oates. Pop culture was the metronome for my childhood. But when she explained that she grew up in northern Maine with hundreds of acres of land and horses, I had to concede that she didn't miss much. We had plenty of time and nothing else to do but walk, so I explained to her the concept of the boy who lived and the evil wizard.

"So Voldemort's a dude, huh?"
"You okay with that?" I asked.
"I like it even more now," she said. "Now when I sign the log books, it will confuse my enemies."

. . .

"My trail name was almost Hiking Home," she said.
"Because you're from Maine. I'm kind of hiking home too," I said. "For a while at least. Once we get past Hot Springs I'll be hiking away."

Starting my hike so close to home made me feel a little guilty. Several hikers I met confessed they were homesick; meanwhile I'd already seen my wife twice, plus my friend was likely to be waiting to see me at the Outdoor Center, and I'd see people I knew at Hot Springs and again at Damascus. I tried not to bring it up often, so as not to make anyone jealous.

"Doesn't bother me a bit," Voldemort said. "When we get up north, the roles will be reversed. Besides, I'm used to being on my own."

The time flew by. Having company was refreshing, and talking to Voldemort was far better than talking to myself. Different people's unique hiking paces tend to isolate us on the trail. When I asked her if I was walking too slow or too fast she said, "I can hike at any pace. So how well do you know this section of the trail?"

"Tellico Gap will be where I first start to see places I recognize," I said. "That's where we used to park and hike up to Wesser fire tower.

Then we'll go down the gorge and into the Nantahala Outdoor Center. I've been there more times than I can remember. Once we cross the train tracks just past the NOC, we're back into unfamiliar territory. So, not much really. Just a few miles."

I had to stop along the way for a call of nature, which turned into a snack by a stream, so Voldemort went on without me for a while. When I arrived at Tellico Gap, a homeless man was there pretending to be a thru-hiker. He had cornered a couple day hikers who were trying to enjoy the view, and after accepting a candy bar he asked if they had any beer.

I had seen him before at a previous shelter, where he had tried the same trick on me. After talking to him for 30 seconds, it was clear he had no idea where Springer Mountain was and no idea where the trail even went. The southern portion of the trail attracts a small number of mostly harmless transients in the springtime, and this one wanted me to vouch for him. "Hey, I know you!" he yelled, pointing at me. "I know this guy! He's all right!"

Not gonna happen, buddy. I waved politely and rushed the next half mile up to the tower, skipping the break I had planned and forgoing any pictures from the gap. After 15 minutes of huffing and puffing, I reached the tower. From its base I could hear Voldemort talking on the platform above, presumably to the owners of the two new packs resting at the bottom. I ditched mine, selected a water bottle, and started climbing the rusty metal stairs.

"Well, I did try to start my own YouTube channel for a while, but it was just videos of me talking, and everyone was like, 'What are you even talking about?' and I was like, whatever, this is just me. So yeah, I talk a lot, but only when I really need to be entertained and no one else will do it, right? Hey! Who's that coming up the stairs? Green Giant, is that you?"

At just over 100 feet, the Wesser Bald fire tower sways in the slightest of breezes, and the winding stairs are almost steep enough to qualify as a ladder. As I cleared the last one I could see Voldemort lying spread-eagle in the center of the platform with a towel over her face. She had stripped to her shorts and a sports bra, and her legs and belly were turning pink as the sun glared from a cloudless sky.

She lifted a corner of the towel to greet me, then dropped it again. Her audience identified themselves as Blue Indian and Droid. Blue Indian was a recent college graduate, lean and tall with short-cropped blond hair. He was about to start his new job handling falcons and other birds of prey at a large zoo in the South, and was near the end of a weeklong vacation on the trail. Droid was still in college. He was seeing how far he could hike before classes started back up in the fall. Voldemort continued to talk about nothing from under her towel, while the three of us took in the view.

The fire tower on Wesser Bald commands one of the most spectacular views along the southern Appalachian Trail. In all directions you are surrounded by monstrous green wrinkles stretching to the horizon. That puddle in the distance is the lake at Fontana Dam, which marks the beginning of the Smokies. It feels like you can see the curvature of the earth from up there. I interrupted whatever Voldemort was saying, and told them about the time I spent a night atop the tower.

"We came up here after a day on the river. My wife smartly set up her tent right down there," I said, pointing to a flat spot near the base of the tower. "My buddy Pimp and I got way too drunk and decided it was a good idea to just roll out our sleeping bags right here on top of the tower."

"Yeah?" Blue Indian squinted behind his dark sunglasses. "How'd that work out for you?"

"It was a damn near perfect night," I said. "Until about 5:30 in the morning, when the rain started. It was just a light drizzle, but we hauled ass down the stairs anyway. Pimp had a one-man tent, and I strung a tarp between these supports." I pointed below. "The tarp kept me dry until it turned into a full-blown thunderstorm. Rain came in sideways. I was soaked, and then the lightning started and we're under a giant metal thing, the highest point for miles! No fucking way did we stick around! We all packed our shit and hauled ass back down to the gap."

I pointed at the trail where we had made our retreat from the lightning, the same way I had come up today. Voldemort lifted her towel again and propped herself on her elbows. Her eyes followed my finger. "The service road? Why'd you come up that way?"

"I always come up that way."

"That's not the AT, man," Droid said. "That is." He pointed to an opening in the trees near the base of the tower. It was a trail I'd seen a hundred times and had never taken. "They both come up from the gap. You just took the easy route."

Voldemort gave me a sympathetic look. "If you want, we'll wait here while you go back and get it."

"Get what?" I asked.

"The part you missed," she said.

"You're kidding, right?" I said. "Why would I walk to the bottom of this mountain that I just climbed, turn around and climb it again? A descent which, by the way, I've done honestly probably six times. For what? Half a mile, maybe point eight, of white blazes?"

"If it was me, I'd do it," Voldemort said.

"Well, I've carefully weighed the pros and cons, and I've decided against it. It would be inefficient," I said. We stared at the horizon while Voldemort baked in the sun. "Hey, did you guys see that lady and her kids?" I asked. Each of them had. When Blue Indian saw the children, they were full of energy and practically running up the hills. Meanwhile Droid reported a death march.

"Those kids are probably already at the bottom," said Voldemort, looking at the gorge. "And this thing looks like a real knee-breaker."

"Good thing they only weigh 40 pounds," I said. She was right; it was an ass kicker.

We stood up to get started, and suddenly I noticed Voldemort's legs. "Dude, you are as red as a lobster. How long have you been up here?"

She told me that she'd been on her back for at least an hour before I showed up. She assured me that she would be okay. She was a lifeguard every summer in college, and that she was used to being in the sun all the time, and that even though she hated kids she loved being a life guard because it meant that she sometimes got to yell at kids, and that she used her life guard money to fund her hike and I told her to stop talking and to get in the shade.

Down we went, and under the cover of trees we made our plan.

▪ ▪ ▪

The bottom of Nantahala Gorge is the lowest elevation on the trail up to that point, 137 miles north of Springer Mountain. Following the white blazes will take you down nearly 4,000 feet over seven miles. If it were flat, we could easily make the Nantahala Outdoor Center by nightfall, but then we would have to pay to stay there. The A. Rufus Morgan shelter was barely a mile from the bottom, and it was free. We could stay there, then resupply at the NOC in the morning and hang out by the falls watching the kayakers until my friends showed up. After eating something, we would climb back up out of the gorge that afternoon.

"The only thing about that shelter is that sometimes it can be kind of a party place," I said. "It's a quick walk up from the NOC and a lot of river rats like to haul booze up there and get rowdy."

"Fine by me," Voldemort said. "I'll drink their beer." We started our hike down. By 2 p.m. the sun was already behind the mountain. Nantahala is the Indian word meaning "Land of the Noonday Sun." When you're all the way down in the notch you only get a couple hours of direct sunlight. The water's freezing too.

The hike down into Nantahala Gorge was the first time my legs were worked to the point of being wobbly. This was more work than running, constantly having to slow myself, braking not only my own weight but also my pack, fighting gravity all the way down the steepest decline of the hike so far. For the first few minutes after each stop, my thighs would shiver unless I stretched. My pack prevented the foot grab which is essential to a good quad stretch, but I didn't feel like taking it off, so I just kept walking.

Every half hour, Voldemort would zoom past me. I would find her a half mile or so later standing on a rock or looking at a bug. I joined her at a break in the trees called "The Jump-off" that offered a view to a similar lookout called "The Jump-up" on the opposite side of the gorge. We gave up looking for it without binoculars. The gap was about two miles wide as the crow flies, but we would have to walk about ten to traverse the sea of green beneath us.

"What's the name of this place we're stopping at tonight?" she asked. "I don't have the guide for the next few days."

"What happened to your guide?" I asked.

"I needed kindling a few nights ago and accidentally ripped out the pages for where I was going instead of where I'd been." She seemed embarrassed.

"Don't feel bad. I accidentally stayed in Helen instead of Hiawassee because they were on the same page. Shit like that's gonna happen. Anyway, it's called the A. Rufus Morgan shelter. I have no idea who A. Rufus Morgan was. I've stayed there like two or three times maybe. We used to night hike to the shelter after a day on the river and then go up to the tower the following day."

"Droid and Blue Indian are probably already there," she said.

Most of our descent was in the green tunnel. At a few places, mainly at switchbacks, we had views below. We could hear the river faintly, but the gorge was too steep for us to see it. Our ears popped and the moist air grew cooler as we continued down.

When we entered the clearing at the shelter, it felt like bedtime.

The shadow of the gorge filtered the late afternoon glow into a pale dusk. Droid and Blue Indian had already set up their tents downhill and far from the shelter. "Don't go anywhere near that thing!" Droid yelled from their camp. "It's haunted!"

Voldemort immediately started toward the shelter, her head thrust forward and her pace quickening, eager to see what he meant. I followed her. "Oh yeah," I said. "I forgot to mention. We never stay in the shelter."

Voldemort stopped short and wrinkled her nose. There was no shelter log, nor was there a broom. The empty remains of a case of Pabst Blue Ribbon were piled in one corner. A filthy crumpled tarp filled the other. A lone millipede vanished between the floorboards. "Look how small this thing is," she said. "You'd have to lay sideways, Green Giant."

"Even Droid wouldn't fit in this thing," I said.

"I heard that!" Droid and Blue Indian had walked up the small hill to greet us.

More garbage stuffed down into the footwell and a cloud of horrible insects with legs longer than their wings, like dragonflies without bodies, further tarnished the legacy of A. Rufus Morgan. "I don't remember this place ever being so trashed," I said, feeling a little ashamed. "When my friends and I came here, we never left any garbage behind. Not all boaters are like this."

Voldemort growled. "What I don't get is this: Your garbage there is now lighter than it was when you carried it in. Why not just fucking take it out, too?"

We all agreed that it was too much for even the four of us to haul. We each had our own trash in our packs already, as we should. We moved down the hill and away from the shelter. A small stream ran at the edge of the clearing, where a few long logs lay circling an ash-filled fire pit. The ground was sloped everywhere, and Blue Indian and Droid had set up their tents in the last two spots that were remotely flat. There was very little grass and the place was picked clean of firewood.

The four of us laughed and joked as much as we could during dinner, but the deep shadows combined with our sore legs to drive everyone into their tents early. I didn't sleep well on the sloping ground, and kept waking up crumpled at the foot of my tent. I would scuttle back up and try to lie perfectly still, but the slightest movement sent me sliding down again. Eventually the exhaustion from the day's steep descent took over and I blacked out.

Soon the birds were singing and we were up again. I felt hungrier than I had been in years, maybe since boot camp. Voldemort had had a rough night too, sliding down in her sleeping bag, and itching from her sunburn.

Droid and Blue Indian had enjoyed a more peaceful rest. When I called dibs on a flat space at our next stop, they told me to hike faster. The birds continued to sing as we broke camp. As we were only a mile from the river at the bottom of the gorge, the mist touched everything. I stowed my dripping rain fly and Droid put on the damp shirt he had hung to dry the night before. We were near the lowest point on the trail so far, and our experience at that shelter was fitting.

■ ■ ■

The day brightened as we left the shelter; it was going to be hot. Mountain laurels were blooming, their flowers like little white teacups just bigger than a thimble. The trail crossed a few little streams and footbridges, and soon the distant shush of the river was joined by the sound of tires on dirt, people laughing, and the occasional rumble of motorcycles. The short walk improved all our moods, mine especially as I began to recognize our surroundings. It was the first time I had been to the Nantahala Outdoor Center without driving.

The trail dumped us onto a parking lot behind the general store, a long wooden building with dozens of kayaks leaning on it. We dropped our packs among the boats and rushed into the bathrooms, excited to wash our hands and faces and throw away our trash. It was a curious thing to be excited to see a trash can.

Across the busy road was a sprawling compound of buildings, with parking lots choked with people and buses rigged to carry rafts. A crowd was forming at one of the outbuildings where paddles, helmets, and life vests were being distributed. Children and adults in wetsuits jostled and shoved to cross a metal footbridge spanning the river.

"Where's your friend supposed to meet us, Green Giant?" asked Voldemort.

"I have no idea," I said. "I haven't had a signal for two days, so I don't know if anyone's even coming. I guess we'll see, huh?"

We tried to stick together, but failed. While I was in the outfitters perusing their meager selection of dehydrated meals, the others scattered. Voldemort wanted a shower, Droid returned to the general store, and Blue Indian, who only had two more days on the trail, went to a restaurant to check out their beer list. For the next hour we moved from one building to another, sometimes running into each other, until finally we arrived at the restaurant, which had a deck overlooking the water.

"Four seats and a beer list, please," said Blue Indian.

The rest of us took a pass on beers, concerned how a belly full of bubbles would feel on the climb back out of the gorge in the heat. We were waiting for our plates and examining our maps when I heard a familiar voice call my name from the other side of the room. It was my friend, Joe Bill.

I jumped up to hug him, but stopped short. "Dude, I smell. You don't want to—"

"I don't care, man. Good to see you!"

He lived about 45 minutes away, about halfway to my house. We had met years before on a kayaking trip and had paddled the Nantahala River together many times. I introduced my friends at the table. "Joe Bill's a veterinarian," I told them. Blue Indian, happy to meet a kindred spirit working with animals, stood and offered a hand. "Droid is studying engineering and Voldemort—er, Megan just graduated with...what was it again?"

"Neuroscience and anthropology," she said.

"I see you've fallen in with the nerds," Joe Bill said.

He joined us at the table and pelted us with questions. "What's your typical day like?"

"It's been almost two weeks, and I still don't know how to answer that yet," I said. "We pretty much walk all day, but that's the only thing the days have in common."

"Seen any bears yet?" None of us had, but we were all happy to discuss the birds, bugs, and salamanders that were everywhere. I asked Joe Bill if he'd talked to Katie and to tell her I loved her and missed her. Then our plates arrived and for a short time the only sound was forks and knives on glass.

Voldemort straightened up in her seat and pointed her fork at each of us. She chewed faster, twirled her finger in a "just a minute" gesture, and swallowed half of her enormous bite. "So here's something interesting," she said, reloading her fork. "Remember that lady with the kids?" she asked. "I ran into a chick at the store who saw them too. She said the kids looked miserable. She talked to her and said they're doing the whole trail."

"Wow, that sounds..." Joe Bill trailed off.

"Crazy?" I said.

"I was going to say impressive, actually," he said.

"No," I said. "Crazy. One of those kids is like four years old." I turned to Voldemort. "Did she say where they are now?"

"I think they're taking a zero here," she said, and explained the term to Joe Bill. "Zero miles, a day off."

Blue Indian added, "I saw them. They looked pretty tired. Someone else told me that one of the kids said they weren't allowed to play near any streams or they'd get yelled at. I wonder what their deal is."

We four hikers had cleaned our plates when Joe Bill pushed his away. Voldemort and I both asked, "Are you going to finish that?" He shook his head and we split what was left in less than a minute.

"So how about that beer?" Blue Indian asked.

"None for me," Voldemort said. "I'm on a budget."

"Not today you're not," Joe Bill said. "I got this." We protested but he insisted. "Gary, you just quit your job, and you three just graduated. Besides, I'm really impressed by what you guys are doing. I really wish I could do something like this. The least I can do is get your lunches."

"Lunches?" I asked. "This is supposed to be second breakfast. What time is it?"

"It's almost noon."

"Aw, shit. Guys, we gotta get moving. We still have like eight more miles today. And it's literally all uphill."

Blue Indian smiled. "So just the one beer then."

"Fine. Just one."

■   ■   ■

I hugged Joe Bill at his car and told him again to give my love to Katie. "One last thing," he said, opening the passenger door. He picked up a bag and handed it to me.

"There should be enough Snickers bars in there for all you guys. Some beef jerky, too. I asked Katie what you liked to eat and she gave me a list. That's all I could find on my way in, though." The bars were starting to melt in their wrappers, but I didn't care. I thanked him and hugged him again, then hurried to catch my friends, who had gotten a head start on the big climb out of the gorge.

As I walked among the boaters, it hit me that I had never taken the trail north from there. I had no idea where to go. I wandered a few minutes before asking a raft guide where the trail was. Before I even finished my question, he pointed me to the train tracks behind the far parking lot. Neither the sign nor the white blaze were easy to spot among the thick bushes behind the tracks, but eventually I found both, and soon my climb began.

Out of habit, I checked my phone for a signal. I expected none and got exactly what I expected. I squinted up at the sun directly overhead and could already feel my ears and cheeks turning red. This place is living up to its name for sure, I thought, unrolling the brim of my hat for more cover.

My next supply stop would be at Clingmans Dome, some 70 trail miles away. This was to be the longest I'd go without a supply stop until maybe the 100 Mile Wilderness in Maine, so my pack was already at its heaviest before Joe Bill handed me three pounds of chocolate and meat. The two full water bottles I brought to combat the heat added four more pounds. I could feel the pack shift with every step, like an angry midget trying to wrestle me off the trail.

Leaning on my trekking poles for support with every step, I slowly realized what I had to do. I had to lighten my load. I had to eat some of that chocolate.

My pack's hip belt was already digging into my stomach, which was full and gurgling from eggs and beer. I happily released the belt and dropped my pack to search for the Snickers bars. In my head, I knew that eating a pound of food I had been carrying in a backpack would not actually lighten my load, merely redistribute it. But I didn't care as I clutched a mushy chocolate bar, tearing at the wrapper with my teeth. Better eat some jerky too, I thought. I didn't want to keep climbing in this heat with the taste of salty meat in my mouth, so I put one more Snickers in my pocket and pressed on.

About five miles into the eight-mile climb I caught up with Voldemort, resting at "The Jump-up," the break in the trees which offered a view to the other side of the gorge. "Good lord, this climb sucks!" I said and plopped onto the rock where she sat.

"No shit," she said. "I just want a fucking nap."

"Seriously. Hey, want some chocolate?" I offered her what was left of the bag Joe Bill had given me.

"No thanks," she said. "I can barely fit what I already have into my pack."

"Really?" I said. "I've never known a woman to turn down free chocolate."

"I'm not like the other girls," she assured me. "Plus I have a package waiting for me at Fontana Dam."

Fontana Dam marks the beginning of the Smokies, and is where Blue Indian would leave the trail the day after next. We'd heard from other hikers that the supply there was hit or miss, which was why I was carrying enough food to get me to Clingmans Dome.

We hiked the next two miles together, up to the shelter at Sassafras Gap. As soon as the wooden box was visible she ran the last few yards, yelling, "Puddin'!"

Puddin' was a large man wearing a tie-dyed shirt. Two weeks into the hike most of the guys were starting to get some stubble; there were even a few real beards. Puddin' had gray whiskers down to the middle of his chest. He stood and smiled at her approach. "Megan!" he called back, and wrapped her in a bear hug, lifting both her and her pack easily. "Damn, girl. You're pink. You been sunbathing?"

"Ugh, I know. And it's Voldemort now," she said. "Some kind of evil wizard who eats babies or something. Puddin', this is Green Giant."

I shook his hand and he greeted me warmly, minus the hug. They had met a while ago, back when I was just getting started. (Hell, I was *still* just getting started.) Puddin' was part of her original trail family, along with Ninja Mike and a few others whose names I didn't catch. Sore shins had forced her to spend a couple days in town, and she'd been left behind. Now as they caught up, I scanned the shelter log for more cartoons, but found none.

"Your boyfriend was just here," Puddin' said.

"Who?" she asked.

"Big Indian? He was with a kid named Robot or something."

"Droid. Oh, we're not together."

"His loss," Puddin' said and winked at me.

I looked at my guidebook. "They're probably going to Cheoah Bald."

Puddin' nodded. "That's the place. You should really consider joining them. It's only another mile and has one of the best views you'll get for a long time—360-degree views and a fire ring."

Voldemort encouraged him to join us, but Puddin' declined. "As much as I'd love to, my old bones are tired and it's a rough mile. Plus you'll have to carry water, and I'm already settled." He motioned to the inside of the shelter, where his sleeping bag was already rolled out.

"Maybe we'll run into each other again," she said, hopefully.

"Probably not, honey. You and those young fellas really pour it on. I've been here since noon and I probably won't get going until noon tomorrow." She hugged him again, and after we filtered enough water for dinner and breakfast, we pushed on once again.

• • •

Cheoah Bald is a clearing the size of a baseball diamond atop a 5,000-foot peak which stands a thousand feet taller than its nearest neighbor. Other than a few trees at the edge of the clearing, there is nothing to block the view. Blue Indian and Droid were setting up their tents when we arrived.

"God damn, what a beautiful spot!" I said.

"I know, right?" said Voldemort, carefully removing her pack and wincing as a strap rubbed against her sunburned shoulder.

It was late afternoon and we were worn out. We had hiked 15 miles that day, descending from one of the highest points so far, down into the lowest point, and back up to another high. I keep a small thermometer on the outside of my pack; a few hours earlier it had read almost 90 degrees. Up here on the bald it was much cooler, and I stood for a minute with my eyes closed, enjoying the breeze.

After I set up my tent the four of us sat on logs around a circle of rocks filled with cold coals. "Looks like it might be clear tonight," I said. Every campsite and shelter so far had been inside the green tunnel, and I hadn't seen the night sky in weeks. "If we can manage to stay awake for a while after dark, I'll give you guys a quick astronomy lesson. I mean, if you don't mind, that is. My second favorite hobby besides hiking is astronomy."

"That sounds pretty sweet," Blue Indian said.

"It would be sweeter if we had a telescope or even binoculars, but I have a feeling just looking with our eyes is going to be pretty damned amazing."

Droid left the circle grinning and said, "I have something that will make this even more amazing." He reached into a zipper pouch on his pack and pulled out a small drawstring bag. "We need to make sure we're safe up here."

Blue Indian nodded. "Yes. Time for a safety meeting."

Voldemort looked up from the pile of stuff sacks surrounding her. "What's a safety meeting? Are we in danger?"

"No, no, no," I said. "Safety is weed. I thought only kayakers said that."

Droid said, "I thought only rock climbers called it that."

"I'm down," Voldemort said.

Droid packed a small pipe for us and we passed it around while the sun dropped closer to the horizon. "Thanks," I said. "Some guys I hiked with at the start gave me a joint I've been carrying around for a few days too. I almost busted it out last night but I still wasn't sure. I mean, you never know who's okay with it or not."

"Dude, we're all in our twenties," Blue Indian said. "We're pretty much down for whatever."

Droid pointed the pipe at me. "Now you, on the other hand, we weren't sure about you, but I said fuck it."

"What's that supposed to mean?" I asked.

"You're like fifty or something, right?"

"I'm forty-four," I said. "There's a shit-ton of smokers in my age group. We're all just weird about it for some stupid reason. None of us gave a fuck in our twenties either."

"That'll change," he said. "So what's your deal?"

"What do you mean?" I asked.

Blue Indian leaned over and snatched the lighter, and Droid continued. "I mean, most hikers are either our age or retired. Are you like, having a midlife crisis or something?"

"I guess it looks that way, huh? No, I just really love to hike and finally got to the point where I could do this. When I was your age— aw, shit, did I just say that? Fuck. Anyway, when I was your age I didn't even know there was an AT. By the time I knew it was a thing, I had a house and bills and shit. So a couple years ago I made up my mind, saved as much as I could, and here I am."

"So what about your job?" asked Voldemort. "Did you get six months off?"

"I quit."

Blue Indian's eyes bugged out. "Just like that?"

"That's really all there is to it. I saved up enough to do this and cover my bills while I'm gone, and here I am."

"What will you do when you get back?"

"I have no idea."

"And your wife? She must be pretty cool to let you do this."

"No, she doesn't *let* me do anything. What I mean is, we have an arrangement where neither of us ever asks permission to do stuff. If she gets a crazy idea that makes her happy, we talk about it and find a way to make it happen. If I want to buy something for me, I don't have to get her jewelry to make up for it. Just stuff like that."

Blue Indian said, "Does she hike too?"

"Oh yeah, she hikes. She's kind of a badass, but she's only good for about two weeks at a stretch. Besides, we can't both quit our jobs. She's running the show from back home. Speaking of which..." I passed the pipe and checked my phone. Still no signal. "Shit. Appalachian Trail Terrible, right? Anyone have a signal?"

"I do," Voldemort said. "Four bars."

"Would I be able to convince you to text Katie for me? Just say hi and that I'm still on track for next weekend. She'll know." I gave her the number and while she typed the rest of us stood and stretched.

On the eastern side of the bald, the sky was beginning to turn the color of a ripe peach. We moved to the west side and stood together, mesmerized by the sunset. The horizon seemed hundreds of miles away, and every inch between us and the edge of the earth was covered green. Deep shadows filled the spaces between countless peaks, lengthening as we watched in silence.

We're going there, I thought. We're going to walk right to the edge of everything we can see. And when we get there, we'll see a new edge and walk to that. And again. And again. For forever. Standing there on that mountain watching the sky catch fire, it felt like we had all of eternity before us to do whatever we wanted, to control where we went, and what we saw, and how we felt. The entire world was ours for the taking.

A dim point of light shone in the periwinkle part of the sky. "That one's called Arcturus," I said.

# 6

# HAPPY GHOST

GREAT SMOKY MOUNTAINS NATIONAL PARK is huge. The park spans half a million acres and contains the highest elevations along the entire Appalachian Trail. It is a UNESCO World Heritage Site and it is the most visited national park in the United States. For northbound AT hikers, the park is significant because some rules apply here that are quite different from the rest of the trail. For instance, it is the only section which requires thru-hikers to purchase and carry a permit, which costs $20. Many hikers are confused by this process or offended by the fact that they have to pay, and you can hear them complain for days prior to arrival.

Another source of friction is that thru-hikers must spend their nights in the AT shelters or pitch their tents next to them. Visitors who only plan to stay a night or two must reserve the shelters in advance, but with their permits, thru-hikers can stay at any shelter they choose. "Stealth campers"—those who pitch a tent or hammock anywhere other than a designated site—are fined and escorted out of the park.

The idea is to minimize human impact. The Smokies are notorious not just for their stunning natural beauty, but also for an abundance of wildlife. Bears, boar, deer, and rare birds exist here in a concentration seen in few other places in the United States, let alone along the AT. This is also the reason for the third restriction likely to cause a tantrum: no dogs.

Voldemort, Droid, and I had no dogs, we knew where the shelters were, and we already had our permits, so when we arrived at Fontana Dam our only concern was to find food. Blue Indian's car was waiting for us, and he offered to drive us into Fontana Village and then back to the park before he went back home to Atlanta to start his new job at the zoo. When we arrived at the lot, we were met by the smell of asphalt sealer and the rumble of diesel engines. Orange cones surrounded Blue Indian's Jeep, and the crew was about to pour the first batch of thick black goo. He ran toward them, waving his trekking poles above his head. "Stop! STOP!"

Droid yelled after him, "Dude, that shit takes days to dry! Just leave it and keep hiking with us!" We watched from a distance. The foreman stopped the crew before the Jeep was completely painted into the corner. He and Blue Indian exchanged some words in what appeared to be a friendly tone, and the foreman slapped him on the shoulder and laughed as another man in an orange vest removed the cones.

Blue Indian tossed his gear in the back and drove to where we stood. "That was close," he said as we got in. "They put up signs two days ago that they were redoing the lot. I told him my car's been here for a week and there's no way I could have known. Dude said that happens every year, and usually it's dry by the time the person gets back so they just work around them."

We drove to Fontana Village, just a couple miles away, and ate cheeseburgers at a restaurant there. Everyone had beer with their lunch except me; that one at Nantahala had practically knocked me on my ass. I figured I had probably lost five to ten pounds since starting, and constantly having an empty stomach made one beer feel like six. That's okay if the only thing scheduled for the afternoon is a nap, but we faced another challenging climb in the heat that afternoon. In fact, we were going to be traveling uphill for nearly three days before reaching Clingmans Dome.

The general store had a decent selection of hiker food, but the prices seemed high and I was glad I had loaded up back at Nantahala, even if it meant that my pack was overloaded for two days. Having eaten my load back down to a more manageable weight, I felt much better about the next three days, especially with that burger in my belly. Megan's package from home was waiting behind the counter, and it contained so much food that it took nearly an hour to repackage everything.

Most of the food hikers carry needs to be repackaged. Pop-Tarts, for instance, are a very popular breakfast staple on the AT. They are inexpensive, contain hundreds of calories, and are relatively light. It's also okay for them to get smashed. A week's worth of Pop-Tarts, however, come in a cardboard box the size and shape of a brick. Peanuts come in a jar that weighs a quarter of a pound empty. Dried fruit and jerky come in a thick, crinkly bag that never closes properly once opened. The best price per ounce for instant coffee is a plastic tub large enough for ten people to share, and so on. This is why a big part of the resupply ritual consists of moving things out of boxes and bags and into smaller bags.

Megan dumped the contents of her care package onto a picnic table in front of the general store and spread it out, covering the entire surface. "Fuck! What am I supposed to do with all this?"

"I hope you guys don't mind," said Droid, changing the subject, "but I'm going to hitch back to the trail and get a head start. I have to be done by September."

"Before you go, take some of these brownies," Megan said. "There must be five pounds here."

Blue Indian and I stayed with her while she repacked, then drove back to Fontana Dam. We thanked him again, and hugged him goodbye. "Man," he said. "I really wish I was going the whole way with you."

"Yeah," we said. "Us too."

When he drove away, I asked Megan, "How many times have you heard that so far?"

"I've lost count."

We double-checked our permits and entered the Smokies.

■ ■ ■

Looking up from Fontana Dam, you can just barely see Shuckstack fire tower. Up close it's 100 feet of steel and wood; from the dam, three miles of trail and 2,000 feet of elevation shrink it to a tiny rectangle made of toothpicks. Megan and I walked along the blacktop over the dam and crossed onto a gravel road that led to the trail. Just before we entered the tree line, a large pickup truck pulled to a stop beside us. The tires were huge, and the abundant chrome was coated with a thin layer of dust. The passenger window slid down, revealing a plump woman with white hair and glasses. Her husband leaned toward us from the driver's seat and shouted over the rumble of his engine, "Hey y'all! Is this the Appalachian Trail?"

"It is," I said.

His wife looked at him, us, and then back to him. "Where's it come out?" she asked.

"Depends on which way you're going, I suppose. That way," I said, pointing north, "goes all the way to Maine."

"Woo-wee!" He whistled. "Y'all goin' all the way?"

"We sure are!" I said, standing just a bit straighter.

"Hot dang! I bet that's gonna take a couple weeks, idn'it?"

Megan spoke up. "Whole lot longer than that. More like six months."

The man and his wife exchanged looks of amazement. "Six months?" he exclaimed. "Y'all must not have kids then."

Megan and I looked at each other, and then I laughed. "Oh, we're not—"

"We just met a few days ago," she interrupted.

The driver's wife raised a hand to her cheek. "So you're doing this by yourself?"

"Yes, ma'am."

"Oh my goodness! You're very brave."

They gazed admiringly at Megan. "I'm by myself too," I pointed out.

"So brave," the man said. "Six months, dang! Well, good luck to both of you. And God bless!"

We thanked them and they rumbled off, leaving a cloud of dust.

At the end of the gravel road a modest sign welcomed us to the AT portion of the Smokies. We were still in the green tunnel, but things were changing. The trail was steeper and the ground was choked with greenery. May apple and thick carpets of ferns and moss covered every flat surface other than the brown strip of dirt leading us north. Rhododendrons were blooming, tiny purple explosions by the millions. Bright orange flame azaleas and red star-shaped flowers called fire pinks were sprinkled among their mostly white cousins, the trillium. It had rained the previous night so the orange salamanders were out. I narrowly avoided stepping in a giant pile of shit.

"Good lord!" I shouted. "Look at this! I seriously would have lost my shoe in this."

"What the fuck shits like that?" wondered Megan. "That's not manure."

"Bear."

"No way."

"Way. Look at how black it is," I said.

"Are you sure?" she said. "That pile's the size of a soccer ball."

"I'm sure. Unfortunately, I do have some experience with bears."

We resumed hiking and I told her about the bear I came face to face with on my shakedown hike at Shining Rock.

"That's crazy," she said. "I want to see one."

"Don't worry," I assured her. "I'm sure we'll see plenty."

■ ■ ■

We didn't see any bears that day, but we did see three wild boars, a female with two piglets. Initially her lumbering black shadow seemed like a bear to us, our expectations playing tricks on our eyes. When the mother saw us, she squealed and bolted—luckily, away from us. I hadn't done any research on boars, and I would not have known how to handle an angry one. (Now that I've had time to read up on the subject, I understand the approved technique is to already have your will drawn up beforehand.)

As we walked on, we saw a man ahead carrying the largest backpack I have ever seen. He was obviously struggling, rocking back and forth with every step and wheezing. By the time we reached him, he had removed his pack and was sitting on a rock. He reached into his pocket for a bandanna and wiped sweat from his shiny bald head. Both he and his pack were overweight. He looked utterly miserable.

"Excuse me," he called to us. "Excuse me. Hi. How well do you two know this area?"

"I've never been here before," I said. "But I do have a map. What are you looking for?"

"I think there's supposed to be some kind of cabin for hikers near here. Do you know anything about it?"

"Do you mean the shelter?" Megan asked.

"Yeah, the cabin!" he said. "Please tell me it's close."

"Actually, it's another three or four miles," I said.

He groaned. "I knew this was a bad idea. I just wanted to go backpacking for Memorial Day weekend. It shouldn't be this hard." He had an old external frame pack, the kind you see in grainy photos from the 1960s, full nearly to bursting. Every loop on the outside had something hanging from it, including a hatchet, a full water bottle, and a frying pan.

"I borrowed all this stuff and now I hate every piece of it," he said.

His head sank and he stared at his feet.

Megan glanced at me with raised eyebrows. "Um, you know it's not actually a cabin, right? It's just a shelter. Like a lean-to. It only has three walls."

"No beds?"

"Not unless you're carrying one." She nudged his pack with her toe.

"How far are you going?" I asked.

"I was going to have my son pick me up at Interstate 40 on Monday, but I think I'll get to the cabin tonight, and then turn around in the morning."

Megan was about to correct him again, but I raised a hand to stop her. I-40 was 80 miles away. He's already decided to turn back, so there was no point in telling him his plan was even more foolish than he realized.

"Where's your map? I'll show you where the shelter is."

"I don't have one."

Unbelievable. It was an hour or two until dusk and he was closer to the shelter than his car back at the dam. Forward was his best option. "Okay. See that?" I said, indicating a white blaze.

"Yeah, I've seen a bunch of those. What are they?"

"That's what's going to save you. Those white blazes let you know you're on the trail." No point telling him what the AT was; just keep it simple. "Keep walking that way and you'll be at the shelter in a couple hours."

He groaned again. "Okay."

"You'll be fine. Looks like you have plenty of water. Make sure you keep drinking it. Okay?"

"Okay." He stopped staring at his feet and looked up. "How will I find where to go?"

"If this shelter is anything like all the other ones, there will be a few people there. You'll hear us. There will probably be a fire. Can't miss it. Just take your time, okay? You'll be fine."

We encouraged him to rest awhile longer and have something to eat, then went on our way. After we crested the next hill and he was out of sight, Megan exploded.

"Cabin? Really?!?"

I joined in, equally exasperated. "How the hell does someone decide that the Smokies is the best place for their first solo backpacking trip?"

"That pack must have weighed 90 pounds! Think he'll really be okay?"

"I think he just learned a hard life lesson, but yeah. He'll live."

As the trail continued to challenge us for the next mile, I couldn't help thinking about the large sweaty man huffing along, taking tiny steps. About halfway up our final climb of the day, I remembered the trick Flat Feet had showed me, the one where you exhale forcefully and flap your lips like a horse whinnying.

"Oh my god, what was that?" Megan called back. I explained to her how the trick helped to push the carbon dioxide from the depths of the lungs, and for the rest of the way to the shelter we made horsey sounds and cracked each other up.

Mollies Ridge shelter was nothing at all like what we expected. Every shelter since Springer Mountain had been a simple three-walled wooden structure with a raised platform for sleeping, maybe a few wood pegs for hanging coats and packs. This thing looked like it had been designed by Frank Lloyd Wright. Stone walls supported a long metal roof with skylights and a chimney.

"Holy shit, this thing has a fireplace! Inside!"

"No wonder that guy thought there was a cabin up here. He probably only saw pictures."

Megan disappeared around the corner to claim her spot along the wall, while I stopped under the covered eating area to meet our bunkmates, who were cooking there. I told them about the bald guy with the heavy pack. They reminded me that the park was full of rangers. One had just been here in fact, checking permits. The big guy would be fine. Even if he had to spend the night out there, there had to be something in that gargantuan pack to keep him warm. Hell, he could even just curl up under the pack.

We found Forager and Lemmy's names in the log book, but no cartoon. I showed off my "Schnozzle bag," possibly my favorite piece of gear. Besides being a waterproof pack liner keeping my sleeping bag and camp clothes dry, it also works as an air pump for the mattress. You just hold the corners and flap it to scoop up air, pinch it shut, and connect its nozzle to the air mattress. Presto! Three times is enough to fill my air mattress for bedtime.

Megan whistled. "That's pretty high tech, Green Giant. I have this rolled up piece of foam. It has some mud on it."

"Yeah, I had one of those when I was in the Marines."

"I still can't picture you as a Marine. You're too nice." She sat cross-legged on the floor of the shelter and began piling stuff sacks around her.

"Thanks," I said. "I get that a lot. Even while I was in. I used to get yelled at for saying please and thank you to my troops." I squeezed more air into my mattress and tested it. "No, I'm not a badass by any means. I wouldn't last three days out here without my gear."

She picked a bag seemingly at random and dumped it into her lap. She shrugged at the spilled contents and replaced them into the bag. "Oh! Me too. I don't even know how to make a fire."

"Really? What about the one you started with your map?"

She laughed. "That was the only part that burned. Unless asking pretty much any guy to make one counts as starting a fire, then no."

"That's a pretty cool superpower you have."

"I know, right? Gets me rides to town and free drinks, too."

I peered over my glasses at her. "You be careful with that."

"Oh, totally," she said. "That's why I have this." She rooted through one sack and then another before producing a 6-inch throwing knife in a black sheath.

"How much does that thing weigh?" I asked. "And what good does it do you when it's buried in some bag?"

"I'm not stupid," she answered. "I clip it to my shoulder strap. I only wear it when I'm hitchhiking. Duh."

"And you still get rides?" I said.

"Wait till you see the shorts."

■ ■ ■

Through one open eye I could tell it was nearly sunrise. I was trying to go back to sleep when I heard Megan's quick footsteps and hushed voice urging me to join her outside. I stepped barefoot into the dewy grass. Right at the tree line stood a pair of four-point bucks. One munched the grass while the other stretched his neck to reach a low branch.

I mimed taking a picture, but Megan shook her head. "Quiet," she whispered. "You'll scare them away. We have deer on my parents' prop—" The big one charged.

I took a step back. "Um, is that thing…Jesus Christ!" She shoved me down into the grass and assumed a battle stance. The thing got to within 20 feet of us, then darted right and vanished behind the shelter.

"What the fuck was that?" she asked, reaching out a hand to help me back up.

The deer reappeared on the far side of the shelter, where it faced another buck, this one with two fuzzy nubs atop his smaller head. Despite his meager rack, the littler one reared up and bolted toward his larger brother, who absorbed the small thump with his shoulder and then bit the newcomer on the ass. The pair then circled around the shelter and rejoined their friend, who was still munching grass.

"Sorry I got your camp shorts wet," Megan said.

On our way out of camp that morning, we met a ranger and told him about the bald guy with the enormous pack. He said his colleague had already radioed him about meeting the man last night; the guy had turned around and was on his way out, doing fine.

The day was full of uphill climbs, and by the end we were at another shelter exactly like the last one—same stone construction, same covered picnic table, same fireplace, even some of the same people. The only difference was that this one was at a higher altitude. The jagged black line of my map's elevation profile for the days ahead climbed and dropped, climbed and dropped, but left each page considerably higher than where it started. It was a stockbroker's wet dream.

At the top of it would be Clingmans Dome and my family. As we huffed up some beautiful green hill together, I told Megan about my sister-in-law Priscilla, who had joined Katie and me to hike at Clingmans Dome a few years ago.

"She has a black belt in karate and was doing some kind of fitness modeling at the time. I think the three of us only did like eight miles that day, but we were struggling to keep up with her."

"She sounds pretty tough," Megan said.

"Not too long after that, she was in a horrible car accident. She was on a road trip and asleep in the passenger seat when they blew a tire and wrapped the car around a pole. No one thought she'd make it; we packed funeral clothes just in case. Name any bone, she probably broke it. Punctured organs, cracked spine and pelvis. Head the size of a watermelon. She spent two weeks in a coma."

I needed to pause. Everything was uphill.

"Fuck," Megan said, her poles clicking behind me. "How is she now?"

"About a month ago, she ditched her cane so she could walk into her dojo and bow to her sensei."

"Now I want to meet her."

I hitched my pack and tightened the waist belt. "Anyway, since she was with us the last time I was on Clingmans Dome, I can't help but think about her and her struggle. While we struggle. You know?"

We wound up hiking eighteen miles that day, the longest yet for each of us.

• • •

I had forgotten it was Memorial Day. It was just the day I'd see Katie again. But less than a mile into that morning's walk, we'd already met two day hikers. By the time the summit was visible we'd lost count of the people wearing jeans and carrying tiny water bottles.

Megan gestured at the observation deck, still a speck from three miles out. "Good lord, that thing is ugly!"

There are many and varying opinions about this structure, which I like to call the Concrete Monstrosity. It is a large flat disc with a quarter-mile spiral approach ramp, jutting out from what is the first alpine environment a northbound hiker encounters.

Rhododendrons and mountain laurel have given way to stunted pines and dead hemlocks. The trail took us over and around moss-covered rocks. Last year's needles were a soft brown carpet that cushioned our soles and muffled every sound. The place smelled like Christmas.

"Hey Voldemort," I said.

"Yeah?"

"Remember Blood Mountain?"

She grunted. "Oh god, yes."

"What didn't you like about it?"

"The way it turned everyone into a whiny little bitch."

I laughed. "Okay. I was going to say something along those lines, but yeah. That was what, like half a day of uphill? We've been going up for four days now."

"Highest point on the AT!" she crowed.

Two miles from the summit, the monstrosity grew as we approached. I took a gamble and pulled out my phone. Only one bar that came and went, but it was enough to fetch a batch of text messages from my mom, my niece Emily, and Katie.

*We're leaving in an hour.*
*We're on our way.*
*We'll be there soon.*
*We're here, where are you?*
*lol where r u ?* (That was Emily.)

I smiled and sent my reply: *Hike south on the AT and you'll find me!*

The next mile couldn't pass quickly enough. Yeah yeah yeah, pretty rock, lovely ferns...shut up bird, I'm trying to find my wife.

And there they were! Katie and Emily bounded down the trail toward us. "Uncle Gary, is the whole trail like this?" my niece asked.

I didn't know what to say. This part was so different from the beginning, but the change had been incremental to the point I had hardly noticed. I'd crossed a hundred big and small mountains already, some with names, most without. I couldn't remember the last time I had seen one of those black and red millipedes, or where the snakes had started. "Just some of it," was the best I could do.

Katie moved in for a hug, then balked and grimaced. Making up her mind, she hugged me anyway.

"Sorry," I said. "No shower since..."

Megan jumped in. "Ooh! I did laundry in a stream two nights ago. Well, not *in* the stream, because you're not supposed to do that. But with stream water. No soap though. So, um..."

Katie said, "You must be Voldemort," and held out a hand.

Megan countered with a hug, which was awkward because Katie's hands had no hope of meeting on the far side of Megan's pack.

"Mom down at the car?" My mom is in her 60s and one of her knees is made of titanium. Of course she was at the car. If I remembered correctly, the view from the parking lot was spectacular.

"Don't worry," Katie said. "She's not bored."

I hadn't seen my car since Springer Mountain, and I almost didn't see it at Clingmans Dome because it was surrounded by a mob.

"Who the hell are those people?" I asked.

"Must be more hikers," Katie said. "There were only four or five when we got your text message."

The back hatch of my Honda Element had been turned into a tailgate buffet. I pushed through the crowd to hug my mom. She gagged. "Oh my god, Gary, you stink. But you're still my baby and I love you. Come here!"

I kissed her cheek and turned to the food in amazement. An aluminum turkey pan full of broccoli and cauliflower. Carrots with blue cheese and ranch dressing. Four homemade pizzas (two were gone already) and a large bowl of strawberries. Four pans of chocolate brownies and two large cans of whipped cream, the spray kind with the red cap.

"It's everything I've been craving. Exactly. How?"

"A little birdie told me." Katie smiled at Megan.

"Remember when you had me text Katie?" my trail partner asked. "We've been besties ever since. I told her you wanted strawberries."

Katie shrugged. "Surprise?"

I was delighted. "As long as it gets me brownies and strawberries, I'm all for it!"

"And whipped cream too!" yelled someone from the mob, and everyone laughed.

A curly-haired guy with a beard and round cheeks picked up a can and gave it a curious look. His friend, with blond spiky hair, urged him to spray some in his mouth. Curly complied, making a bit of a mess, white foam collecting on the edges of his beard.

"It's whipped cream, Lemmy," said the spiky-haired guy. Lemmy tilted his head and overdid it, whipped cream blasting over his beard and filling his nostrils.

Katie shrieked. "Oh my god, you're Lemmy!"

He coughed and laughed at the same time, propelling whipped cream and whatever else was in his beard all over us. He pointed at his closed mouth and nodded, blinking and blushing. One of the other hikers asked me how we knew Lemmy.

"We don't," I said. "Until now, that is. I've only seen the cartoons in the log books."

"We're your biggest fans!" Katie exclaimed.

Lemmy wore a serape with yellow, blue, and red stripes and "Colombia" embroidered on the left breast. He used it to wipe his hands and mouth.

"I can die now," he said, his voice unmistakably foreign. "I can die happy! I have this…whipped cream. And I have fans." He chuckled, his shoulders heaving. "And two of them are girls!" he added blushingly, followed by more shrug-chuckling.

The girls especially seemed to like this, and when they giggled he blushed more. "When I die, I will be a happy ghost!"

Someone crunched a carrot and pointed at Lemmy's serape. "You told me you were from France."

"Oh. That was before Columbia. I only visited there." While the two of them straightened this out, the hiker who had asked me whether I knew Lemmy told me that he was actually from Israel.

Megan asked my mom what she thought about my AT hike. Mom flicked a hand dismissively. "Doesn't surprise me a bit. All he and his friends ever did growing up was walk around the neighborhood at night. Not getting into trouble or anything, just walking."

Each tray or bowl reached the point where nobody wanted to take the last serving, and most of the crowd thinned out. There were still tourists everywhere, but most of the hikers were moving on; from the dome it was either ten miles to the next shelter, or hitch into Gatlinburg.

We invited Lemmy to hike with us and he agreed. "Aw shit," I said, suddenly realizing a hitch in the new plan. "I was going to suggest Katie take us to Gatlinburg for resupply, but there's no way we'll all fit in here."

"You're not going to Gatlinburg," Katie declared.

"Why not?" I asked.

"Why would you go there when home is just a short drive away?" She moved closer. "Of course, you'll need to shower first. Twice."

"What about Mom and Emily?" I whispered.

"They rented a cabin a mile down the road."

"Oh. Oh! Yes, excellent idea," I said. "I can do laundry, we'll have breakfast in the morning. Yes. I agree."

Megan said not to worry about her and Lemmy, they'd hitch to Gatlinburg and back to the trail in the morning. With so much holiday traffic, it would be easy. We would all meet up the trail the following night.

"If that actually happens, it'll be the first time," I said skeptically.

"Go on," Megan insisted. "We'll catch you. Go have fun."

We didn't say goodbye, because you're not supposed to do that so I said, "Happy trails," and then climbed into the car with the girls and the food.

As we turned out of the parking lot, Emily opened her window and whispered to my mom, "Grandma, Uncle Gary smells like pee."

# 7

## PANTRY

SO MANY NIGHTS on the trail I missed Katie. I missed our warm, soft bed. Now that I was in it, I spent the night kicking and squirming. The quilt was too heavy and some naked person kept touching me. I kept thinking the sun was rising only to turn and see floating green numbers by the bed. I'd gotten accustomed to sleeping in a room this size, only minus an entire wall. That's where the wind and the crickets were supposed to be. Their absence was like an itch. I wasn't supposed to be here.

"Do you toss and turn like that on the trail?" Katie asked me at breakfast.

"Not even close," I said. "As soon as it gets dark, I'm out, and I don't remember a thing until I hear the birds."

"No dreams?"

"Almost never." I sipped my coffee. "This is so good." We sat quietly for a minute just looking at each other. I was in the place I dreamed about and all I could focus on was the unnatural hum of the refrigerator. "We should get going."

While I packed, I talked. "You know how everyone on the internet and all the books say 'it's the people' over and over again? I kind of get it now."

Katie handed me a clean shirt. "Go on."

"I mean, I knew it wasn't going to be complete *wilderness*, but I haven't camped alone more than a couple times. I'm already losing track of how many people I've met. And most of them have been pretty cool. Thing is, after a couple days they all either drop out or pull ahead. I heard Big Ups is already in Hot Springs."

"Really? How do you know?"

"Hiker grapevine. A section hiker coming south passed him going the other way a couple days ago. He asked the guy to tell us he said hi."

"Aw, Big Ups is so nice!"

"So was that sectioner. He told us he had about 12 other hellos to deliver. Had to start writing them down."

"Don't people use the log books for that?"

"Yes, and every other means available too. I've seen notes impaled on tree branches or left under a rock right on the trail. I saw where someone wanted their friend to know he took a side trail, so he made his initials out of rocks and an arrow out of sticks to point the way. People are pretty creative out there. It's almost like we have a sixth sense about where everyone is."

"Do you and *Megan* pass notes?" she teased.

"Yeah, because we're boyfriend and girlfriend," I replied. "I know *you* know, but it's funny how many people have assumed that. No, we don't pass notes. We don't have to. I think this is the first time we've been more than ten feet apart since we met."

She raised an eyebrow.

"Okay, I'm exaggerating, but only a little. We were going up something called Jacob's Ladder the other day, this fucking relentless monster of a steep climb. There were a couple places where I could reach out and touch the trail in front of me, it was so steep. We were pulling ourselves up by roots and branches. Sweat was pouring down my face, I was huffing and puffing the whole way, and there she was, right on my heels the whole time. Almost step for step."

"Wow, that's pretty impressive for a guy your age." Katie looked me up and down. "You're as fit as a 22-year-old girl."

"And you know what she was doing the whole time? Talking. Talking about nothing. Non-stop. I asked her if she wanted to pass me, you know, if I was holding her up, and she said no. Went right back to whatever it was. I can't shake her."

"Are you trying to?"

I thought about it. "Not really, I guess. She's entertaining at least. I forget where we were, but we had to stop once so she could do a handstand up against a tree she really liked."

"So they don't all drop out or pull ahead."

"I guess not. She actually listens to my advice too, which is nice. Did you know this is her first backpacking trip longer than an overnight?"

"I think you mentioned that."

"I think she'll be good on her own by the time I flip."

"I think she was good on her own before you came along."

"I know. But just barely." I closed the top of my pack and looked at the door. I was so happy to be there, but I needed to feel the sun and the wind. There were too many walls.

Katie snapped me out of it. "Speaking of flipping, I did some math. I calculated your average daily mileage, and if you keep your current pace, you'll be in New Jersey in August."

"Shit. That's what I came up with too."

As much as I loved the idea of being whisked up to Maine in August, I wasn't thrilled with the idea of then walking south through what I'd heard was the most dramatic and breathtaking part of the trail, only to finish at some random bridge or deli in New Jersey. The sign atop Mount Katahdin is sometimes referred to as the sandwich board, perhaps I could get my photo taken standing on the one outside Tony's Subs, or wherever the hell I'd be.

We discussed her picking me up sooner, possibly Harpers Ferry, and decided to leave a decision on where to flip until later. My sixth sense was telling me that Megan and Lemmy were probably trying to hitch back to the trail from Gatlinburg, and that if we left now it would increase my odds of actually seeing them again.

Along the way we picked up my mom and niece and stopped at a grocery store so I could get enough food to carry me the next few days. The drive back to Clingmans Dome was dizzying. The road launched us over some of the highest peaks in the Smokies. I was getting the same views I was accustomed to on a daily basis but delivered at a speed which was impossible to process. Sleeping in my own bed, zooming along in a car, the blinking lights and beeping registers at the store—it was all too much. I needed the green tunnel. I closed my eyes until we were there.

I stepped into a parking lot full of cars, but this time there were no hikers. The ones who had camped nearby had already passed through, and the ones coming back from town wouldn't be here for a while. No Voldemort. No Lemmy.

The AT picked up near the base of the Concrete Monstrosity, a quarter-mile hike from the car. I hugged and kissed everyone after posing for more pictures and stepped into the crowd of weekenders clambering their way onto the big spiraling ramp. I continued past it and dropped over the edge as fast as I could, down into the cover of pines which muffled the din coming from the dome.

Stopping at a rock to put my foot up and rub my shin, I thought, when did this start to hurt? So far I hadn't needed a single pain reliever of any kind. It was best to not mask this new pain, I decided. It was only a minor ache, and if it got worse, I'd like to know. Strong as a 22-year-old girl, that Green Giant.

■ ■ ■

As I walked alone, the small ups and downs delivered balcony views of the same vast green arenas I had seen on that morning's drive, only now at the correct speed. When the trail went up, I was surrounded by a carpet of soft brown needles, green spruce, and black balsams. Rocks leaned like crooked teeth. When the trail went down, I was surrounded by a canopy of wide green leaves, and softwoods like poplar and beech. The lower beech forests were protected by barbed wire fences surmounted by metal ramps full of holes designed to prevent crossing by hoofed animals, particularly an invasive species of wild hog.

The portion of the AT that goes through the northern half of the Smokies straddles the border between North Carolina and Tennessee. Most hikers, myself included, are as excited to make that third state line as they were to make the first. Less than an hour later, you're back in North Carolina. Not quite as exciting the third or fourth time. For those few days of hiking, most people stop paying attention.

There is one exception, and that is the parking lot at a place called Newfound Gap on US-441, with the same spectacular views as Clingmans Dome minus the crowds. There are bathrooms, and a sign in the middle of the parking lot shows North Carolina on one side and Tennessee on the other. A guy on a Harley kindly agreed to take a picture of me on each side.

Beyond the lot the trail was narrow and climbed gradually so I didn't have to exert much. I didn't encounter any other thru-hikers the rest of that day. When I arrived at Icewater Spring shelter, I figured I had the place to myself.

The shelter wasn't far from the trail, just a few steps. It occupied a small corner of an acre or so of clearing, a grassy peninsula with 180-

degree views of green peaks skirted by shadowy folds receding to the horizon. Gray clouds filled the sky.

I heard the click of trekking poles approaching from the south. How strange, I thought. I already know who it is. I recognized the cadence.

"Green Giant!" The voice was unmistakable.

"Voldemort! How was Gatlinburg?"

She threw her pack onto the shelter floor. "Ugh. I've never been so glad to leave a place in as long as I can remember."

Gatlinburg is a shining beacon of commercialism in the middle of a vast wilderness. The town's official nickname is "The Gateway to the Great Smoky Mountains," which is appropriate because the border between the forest and the city is as sharply defined as a gate. The road into town winds through trees, rocks, and waterfalls. There is a small sign marking the city limits, and ten feet later you are bombarded by flashing neon lights, expensive parking, and animatronic bears playing harmonicas and trying to sell you beef jerky and imitation moonshine. The speed limit through town is 20 mph, but it's rare that any car has enough room to accelerate to even half that speed. Every crosswalk is packed with waddling tourists overloaded with bags or pushing strollers. If you need a shirt or coffee mug that says "Paddle faster, I hear banjo music," you can buy one next door to the Ripley's Believe It or Not museum.

"I know," I said. "I've been there. I'm much happier with where I spent the night. It was weird though. Being in my own house felt like cheating, even though it was less than twenty-four hours."

I watched Megan pull the drawstring at the top of her pack and then flip it over, spilling the contents into a pile on the shelter floor. "Hey, where's Lemmy?" I asked.

She looked up from the pile and snorted. "He's still in Gatlinburg. When I left this morning he was still in his underwear. I think he might be the most disorganized person I've ever met." She held one of her stuff sacks to her ear and shook it, frowned, and tossed it back into the pile.

"What did he think of the place?"

"Oh, he loved it. Like a kid at Disney World."

"Did you hear he's not from Colombia?" I asked her. "He's from Israel."

She opened another small sack and felt through its contents. "So what?"

"Exactly. He seems like a cool guy. Who cares where he's from, right? Unfortunately not everyone feels that way."

She raised an eyebrow.

"A few years ago, Katie and I went to Peru."

"Oh how cool, that's awesome! Did you see llamas?"

"We did. But listen. We were part of a tour group, and there were people in it from all over. Australia, South Africa, Spain…it was a pretty diverse bunch. So anyway, when they met us, almost every one of them said they were so relieved to meet us, not because we were Americans, but specifically because we weren't Israelis."

"They really said that?"

"Yeah. We prodded a little, and they just said more stereotypical crap. Like how they're all loud, how they're all selfish and annoying, and so on. We changed the subject and it never came up again. I've traveled a lot since, and I haven't seen that specific prejudice often, but it is out there."

"Well, he's gotta know by now that hikers aren't like that, right?"

"You would think so, but then again he's been on the other side of it for 20-plus years. If he wants to tell strangers he's from France, I say let him."

"Well, either way, he loves Gatlinburg," she said. She shook another bag by her ear. This one rattled, and she smiled.

"What are you looking for?" I asked.

"Something for your ankle. You've been rubbing your shin this whole time, and your ankle is swollen too."

I hadn't noticed. She told me to remove my sock and I did.

"Look how purple it is. Did you roll it, or bang it on something?"

"I don't know," I said. "It just started to ache today coming down Clingmans Dome. I would remember rolling it."

"Rub this cream on it. It's a prescription-strength, so don't get caught with it. Hopefully it will help."

While I rubbed the cream into my shin, Megan sat beside me. She took off her shoes, crossed a foot over her knee, and drew her knife, using it to pick dirt from under her toenails. She caught me staring, sniffed her armpit, and said, "What?"

"Nothing," I said. "It's just… Look at us. How is this acceptable? If we were at a bus stop I would have run away from you."

"Yeah, well, I would have pepper-sprayed you first."

Sunset was hidden behind a stack of dark clouds. We were asleep in the shelter when I heard something large crashing through the bushes behind us. The disturbance quickly revealed itself to be human; what I thought might be hooves was actually the pounding of two heavy wooden walking sticks. Between them a single white headlamp blazed.

"Is that Green Giant?" the headlamp asked. "And Meeee-gan?"

She poked her head out of her sleeping bag. "Yes, Lemmy. It's us."

"I am so glad to find you!" he said.

I closed my eyes again and fell asleep to the sounds of Lemmy unpacking, Lemmy boiling water, Lemmy eating, and finally the soft scribble and swish of pencils on paper. At some point that night it started to rain, and when we awoke, Lemmy's tent was pitched. His rain fly was loose and flapping in the breeze.

. . .

When Lemmy finally stuck his head out of his tent, Megan and I were nearly finished eating breakfast. He squeezed his eyes shut, and then opened them wide. He stared up at us through long thick lashes. "Is that coffee?" He smiled.

I swallowed the last of it. "Yep, and it was delicious. Would you like some?"

He thought a moment and asked, "Is it instant?"

"Do you think I packed a French press out here? Of course it's instant. Do you want some? I have extra hot wa—"

"No, I don't like it." *Eet.* He stood from his tent, let the flap fall behind him and walked to his pack. "I have one," he said.

"One what?" I asked.

"French press. Do you want some?"

I couldn't tell if he had mastered deadpan sarcasm in his second language. "No, thanks. I'm good."

The log book was on the table in front of us and I opened it to make an entry before we left. Lemmy watched me turn the pages, and when I reached the one full of bears, he spoke up. "Eet's not done yet."

"It's still very good," I said. He had real talent. Two of the three bears were done in bold lines; the third was barely a ghost, with short, light strokes that gave him a thin, feathered appearance. The trio was gathered outside a shelter trying to work out the food-on-pulleys problem. There was no color yet, and even though the faces were depicted by only a few quick lines, their expressions were already clear. The first one was frustrated, the second one was the hungriest, and the third might be clever enough to pull it off. "Is this Episode

Three?"

He sat next to me. "It will be! I am telling a story in all of the books, so that if you walk to Katahdin behind me you can read the whole thing!"

Megan stood. "That's really cool, Lemmy. How does it end?"

He unfolded a leather pouch revealing a full set of colored pencils. "I don't know. We will have to find out."

He was still coloring when we left, and promised to meet us at the next shelter. Along the way, Megan and I came to a fork in the trail. The AT continued to our right, while the left fork followed a blue blazed trail to something the sign called Charlie's Bunion. Some previous hiker had written on the sign in black marker, "Do this!" Another had circled it, added an arrow, and written, "Totally worth it!" Megan took off her pack.

"What are you doing?" I asked.

"I'm leaving my stuff here. If we're coming right back, why would I carry my whole pack both ways?"

"Why are you coming back here? The guidebook says that this side trail parallels the AT and then rejoins it in two-tenths of a mile." As soon as I said the words I knew her reason.

"I can't—"

I said it with her. "Skip any white blazes. Right. I remember." I put the guidebook back in my pocket. "Well, I've been impure since I skipped those eight-tenths of a mile back at the fire tower. I'll see you up where they rejoin."

I took the left fork and heard her follow. "I'll bring my stuff with me just in case. I probably shouldn't leave it."

Charlie's Bunion lived up to the hype scrawled on the sign. The side trail was mostly level, carved into the side of an ever-steepening rock wall. At the final bend, we found ourselves on a boulder pile at the top of a dizzying cliff. The neighboring peaks looked close enough to lean out and touch; the narrow gaps between concealed thousand-foot drops beneath low moving clouds.

As I stepped closer to the nearest deadly drop, my new perspective revealed a large flat ledge only five feet below. "Well, that's it for me. It'll never get any better than this." Without looking back, I stepped over the edge.

Megan yelled, "What the *fuck!*" When she saw me crouched safely below, we both laughed.

"That looked really cool," she said. "Get a picture of me pretending to hang from the cliff."

We spent the next hour climbing and posing, eating and laughing. She handed me my camera and while we snacked I scrolled through the pictures. She caught me at a weird angle on this one, I thought. There's no way I'm that thin. My clothes hung from me. Must be the wind, I thought. The next one was the same, and the one after that.

I snapped out of my fit of self-absorption when a day hiker coming from the north joined us. I asked him, "How far until this joins back to the AT?" I pointed the way he'd come.

"Less than two minutes," he said.

I asked Megan, "Do you want me to wait for you there while you circle back? Or should I just meet you and Lemmy at the next shelter?" It would take at least ten minutes to get back to the sign, and then probably about the same to get back.

She frowned. "It seems silly now that I'm here."

"It seemed silly before you were here."

"And I'm still moving north. On foot."

"Right…"

"Ugh. I can practically see it from here. Let's just go." She lifted her pack.

"Are you sure?" I said. "Hike your own hike, and all that."

"I'm sure. Just don't tell anyone, okay?"

"Sure," I said. "I won't tell a soul."

■　■　■

Lemmy kept his promise and caught up with us. Each night, Megan would take the spot on the floor closest to the wall and I would position myself as a barrier between her and any potential creeps or weirdos. Each night, Lemmy arrived in the dark and pitched his tent just outside the open end of the shelter.

At breakfast I said to him, "Lemmy, you know if you just stayed inside the shelters with us—"

Megan interrupted, "Like you're *supposed to*."

"If you stayed in the shelters with us, you'd be ready a lot quicker in the mornings, and then we could actually hang out for more than five minutes each day."

"I don't feel good in them," he said. "It's too open. I feel like the wolfs will get me."

"Wolves," Megan said, emphasizing the V. "And there aren't any."

"Then whatever makes that sound every night."

"Those are owls, Lemmy," I said. His mouth formed an O. "Besides, tonight you don't have any choice."

"Why not?"

"It says here in the guidebook that Davenport Gap shelter has no tent sites."

"I will find one. I will make one."

"There aren't any cables to hang our food either. The open end of the shelter has a chain link fence instead of a wall. The humans and the food all stay inside and we latch the gate."

"I don't want to sleep in a cage!"

"Think of it as a gated community," I said.

"I think it is like the movie *Jaws*, but with a bear."

"Well then, you'll have material for your next comic."

The trail since Clingmans Dome had kept us between five and six thousand feet, with only a few relatively small climbs and descents. Exiting the Smokies would take us back down to land lower than we'd seen since Fontana Dam. Over the next 14 miles of hiking, we'd given back nearly a mile of elevation.

It is easy to assume that hiking down a mountain is more forgiving than hauling yourself and your gear up a mountain. The truth is both activities can be equally strenuous, for different reasons. Hiking downhill, especially a steep downhill, is often more difficult. With every step you must exert effort to arrest your ever-increasing forward momentum. Your body, your pack, and gravity are all conspiring to pull you down faster than you intend, and if you relax for more than a few seconds, you'll find yourself running, struggling to keep your bottom half moving as fast as your top half. Failure to do so will send you sprawling.

The effort from constantly braking aggravated the mysterious new ache in my shin, and consequently my friends finished their day about an hour ahead of me. When I arrived I could hear them in the shelter, talking and laughing with someone.

It was starting to become easy to identify thru-hikers, the male ones at least. Just look for three to four weeks of stubble and a bad haircut. Nightwalker had the belly of someone just starting his hike, but the calf muscles and beard of someone who's been on the trail for years. I studied the chain link fence, and Nightwalker stood to show me how to work its locking mechanism. "I've already met Voldemort and Lemmy, so you must be Green Giant."

Lemmy's voice came from inside. "Hey! Buddy!"

"Hey there!" I shut the gate behind me. "Good thing nothing was chasing me." Lemmy smiled and asked for the log book.

Nightwalker handed me a GPS the size of a shoe. "Check that out."

"Good lord, this thing must weigh two pounds!" I handed it back. "You do know about the white blazes, right?"

He pressed a button, lighting a number-filled screen. "This puppy's accurate to within a millimeter. Beyond military grade. I'm verifying data for next year's edition of the guidebook."

I touched my pocket. "This guidebook?"

"The same."

"Oh, well then I apologize for almost calling that thing a useless brick."

A hiker is actually moving in three dimensions. We're all very aware of the up and down dimension. That's the one that we really feel, so much that often we forget about the other two: east/west and north/south. The good thing about the AT is that you can ignore those dimensions, because they don't matter. Once you leave Springer Mountain, you just follow the blazes until you get to Maine. If you accidentally go backwards, you'll run into someone soon enough.

The guidebook caters to the thru-hiker spirit of minimalism. Other than street maps of nearby towns, there is no top-down view of the AT anywhere in the book. Each page contains a profile of the next 20 or so miles. One thick black line inches its way across the page; as it goes up or down, so do you. Everything since Clingmans Dome for example, had been a little wiggle near the top of the page. Today's page started at the top left and took a hard dive right. Sitting here in the unlit shelter, I squinted at one of the guys who helped draw that line.

He told us there were a bunch of people up and down the trail doing this, and his part was "only a couple hundred miles."

"After that, I'll go a little further and then flip-flop. Not sure when; we'll see where I am and how the weather is."

"That's a good plan," I said. "I'm kind of doing the same thing."

He asked when I started and I told him May 10. He performed some quick math. "Why would you flip-flop?" he asked. "You're on pretty good pace to get to Maine before they close Baxter State Park for snow."

Megan agreed. "I said so! I tried to tell him."

It was true, she had. I had already disrupted my home routine simply by being here; I cringed at the thought of asking Katie to rearrange things yet again. "I'll think about it."

Nightwalker sat next to Lemmy. "So, no trail name yet?"

Lemmy closed the log book. "I used to have one back at the start. Someone called me Taj Majal because my tent was a palace."

"What tent did you have?"

Lemmy blushed and turned his attention to his pencils. He put them away and looked at us. "Before I did this, the only thing I know about camping in the woods is from TV and movies. So when I went to buy my things for this, the guy at the store, he knows: I am wounded prey! He sinks his teeth into me." *Teef.*

Lemmy tucked his chin and deepened his voice. "'You need the biggest tent! And the biggest pack! And we can fill it up for you!'" He continued as himself. "He sold me a tent I could stand up in. It was like this shelter. So someone named me that."

"But no one calls you that now?"

"No. I have a better one, but they tell me you are not allowed to make your own."

"What if you could?" I asked. "Would it be Happy Ghost?"

"No." He stood, puffed his chest and spread his hands, framing an invisible marquee. "The Legend!"

Megan said, "Lemmy just seems, I don't know. To fit," and dumped her pack.

■   ■   ■

So many nights on the trail I missed Katie. I missed our warm soft bed. Now that I was in it, I spent the night kicking and squirming. The quilt was too heavy and some hairy person kept touching me. When did Katie start wearing a bulky watch, I thought. And why do her knuckles smell like oranges?

I carefully lifted Lemmy's hand, which was pawing at my face. Now I see why we keep you in your tent, I thought. The sun was almost up, things were starting to chirp, and I had to pee. No point trying to go back to sleep, so I wiggled out of my bag as quietly as I could and stopped at the chain link fence.

My attempt to lift the latch without disturbing the wires was bomb squad-worthy, but I still rattled the cage. Everyone stirred.

"Sorry, guys." I pushed the door and the hinge squealed, briefly interrupting the stirring songbirds. Nightwalker's head appeared from his bag. "I just stuck my wiener through one of the holes when I had to go at three o'clock."

Megan mumbled, "I wish I had a penis."

Nightwalker nodded toward Lemmy. "If this other fella would get up and leave too, that could be arranged."

"You know she has a knife?" Lemmy said. "You might not get your penis back." He cracked himself up and his shoulders bounced with each laugh.

Based on their tone and some of the horrible things we'd all said to each other after the whiskey came out last night, I wasn't worried. I shuffled off to the privy, and when I returned everyone was eating or packing.

I opened the log book to the most recent page, where I found a lanky hiker wearing a feathered cap. He was punching and kicking at the fence keeping him out of the "sheltar." He has squinting, teary eyes and exclamation points flying from his head. In the second panel the exclamation points had turned to blood. A fanged teddy bear with black sleepy eyes now wore the feathered hat as it licked red chunks from its claws. Three terrified hikers huddled in a corner, safe behind the fence. The sign above the fence was blank.

I touched the sign. "What goes here, Lemmy?"

"Ah! This is why I need you. What is the word that means a closet where you keep food?"

Megan's hand shot up. "I know! Pantry."

"Ah, yes! This is it!" He filled in the missing word and added some shading to the sign.

I leaned over his shoulder. "You forgot one more detail, Lemmy. This bear that mauled me at the shelter, you forgot to draw his watch."

# 8

## DISCO

WE WERE HEADING NORTH out of the Smokies, down to the Pigeon River and under I-40. Nightwalker had a shorter day planned than we did. He was stopping at Standing Bear Farm, a hiker hostel where the three of us would just resupply and move on. He was still getting up as we left, so I wished him happy trails, figuring we wouldn't see him again.

Megan passed me without stopping as I was filtering water. "I'll take web duty," she said. Each day someone has to be the first person to walk on the trail. That person, like it or not, is responsible for clearing the fresh spider webs that formed overnight. The big ones are easy. Heavy with dew, they sparkle in the sun. Usually you can duck under them, but sometimes they need to be swatted down with a trekking pole.

The lone strands, or works in progress, are too new to collect dew, so they hang unseen right at lip level. I learned pretty early to lean my head forward and let the brim of my hat do all the work. Sometimes I would catch an inchworm, let it swing while I walked, and then touch a bush with my hat, transporting him to safety.

"What's the hurry? That's usually my job."

"I think Forager might have stayed at the hostel last night. They might still be there."

She'd mentioned that name before. He was in the books a few

times while I was chasing Lemmy. "Part of your original crew you met back at the start, right?"

"You got it."

Cut off from the routine of our former daily lives, and with no radio, internet, or TV, keeping track of where everyone was became a real pastime. All you had to do was look in the shelter logs and read backwards. The further back you went in the book, the further ahead in miles the people were.

I had my own list of log book celebrities I was stalking. There was no way I'd catch them; these people were weeks ahead. Someone named Engineer, for instance, was making highly detailed sketches depicting his version of trail life rendered in blue or black ballpoint pen. Someone else named Color Bandit was a few days behind him, filling in Engineer's drawings. A whole crew traveled under the name of "Shrimp Gang"—they each had their own wildly colorful trail names, but rarely used them, sticking to their gang name.

Once somebody was behind us, their location was anyone's guess. Our only hope of word from behind would be if a faster hiker passed them and caught up to us. Now that I thought of it, though, no one had caught us or passed us. Maybe there wasn't anyone behind us at all. Maybe we were last.

Less than a mile past the river the trail crossed a gravel road. It wasn't obvious from the road where the trail resumed, but the guidebook said left, so I turned left. The forest thinned and I could see a few tents pitched in a clearing ahead. A small stream followed the road to my right. A few of the trees along the water held well-constructed, brightly-painted tree houses; cozy cottages complete with doors and curtains had been hoisted into the branches. A group of chickens had gathered in the shade below, scratching at the dirt and occasionally each other.

I crossed a footbridge and approached the bunkhouse, a long single room with a door at each end. The room was unlit, and from the porch I could make out a dozen or so beds and several vaguely human shadows. Unsure whether I'd been noticed, I announced my presence. "This must be the right place," I said. One of the shadows lurched toward me, pushed past, and vomited into the bushes. A second later her friend arrived to hold her hair.

I stepped back as a third shadow exited, moving with less urgency and not headed for the bushes. Black curls hung to his shoulders and a blue tie-dyed shirt covered all but the very bottom of his hairy belly.

The girl in the bushes retched and burped. He held out a closed fist and said, "Bad Dinner."

I looked at the girl, then back to him. "What was it?"

He laughed. "No, *I'm* Bad Dinner." The fist was for me. I bumped it with my own. "Never shake hands. That's how Norovirus gets spread."

I was pretty sure that the microbes responsible were capable of surviving on knuckles as well, but I kept quiet; it is often fruitless to dispute hiker-based medical advice. I introduced myself and asked if the girl would be all right.

"Eventually. It's just Noro. People freak out like it's the plague, but she'll just have the shits for a few days and then wake up fine."

There was no room in my schedule for even a single day of the shits. I kept a tiny squeeze bottle of hand sanitizer in an outside pouch and applied some. "So, do you work here?"

He laughed and flipped his hair. "Nah, man. I took a zero here yesterday. Just now getting packed."

"Taking a zero" means staying put, walking zero miles. Zero can be a noun, a verb, or an adjective. You can zero somewhere, take a zero, or have a zero day. There are also variations, for example the "nearo," which means only hiking a few miles into or out of a town or hostel.

Bad Dinner asked me if I was stopping here, and I told him I was just resupplying and would continue to Hot Springs for my first official zero. He seemed impressed. "Your first? Damn, dude, that's hardcore. I think I've had six or seven already. Hell, I'm not even sure how long I've been here. Hey, Rocket! How long have I been here?"

"I don't know. Who the hell are you?"

. . .

Rocket wore camouflage pants cut off at the knees and a gray tank top. His dirty blond beard matched the frizz that hung past his shoulders. He held a bundle of wood in one hand and a bottle in the other.

"Rocket runs the place," Bad Dinner said. "He'll take care of you."

Rocket dropped the wood beside a stone fire ring and held out the bottle. He raised his chin and clarified the offer with a grunt. "I like to wait until noon, thanks," I said. He took a swig for each of us and wiped his mouth on his arm. "C'mon. I'll show ya."

The kitchen was in a shed behind the bunkhouse. The space was small and tight. Stacks of mismatched plates and cups filled the shelves. A cardboard sign with handwritten warnings was taped to what appeared to be one of the earliest microwave ovens. Rocket pointed. "The water from the sink's real good."

The laundry was outside and behind the kitchen. It was a porcelain tub and a washboard. The resupply shed had envelopes hanging by the door, where you could write anything you took and leave cash in the envelope provided.

"There's some frozen pizzas in the shed too. You can cook them in the kitchen. Close the door when you go in, because the chickens will try to follow you and they like to shit all over creation."

I thanked Rocket and he wandered off, and I headed for the resupply shed. Megan was inside; her pack was leaned against the wall by the door. As I pulled the handle she shouted, "Stay out!"

"Why?" I yelled back, shutting the door.

"Oh, sorry. I thought you were a chicken. Come in."

The interior was stifling, at least 15 degrees warmer. A dim fluorescent bulb hummed overhead and warm sunlight leaked in through small windows behind full shelves. Row upon row of Pop-Tarts, Snickers, jerky, granola, raisins, ChapStick, rope, and Band-Aids surrounded us. Jars of peanut butter, no more than any two the same size or brand, were piled into a box with a handwritten sign indicating the price. Some shelves had hats and gloves, and there were three pairs of mittens next to one left shoe. Megan sat in the corner with her piles of food.

"Find everything okay?" I asked.

"I think so. How many days do you think it will take to get to Hot Springs from here?"

"Well, it's thirty or thirty-five miles, so…" I paused to calculate. "The rest of today, plus one more full day, plus another half day? We should get there around noon day after tomorrow, so we'll need two…two-and-a-half days' worth of stuff tops. Not bad, actually."

She stared past me. "Yeah. I should get five."

"Wait, what? Why?"

"Well, every time I've done resupply so far, I've eaten almost everything within the first day or two. Especially these!" She held up two boxes of Little Debbie Oatmeal Cream Pies. "Oh my god, I can't stop eating these! Do you think they'll care if I start eating before I pay?"

I pointed to a box which read PAY 4 FOOD HERE. "I don't think their accounting system is very strict. Do you mind if I open this door? It's getting crazy hot in here." I opened the door, kicked a chicken, and shut the door. "Never mind." I picked up an envelope and took a crayon from the cup provided.

Megan and I scratched our heads and worked at getting our food right, given our limited and unusual choices. Breakfast for the next few days would be Pop-Tarts. They were a special red white and blue edition, for the Fourth of July. It was still over a month away; these were from last year. I selected a few dehydrated pasta sides. That covered breakfast and dinner. Now the hard part.

There really isn't such a thing as lunch on the trail. It was the time of year when 12 to 14 hours of daylight separated breakfast from dinner. The best way to cover that period nutritionally is to munch and snack all day long, and the trick is to do this without overburdening yourself. Carry too much food and the extra weight slows you down, meaning more meals are consumed between resupplies, which means carrying even more food. Carry too little, and the result is far worse.

I tried to estimate how many times per day I might like a snack and made that many piles of candy bars and beef sticks. I added a few more just in case. "Look at this. Look at this garbage. If I ate half this stuff a month ago I'd have an upset stomach for weeks. Is there any kind of fruit or vegetables around here?"

"I don't think so."

"I would fight a pregnant cougar for a single bite of a real apple right now."

"There's gummy worms. It says fruit-flavored right on the package."

I managed to squeeze my piles into a bag small enough to carry and tallied it up. "What if we need to—"

"Make change?" Megan interrupted. "Yeah. I don't know. I guess we go find Rocket."

He was easy to find. When I returned to the bunkhouse, Rocket had a pretty good-sized fire going, despite it being the middle of the day and almost 90 degrees in the sun. His bottle from earlier was gone, and now he held a Mason jar filled with clear liquid. He handed it to me when I asked him to break a twenty. He slapped my shoulder and insisted. "You got no excuse now, boy! It's been noon for damn near an hour!"

"Corn mash?" I said.

"Only the best!"

What the hell, I thought. Corn's a vegetable.

■ ■ ■

The fire grew and someone produced a banjo. Voldemort was making a good run at matching Rocket shot for shot and Lemmy ran in circles. He was chasing a rooster that Rocket told him they would kill and cook "raht here on this here FAHR!" But only if he could catch it.

Bad Dinner stopped by on his way out. "This is what they call the Vortex, Green Giant. You're getting sucked in." I remembered the girl by the bushes and stood up.

Megan poked the fire. "I could use a day off."

"Hey Bad Dinner," I said. "Did someone named Forager come through here over the last few days?"

"Yeah, he and his dad left right before you showed up."

Megan jumped up. "Fiddlin' Jim was with him?"

Someone in the kitchen yelled, "Fuck that guy!"

I looked at her and mouthed, "Who?"

"Fiddlin' Jim and Forager! They're father and son. Jim snores."

"Hah!" From the kitchen.

"You have no idea," added Bad Dinner.

"That's my place," said Rocket, pointing to a small cabin. "He was over in the bunkhouse. But the fucker still kept me up all night." He spat, and then snickered.

"And we want to catch these guys?" I asked. Megan looked at me, then Lemmy, then back to me.

"Okay, you convinced me. I'll get my stuff. Lemmy, put down that chicken."

I took the lead to start, and Lemmy and Megan caught up when I stopped to look at a red eft. Lemmy was curious, so I told him the story of how they travel many miles, transforming numerous times along the journey.

"Do you know what this reminds me of?" he said.

"Let me guess," I said, a bit bored with the obvious. "It reminds you of us."

"What? No. That is stupid. It's a Pokemon! Look how bright he is. And he mutates." He pointed a finger at the eft and shook his other fist at the sky. "This isn't even my final form!"

Megan was above us, headed the opposite way along a switchback. "What the hell is he yelling about?"

"Just keep walking," I said, and did the same.

Lemmy stayed close behind. I could feel his big sticks and heavy boots each time they hit the ground. "Green Giant, you know so much about this thing" —*fing*— "the eft. How do you know so much?"

"I'm from here."

"Where?"

"Okay, you know we're headed to Hot Springs next, right? My house is less than an hour from there."

This excited him. "In the mountains?"

"Close enough."

"Do you know what this flower is?"

I told him it was a rhododendron. We practiced saying it a few times and he asked if they always bloomed like this.

"Good question! They only bloom for a few weeks each year. But here's the thing: that's only true if you stay in one place and watch the same bush for two weeks."

"But we are always moving."

"Exactly. Warm temperatures trigger the bloom. Right now, two hundred miles north it's not warm enough yet. But when we get there in two weeks, it will be. Which means we'll get at least a month of the green tunnel sometimes being the purple tunnel."

"That is so cool!"

"And check this out. At some of the higher elevations, the flowers are white instead of purple."

"Whoa!" His enthusiasm was contagious. I'd been walking past these flowers for years; suddenly they were fun again.

"What tree is this kind?"

I could answer less than half his questions, but he didn't seem to care.

"Do you know the birds and the bird sounds, too?"

I told him that I knew some of them and we could practice, but there weren't any out right now, probably because it was hot and they were resting. When we ran out of birds for me to imitate he asked me about the rocks and ferns and mushrooms.

"I have to pee, Lemmy. You go on ahead. See if you can catch Voldemort."

"No, I don't want to," he said. "She talks too much."

. . .

To get to Groundhog Creek shelter, we first had to climb Snowbird Mountain. At the top, in addition to nice views, there is an FAA tower used as a navigation point for commercial airlines. It's a round single-story building behind a locked fence, with a white metal cone about 30 or 40 feet tall sticking out from the roof. The whole thing hums. Signs on the fence told us to keep out, so we took a few pictures and then moved on, dropping down the north side of Snowbird Mountain and into a place called Deep Gap. This was either the second or third gap with that name. There had also been a few Low Gaps and a couple Sassafras Gaps, too.

I was the last from our group to arrive at the shelter. There were already at least 15 people there in groups of threes and fours.

A young, clean-shaven hiker named Snail Trail was the first to introduce himself. He offered a fist bump as I took off my pack. "Good to meet you, man. At first when I heard you were hiking with Voldemort, I was like, aw yeah, Green Giant's banging that! But then when she mentioned something about your wife, I was like, aw damn!"

I returned his fist bump. "Don't feel bad for me, Snail Trail. Did you miss the part where I get to have a wife?"

"Oh yeah, right on!" He disappeared into one of the circles.

I met a guy called No Filter, not because he didn't filter his water, but because he apparently had no filter between his brain and mouth. I met Short Bus and Man Calves, brothers who were both linebackers and who planned to lose 100 pounds each by hiking the trail. One got his name from his enormous leg muscles, while his brother earned his name by committing a continuous string of innocent errors. One such mistake involved getting lost on the AT, which is next to impossible. Short Bus was trying to find a water source the guidebook said was to the left of the trail. He got mixed up, thinking west instead of left. The AT does not run due north, especially in rough terrain; he wound up miles up the side of some mountain before figuring out his mistake.

Bad Dinner was at the picnic table playing cards with someone while a group of four or five watched. Megan was seated on some rocks talking to a pair of hikers who had to be Forager and Fiddlin' Jim. Both men wore their hair short and had shaved their faces within the last few days. Forager wore khakis and sandals with a plain short-sleeved button-down shirt and mirrored aviator sunglasses. Fiddlin' Jim wore cotton gym shorts and a sleeveless tee. He had the arms of a much younger man. A single black feather stuck out from the bandanna he wore around his head.

There are certain questions which naturally come up when hikers meet for the first time. When did you start and what does your trail name mean are usually the first two.

Forager said, "Dad plays the fiddle, and I find food."

"At the same time?" Lemmy joked. "Is this part of your act?"

"I'll show you," Forager told us. He unrolled a small bundle on the ground to show it was full of plants. "These ones are ramps. Smell them—they taste like onions. These are milkweed pods, and here are some fiddleheads." Those were tiny rolled-up leaves which eventually unfurl into broad-leafed ferns. "You boil 'em all together."

"Not bad," I said. "That's not all you eat, is it?"

He and his dad laughed. "Not hardly. I'll add this to pasta."

That reminded me that I still needed to fetch water. I asked where the source was and several hands pointed the way in unison. Bad Dinner called out, "Hey Green Giant, if I beat you at Rock Paper Scissors, will you get me some water too?"

I would have done it anyway, but he was a gamer so I indulged. Paper covered rock and he handed me two empty bottles. "Do you want me to filter it, or do you have tablets?"

"Neither. Just fill 'em up. I'll drink it as-is."

"You're insane."

"That's irrelevant, but yes, I drink straight from the spring. If you get the water right out of the earth, nothing's had a chance to piss or shit in it yet. It's clean. As long as you don't mind a little sediment, but that's what your mustache is for, right?"

"I wouldn't know." I, like most hikers, stopped shaving the day I started the AT. I had been on the trail for the better part of a month, the longest I'd gone in my adult life without shaving, but it didn't seem to matter. Thin patches of auburn fuzz covered parts of my cheeks, neck, and chin. Something was growing on my upper lip, but so far Katie had been the only person to get close enough to see it. Everyone else looked like they were ready to appear in a ZZ Top video; I looked like I was on *rumspringa*.

Even before I could hear the water, I knew it was near. Springs are usually located in cool, humid draws, and after weeks of getting my water from them, my mind began to form the association automatically. Even if I was deep in thought, stepping into cool patches like this made my water sense tingle.

I enjoyed an extra moment of solitude at the spring before I walked back to the shelter. I handed Bad Dinner his cloudy bottles and he drank one down immediately. "I've hiked over five thousand miles and I've never been sick from water," he said proudly.

"So this isn't your first thru-hike then?" Megan asked.

Bad Dinner introduced his cards partner as his girlfriend. "I hiked the whole thing alone last year. This year we're hiking together, but

I'm only showing her the cool parts."

Megan snapped back. "Only the cool parts? So you mean the whole thing, right?"

Bad Dinner laughed. "You'll see. Until you get to the Whites up in New Hampshire, everything after Hot Springs is boring and repetitive."

"Boring and repetitive?"

"Boring and repetitive."

■   ■   ■

The hikers who had arrived early had filled up the good tent sites, which left us in the box. There was plenty of room, and I was only one blink or two away from sleep when I heard Lemmy sit up and gasp. He was still wrapped in his sleeping bag, and for a moment I saw him as a curly-haired caterpillar rearing up in the dark. "What is it?"

"Green Giant! Do you see this?"

I propped myself up on my elbows. The fireflies were out. They're common in the Eastern US. We get them in our yard back home. They'd actually been out several times that week, but Lemmy hadn't seen them because he was usually in his tent.

"Yeah, it's the lightning bugs, Lemmy. Aren't they cool?"

"Look! They're coming into the shelter!"

I rose up off my elbows and rubbed my face with both hands. *This is the first time he's ever seen fireflies.* I can't even remember how old I was the first time I saw them; they were just always there. A big part of every summer growing up was running outside after dinner to fill glass jars with the easy, glowing targets, hanging lazily in the air just waiting to be plucked by tiny child fingers. The grownups watch from the porch as the kids run and giggle. *This is how he must feel right now.*

"It's like we're floating in the stars!" He squirmed and wriggled one arm out of his cocoon and held out a finger. One landed on it. When its little butt flashed, Lemmy jumped. "Do they bite?"

"No, Lemmy. They're totally harmless."

There was another flash and the bug floated off. Lemmy pawed at the zipper and unfolded himself from the bag. He crab-walked to the edge of the platform and ran out into the night in his socks. Glowing dots danced around him. He pointed to the tree line and said, "I feel like we should see some elfs come into here, or a unicorn!"

More fireflies had joined us in the shelter, and the place dazzled and flashed. "It's like a disco in here!" I yelled. "Look! They're in the trees now, too!"

The sparkling began at the lower branches, and as they filled up, each wave of light landed higher and higher, until the trees were full of stars and looked like Christmas. "This is so epic, Green Giant!" Lemmy spun to the picnic table and landed on his back. The loose end of one dirty sock dangled from his toe. "It's like we are floating in the whole galaxy!"

Exhausted from our long day, I put my head down and turned over. "Don't fall asleep on that table," I said. "The whole galaxy's in here too."

While he was zipping himself back into his bag, he asked me, "Green Giant, why do they do this? Why do they blink?"

"It's a mating call," I said. "I think it's the males that light up. That's how they attract females. It's a chemical reaction in a bioluminescent molecule on the surface of their abdomen. It's triggered by hormones."

"So we are surrounded by a bunch of bugs that are saying, 'Hey baby, come fuck me!' Is that it?"

I sighed. "Yes, Lemmy. That's it."

His voice deepened and he whispered, "Hey bay-bee! Look at my glowing butt!" I stifled a snicker. "Let me shake it for you, baby!" He kept this up for a while, using different accents, making imaginary bugs flirt with one another while I tried not to laugh and wake the others. He finished in a high falsetto. "You have the brightest ass of all! I choose you!"

A moment or two passed and we shared an aftershock of giggles, then fell silent as the bugs continued to strobe above us. I was only one blink or two away from sleep when I heard Lemmy crack himself up again with one of those laughs that made his shoulders bounce and his face turn red. I imagined his cheeks glowing in the dark. "What is it Lemmy?"

"All these bugs hooking up tonight. It *is* like a disco in here!"

Fiddlin' Jim's snoring shook the floor. "And Jim is dropping the bass."

# 9
## ZERO TOWN

MEGAN STOMPED up the trail. "How dare that guy! The entire AT is incredible! Every inch of it. 'Flat and boring.' What's he know?"

Forager was right behind her. "Actually, it's 'boring and repetitive.'"

"Yeah, well, you're both wrong."

The two of them took off at a quick pace, Fiddlin' Jim and I following behind. Lemmy was still at the table working on a cartoon when we left. I bet I knew what it was about.

I can't personally verify if Jim's fiddling skills are worthy of his name. He was a practical man, and despite being as fit as a fiddle, he wasn't willing to add the extra weight of one to his pack. "Besides," he told me, "keeping the damn thing dry is a pain in the rear. We find one of them guys carrying a plastic ukulele, I'll show 'em how it's done!"

Fiddlin' Jim was 65 and had just retired. He and his son—Forager—were hiking the AT together to celebrate. He was from Minnesota and you could hear it, as he spoke slowly and always enunciated. It was a nice change.

"So you guys finally found a trail name for Megan, huh? You know Snail Trail back there wanted to call her Fire Butt or something. I think he might be kind of sweet on her."

Oh, Jim.

He told me about teaching his son how to forage for edible things in the wild, the way his father had taught him. They weren't doomsday preppers or anything like that, just regular blue collar guys who grew up outdoors. Who could make stone tools and kill dinner.

Now it was my turn to be Lemmy. "Hey, Jim. See that tree?" I pointed at a young sapling; it looked like it was turning into sawdust and splitting apart from within. "What makes them do that?"

"Ah geez, Green Giant. That's an American chestnut, or what's left of one. They all have the blight now. It started in the 1900s from a ship full of Chinese chestnut. That stuff is resistant to the blight, which it brought over."

"I remember now. Didn't they used to be huge, too?"

"Oh, yeah. I saw a picture once of one that had like ten guys standing around it holding hands and they barely fit around the trunk."

"Man, that's too bad."

"They're finally doing something about it though. They've been crossbreeding the American with the Chinese to get the gene that resists the blight. And then they cross the offspring with a pure American, and again and again, until they have a tree that's like ninety-nine percent American chestnut but won't die to the blight."

"That's great," I said. "Who's doing this? Who's 'they?'"

"I don't know. Scientists."

"So if the blight's been around more than a hundred years, and it kills the tree, how do we still have any at all?"

"It doesn't kill them for a few years. They only ever get this big. Some reproduce, but there are no mature American chestnuts left. Ah, like maybe a hundred. But there used to be billions. Right here. The Appalachians were covered with them."

We were in a forest all right, but now that Jim had told me this, I became acutely aware that every tree in it was thin enough to hug. A few might require two or three of us, but there were no ten-man trees of any kind to be seen. Oaks, poplars, locusts, all small compared to what Fiddlin' Jim had just put in my head.

"We really logged the shit out of this place, didn't we?"

"We sure did."

I enjoyed Jim's pace as much as his company. The mysterious purple bruise and the pain which seemed to follow it had crept down and settled at the top of my left foot. It didn't hurt to touch at all, but my shin felt weak and ached any time we went downhill. It was only a minor annoyance, but it had gone on for a few days at least. So I slowed a bit.

Which meant that Voldemort was now on Forager's heels instead of mine. She could have easily been up front, way ahead of all of us, but then who would she talk to?

I asked Jim what he thought of my shin. "I wouldn't worry too much. Everybody says right around a month you'll start to get aches that last a couple days or weeks and then just go away. You pulled something and your body is healing while you walk."

I had finally started taking something for it. I picked up some Advil back at Standing Bear and had been allowing myself one or two a day.

"We should be getting our trail legs by now, don't you think?"

"Trail legs" is the term hikers use to describe a state of maximum physical fitness, balanced with a heavy dose of Zen. After a few weeks of hiking up and down mountains, your legs cycle through an initial state of shock followed by a rebuilding phase, and eventually you end up with the most muscular thighs and calves you've ever had in your life. Along with this comes the ability to simply zone out for 12 hours and then snap out of it 20 or 30 miles up the trail. We weren't quite there.

"Have you guys done a 20 yet? Megan and I have tried a couple times but either went too slow or the spacing didn't work out."

Now that we were out of the Smokies, we had more freedom regarding where to spend each night. Shelters almost always had water sources, but sometimes shelter-hopping meant the difference between a 9-mile day and a 25-mile day. There might not be water at tent sites, but those gave us the option to stop pretty much whenever the mood struck. Breaking 20 miles at this point was nothing more than a matter of willpower and a little extra planning.

"We haven't done 20 yet either, Green Giant. Maybe after we fill our bellies up in Hot Springs we'll give it a go."

∎ ∎ ∎

I had my back to her, but I could tell by Lemmy's face that Megan had put on the shorts. I should have closed my eyes when I turned around.

"Good lord, Megan. I think those are illegal in most states."

Forager joined me at the table. "Why in the world are you wearing those? I mean, I'm glad you are, but why?"

She already had her pack on. Her alarm had gone off at 4 a.m., and then again at 4:30. She had already eaten, braided her hair and visited the privy before any of us had stirred. We had just begun eating and gathering our things and she was ready to go.

"Because while you suckers are standing by the road with your thumbs out, I'll be in Hot Springs eating pancakes, that's why."

Jim was in the shelter rolling his sleeping bag. "The trail goes right through town," he said.

Megan turned. "No, you're thinking of Damascus."

I said, "You're both right. Where's your guidebook?"

She turned again. "Oh, wow! Look how the light comes in through those trees there. Really pretty. Well, better get going."

"Megan, do you have your pages for today?"

"We started the fire with them last night."

"Really? Again? Okay. Mine are way over there. Lemmy, do you have yours? I bet Lemmy has his. The most disorganized person you ever met."

"I do have it," he said. "But it is the book for southbounders, so you have to read it backwards."

"That'll work. Thanks."

Hot Springs was exactly as I remembered it. So far I'd been over small parts of the trail I'd recognized from before, but this was the first (and only) town along the trail I'd already visited. I had made the 45-minute drive from Asheville many times; this time I had walked the better part of 300 miles to get there.

The trail enters the south end of town by dropping down Deer Park Mountain and into the backyard of Laughing Heart Lodge. Just a few steps more and the white blazes are on the telephone poles that line the town's main street. The French Broad River runs wide and deep at the other end of town, four blocks north. I showed Megan. She dropped her poles and undid her pack straps, slumped her shoulders, and let her pack slide to the ground. Then she pouted.

The mineral spring that gives the town its name is the only one of its kind in North Carolina. It was originally discovered by Native Americans, and of course European settlers built a hotel there. The myth of the spring's healing powers brings just enough visitors to keep the town's three restaurants open. The hikers take care of the bars.

Megan's mood improved when she saw Katie waving in front of the outfitters. I was okay with being the second one to get a hug.

"I'm assuming you didn't get my messages. That's okay. Hi!"

Lemmy introduced her to Fiddlin' Jim and Forager and I explained that none of us had had a signal for days.

"Of course, that means we had no way to arrange lodging. And I hope you understand, but I can't go home tonight. I want to but—"

"I understand. We have a room at the Alpine Court Motel. You are zeroing tomorrow, correct? They have vacancies if the others want rooms too."

"This is incredible! Can we go there now? I haven't showered since last week."

The others opted for the hostel, while I enjoyed the rare luxury of a room with a door, bed, and bathroom. The shower was a simple chrome pipe behind a plastic curtain that was too small, but the water was instantly hot. I turned the knob to cold. The water was cold. I turned it back to hot. Hot again. "This is incredible!"

Katie called back from the other room. "You know what else is incredible?"

"What? Come in here."

She stood by the sink. "This is as close as I get."

"I don't blame you. I don't even want to be in here with me."

"What's incredible is the way your pack stinks."

"I honestly hadn't noticed. But you know, I can smell day hikers before I see them now. Just before they round the corner it's like stepping into the shampoo aisle at the grocery store. But me? And other hikers? Nothing."

"Yeah, well your pack smells like a homeless person."

I turned off the water and she handed me a towel. "I'm sorry. I live in the woods, you know? Plus, I think I need to replace it anyway."

"Why?"

"Every day I notice that I'm pulling the straps tighter. Pretty soon I'm going to run out of strap." I hung my towel and said, "Now that I'm clean, do you want to take a shower?"

"There's no time. A whole bunch of your friends are waiting for you at the restaurant. Get dressed."

"Okay, but I'm not putting on deodorant. It burns. What time is it?"

"Almost three."

I thought a second. "What day is it?"

At the restaurant, we pushed together tables as my friends from home met my trail family.

My good friend Travis was the one who bonded most closely with the hikers. He's a musician like Fiddlin' Jim, likes the same Japanese cartoons as Lemmy, brews his own beer like Forager, and is just hyper enough to hold his end of a conversation with Megan. Before he left, Travis gave me a hug and slapped me on the back. "Hey man, I really like your hiking friends. Maybe we'll figure out how to get me on the trail with you guys for a few days."

I told him I'd really like that. I also told him that about 30 other people had said the same thing, and that so far the only person who had managed it was Mark, who dropped me off at the beginning. Frankly, it was hard knowing where I would be at the end of each day, let alone planning a meeting weeks in advance. (How in the hell Katie was nailing my arrivals so precisely was beyond me.) So I told Travis that I hoped we could work something out, and reminded him that I was now walking away from home, so the longer he waited, the farther he would have to drive.

It was getting late and all the food and beer was making me drowsy. It had been a crazy day and I was worn out, and relieved to think that tomorrow was my very first zero. Finally I could take a break and just do nothing for a change.

■ ■ ■

Zero Day To Do List:
1. Breakfast
2. Laundry
3. More food
4. New pack?
5. Resupply—how far/how many days?
6. Nap? Swimming?
7. Write in journal
8. More food/dinner
9. Beer and music w/ gang?
10. Sleep! (Ice cream?)
11. Post cards—DON'T FORGET

8:00 a.m. Had first breakfast in room. Last of last year's Pop-Tarts. Second breakfast at Smoky Mountain Diner. They have a "plate of everything"—every breakfast food on one plate. Potatoes, bacon, eggs, and toast all mixed. Onions and ham. Everyone ordered dessert.

9:00   Fiddlin' Jim and Forager will combine laundry and use the wash at hostel. Lemmy, Megan, and I will share a machine at laundromat downtown and hang out with Katie.
9:15   Waiting for Lemmy. Megan just left to find him.
9:25   Lemmy is here. Now waiting for Megan. Katie becoming impatient.
9:52   In bathroom at laundromat changing into long johns and raincoat. Everything else gets washed.
9:53   Ignore suspicious looks from regulars.
10:00  Lemmy and Megan can get their own machine. Starting load without them.
10:04  Lemmy and Megan just showed up. I bought the last individual box of soap in the place. Lemmy and Megan leave to find soap.
10:14  Sitting with Katie and guy who works here. He is 77 years old. Chain smokes Camels. Raised bees and homing pigeons growing up here. Neat guy!
11:00  Great stories from laundry guy. I'm starving. Lemmy and Megan still missing. Saw Forager at bar with his dad. Going there.
11:15  Something just exploded outside and no one seems to care.
11:16  Our server just told us there is a Civil War reenactment going on in the field across town. We'll have a quick bite and go check it out.
12:42 p.m.  Really good IPA on tap here.
1:22   Stuff is still exploding out there. Let's go!
1:47   Just caught the end of the Civil War reenactment. I can't imagine walking this far and then being in any shape to fight. Women dressed as field nurses are bringing ice chips to the pretend dead guys. Hot as hell out there.
2:00   Field filled with fog and fake fatalities, film at five! Beer making me sleepy.
4:18   Just woke up in motel room. Katie is still asleep. Is there still time to shop for a pack? Shit, just realized it's Sunday and the post office is closed. Time for a second shower.
5:03   If I weren't so damn hungry I would have taken a longer

shower. Outfitters is closed. New pack will have to wait. Shit, now what about resupply? Katie is awake; I'll look at the map and figure it out while she showers.

5:15   Katie is ready to leave for dinner. I just found my map. I'll figure it out at dinner.

6:48   Everyone is here except Fiddlin' Jim and Forager. Still have not decided where to eat.

8:07   We are finally all here.

8:12   Waitress is moving tables and chairs out of the corner next to us.

8:17   Man in Hawaiian shirt now setting up amplifier in corner next to us.

9:04   Check arrives. Math begins.

9:28   It's dark out. Sudden urge for bed. Ice cream place is closed. Everyone else wants beer. Forgot to resupply.

10:09   Katie is asleep.

■ ■ ■

"I'll have a coffee and a water to start, please."

It was Monday morning and I was alone in a booth at the diner where we'd all had breakfast the day before. The rest of the gang was probably still asleep at the hostel. Katie had left a couple hours ago, and because she had thought to bring me enough food to carry for the week, my work in Hot Springs was done.

I thought about getting the everything plate again, but I'd learned my lesson back at the NOC. They don't build trail towns at the tops of mountains. The trail out of town is always uphill, and the day was shaping up to be another hot one. I ordered pancakes and a side of bacon and waited.

Five locals in overalls were yukking it up with the waitresses behind the counter. When I took my seat they were talking about tree removal services. When my coffee arrived they were explaining how the president wasn't able to take our guns away, so instead he was making bullets illegal. With my pancakes came an assertion that the cop who gave that one guy a DUI had it in for him ever since that thing with his sister.

While I ate, I scanned the room. Other hikers started showing up for breakfast. I recognized a few of them and waved, but most were unfamiliar, men in their mid-20s with old haircuts and new beards. They were all disheveled, yet I could tell who had just come from the trail and who woke up in town.

Hot Springs is a trail town, and the walls in the Smoky Mountain Diner make that clear. Near the front door is a corkboard filled with postcards from hikers. Shots of smiling faces standing at the famous summit sign at the top of Mount Katahdin were interspersed with business cards advertising local shuttle services and gear repair.

On the wall across from my table hung a poster titled "The End of the Journey." A thru-hiker has collapsed to his knees at the summit sign on Katahdin, gripping it for support, resting his forehead on the board. He is spent. The hair on my arms stood up, and a shiver hit me so hard I dropped my fork. *This is what I want.*

I wanted to know what it felt like to give everything I had and just barely make it. I wanted the feeling of accomplishing something I hadn't thought I could do. I wanted to be humbled and crushed by this. In the future, when I thought back to Mount Katahdin, I didn't want it to be the place where I had started walking south toward some random parking lot in New Jersey. I wanted the dramatic finish.

It seemed like my hike was going to last forever, but I knew it would be over all too soon. Who knew when I might see Lemmy and Voldemort and Fiddlin' Jim and Forager again. If I flipped, they'd be gone, except for the moment we passed. I imagined hiking south with their Bizzaro World doppelgangers—a no-nonsense businesswoman with her hair in a bun, a Palestinian card trick magician, Tuba Tim and his son Starvin' Marvin, who was always losing his food.

No thanks. I had to go all the way.

I signaled for the check and walked to the bathroom, pausing by the poster. Nearby was a framed newspaper article featuring a familiar face. The headline read BUTCHER TREKS CONTINENTAL DIVIDE FOR SUNSHINE FOUNDATION. The story covered the adventures of retired U.S. Army Officer Gene Butcher, who hiked all three of America's longest trails to raise awareness and funds for a charity that helps sick children. It was none other than Flat Feet, the man who named me. He even signed the framed article that way.

Gene had gotten off to a late start, both in hiking season and in life, which led many to believe he might not make it. The Continental Divide Trail goes from Mexico to Canada. He was almost stopped by heavy snow many times. He encountered grizzlies, freezing rain, and drought. And he made it.

I still remembered the word he told me. "Perseverance." He had it in spades.

I stomped my foot at the picture and whinnied like a horse. I laughed and forced the air from my lungs, making a raspberry with my lips. Everyone in the place turned to stare at me, except for the other hikers.

■   ■   ■

Getting out of Hot Springs via the Appalachian Trail is confusing. I walked four blocks to the north end of town and the next white blaze was painted on the bridge over French Broad River. The river is indeed broad, and by the time I reached the other side, I was already in the zone. Ten minutes later, I realized that I was still on the road and hadn't seen any blazes. Time to check the guidebook, I thought.

Sure enough, I'd missed the turn. Immediately after the bridge, I should have hopped the guardrail, scrambled down a steep dirt embankment, looked past the NO TRESPASSING sign, and then I would have seen the next blaze. I did all these things and the trail turned again, taking me close to the edge of the water. The river splashed to my right, and to my left stood a steep rocky cliff hundreds of feet high. That must be Lovers Leap, I thought. The guidebook showed a good flat stretch followed by a steep climb, so this had to be it.

Another mile of climbing up a switch-backed trail, and I was up at what I thought had been Lovers Leap. But I had been mistaken, and the climb was only beginning. Two or three more switchbacks and I would be at five times this height. The way was rocky and in a few places I had to grab onto a root or branch to make the next step. On one grab, a pine bough brushed my face and just missed my eye. I wasn't wearing glasses anymore. They kept fogging and would probably break soon anyway, so I had determined they weren't worth their weight and had given them to Katie to take home. I could squint when I needed to.

The climb would have kicked my ass a month ago, but now here I was at the top, and had barely broken a sweat. The sun was hot but the breeze countered it. I could feel my feather catch the wind and tug at my hat.

The river slogged below. Walking by the rapids earlier, their pounding roar drowned the sound of my own footsteps. Up on Lovers Leap they were thin white ripples that hardly hissed. I could see the little town along the other bank and part of the bridge where I missed my turn.

Megan and the others were probably still somewhere down there. We had started to realize that staying together didn't require the precise planning we'd originally thought. There were only so many stopping points between here and the next shelter, and there were only so many shelters between here and the next town. We spread out sometimes, but eventually we bunched right back up. Even on zero days.

This newfound laissez-faire approach seemed to apply to each of us except for Megan. She was like a border collie; she always knew where everyone was at all times. Whoever was still down there with her had probably already been rounded up and they were marching this way. She wouldn't need to look at a map. Her plan would be walk north until she got to wherever Green Giant was.

I was about to leave when I heard kids approaching. They were four Boy Scouts on a day hike with their parents, whom they had outpaced miles ago. "Are you hiking the whole trail?" one asked me.

"Yes sir," I said.

"Oh, good," he replied. "Maybe you can help us to settle an argument we've been having."

This was my chance to shine. Surely he was about to ask me a survival-related question. I hoped it was about navigation. I'm good at that.

"How would you kill a werewolf?"

■   ■   ■

I was the first to the shelter after all. Good, I thought. More work for Voldemort. Maybe they'll tire her out.

Besides the Boy Scouts, I'd only seen one other person. She was returning from a weekend hike and asked me if I knew about the weather. I told her that I didn't even think to check. It no longer mattered.

Maybe I'll write something like that in the shelter log, I thought. *I don't check the weather anymore because it doesn't matter.* I wasn't feeling very creative, but it was the best I could do on short notice. Just in case the gang decided to sleep in tents, which they never did, it would at least get my name in the book.

Before I found a blank page for my entry, I saw a name that made me stop.

Two days ahead. One word, no note. *Droid.*

I saw Droid's name and it took me back to that night on Cheoah

Bald, the night with the incredible sunset. That time we saw the stars. I remembered being nervous before I started my tour of the sky that night. I've spent years as an amateur astronomer and I know the constellations well enough to navigate by them. When I start talking about the sky at night, I become excited. I speak fast and wave my hands. And I go on. I assumed that if I became a bore someone would let me know.

No one stopped me and I talked for an hour, answering questions, telling stories and pointing. Without a telescope, the best way to indicate faint stars is to put your heads together and point. The closer your eyes are to theirs, the closer your finger gets to what you want them to see. We all put our heads together that night. We connected under that incredible sky. And now we were as scattered as the stars themselves.

## TRAIL LEGS

THE GANG REASSEMBLED at the first shelter north of town, and by dark we had a guest. Bandit was a major pain in the ass. He bragged about his numerous periods of incarceration and how it was never his fault. He blew cigarette smoke in peoples' faces and hacked, coughed, and spat phlegm on the shelter floor. He sat on the picnic table in his underwear. We had to get away from him.

The next morning, we all packed wordlessly and left as early as we could. But at the end of the day, 15 miles later, he was with us again. This time he lectured us about the various secret societies that controlled the world. They tracked our movements by using the magnetic strips on our driver's licenses, which is why he didn't have one.

The morning after that, we all left early again. Seventeen miles this time. When he caught us that night, he told us about how he was suing the Smoky Mountains National Park for making hikers buy a permit. "That's what our tax dollars are for. Making us pay for a permit is a breach of contract. Not like I pay taxes though. Taxes are bullshit!" He spat.

"I'm going to change his trail name," I told Megan. "We should call him Tick, because he just latches on and sucks."

Since Bandit didn't carry a tent, we plotted to hike past the next shelter and camp under the stars.

But the next day brought a severe thunderstorm, so tenting was not a very good option. Instead we found ourselves trapped in a box subjected to stories about how lizard people helped fake the moon landing or something. I don't know, I'd stopped listening.

He stayed with us for the next 75 miles, all the way to Erwin, Tenn. We had just finished resupplying at the hiker hostel and were leaving when he arrived and started arguing with the proprietor.

We pushed on to the Curly Maple Gap shelter a few miles up the trail. He didn't join us that night, but unless we could get at least one shelter between us he was sure to catch up again. So we decided to go big.

■ ■ ■

Breakfast was pleasantly calm at Curly Maple Gap shelter. There were no conspiracy stories and no one hawked loogies while we ate. We decided to keep it that way by skipping the next shelter and staying at the one after it.

I walked with Lemmy. As the long day wore on, we started looking forward to a road crossing where we could refill our water, but when we reached the crossing we couldn't find the source. The guidebook said to turn right and walk a quarter mile along a gravel road to a spring. We were standing at a five-way intersection of gravel roads.

Each guess, right or wrong, would cost us a half-mile round trip. The guide said another source was three miles ahead, so instead of adding miles to an already long day, we decided to keep going.

Across the road where the trail picked up again, we saw an elderly couple loading the trunk of their car with day packs and trekking poles. They waved us over. "Are you two hiking all the way?"

"Yes ma'am," Lemmy said.

They offered us some water which we gladly accepted. "We hiked the trail in 1974," the woman told us. "I bet your experience is very different from ours."

"Look at my shoes," I said, showing one difference. Back then everyone wore boots; now almost no one did. Lightweight trail runners were the footwear of choice. They say you'll take five million steps between Georgia and Maine, and the amount of energy required to lift a shoe that many times is significantly less than lifting a boot.

"Those look pretty new," the man said.

"They are. I just got them yesterday. Even cooler is *how* I got them. The pair I started with were getting pretty worn out. I managed to get a cell phone signal a few days ago, so I hopped on Amazon and these were waiting for me at the mail counter in Erwin."

They smiled. "That really is amazing," the man said. "I can't even imagine what it must be like to hike now."

"Do you still think about it?" I asked.

The woman answered. "It's been 30 years, and not a day goes by."

"Not one day," her husband added.

"It has a way of staying with you."

The couple gave us enough water to fill up completely, so we wouldn't have to stop again until we caught up with the rest of the gang. The Clyde Smith shelter was just a few miles ahead, which would make that day our longest yet, at 22 miles. I don't know if it was my new shoes or if I was just jazzed to hit our first 20, but I was feeling pretty good.

For the next few hours as I walked I kept thinking about that couple we met. Thirty years ago they had stepped right where my feet were. A hundred miles from now, they had been there too. A thousand miles from now. Any time I looked down.

I tried to imagine a future with all of these experiences 30 years in my past but I couldn't. Time was already becoming hazy as a concept. I could tell you the town, shelter, or mountain where something happened, but not when. Last night or last week, it was all the same. I kept forgetting what day it was because I just didn't need to know. In fact, I kept forgetting it was June. But as I mulled it over, I figured out that today marked exactly one month on the trail. By the time I arrived at camp I was buzzing with energy.

When we got there, Megan yelled, "Is that Green Giant?"

I yelled back, "And Lemmy, too!" She was sitting by a small fire with Forager. Fiddlin' Jim was on his back doing stretches in the shelter. I dropped my pack, checked for ticks, and then joined my friends at the fire. "Who wants to do something epic?"

Lemmy's voice answered from inside the privy. "I always want to do something epic!"

Forager nodded. "Go on."

"Okay. So, first, congratulations on 22 miles! Everyone feel good? Me, too. As of right now the plan is to do what? Eat and then go to bed. Rest our bodies for eight hours, get up and hike again, right? Short day tomorrow by comparison, 17 or so, right?"

"I think I know where you're going," Forager said.

"So what if we still did those things, only in a different order?"

Megan stood up. "You mean hike instead of sleep? Oh my god! Are we going to get to see a sunrise? I love sunrises!"

"That's the plan. Instead of dinner, then sleep, then hike, we go dinner, then hike, then sleep. If we roll out of here around 10:30 tonight, we'll get to the top of Roan Mountain just in time for sunrise. We watch the sun come up from one of the highest peaks on the AT. Then we get to the Overmountain shelter before lunch. We stop there and basically take a zero, only at a shelter."

Forager pulled his pot from the fire. "Is that the old converted barn?"

"It is. The guidebook says it sleeps 24. It's two stories tall and has a 'commanding view of the valley below.'"

"I want to leave now!" Megan said.

"If we leave now, we'll get there at two in the morning. Then what? Let's have dinner first. Who's in?"

"I was on board as soon as you said 'epic,'" said Forager.

"How about you, Jim?" I called into the shelter.

"No thanks," came the reply. "I just finished setting up my bed. I'll catch you guys at the barn tomorrow."

As dusk fell we ate our dinners and talked about how great the sunrise was going to be. Forager opened a flask of brandy, and soon it was dark. I was getting the tiniest bit sleepy when it was time to go.

■ ■ ■

"We're ready!" All three of them had their packs on.

"Guys, it's 9:30. It's just barely hiker midnight." "Hiker midnight" is whatever time it gets dark. No matter how much energy hikers bring to the shelter at the end of a long day, the revelry rarely lasts an hour. The body knows that dark means sleep; our tiny headlamps have no chance of fooling the brain, and we all shut down. Hiker midnight. Our friends back home are just settling into the next episode of their favorite binge-watch while we're sound asleep.

Fiddlin' Jim was already snoring. The full moon was just rising, and in its light I could see the circles under Lemmy's eyes. "He kept me up all night, Green Giant! I hate this sound."

The previous night had been bad. Having spent a decade in the military and twice as long camping, I've slept in close proximity with hundreds of people. I've encountered snorers and screamers, sleepwalkers and sleeptalkers, even a bedwetter or two, and no human being has ever disrupted his neighbors' slumber more thoroughly than

Fiddlin' Jim. Everything will be perfectly quiet, nothing but breeze and crickets, when Jim, dead to the world, lets out a sigh and stops breathing. After a moment or two of silence, he starts gagging, quietly at first, a sort of muted gurgle. We can hear him struggle as if he's drowning. Then, with a snap, his vocal cords release, a dam in his throat bursts and air floods in. His teeth slam shut with a clack and his lungs force the air out through his nose. Now that his body remembers how to breathe, his engine idles with plenty of gas, rumbling enough to shake the shelter floor. All night long.

"It sounded like he was being strangled," I said. "I hate to break the news to you, Forager, but I'm pretty sure your dad was clinically dead eight or nine times last night."

We geared up and moved out. The moon helped us to see in clearings, but much of our walk was in the black tunnel, so we kept our headlamps on. Less than a mile from the shelter we came to a rocky knob with a view. From here, we would descend 1,000 feet and then go back up 2,500. That final big climb would take place over five miles and get us to the Roan Highlands.

The wind was picking up, and Megan pointed out some clouds in the west. "Did you check the weather before we left?"

"You know I don't check anymore. Did you?"

"I did. We have a 60 percent chance of thunderstorms overnight with a low in the 50s."

Forager's voice carried a hint of concern. "Why didn't you mention that before we started this?"

"I thought you knew something I didn't. Besides, we have a 40 percent chance of *not* thunderstorms overnight, right?"

"I don't think that's how that works," I said. "Now I think I hear thunder, too."

"That's not thunder, that is Jim snoring," Lemmy corrected me. "We can't go back!"

Once we got off the knob and began our brief descent, the wind decreased and we stopped thinking about rain. Instead, we thought about the swarms of moths that our headlamps attracted. They fluttered in front of my face, avoiding my frantic swatting. One landed on my sweaty cheek and its wing got stuck. I had to help it. Another rested in the exact center of my headlamp, casting a giant moth shadow wherever I looked.

"Point your headlamp at the clouds," Lemmy said. "We can use it to call Mothman!"

Forager held up a hand to stop us, then pointed to our left. None of us saw it, but we all heard it. Something big was moving through the trees, either toward or away from us, we couldn't tell. "It's a bear!" Lemmy shouted, no fear in his voice, only joy.

To scare it away, Megan began stomping and shouting, and we joined in. Lemmy clacked his big wooden sticks while I made my trademark pole antlers and yelled, "Git!" Forager bellowed at the sound in the dark, and soon we were all jumping and yelling and laughing at nothing in the woods by the light of the moon.

It was only 11 p.m. Six more hours until sunrise and only five miles to go. Even uphill in the dark, we'd still be hours early. Megan suggested that we look for a place to make a quick camp and set an alarm for sunrise, but the rest of us figured that would hardly leave any time for rest, given how long it'd take us to make and then break camp.

Lemmy continued up the trail without waiting for us, so we followed. He had the right idea. The closer we were to the top when we stopped, the more likely we were to follow through with this ridiculous plan. If we did eventually stop and get some sleep, it would be easier to drag ourselves to the sunrise spot if we had a short walk to get there, instead of the five-mile climb still ahead.

The first raindrop hit my face. "Just a light sprinkle," I said.

■   ■   ■

Forager shouted something from up ahead, but all I could hear was the hood of my raincoat slapping my ear in the wind. He shouted again. "I! SEE! LEMMY!"

The rain pelted my face and I had to squint to see, but there was definitely a light shining through the trees. The headlamp looked down, then up, then down again. Looking for something in his pack.

Megan waved an arm, pointed right, and walked toward the light. Lemmy had discovered a big rock leaning up against a bigger rock, and it looked like he was using them as shelter. There was just enough room for three people.

"You guys go in. I need to check the map anyway." I hunkered outside by the rocks and confirmed that we were near the top. The series of wide balds with expansive views were a mile or so further, and somewhere in between I thought I saw the car symbol and maybe a trash can, but the wind refused my efforts to steady the map. I folded it neatly, returned it to its Ziploc bag, and shoved that into my soaking wet pocket.

"I have to keep moving." I leaned into their cave. Their headlamps converged on my face, and I was blind.

"Goddamn it, guys." I looked down. "If I stop and sit, I'll fall asleep. I don't want to spend the night under a rock. You're all faster than me, so I'll see you when you catch me. You're not planning to stay here, are you?"

The three lights shook "no" and I continued. "If I stop, I get cold. My shirt's wet from sweating to keep up with you, so I don't even know why I'm wearing this thing, the goddamn moths are driving me crazy…" I stood up. "Be safe, guys."

I was about 20 feet away when Megan yelled, "Hey Green Giant! I have a great idea! How about you go stand on top of the highest point for miles during a thunderstorm!"

I would rather die by lightning than spoon Lemmy under a rock, but I kept that to myself.

It was only ten minutes later when I saw three lights on the switchback behind me. Forager said, "We just sat there for a while, and I was like, what the fuck are we doing under this rock?"

"I was only trying to use the bathroom," Lemmy said.

"Jesus Christ, you people." I let them get ahead and we marched on into the storm.

"We'll be above 6,000 feet," I said. "I think we're going to get above this." I had been watching the moon all night, and its veil of storm clouds was persistent but thinning as we climbed.

Three times we thought we were at the top, when the trail bent sharply, leading us up the next false summit. The storm had changed to a blowing mist when Lemmy yelled, "I see an overhang! We can get under it!" He ran.

We followed and soon our feet were on asphalt. It was a map board in a parking lot. Lemmy stood by it, shivering. Megan helpfully pointed out that he was on the windy side, and he joined us as we huddled on the sheltered side. It kept our upper bodies out of the wind, but our legs were still exposed. Forager tapped my shoulder. "Look. Bathrooms. Let's get on the other side of that."

We ran to the bigger shelter, dropped our packs, and crouched behind the wall, finally out of the wind. I hugged my pack, trying to get warmer. It helped a little, but I was still cold. "What are the odds that one of these doors is open?"

The wall we huddled against had four identical doors, each displaying both the male and female bathroom stick figures. Everyone grabbed a handle. They all opened.

Forager shut his. "I am not sleeping in a shitter."

"I'm going to change into dry clothes and try the hot water. I'll be around the other side." The windward side of the building also had four bathrooms, and I wanted to spare them any unpleasant sounds I might need to make.

The instant I emerged from the protective shadow of the building, I was pushed by a current of cool mist. I hurried to the other side, opened the first door, and entered, setting off a motion-activated light. I turned on the hot water. It was hot.

I stripped naked in the tiny room and put on dry clothes. They were all I had. If that weak mist turned back into an actual storm, I would just put the wet stuff back on. The hot water felt so good, I washed my face and hands twice. The hot air dryer worked too. Finished cleaning up, I sat on the closed lid of the toilet and leaned forward, elbows on knees. Holy shit, that felt good.

Stretching my back felt so glorious, I groaned. I placed my pack between my knees, folded my arms atop it, and rested my head there. My skin was no longer cold, but my insides still were. It was so nice to have warm dry clothes, I thought. And a simple thing like hot water was amazing when you really thought about it. The wind outside was soothing and I closed my eyes. Just for a second.

The motion activated light turned itself off. This does not help, I thought. All I have to do is wave my arm. I'm not going to though, am I? My arm was so heavy, and it felt so wonderful to just not move.

If I died right there, would I be a happy ghost? I didn't care. Even if I went out like Elvis, it would still be better than spooning Lemmy in some weird toilet cave. I tried to not activate the light and fell into sweet, sweet blackness.

■   ■   ■

I'm happy to say it isn't very often that I wake up confused and sitting on a toilet. Peeling my face from my forearm was enough to trigger the motion detector. The sudden bright light startled me to my feet only to discover that both my legs were asleep, so I collapsed to the floor. I considered just lying there and waiting for the light to go back out, but something in my pack was jabbing my rib. I got up.

It was 4:30 a.m. I had been asleep about 45 minutes, and now I felt more tired than if I'd stayed up.

Outside the wind had decreased but a thick mist still hung in the air. At 6,000 feet this was not fog; we were in a cloud. Lemmy was curled in a ball under his sleeping bag and raincoat. Megan and Forager had constructed a couch from their foam pads and were snuggled under a blanket.

I kicked Forager's shoe. "You don't have to go home, but you can't stay here." He met my grin with one open eye and Lemmy moaned his disapproval.

"Come on," I said. "Even with your blankets that brick wall is going to suck all of the heat right out of you. You'd be even more miserable in half an hour. I'll make coffee."

It didn't take long to get some water boiling and we mixed powdered cocoa in with our coffee. "Poor man's mocha," Megan said, unwrapping a Pop-Tart. "Hey Forager, I think I saw some snails over by the parking lot if you want some protein with breakfast."

A sign in the parking lot read TOLLHOUSE GAP, which confirmed that we were very close to the top. But it was tricky to find the trail walking inside a cloud. The beams from our headlamps stopped short in the thick mist.

We walked the perimeter of the lot until we found the white blaze on a pole at the other end. It led us into the cover of pines. The trail stayed very close to the summit for the next mile, making a few small ups and downs. We passed Roan High Knob shelter but didn't go in, assuming it was full of sleeping hikers.

"Well guys, that was it." One of those small ups had been the summit. Visibility was 50 feet at most. "Sorry."

Forager leaned on his poles. "So, what now?"

"The barn is still seven miles from here. Good news though, it's mostly downhill. There are three big balds between here and there, and it'll be daylight by the time we get to those. If we get really tired, there's even one more shelter before the barn. We do what we always do. We go north."

North led us down the other side of Roan Mountain, a thousand foot descent through rocks and stunted pines. The sun came up, turning the mist from gray to white. A colossal round shadow loomed in the haze, one lone mountain, a backlit, nearly perfect semicircle 500 feet high and covered with rhododendrons in full bloom.

No one said a word. Single file, we climbed the first bald and the sun climbed with us. The mist thinned and the flowers caught more light. From the top we could see the other two giant balds, stretching over a mile into the clouds. We were surrounded by millions of pink and purple starbursts. The wind blew and sent petals flying. The sun found an opening behind us, and every place our shadows touched the mist, they were surrounded by rainbows.

■ ■ ■

Overmountain Gap was the site of a skirmish against the British in 1780, but the real draw is the barn. It sits on several acres of land at the edge of a steep drop that looks across a deep wide valley. The first floor has a covered area and a long sleeping porch facing the valley, with two platforms each capable of holding half a dozen sleeping hikers. The upstairs is fully covered, with wide windows opening to the same spectacular view. It is a popular location, only a few miles from the nearest road, and it is almost never empty.

When we arrived at noon, it was empty. And the sky had cleared completely. We had the full show to ourselves.

"Anybody know how far we just went?" Forager asked, unpacking his sleeping bag.

I did some calculations in the guidebook. "Holy shit. Are you ready for this?"

"Bring it on, Green Giant."

"We were at 22 miles when we had dinner last night. And we just put another 15 on top of that, giving us a total of 37!"

We cheered and high-fived each other, then counted six shelters we had passed on our marathon trek. Megan pounded her fist on the platform. "There's no *way* Tick will catch up with us now!"

Lemmy cooked some soup and Forager made a fire to dry his shoes. For her lunch, Megan spread chocolate sauce on a tortilla and filled it with peanut M&Ms arranged according to the spectrum. "This is for all the rainbows we saw on the way here," she said.

"Congratulations. No matter what happens, now you can always say you walked 37 miles in one day."

"And no matter what, now you can always say that you slept in a shitter."

Less than an hour later, we were all asleep. We never heard Fiddlin' Jim arrive, or the 12 other people.

## 11

## SALAD DAYS

THE SUN ROSE over my feet. I could see it behind my closed eyes as soon as its first rays crested the horizon. Overmountain shelter is so close to the edge that I couldn't see the ground between the barn and the drop-off. It felt like I was floating above the valley.

Voldemort wasn't in her usual spot by the wall. She was on the other platform spooning with Forager. Lemmy was spooning me, so I jabbed his rib with my elbow and he jerked away. He would have kicked me had he not been zipped tightly in his bag. The boards upstairs shook, the unmistakable sound of Fiddlin' Jim snoring. Unfamiliar hikers filled every remaining space on both platforms. Someone had suspended a hammock above the picnic table. I leaned forward and counted three tents in the field to our left.

I checked my phone. It was 6 a.m. We'd slept 18 hours. I stood and stretched, and my spine cracked, bringing relief with each pop. My legs felt strong, ready to go again. Other than being unusually hungry, I felt fine.

My water would come from a piped spring a quarter mile from the barn. It was in the direction of the trail, so I decided to have breakfast there to avoid backtracking. No unnecessary miles.

The trail carried me up the same mountain the sun had risen over. From the top, the barn was a red speck in a sea of green. I shaded my eyes and squinted. I could barely make out Lemmy and someone who might have been Voldemort. I cupped my hands and yelled "WOOOOOOO-HOOO!" The faint "woo-hoo" that came back might have been them, or my echo.

I didn't need to wait, because we all knew where we were going: up and over Little Hump and Hump Mountain, two more big balds like the three we had crossed in the fog the previous day. Today was sunny and clear, and the high grassy meadows offered far-reaching views into the wrinkled landscape behind me. Ahead lay an easy day of mostly downhill through the green tunnel and past a sign that said LEAVING NC. We were no longer straddling the border; there would be another couple days of Tennessee, and then we'd be in Virginia.

There had been a lot of talk about Virginia. The AT touches 14 states, and Virginia contains more miles than any other: over 500. That was more miles than we would walk just to get *to* Virginia. It takes so long to cross that the term "Virginia Blues" has been around as long as the trail. Instead of ghost stories, hikers sit around campfires and scare themselves with stories of people who went insane in Virginia. "They walked 25 miles, ate dinner and went to bed tired...*and then they did it again! Oooooooh!*"

Yeah, but they walked 25 miles, right? I flipped to my guidebook's Virginia section and saw how this was possible. It looked like a few Smoky-sized hills after Damascus, and then a whole lot of horizontal. The elevation line rose from the edge of the page to about 3,000 feet pretty quickly, and then stayed there for the next three or four pages. It looked like each page corresponded to a day, and each day maybe once or twice the line would dip a few hundred feet into a V marked with a water symbol or a small town.

I couldn't imagine anyone getting the blues from that; it sounded like paradise. Aside from shelters, towns, and tent sites, very little of my life had involved flat ground lately, and I was looking forward to some. A certain amount of adrenaline had come at the end of our big day, and after that a wave of endorphins followed by the deepest sleep I'd ever experienced. There was also a twinge of smug satisfaction I got from tearing out two days' pages at once.

Bad Dinner had called it "boring and repetitive." If that was what Virginia had in store for us, then I was ready. We had Lemmy's colored pencils, and if my hunch was correct, there was love in the air. I was certain that we had nothing but good times ahead.

■ ■ ■

"Good lord, Green Giant, that's disgusting! Does it hurt?"

Voldemort pointed at my right big toe. The nail was completely black.

"No, it doesn't. In fact, watch this." I poked it and it moved. When I pressed down and moved my finger, the toenail slid around like wet wallpaper. "Can't feel a thing."

"Oh, that is coming off. Soon," she said. "And it is going to hurt!"

We were at Mountaineer Falls shelter. We had our own waterfall about a hundred yards from the wooden box we called home, and when we were quiet we could hear it.

Fiddlin' Jim was the last to arrive that night, several hours later than we expected him. He was smiling and appeared to be walking normally, so we asked him what caused the delay.

"Oh, I stopped and took a nap."

"Where?" There weren't any shelters that day other than the one we were in.

"Under a rock."

"Under a rock? Why?"

"Aw geez, I was tired. I was sitting there eating an apple around two or three. And it just got so hot, you know? So I see this rock over there and it's pretty shady, so I think maybe I'll go sit over there for a minute and cool off. So I did. And pretty soon I start getting sleepy, you know, so I just closed my eyes for a second and I guess I dozed off."

Forager joined us. "How long were you out, Dad?"

"Aw, well, you know, I woke up after a bit and I don't know what time it was. But then I was cold, so I pulled a bunch of leaves around me and piled them up for a blanket and went back to sleep. I woke up again a while later, this time because I heard voices. Some people were having lunch on top of my rock!"

"Oh shit! What did you do?"

"I couldn't do anything! Could you imagine if I jumped up out from under that rock with dirt on my face and leaves in my hair? 'Don't be scared! I'm Fiddlin' Jim! I won't hurt ya!'" He danced a little jig and hooted with glee.

That night, I fell asleep to the chanting of cicadas. The next morning, I awoke to the sound of a hummingbird zooming through our camp. Again I was the first one up, and felt well rested—either Fiddlin' Jim didn't snore or I had gone deep. I packed and ate quickly and was ready to leave just as the others were sitting up and stretching.

"Don't forget to go for a walk today," I said, and started north without them. Everyone knew where we were going, and half of them would beat me there anyway.

The ache in my shin was mostly gone, but there was a new problem. My pack no longer fit. When I had mentioned to Katie I might "run out of strap," I was joking. I didn't think it would actually happen, but I had tightened every strap to its limit now and still couldn't get the snug fit I needed.

Modern backpacks employ a design that relies on a wide padded hip belt. The majority of the pack's weight is supported by the belt, and as a result the legs bear most of the burden, not the back or shoulders. Shoulder straps are there only to keep the pack's center of gravity close to your own and to stabilize the load.

As I lost weight, my shoulder straps were the first to go. As I walked, the pack swung like a metronome. It was like giving a piggyback ride to a child who keeps pointing at things. A few days later, the hip belt reached its limit. Now I was giving a piggyback ride to a kid who wasn't holding on with his legs. This was okay for about an hour, but not for all day. The bouncing weight fatigued my shoulders and rubbed them raw. So I took more breaks.

Usually about an hour or so into the day's hike, we would start to get hungry again and stop for second breakfast. I was still alone and on spider web patrol, so I sat by the trail to enjoy a snack. I leaned my poles against a tree and when I removed my pack they fell, making a clatter as they slid and scraped on a rock. Something in the tree above me rustled. I jumped up and backed away from the tree.

It was a small black bear I had startled, trying to get down and run away. The bottom branch was eight feet up, and the bear jumped. It looked like it weighed almost 200 pounds, but it landed almost silently, glancing briefly over its shoulder as it retreated deep into the woods.

I closed my hanging jaw and wished Lemmy had been there. He was the only one of us who hadn't seen a bear yet, and since it was dark when we heard whatever made all that noise coming up Roan Mountain, no one could prove it was a bear and Lemmy said it didn't count.

A mile further, I was still thinking about the bear. I wanted to let my friends know, but I didn't want to wait until they caught me. I tore a sheet of paper from my notebook and wrote a note: *Just saw a bear about a mile south of here. –Green Giant.*

I placed small rocks on the corners so it would not blow away and continued north.

• • •

The day before Damascus, I woke up excited. Megan had received word from Katie that my friend Travis was going to make good on his promise back in Hot Springs, and would be joining us for a couple days. He was going to leave his truck at a trailhead and hike about three miles to the shelter with us. Then, the following morning, he would walk into Damascus with us, stay the night, and get a ride back to his truck from Katie when she left. She would join us on the second day.

I always enjoyed seeing people from home, especially Katie, but this was to be the last time. They would both have to drive three hours to get there. Every week was taking me about a hundred miles further away from home.

We were still a few miles from where we planned to meet Travis when Voldemort asked, "Do you think your friend will bring us any trail magic?"

"I guess we could ask him." I gave her his number and she texted him: *Gary says bring food.* When he texted back asking for specifics we replied: *Bring all the food.*

We reached the meeting place first. Ten minutes later, a green Toyota truck parked in front of us.

Travis yelled "Come and get it!" and threw two plastic grocery bags onto the picnic table. We tore in and spread the contents. Like vultures reveling in the guts of a fresh kill, we ripped open the chips with our teeth and sucked chocolate from our fingertips. Voldemort held out a bag of barbecue chips she and Lemmy had partially devoured and I declined.

"No thanks," I said. I turned to Travis to explain. "Once your hand goes in the bag, the bag is yours. Otherwise that's how Noro spreads. Nothing personal."

"You don't have herpes or anything creepy, do you?" Voldemort asked Lemmy.

He finished twisting his pinky finger in his mouth, and eyed the bag. "Mmm, no? I don't think so. Why?"

"You do now."

As we tore into the food, a thin bearded man climbed out of the back of Travis's truck. He had a teardrop tattoo under his left eye.

When he held out his hand and nodded at me I poured him a serving of chips from my bag. "Thanks, bro. And thanks for the lift." He nodded at Travis, shouldered his pack and took the trail south.

"Travis, who was that?" I asked.

"I'm not sure. The dude had his thumb out so I picked him up. Besides, he sat in the back. Too much shit up front." He turned his attention to Voldemort and Lemmy.

"It's good to see you guys again."

Voldemort pointed at her bulging cheeks and gave him a thumbs up. "Mmmf!"

He removed his own pack from the truck and asked, "Are we waiting for anyone else?"

I explained that Forager and Fiddlin' Jim were up ahead at Abingdon Gap shelter, three miles north from where we stood. "And then it'll be about ten miles from there into Damascus in the morning—"

Travis interrupted. "In the *morning*? Dude, I can do ten miles for sure, but it'll take me all day!"

"Nah, you'll be fine," I said. "Trust me. You're carrying next to nothing; there's one little hill and after that it's literally all downhill." I reminded him that he also had the luxury of being able to rest for the next whole week if he wanted. This was a one-time thing. "It'll be a piece of cake."

Minutes later we were fully loaded and on the trail. I brought up the rear while the other three jockeyed for the lead, laughing and chattering the whole way. I didn't mind being in the back. It felt good to just walk and breathe for a change. It's noticeable how much more effort it takes to hike while holding a conversation. I kept close enough to chime in occasionally, and it felt like just as we were warming up, we were there.

Abingdon Gap shelter is a standard wooden box with a slanted tin roof. Out front is an average shelter scene: a picnic table, a fire ring, room for some tents, and a bunch of trees. Behind the shelter there is a shoulder-high rock wall and a view of the valley below. The evening was overcast and provided a less-than-spectacular sunset. At least it was warm.

Fiddlin' Jim hadn't snored for a few nights, which meant we were due for a doozy. I set up my tent as far away as possible. As I was zipping the fly, Lemmy began dumping the contents of his tent bag on the ground inches away from me. I stood up. "Do you need help with that?"

"No," he said. "I can do it."

"Oh. Okay," I looked down and flicked his rain fly off of my toe. "I was just wondering why you dumped your tent and stuff, like, right here, when there are," I pointed everywhere, "a million perfectly flat spots all around us."

He shrugged and fumbled with his tent poles. "Yes, but this is the best spot."

I gave up and returned to the fire where Travis and Megan were in hysterics about something.

"Megan stepped in shit," Travis said, and stifled a laugh.

"Yeah. Shit," she said. "And not just any old shit."

"Nope," Travis added.

"Yeah. Human shit."

"Oh my god," I said. "I mean, are you completely sure? It wasn't animal?"

"Oh, no, I'm sure," she said. "I've buried enough of my own to recognize human turds by now. This was the real thing."

I looked at her bare feet. "How?"

I was embarrassed. My friend was our guest, and this was not how I wanted him to imagine us out here. We weren't *complete* savages. So far 99 percent of the shelters and privies had been well maintained and cared for. There had been trash in the one back at the NOC, but that was the exception. Sometimes there were foil pouches or cigarette butts in the fire rings, maybe some unwanted food or gear left on the picnic table, but never anything like this. Maybe someone was sick, I thought. They couldn't make it to the privy in time. Or, maybe someone was just an asshole.

"Oh, don't worry, I cleaned up."

Travis said, "It gets better."

"Go on..."

"I was only wearing my Crocs." We all burst into groans. "Yeah, and then Travis goes, 'Hey, that's a Croc of shit!'" He said it with her in unison and they cracked each other up again. "Oh my god, I'm going to write that in the log book."

"No wait!" Travis stopped her as she reached for the log book. "Write this instead: 'Shit happens, but fecal matters.'"

The poop jokes continued as we boiled our noodles around the fire. As we ate, we reviewed our plans for the following day: 10 by 10. That is, 10 miles by 10 a.m. The Blue Blaze Cafe was rumored to have the best pancakes in town, and if we could do 10 by 10, we could have second breakfast there. Forager did the math and set an alarm for 5:30.

Lemmy had finished setting up his tent and joined us at the table. "Where are we going to stay, guys?"

Everyone pulled out their copy of the guidebook and turned to the same page. We agreed, based on the name alone, we had to stay at Crazy Larry's.

■ ■ ■

Thunder exploded above us and I yelled to Travis, "This is what we call getting the fire hose!" His feet continued to splash just ahead of mine, and he held out a thumbs-up without turning around.

The drizzle started the moment we exited our tents. We aren't supposed to eat in the shelters because it attracts mice, but every time it rains, everyone does. Before we finished eating, the rain pounded the tin roof so hard that we had to shout to hear each other.

The thunder started about a mile into our walk. Allegedly the sun was up.

Despite the rain, the group's mood was up too, and we splashed in puddles on purpose. We were so wet we couldn't get any wetter, and we no longer cared. The climbs and descents had become more gentle over the past few days, and on that morning the difference was especially pronounced.

We emerged from the green tunnel to find ourselves at the edge of a grassy meadow. A barn and farmhouse were nestled in the valley to our left. To our right, the field was dotted with cows.

Travis pointed to the fence at the far end of the pasture. "Do I see a white blaze?"

The only thing between us and the horizon that wasn't grass or cows was the strip of dirt which stretched from our feet and into the herd. "Yep."

He inhaled deeply and took the lead. "Smells just like home! Hey, Voldemort, watch your step."

There were brown cows, black cows, white with brown spots. Babies, calves, and bulls plodded around us. Most didn't care, but a few stared us down while we passed.

One of the babies galloped up to Lemmy and sniffed. "Don't try any funny business, cow. We will eat you. And wear your skin." He pointed at a bull. "And we will use your head to decorate the front of ridiculous cars!"

■ ■ ■

Damascus, Va. is probably the most famous trail town along the AT. It is one of only a few places where the trail actually goes through the town, and there is no denying the impact this arrangement has had. The place is known informally as "Trail Town, USA" since several other famous trails intersect there, including the Virginia Creeper Trail and the Trans-America National Bicycle Trail. Each year in May it is the site of an extravagant festival called Trail Days.

Trail Days is homecoming for AT hikers. Past, present and future thru-hikers converge here for a long weekend of music, food, and reunion. Bands perform for small crowds all over town. Gear vendors, authors, and artists set up booths alongside fair food staples like deep fried Oreos and funnel cakes. There is a talent show, and the highlight of each Trail Days festival is the thru-hiker parade.

About 15,000 people had filled Damascus, a town slightly bigger than Hot Springs, while I was 400 miles south in a shelter with Big Ups and Floats watching a mama bird feed her babies.

There were considerably fewer people in town when we arrived. Each storefront along the main street had its own neat row of backpacks lined up out front. The Blue Blaze Cafe had the most. This is where the pancakes were.

We pushed some tables together and bombarded our waitress with orders. There were six of us, and two other groups about our size. She was obviously used to an even larger volume and handled us with ease.

While we waited for our food, we scouted the walls for electrical outlets. Even without cell phone reception, we still listened to music and took pictures with our phones. In addition to a wall of packs in front of every store, there was always a bank of smart phones charging by every front door.

When the stacks of pancakes arrived, it felt like I'd won the lottery. She placed them before me, six perfect circles of soft spongy fluff, popping with blueberries. I coated each cake with butter, which quickly melted and vanished, totally soaked up. Starting with the bottom pancake and working my way up, I separated the stack with my fork and applied generous syrup. I held the slippery mess in place with my knife and slid my fork through each layer, feeling it yield and give, yield and give until I'd cut through all six. I made a wedge with another cut, stabbed it through and soaked up more syrup. A sticky amber string clung to my fork and rode from the plate to my mouth and then dripped on my chin. My eyes rolled back into my head and I dropped my fork. I folded a piece of bacon and shoved the whole thing in with my fingers. While I chewed, I worked on preparing the next bite.

I felt stronger with each bite and could not get them into me fast enough. Ten miles ago, I had munched a Clif bar while walking in the rain. This was heaven.

For the next 20 minutes the only sounds were chewing, grunting, and forks on plates. We finished, pushed our chairs back, and sighed. Forager said, "Let's go find Crazy Larry's and get cleaned up for lunch."

Crazy Larry's place was only a short walk from the cafe. Crazy Larry isn't actually crazy, although I'm sure we almost drove him insane. The hostel is actually just his house. He greeted us on the porch and took us into his living room to explain the arrangement. There were a few bedrooms for us to choose from, a bathroom with a shower, and the laundry was in the back. Travis and Lemmy shared a room and I took the back porch. Voldemort threw her pack in the room where Jim and Forager were staying before disappearing into the shower.

The rest of us moved to the front porch to wait our turn. The beer store was practically across the street, so it only made sense for us to crack a cold one while we waited.

Everyone's trekking poles were grouped into a quiver which leaned in one corner of the porch. Travis picked up one of Lemmy's heavy wood sticks. His hand barely closed around it. "Dude, where did you get these?"

Lemmy opened a can of beer and took a sip. "I found those in Georgia."

"And what are these carvings? Is this one a bear?" Until Travis asked, I hadn't noticed the figures etched into the sticks.

"Every time something memorable happens on this hike, I carve it into the stick. I call them my 'memory sticks.'"

"So it this one a bear?"

"No, I have not seen one yet. This is a skunk." Next to the skunk was a triangle for the first time he slept in a tent. A cloud with dots beneath it represented a hail storm. I remember that storm, I thought. We hadn't met yet, and he was just ahead of me.

"I will carry them all the way to Katahdin!" He pronounced the name of the mountain as three separate words: *Kah*, *tah*, and *din*.

Travis put the sticks back. "That's really cool, Lemmy. So, you're from Israel, huh?"

He sipped at his beer and gave me a sideways glance. He squirmed in his seat. "Yeah." He took another drink. "I lived in lots of places though."

"What did you do before hiking?"

"I was in the army. I was a medic. I just got out, and now I am traveling the world before I go to school."

"What for?"

"How do you say it? It's when they are making a movie, but they draw pictures of it first? So the camera knows how to make the scene?"

"Storyboarding?"

"Yes! That is it. I don't know where to go yet though. First I have to do this."

Fiddlin' Jim handed out more beers and Travis selected some fast jazz to play for us on his phone's speaker. Voldemort joined us on the porch, clad only in a towel. Lemmy handed her a beer. "Thanks!" she said. "Who's next?"

The door opened again behind her and Larry looked at us. He slid one index finger across his throat while shaking his head side to side. "Guys, guys, guys. What's it say in the book next to my name?"

One of the reasons we chose Crazy Larry's was a note in the guidebook that said "drinking in moderation."

Since I was the one who had arranged our stay, I took it upon myself to act as our representative. "Larry, we're sorry."

He cut me off. "Guys, it's barely noon, and there are cans and bottles all over the place, she's half naked…turn that down."

Travis turned off the music.

"Not off, just down. Here, use these." He handed us a stack of red plastic cups. "You're going to get me shut down."

I tried to apologize again, but he was already gone. Forager opened a beer. Travis handed him a cup, which he declined. "I'm going to take this into the shower with me."

Lemmy took the cup instead. "He said to use these. So I will use it."

Megan gathered empties into a box and said, "Looks like I've got some catching up to do."

It took about three hours for the six of us to get showers and wash our clothes. We hung our tents on drying racks that Larry provided in the back yard and spent the rest of the afternoon exploring the town.

That didn't take long, and after a large and satisfying dinner at the Blue Blaze Cafe, we walked another half mile out of town to the Damascus Brewery.

While we were inside the pub it started raining again. The fire hose is only fun when you're in the woods, so we decided to wait it out. The rain outlasted us, and when the pub closed the bartender offered us a ride back to Crazy Larry's.

We didn't see Larry again that night, but he had to hear us come in. By the time I was ready for bed, Travis and Lemmy were in a heated card game. Travis sat at the dinner table, looking over his fan of cards. He watched Lemmy, who was at the counter in his socks and boxer shorts staring into a large bowl of green vegetables. "I made this salad for my friends."

"Lemmy, it's your turn."

"I made this salad for my friends, and no one is eating it."

"Lemmy it's your turn."

I walked through the kitchen and onto the back porch. I pulled my sleeping bag up and over my head and drifted off to the sound of my friends trying to decide whether to eat salad or play cards.

## UP, UP AND AWAY

"Did you remember to bring it?"

"I did," Katie said. "It's in the car. Should I go get it?"

"You should. Do you mind carrying my old pack out, too? I'd go with you but..." I was naked.

"Dude." She was disgusted. "It fucking reeks. Put it in a trash bag first."

It was no surprise to see that she had one ready. I rummaged through every empty pocket for the last time and pulled the drawstrings on the vanilla-scented plastic bag. Watching Katie carry it out the door and downstairs to the parking lot of the Dancing Bear Bed & Breakfast was like saying goodbye to an old friend.

The B&B where I had just showered was a few blocks away from Crazy Larry's. There had been no alarm that morning, nor had there been a chorus of birds. Crazy Larry, who's not so crazy after all, lured us all boogery-eyed and stumbling into the kitchen with the smell of bacon.

He let the strips sizzle just long enough to crisp the edges and then snatched them from the pan, diced them, and added them to his blueberry pancake batter. All four burners were going, with scrambled eggs and potatoes on the other two. He heaped giant plates of food before us, and we were each working on our second serving when Katie arrived. Larry was happy to meet the wife of a hiker and offered her a chair and a plate.

After breakfast, she joined us for a trip to the outfitters a few blocks away, where after much deliberation I selected my new pack. Completely empty, it weighed three pounds less than my old pack. In addition to switching brands, I had moved a size down, meaning the straps now fit. It was the only thing I was wearing when Katie came back into the room.

"You're not going to hike like that, are you?"

"I might. In about a week."

"Oh that's right! June 21st!"

I took off my pack and put on shorts. June 21st, in addition to being the summer solstice, is also for some reason the day that hikers everywhere—not just on the AT—hike naked. "I guess it depends on who's around, you know."

"Yeah, I know." She looked at my shoes by the door. "We have an important matter to discuss."

I pulled my shirt on over my head. "What?" I sat on the bed and repeated, "What?"

Oh shit, I thought. She looked serious.

"You smell like piss."

I was not expecting that. "I'm sorry? What?"

"Yeah, I thought I noticed it a while ago, and it's getting worse."

"Me? Or my gear? Because I noticed my pack had a hint of ammonia."

"A hint?" She laughed. "It smells like a goddamn litter box and so do you."

"Well, I promise I'm not peeing myself. What could it be?"

"You need more protein. I looked it up."

"Of course you did. So how will that help?"

"Come here." She stood by the full length mirror on the back of the bathroom door. She put her hand on my back. "Look."

There aren't any mirrors on the trail; I had no idea who I was looking at. My cheeks were sunken, and my patches of facial hair had mostly connected. It still looked glued on, but it was starting to resemble a beard.

My neck stuck out from my shirt like a broomstick in a barrel. My shoulder seams were slowly working their way down toward my elbows. I had been slightly pear-shaped the day I left Springer Mountain; now I grabbed the bottom of my shirt and gathered it at the waist, revealing the V-shaped torso hidden within the folds.

Not everything had shrunk. The bottoms of my shorts were almost pinched around my legs. My thighs were a thick bundle of ropy muscle coated in stubble; the constant swishing of my pants had eroded the hairs away. My calves looked like upside down bowling pins. I flexed. "Nice gams, huh? Looks to me like I'm getting plenty of protein."

"Your bottom half is. But it's eating your upper half to get it."

I struck a double bicep pose. My arms were lost in hanging folds of cloth.

"You're doing a couple thousand reps of one-legged squats every day. With weight on your back. When the muscle being worked needs protein to regenerate, it gets it any way it can. If there's not enough in your diet, your body will metabolize its own muscle tissue to make up the difference, starting with the ones being used the least."

"My legs are eating my arms."

"Yep. And the byproduct of that process is ammonia. It comes out in your sweat."

My shirts got a daily wash in streams or rain, so they weren't so bad. But my pack straps and all of the padding were pretty much saturated all the time. Sometimes their briny stench even made me gag. "Sounds like you've done your research. What's next?"

The bags she'd carried from the car were by the door, along with the thing I asked her to bring. She put the bags on the bed. "I added protein bars to your resupply. I had a hard time finding ones that weren't coated in chocolate, so they might be messy. Sorry."

"Don't apologize, that's great! Thanks!"

"Also, they make foil pouches of tuna that are pretty light. Start dumping one into your pasta each night. We'll get you some beef jerky at the grocery store and that should help."

"You're the best." I thanked her again and we kissed. "And thanks again for bringing this!" I moved some things around in my pack and slid it into the bottom. "How much does it weigh?"

"Six-and-a-half ounces. That's after I took out the instruction booklet. You know how to use it."

"The guys are going to be so surprised."

"So when are you going to bust it out?"

"I can't really plan with this sort of thing. When the time is right, I'll know."

． ． ．

Damascus isn't very big, and if you spend more than an hour there, you'll run into the same people multiple times. There were a few familiar faces in front of the Dollar General. Travis was unwrapping an ice cream sandwich. Lemmy and Megan were each carrying half a dozen plastic bags bulging with their food for the upcoming week. Forager and Fiddlin' Jim were back at Crazy Larry's.

Lemmy's bags clanged when he dropped them. "Hey! Buddy! I like your new pack!"

"Thanks. I like your new shirt." He was wearing a black T-shirt with a cartoon monkey eating a banana on the front. It seemed like Lemmy bought a new shirt in every town along the trail.

Other hikers, though oddly dressed by normal standards, were at least consistent. Voldemort, for example, was wearing her non-hitchhiking shorts and her usual sleeveless hot pink button-up shirt. (She always reminded me that it was "neon coral" and I always got it wrong on purpose just to mess with her.) Seeing the same people wearing the same thing in the same woods every day added to the timeless nature of the hike. With Lemmy, you never knew what to expect.

"So what's in all the cans?" I asked.

"It's sardines!" He opened the bag to show me his prize. "If you buy twelve, they are one dollar each!"

"Those look pretty heavy to me."

"They will be lighter when they are empty!"

Katie and I ducked into the dollar store for most of the things I needed for the upcoming week. I needed protein, but I didn't want to carry—or eat—four pounds of fish. I remembered passing a full-size grocery store on our way to the brewpub the previous night, and we decided to drive there after finishing here. When we exited, the gang was engaged in loud happy conversation with some hikers I'd never seen. Lemmy said, "There he is," and two ran up to me.

"Green Giant!"

I was at a loss. "That's me, hi."

The one who somehow knew my name introduced himself as Hungry Horse. He looked to be in his mid-20s and wore glasses and a baseball hat. His short red beard was thick and neat.

His friend was Dingo. "We've been chasing you since Springer!" A blue headband held back black curls that were just starting to go wild, like the hedges around a newly abandoned mansion. "I mean, not *chasing* you, but—"

Hungry Horse finished for him. "We started the day after you, and we've been one day behind ever since."

Dingo picked it back up. "We almost caught you back at Erwin, and then you guys did that 37-mile night hike. We've been reading you guys's log book entries."

I was flattered that anyone would be excited to meet me, but the idea of being followed was a bit unnerving, even if it was all for fun. I wondered how Lemmy felt when we mobbed him back at Clingmans Dome. "And here we all are," I said, introducing Katie.

Another friend was still talking with Voldemort and Lemmy. "Green Giant, meet Bones," said Lemmy. "I met him the day at Springer Mountain and I have not seen him again until today!"

Bones was aptly named. He looked healthy, quite handsome really, but alarmingly thin. A smiling, bearded skeleton. Bones and Lemmy were busy catching up and I still had more shopping to do, so Mrs. Green Giant and I excused ourselves to fetch her car.

On the drive to the grocery store, I said, "We have another serious matter to discuss."

She answered with, "You're not going to flip-flop. You're going north, all the way to Katahdin." It wasn't a question. She was right.

"I see how much fun you guys are having. I've only met them a few times, I can only imagine how close you all are. It would be like starting over. Could you handle that?"

I couldn't.

"There's plenty of time, too. If you keep your daily average, you'll still make it with a couple weeks to spare. Did you know that they're closing Katahdin two weeks later this year?"

I didn't.

"I already canceled the vacation I was going to use to take you up there. Once you get closer to Katahdin I'll use it to come get you instead." She pulled into a parking spot and stopped the engine. "Anything else about that we need to cover today?"

There wasn't.

The store had just what I needed. I found the tuna packets that Katie had suggested, plus a small bottle of olive oil. Voldemort had recommended adding it to pasta and ramen for the extra fat. Someone else had told me to put peanut butter on everything so I bought that too.

On the way back to the B&B, we spotted Bones walking toward the store. Katie thought we should give him a ride, so she dropped me at the B&B with the room key and drove back to get him. I was still moving food from big bags to small bags when she returned. She left the bathroom door open and started the shower, pulling the curtain shut behind her. "I really like Bones. He's nice."

She had gone back into the store to hang out with him and show him where to find the things we had asked for help with ourselves. Then she had dropped him off at his hostel before coming back to the room.

I was studying my map when she stepped out wearing only a towel. "Got any plans for after dinner?"

"I told Lemmy and Travis I might play a game with them over at Crazy Larry's. Other than that, no."

"Go look out that window," she said.

I drew the curtain and looked down. "A hot tub. Hmm. I don't know. Those things are giant petri dishes."

When I turned around, she dropped her towel. "Still feel like playing cards with Lemmy and Travis?"

I didn't.

■ ■ ■

Voldemort and I were on the trail out of Damascus. The first mile or so is also the Virginia Creeper Trail. It is also a bicycle path, and on that day it was full of pedestrians, bikes, and couples pushing strollers.

"How's your toenail?"

"It still doesn't hurt, but it looks worse, like a marshmallow that's been in the fire too long. It has a black crusty exterior with white goo underneath. I do have one new weird thing, though."

Before I could explain, a middle-aged woman interrupted us. "Hi. I'm sorry to bother, but are you hiking the whole AT?"

"Yes," I said.

"That's amazing." She stared at the fine gravel beneath our feet. "It must have taken a really long time for them to pave the whole thing like this."

Voldemort snorted. She was incredulous. "It's not paved! Out of 2,000 miles, like ten of them are paved. This is one."

"Oh, I'm sorry. Are you a thru-hiker too? You don't look like one."

"That's because my beard hasn't come in yet," Voldemort retorted. With that, she laughed and left.

I shrugged my apology and ran to catch up with her. "So anyway..."

"You were about to tell me something weird. Is it more stuff about your feet?"

"Maybe. I think it could be these shoes though. Every once in a while I feel like my socks are bunching up right here." I tapped the sole of my shoe with the end of my trekking pole. "Just behind my toes. But when I take off my shoes to fix them, they're perfectly smooth."

"And does that hurt?"

"No, it just feels weird. Like nails on a chalkboard. It's hard to explain. Anyway, last night I felt it walking down to the hot tub. I was barefoot."

"Yeah, I think my grandpa has the same problem."

"Very funny."

The paved path continued, but the AT made a sharp left across the road and up the side of a mountain. She was hot on my heels, if that could be said of two people moving so slowly. A visible ring of "town fat" circled each of our bellies, making our escape from the Vortex that much harder.

"I've got some good news," I said. "I'm not flip-flopping. Katie and I talked about the logistics and it looks like it'll work out."

"That's great! Do you think she'll climb Katahdin with us?"

We hadn't discussed it, but I was sure she would be up for the task. That morning we'd spent stumbling through rainbows on Roan Mountain, Katie was busy running a half marathon back home.

"Probably. She's pretty badass, you know. You are too."

"Aw, thanks, Green Giant."

"I'm serious. I was thinking the other day about all the things I've climbed with Katie and Mark, and all the stuff you and I have done, and it's right up there. In fact, I started tossing some numbers around and I'm pretty sure you are now the person I've hiked with more than anyone else."

"Ever? Even Katie?"

"Even Katie. We've been on a bunch of hikes together, but mostly three or four day stretches here and there, a few overnighters, but that's it. If you add them all up, you're either pretty close, tied, or about to pass."

"What about the Marines?"

"Doesn't count. That was always like me and 50 other dudes."

"Wow. That's pretty neat now that I think about it. Good thing we get along, huh?"

"Good thing. I was pretty worried about you at first. Now, not so much."

The next climb was steeper than we expected. At the top she said, "You know I'm pink blazing Forager, right?"

I hadn't heard the term before. I knew that blue blazing meant taking a side trail (the trees were usually blazed blue instead of white) and that yellow blazing referenced the dashes on the highway one might see when skipping a section by car. I had even heard of aqua blazing; for instance, a popular alternative to hiking the Shenandoahs was to raft on the river instead.

"I think I know what pink blazing is. So how's that working out for you?"

"It sucks. We're constantly frustrated. Even if we didn't both smell like ass all the time, which we do, no shelter is ever empty. And even if one was, they're full of mice and bugs. I mean, I'm not exactly a candles and bubble bath girl but I do not need spiders in my hoo-ha either.

"And then we get to town and it's impossible to find time alone together. And when we finally do, we have to worry if people can hear us or if someone's going to walk in. It's like we're kids again."

That's because you still are, I thought.

"I noticed you and Katie didn't show up to play cards last night. How was your conjugal visit?"

"Oh, we just did old people stuff. We paid bills with checks, put on *Matlock* and went to bed early. So, you know. It was boring."

It wasn't.

. . .

Long before Damascus, people started talking about the ponies. A day or so north of Damascus is Grayson Highlands, nearly 5,000 acres of high altitude meadows with 360-degree views. The area is near Mount Rogers, the highest point in Virginia. The meadows are home to herds of wild ponies.

I was embarrassed to learn that ponies are not baby horses. Baby horses are called foals. Ponies are three to four feet tall when fully grown. It was a relief to learn that other adult hikers were also just now learning the same thing.

To get to the highlands we would need to climb a few big round balds first. Before Virginia these were scarce, a welcome break from the green tunnel. Right at the state line their frequency increased, and now I looked forward to our brief shade breaks under the trees.

Lemmy and Voldemort were resting on a log in the shade between balds when I caught up with them. "You guys ready to see some ponies today?"

"I want to ride one!" Lemmy replied.

"I know you're joking, but you know you're not supposed to touch them at all, right?"

"What if they touch me first?"

"Then you go get a grown-up. How are you guys doing? We have a lot of climbs today. It's getting pretty windy up there." It was calm where we sat, but the treetops were bending. "Where's Fiddlin' Jim and Forager?"

Megan pointed north. "Those two really got their speed on this morning."

Lately, Fiddlin' Jim and Forager would already be at the shelter when everyone else arrived. There was usually a fire with a nice bed of coals and something cooking. Jim could catch fish with a bootlace and a paper clip and Forager knew which leaves to wrap them in before tossing dinner on the embers.

"All right, I guess if we don't catch them at the ponies, we'll see them at the shelter. You guys should stay near me. I have a surprise for you when we get up there." I looked up at the bending branches. "Here I go!"

I left them with their packs still at their feet. She was disorganized and he was slow. Good, I thought. That will give me time to set up.

I stretched my legs as I walked. This was the first time since Georgia that I could finally stare straight ahead and just go. There had always been roots or rocks to pay attention to, branches to dodge or streams to cross. Here, I was still climbing but I could see. I could see all the way to the horizon. I could see clouds stacking.

It's got to be now, I thought. This thing would probably scare the ponies anyhow.

I dropped my pack and fished it out. I unzipped the pouch and laid out the string, poles and brightly colored nylon. I knelt to assemble it, keeping my knees on the parts I wasn't ready for, to hold them in the wind.

Lemmy was first to arrive. "What is this?"

I snapped the last two pieces together and held it up for him: a rainbow-colored stunt kite with a four-foot wingspan. "Here, you take this. I'll hold the strings. Go that way."

He was stunned. I told him a second time and he obeyed, dropping his pack beside mine first. He held the kite and walked backwards. "How did you... Where did..."

Voldemort crested the hill. "Where the fuck did you two find a kite?"

"Green Giant made it appear. He is some wizard! What kind of person brings a kite on the Appalachian Trail?"

"Lemmy, watch out!" I dropped a string and pointed at a heap of manure, which he barely dodged. "Now, stop. We don't want to tangle the strings."

I picked up the one I dropped. "Why are there two?" he asked.

"Hang on, you'll see. Okay, stop. Right there. We have to wait for just the right gust."

Megan added her pack to the stack and crouched near the pile Lemmy had almost stepped in. "Hey, Green Giant."

"Hang on, the wind's picking up. Get ready..."

"Hey, Green Giant. I don't think this is horse shit."

"They are ponies," Lemmy said. "Not horses."

"Lemmy, pay attention! When I say throw, you throw that thing straight up. Raise the roof, got it? Here we go... One, two, three, THROW!"

He got it right on the first try. The stunt kite is one big wing, a rainbow-colored stealth bomber with no tail or ribbons, and as soon as it left Lemmy's hands it caught the wind and pulled all the slack out of the lines. It took off like a rocket straight up, buzzing in the wind like a giant hornet. When it was directly overhead, it soared like a fighter jet at cruising altitude. "Okay guys, watch this."

I held one string in each hand, controlling the right and left wingtips. A gentle tug on one would cause the kite to dart in that direction. "I haven't had it very long, so right now figure-eights are the best I can do."

With alternating tugs, the kite pirouetted 150 feet above us, making crazy energetic eights while we watched. I caught on that if I made half of the eight bigger and bigger, I could get the kite to nosedive to earth, turning at the last second before zooming back up into the blue.

On the third or fourth big loop the kite nosedived into a blueberry bush. The strings fell slack in my hands.

"Again! More!" Lemmy cried out, running toward the crash site.

"That's bullshit," Megan said.

"It's no big deal," I said. "Lemmy will help me get it back up in no time. Hey, Lemmy, do you know what a fluffer is?"

"No, I mean the pile! It's literally bullshit. Look!"

Cresting the top of the hill was the silhouette of a head with horns. It was moving slowly and chewing, which was better than stomping and snorting, but it was eyeballing the same thing Lemmy was running toward: this strange bright bird that just crashed in his field.

"Lemmy! Stop."

He did, and the bull moved in. It approached slowly, but there was no doubt where it was going. It had a numbered yellow tag in one ear. Lemmy backed away slowly. "Easy there, Number 812. Easy, big boy."

The rest of the herd followed. By the time the lead bull reached the blueberry bush, at least ten other cattle crested the hill. Some calves, some cows, they formed a circle around the orange and yellow and purple thing flapping in the bush. The bull mooed at it.

"Lemmy, go stand by Megan."

One of the cows sniffed at it and jumped back when the bull head-butted the bush. It mooed again.

None of them are standing on the strings, I thought. I wonder if I can get it loose from here and pull it back to us. I tugged the strings and it shook the bush. The bull mooed and swatted with a horn.

The kite shook free, and with the strings tight it rode the breeze, about ten feet up. It buzzed and fluttered right above the herd's heads and all hell broke loose.

The cows scattered like extras in a disaster movie. They ran in every direction, mooing and tripping over bushes. Lemmy dove behind his pack for cover. The kite soared again.

"Don't look down," I shouted. "If we get trampled, I want this to be the last thing we see!"

. . .

When we arrived at the shelter, Fiddlin' Jim and Forager were already settled in. There was no fire, and there was no fish. Instead, the two of them were hunkered down behind a rhododendron bush. (These ones weren't blooming, and their leaves were smaller.) Forager's phone was in his dad's cooking pot to amplify the tinny blues it was playing. They each had a flask, and they giggled and slurred their greeting.

Jim offered me a swig. "How'd you guys like them ponies? That was pretty neat, huh?"

Lemmy shrugged. "Eh. They were okay. Everybody sees the ponies. We got to fly a kite with cows!" He returned to the shelter where I could hear Megan unpacking.

I stayed behind the bush until my hunger got the best of me and joined the other two at the table.

Megan was putting things away. "How do I smell?" she asked.

"I think you're asking the wrong person."

"You smell like you have been near animals all day," Lemmy said. "Soooo, I would say, like normal." He barely made it to the end of the sentence before snickering at himself. He blushed and used one closed fist to hide his smile.

"You smell fine." I looked toward the music and laughter. "Got a hot date? That's a four-star bush. Very exclusive; only seats three."

"I do, actually. I think I'm spending the night at Forager's place."

"You guys are going to share a tent?"

"Gonna try to."

Most thru-hikers' tents had barely enough room for one. "Good luck with that."

"Thanks."

"And hey, make sure those guys eat some food. I don't think their original plan was whiskey for dinner, but they're headed that way."

"Will do. Good night, Green Giant."

While Lemmy and I ate, a few late arrivals joined us, and after I hung my food, I was soon in my bag. I must have been exhausted because the next thing I heard was the birds. Lemmy was still asleep, the newcomers were still asleep, and the three people in the two tents behind the four-star bush were still asleep. One of the tents bulged ridiculously, a nylon sack full of knees and elbows.

My shelter pack-out routine was becoming pretty smooth, and because it was already too warm for coffee, I was ready to step off in 15 minutes. As I was leaving, the bulging tent unzipped. Voldemort's head popped through a slit and blinked at me.

I touched the brim of my hat. "Don't forget to go for a walk this morning!" She grunted and the zipper closed.

I needed this head start every morning for two reasons. The first reason was all around me. Horizontal shafts of golden light filtered through the morning mist. Spider webs hung like hammocks, sagging with dew, the entire world reflected upside down in every drop. And it was all mine. Mine and the birds.

The second reason was that all the rest of the gang were so much faster than me. Even the old guy. It was taking me 12 hours to travel as far as they did in ten. Endurance wasn't an issue; my legs, heart, and lungs were handling these 20s with ease. It was that damn bunched-up sock thing that was slowing me down. I would stop to fix them, and there was nothing to fix. I rubbed my feet. The shin thing went away after a couple weeks, I thought. So will the invisible sock thing.

So I would get started about an hour early and walk slower. That seemed to help. Throughout the day, one by one or in pairs, they'd pass me. We'd stop, hang out a while, and then move on. The last one would pass me by the end of the afternoon, and an hour or so later I'd get to the shelter and we'd all share stories from the day. Hiking apart was nice that way.

By the middle of the day, the terrain had really evened out, as I'd expected. But Virginia had a surprise in store. The first day of summer was near and all of the plants were way ahead of schedule. The grass in grassy meadows was waist high. Blackberry bushes and small spindly rhododendrons crowded the trail. For the first time, I had to hunch or even crouch as I walked, pushing branches and leaves and stalks and flowers and berries and thorns away from my face, just so I could even see where to put my foot. It was flat, but it was not boring.

When I emerged from the thicket, I checked for ticks. A quick visual scan of my arms and legs revealed nothing. I rolled my socks down to my ankles; no hitchhikers. I rolled my sleeves and poked around my armpits; no stowaways.

Just in case, I'd better remind those guys, I thought. I ripped a page from my notebook and wrote: *Check for ticks!* I drew my best tick and added a circle with a line through it. I impaled the note on a branch at eye level and continued north.

Nobody passed me, and when I arrived at the shelter, nobody was there.

Those guys looked pretty hung over, I thought. I bet they got a late start. I started a fire and ate dinner alone. Horizontal shafts of golden light filtered through the smoke and I had it all to myself. The birds weren't interested.

By the time it was dark, I began to wonder. I had passed another shelter earlier in the day, but that would have meant a super-short day for the crew. Lemmy went to bed early last night, so he had no excuse. They'd probably night hike, silly fuckers. I added a few big logs so they could see and still have coals. It was time for Green Giant to go to bed. It was hiker midnight.

I rolled out my bag and sat on the boards. I took off my shoes and socks. I shined my headlamp at my feet and in the span of one second I was startled, horrified, and then fascinated. My right big toenail was gone. The black crust, the white goo, gone. The top of the toe was covered by a thin transparent shell, like a dragonfly's wing. I touched it. It only hurt a little.

It had to be around here somewhere, I thought. I turned my sock inside out and shook it. Nothing.

I thought, when the hell did that happen? I never felt it go.

# 13

## BREAK

I BET THE GANG got soaked last night, I thought. Unless they stopped at that shelter midday, surely they tented in that rain. If they'd gotten up early with me we'd all be dry, not just me. Oh well, I'll get mine soon enough.

I took my time getting ready that morning. I had the shelter to myself and there was no one for me to disturb, so I made no effort to be quiet. There was no one to confer with either, so I made my plans aloud.

"Okay, Green Giant, depending on where they stopped last night you are either five or ten miles ahead. That's only two or three hours the way those guys hike. But," I checked the time, "they won't start for at least another hour. Which means…"

I chose a stopping point about 15 miles north of where I stood. Compared to the miles we'd been cranking out lately, this would be a short day for me. For my friends a few miles back, it would be a normal to above-average day. I wrote my plans in the log book and added, *I'll have the fire ready.*

I lingered around camp, which was a nice change. I sat on the picnic table and sipped coffee. The sun had only been up an hour and already it was warm. My right big toe was pretty tender where the nail had fallen off; I wrapped it with gauze and tape and carefully pulled on a sock. I winced.

Getting that shoe on is going to be tricky, I thought. Oh yeah, and walking. Better take a couple Advil preemptively.

I did these things, stood and stretched and paced a bit to test putting weight on that toe. It was relatively painless, and I was out of stall tactics, so I left. Slowly. There was no way I'd keep the lead for long.

After an hour or so of hiking I felt warmed up and forgot my toenail completely. Without realizing it, I settled back into my normal hiking speed and zoned out for a while, enjoying a series of rolling hills broken by periods of green tunnel.

My hiking trance was interrupted by voices calling my name from above. "Hey Green Giant!"

"I told you that was him."

I turned left and saw three young men sitting on a boulder about ten feet high. Two of them I recognized from Damascus: Dingo and Hungry Horse, the guys who had started at Springer Mountain a day after me. "How's it going, guys? Who's your friend?" My first thought was Bones, but this guy was too muscular.

His name was Johnny Oak, and he was shirtless and wore Ray-Bans. He was one of those rare hikers who kept a clean-shaven face. Dark curls hung in his eyes. "What up, Jolly Green? Sweet pack." We had the same pack.

"Actually there's no 'Jolly.' I mean, I am jolly. Most of the time, at least. But yeah, great pack, huh? I just got mine."

"Where's the rest of your crew?" Hungry Horse asked.

"Somewhere back there. I saw them yesterday morning. They looked pretty rough." I mimed sipping a bottle and screwed up my face.

"Might as well chill with us for a minute then," Dingo said.

Johnny Oak asked me how far I was going that day, and when I told him, he said they were headed there too and that was that. He also revealed that they were up on the rock to conduct a "safety meeting" and asked if I would care to join. Of course I would.

I climbed up onto the rock. These guys seem pretty cool, I thought. We're going to have a lot of fun together when the gang catches up tonight. And Johnny Oak, Dingo, Hungry Horse and I did have a lot of fun together that night. Just the four of us.

■   ■   ■

I usually like to know someone for a while before we spend the day naked together. But on the AT, where everyone you meet lives in the woods and carries everything on his or her back, friendships form faster than they would under normal circumstances.

I was taping my toe when Johnny Oak put his bare foot on the bench beside me. I looked up and was almost hit in the face by his penis. I jerked my head back with such force that I fell off the bench and into the shelter behind me.

He laughed. "Double-G! It's June 21st, bro. Time for the great outdoor pants-off dance-off."

Dingo offered me a hand. He was nude, too. "Holy shit, I forgot." I said. "It is Hike Naked Day."

Hungry Horse was still wearing his shorts, glasses, and baseball cap. Anyone stumbling into our camp would assume him to be the director of a very strange film. "What? I'll do it too. This bench has splinters."

"You have to go at least one mile for it to count," Dingo said.

Johnny Oak put on his sunglasses. "I'm walking like this until it gets dark or I get arrested."

"I guess I'd better strip down too," I said, and retreated to the stream behind the shelter so I could get naked in private. I don't know why I'm back here, I thought. I'm just going to walk back out there in the raw anyway. Leaving my shoes on, I removed my shirt, my hiking shorts and my underpants.

Motivated more by silliness than by modesty, I removed my hat and placed it over my front parts, cinching the chin strap around my waist and tightening it just above my butt. I walked back around the shelter and entered, stage left. "What do you think, guys? Feather up or feather down?"

Hungry Horse was now out of his shorts too. "Depends on who's around, I guess."

For a brief moment, I was glad the rest of my crew wasn't around.

Johnny Oak started toward the trail. "All right boys, let's get this sausage train a-rollin'."

The first day of summer was as hot as expected, and surprisingly dry. The guidebook suggested that some streams in Virginia might be intermittent, with a flow heavily dependent upon rain. The amount of rainfall felt normal to me, but then I was just passing through. What did I know?

Every stream I passed that morning was a wide dry ditch filled with rounded river rocks. These things must rage in the early spring, I thought. When the snow melts up high, there must be two or three weeks every year where they are almost dangerous. Today, just rocks. I carefully hopped among the flattest ones I could find, pretending there was water there anyway, making a game out of it. I almost lost my balance at the other side, surprising a sleepy group of hikers camped by the dry bank. I offered them a tip of my hat, which was awkward considering where it was.

Around lunchtime I caught up with my new hiking buddies at a gravel road in the middle of the woods. There were no cars because there was no parking lot. There was no trailhead and no sign. Just the trees, the hot gravel, my three naked companions, and a case of beer.

"This is a mirage, right? Because if it is, it's a shitty one. You guys are supposed to be hot chicks."

Dingo handed me a can. "Here's the hottest thing out here." It was warm. The handwritten sign on the box he pulled it from read TRAIL MAGIC FOR HIKERS. "There weren't any empties, so it must be fresh."

I pointed the can away from my face and popped the top. Foam sprayed in a jet and I caught the overflow with my mouth. I flicked the extra drops from my hand. "Hot or not, that hits the spot. I am thirsty as hell right now." I drank the beer too quickly and belched.

Dingo opened another. "Honestly," he said, "I'm just as excited for the calories as I am the buzz."

I agreed. "Good point. How many are left?"

We had another each, then stomped the empties flat. The rule was: You drink it, you carry it out. Whoever drinks the last one takes the box. We left that task, plus nine warm beers, for the next group. I counted two times four, and imagined Lemmy and Voldemort racing Fiddlin' Jim and Forager for that one leftover beer. No one wins that game, I thought. I wiped my sweaty forehead with my forearm.

As usual, Johnny Oak was first to cross the road. "I'm ready to book it, guys. I saw in one of the log books that there's a church group not too far ahead. I want to catch them. You coming?"

"I think I'm going to put my pants back on. I'll catch up."

I was also feeling the nagging urge to unbunch the bottoms of my socks again. I had almost reached the point of ignoring it; every time I checked there was nothing to see but perfectly smooth socks. Until that one time there was actually something to fix. The bandage from my toenail had worked itself free and somehow migrated down to the arch. Of course, that didn't explain why the other foot felt weird too, so now whenever I removed my shoe it was a gamble.

This time is was smooth socks and one new red toenail. Four lemons and a cherry: worst slot machine ever. I put my shoes back on.

When we finally caught up again that night, clothes back on, we built a huge fire and commiserated about the lack of water that day. There had been some real low points that afternoon. After the beer buzz wore off, the heat made everyone tired and grumpy. It was the first time I'd come close to running out of water on a hike in years. The distance between sources that day ended up being 16 miles.

"I was thirsty enough to drink pee," I said. "But not mine. Someone else's more hydrated than me."

The four of us lay side by side in the dark that night and fell asleep quickly. We had worked together, sweat and climbed and laughed together—hell, we had spent the day naked together.

In the morning, I found that we all had the same shelter routine: fast and efficient. We took advantage of the terrain and knocked out some big days, never dipping below 20. I was no longer worried about my crew catching me; based on the shelter spacing I was pretty sure I knew right where they were.

One night I wrote in the shelter log, *Only miles. No smiles.* When Dingo asked me what it meant I explained. "It's a spin on some graffiti we saw a while ago: *It's not about the miles, it's about the smiles.* I actually like the quote, but Voldemort was pissed that someone wrote it in black marker on the floor."

"Rightly so."

"Yeah, so we used to say it backwards to each other as a joke." I signed my name in case there was doubt.

"Those guys sound pretty cool. Can't wait to meet them all."

"Pretty soon." I opened my guidebook and pointed. "I'm pretty sure they're right here. And if we do a short day into Woods Hole Hostel here they'll either catch up that night or we'll see them as we're leaving the next morning."

"Excellent. I can't wait."

"Neither can I."

• • •

The guidebook describes Woods Hole Hostel as a "slice of heaven, not to be missed." There's nearly a full page more, but we were reading by headlamp at the end of a 24-mile day, so that first sentence really sealed the deal.

Dingo was the only one with a signal, so he made the reservation. I gave him Katie's number and asked him to text her our plans. She and I had no more visits scheduled, but Katie was still tracking my progress in anticipation of arranging upcoming mail drops. Plus, you know, love.

Our hike that day was only seven miles, although the first two included a steep 1,500-foot climb. The guys arrived before me despite my early start. I spent most of that big climb placing my feet gingerly. The red toenail was blackening, and now both pinky toes had somehow bent themselves sideways. At least I wasn't getting the weird sock thing anymore; the bottoms of my feet were numb. If only the tops were numb too, I thought. Then I could really get some work done.

Early in the afternoon I found a hand-painted wooden sign at a gravel road. It told me to go left another half mile to the hostel. Woods Hole is on a 100-acre property surrounded on three sides by national forest, with almost a thousand acres of privately owned land on the other side. At the heart of the place sits a chestnut log cabin built in the 19th century—remember, there aren't any chestnuts anymore.

Neville and Michael run the place. Neville's grandparents, Tilly and Roy Wood, first turned the old cabin into a hostel years ago. When I arrived, I found Dingo and Johnny Oak smiling and seated in big comfortable chairs on the wraparound porch down at the bunkhouse. An acoustic version of "Norwegian Wood" was coming from the kitchen. I whistled. "Nice place. Anyone home up at the big house?"

The music stopped. Hungry Horse answered from inside. "They left a note, should be back soon. There's food and a ledger in here. Good stuff, too!" The song continued.

I threw my pack on the deck next to the others and fell into a couch. "Is there ice cream?"

Johnny Oak nodded. The song finished and he clapped. I craned my neck to see into the kitchen. "That was you? Holy shit!"

Hungry Horse strummed a chord and put a guitar on the table. "Thanks. This was on the porch. Any requests?"

"As long as it's that good, anything."

I moved to the hammock and a few songs later we heard Neville's car pull into the driveway. She had just taken the previous night's guests to the nearest town for groceries and then back to the trail. Her car was full of new hikers who were eager to join us at the bunkhouse.

After introductions, Neville brought us huge cutting boards piled with loaves of bread and bricks of cheese. "The bread is homemade and so is the cheese," she told us. The hostel revolved around sustainability. Chickens, cows, sheep, and vegetables were in the fields and on the menu. If you ate it at Woods Hole Hostel, it was probably grown there, or at least nearby. They even made their own soap.

"How do you do it all?" I asked. "It's not just the two of you?"

"Everyone who stays, helps." The way she said this was pleasant, but she didn't blink when she said it either, and everyone nodded.

A young man with a full beard entered the room. His overalls were splashed with blue paint. He held a bucket in one hand and a blender in the other. "Nev, can I mix paint in this?"

She turned slowly, and again without blinking said, "Michael, I don't think that's such a good idea."

"But it's milk-based paint." He blinked. He left.

"Sometimes things get a bit frantic around here, so everyone's help is welcome."

We devoured the cheese and Hungry Horse played something classical that I recognized but couldn't quite name. We spent the rest of the afternoon in the kitchen with Neville assisting with dinner. There were pizzas made with sausage from the pigs who had eaten last year's scraps. Pans of pasta and vegetables overflowed beside several large walnut salad bowls. There were plates of homemade bread, with dipping oils and honey from the bees just over the hill.

Before we ate, we stood in a circle around the table. Neville said, "I want us to all join hands. Before we eat together, please tell the group your name. Say where you're from, if you like, but do say one thing that you are thankful for."

The hiker in the kilt started, followed by the girl with the buzzcut. The guy with one fingernail painted purple said his piece and then it was my turn.

"I'm Gary." My new hiking companions looked surprised. Everyone had used their trail names. I don't know why I didn't, it just came out. "I'm from North Carolina, and I'm thankful for my friends." How far back were they? I'd forgotten how long it had been since I had seen them. Maybe that was it. I was Gigante Verde now, or G-Dub, or G-Money, or whatever name of the day Johnny Oak came up with. Maybe the new challenge would be for him to come up with a hundred more between here and Katahdin.

I looked at them, but I didn't say their names, just in case. I had trailed off and they were already nodding at the guy with the mohawk and tattoos. But Neville was looking right at me. I think she knew.

■ ■ ■

We enjoyed our stay at Woods Hole Hostel so much that we made special arrangements to stay a second night while still making miles. We would leave our heaviest gear at the hostel, and Neville would drive us to the next town, ten miles north. We would buy our groceries there and then hike south, back to the hostel where we could enjoy another night with the cows and the ducks and the amazing food.

Initially, Neville had a rough time convincing us to do this. "It feels wrong," Dingo said. "I know we're still walking, and still passing every white blaze. But we're going the wrong way!"

Once we managed to convince each other that it wasn't cheating, we jumped in the car and soon forgot the whole exaggerated moral dilemma. I was happy to walk another short day, especially with a lightened load. My feet loved it, too.

During our second night at the hostel, I stood on a hill and had enough signal for a brief talk with Katie. She had not heard any news from the gang. Over dinner I threw their names around during trail gossip, but no one had even heard of them.

The following morning Neville gathered us on the lawn. She led the group through a yoga routine and then we had breakfast. After everyone was fed, she drove us ten miles north to town again. This time we brought all our gear; those ten miles were behind us as of yesterday.

The Vortex was strong. Our stay had been incredible, our packs were full, and the climb was steep and hot. I had never tried yoga before and our session that morning relaxed me and loosened me up. I was definitely not "fired up and ready to crush mountains," as Johnny Oak put it. So I took my time.

We had another relatively easy day planned, so I surprised myself when I stopped short. Right there on the trail not ten feet away was the cutest little campsite I had ever seen. It was barely a 20-foot wide circle of flat packed dirt surrounded by sparse trees and ferns. Two chairs made from flat rocks and a small stone table sat beside a fire ring. One chair in particular called to me.

At first, I told myself I was only going to sit on it for a second. See how it feels. It was sturdy and the flat granite was cool on my back. I leaned forward and straightened the edge of the fire ring. I spied the perfect branch for my food bag.

Already moving in, I thought. There were enough rocks to construct a small windbreak behind the fire ring too. That would be next. Already remodeling. Still two hours from sunset, the woods were already dark. Crickets were chirping and the tiny circle of light from my fire was the entire world, a flickering orange disk floating in a dark sea of rustles and chirps.

I thought about Dingo, Hungry Horse, and Johnny Oak. If I was where I thought I was, the shelter we all agreed upon was just a few miles ahead. I'd probably walk up on them packing in the morning, or catch them at the next one at the end of the day. It seemed like no one tented anymore, which made it easier to guess where people might be.

This is nice, I thought. It's like I'm on a vacation. I'm taking a little backpacking trip in the middle of my hike. I warmed my feet by the fire and enjoyed simply being alone for a few minutes. Punch me out — I'm on break.

■ ■ ■

Those motherfuckers, I thought. I reread the note: *Green Giant: We got here early, headed to the next one. Night hike? Catch up! –HH.* The next one was almost ten miles from where I stood. I closed the book and put it back in the shelter. Those sons of bitches. That ten miles plus the five I just did from my cozy little fire ring separated us by a whole day now. Night hike my ass. Screw those guys.

I didn't stay mad for long. After all, we had shared a lot of firsts together, they were cool guys, and we did have plans to take a zero up at Daleville in a few days. Maybe I'd catch them on the second day and make up my zero the next time.

Hungry Horse's gentle goading had worked. I was now suddenly "fired up and ready to crush mountains." Which gave me an idea. I opened the log book again and wrote: *This message is for Fiddlin' Jim and Forager ONLY: Ditch the girl. She's slowing you down. There's a reason they considered women to be bad luck on sailing ships. Put on your headlamps and get up here with all the cool people! –Green Giant.*

I added a smiley face, in case it wasn't obvious that I was joking. This needs something, I thought. I added a patchy beard and gave him a hat with a feather. There, I thought. Perfect.

My burning desire to crush miles lasted about as long as my misplaced anger. By midday I had already taken three breaks to rest my feet, so I redirected some of that anger toward them. At the end of the day it was just me and another empty wooden box in the forest. Some asshole had tossed the entire log book into the fire the night before. I was too tired to write anyway.

Between here and Daleville lie some of the best miles that Virginia has to offer. I hiked to Dragon's Tooth, a colossal granite spike atop a rocky ridge with a far reaching view of the valley below. The path to it was miles of sharply angled boulders that caused me to tilt in every direction except the one I was trying to go. I rolled my ankles repeatedly, and my feet slid around inside my shoes, surpassing the limit of what their numbness could mask.

I stood beside the monolith and posed for a picture, hoping my grimace would pass for a smile. On my way down the other side, I allowed myself to curse and swear loudly at the rocks, surprising a young boy and his father as I rounded a corner.

I hiked to McAfee Knob, which is hands-down the most photographed vista on the AT. McAfee Knob is a cantilevered platform of rock which juts out like a diving board over a frightening chasm. It is perfectly safe and stable—it could support a herd of elephants—but when photographed from one famous spot, the hiker posing on this ledge could easily pass for a true daredevil.

The night prior to McAfee Knob, I shared a shelter with a Boy Scout Troop and a class of fraternity pledges. The pledges brought a bundle of pine boards for the fire pit, presumably because they didn't think there would be wood in the woods. They lit the boards on fire and then produced some steaks, which they impaled on long sticks and dangled in the flames until the thunderstorm began. The rain turned the trail to mud, and the spectacular view from the knob was entirely shrouded in fog.

Throughout this I managed to keep a pretty good average per day, but I still found myself 19 miles shy of Daleville on a Saturday morning. The outfitters there would be holding a care package from Katie. They would close at 4 p.m. and not reopen until after the weekend. It was going to be close.

The only way I could think of to hike 19 miles by midafternoon was to start early and not take breaks. So I was up before the sun and had second breakfast on the march. The little springs and waterfalls which usually held my attention had to suffer my neglect as I was pulled forward by an urgent deadline.

Should I go to the outfitters first, or to the hotel first? I guess it would depend on which one was closer to the trail. Without stopping, I reached into my pocket and looked at my pages. Hotel first—got it. Then I guess I dump my pack, head to the outfitters... Shit. Find the guys first, split the room. Hey, I just saved money by not joining them for the first night.

It was 3:45 when I walked into Daleville. The outfitters closed at 4, so I hiked past the hotel. As soon as I was out from the trees and onto the pavement I began to sweat. I stretched each stride to the maximum. My heels pounded the asphalt as my poles clicked faster. Cars zoomed by while I paced at the light. I made it with minutes to spare. Cookies, new shoes, and a handwritten love letter. Totally worth it.

I had to backtrack to the hotel. There wasn't room in my pack for the box of goodies, so I cradled it while I circled the pool looking for familiar faces. There were hikers all over the place, but none whom I recognized. I asked around until I found someone who had seen Hungry Horse and the guys. They'd already been here and gone.

Goddamn it.

The only good thing about missing them was that they'd vacated the last available room, which was now mine if I wanted it. A double. Fuck it. I'll take the double.

I put my box on the counter, signed the register, and paid for the room. As I picked up my box, I saw that it had been sitting on top of a log book just like the ones in the shelters. On that day's page I drew a smiley with beard, hat, and feather, then thanked the clerk for my key and carried everything to my room on the second floor.

When I opened the door, the air conditioning gave me goosebumps. My shirt was soaked from racing to the outfitters. I hadn't had a sip of water since lunch and my feet were on fire. I dropped everything onto the floor and collapsed on the bed farthest from the door.

I could just go to sleep right now, I thought. No shower. No barbecue. No ice cream. Just this bed, this air conditioner, and the hum of the mini-fridge. I'll just close my eyes for a second.

The phone rang.

Son of a...

"Hello?"

"Hello, sir?" asked the desk clerk. "This is Gary, yes?"

I had been so close to being asleep. So close. I grumbled, "Yes."

She covered the phone with her hand, asked someone a muffled question, and came back a second later. "Are you Green Giant?"

I sat up. "Yes." Why was the desk clerk calling me by my trail name? I didn't sign my credit card slip that way, did I? Was I that tired?

"There's someone here who would like to speak to you."

She handed the phone to someone else. "Hey, buddy!" It was Lemmy. "Deed you miss meeeeeee?"

## NEW RULES

I OPENED THE DOOR and there he was.
"Buddy!" He pushed past me and dropped his pack. He plopped onto the bed nearest the door and lay spread-eagle. His boots were caked with mud.

"Lemmy, this isn't a shelter. And even if it was—"

He sat up. "I thought I would never see you again, Green Giant!"

"I missed you too, buddy." I pointed to the still-open door. "But I need you to knock the mud off those boots."

"Ooh, already we are sharing a room and we are knocking boots! What will Katie think?" He snickered his way to the door, threw his boots outside, and shut it. "Nobody will steal those." He dumped his pack and removed his socks.

"Man, am I glad to see you." I told him. "What's it been, 11 or 12 days?" I could remember where I'd last seen him, just not when. "So? What's up with Megan and those guys?"

He looked up from his pile. "Those two are professional pink blazers. They take a zero at every town."

"What about Jim?"

"He gets a room, they get a room. They are going to run out of money before they run out of miles."

"Well, how far back are they?"

He moved some bags from the floor to the bed. "I don't know. I left them a week ago and try to catch up with you. I would think"—his voice dropped an octave and he shook his fist— "today I will catch you, Green Giant! But then you would go *five* more miles." He spread out more things on the bed.

"Well, you got me." I smiled at him and his mess. "I'm going to go do laundry. Do you want to go with me to the barbecue place after? Wait—you can do barbecue, right? I've seen you eat bacon."

Lemmy shot me a stern look and kept unpacking.

"What? I don't know these things." I pointed. "Okay. That's my bed. I want you to imagine an invisible line down the middle of this room. Your side, my side. Got it? Good. I'll be back in an hour."

I took a towel from the bathroom, said goodbye, and closed the door behind me. The laundry room was down a flight of metal stairs, around the swimming pool and down some more stairs. I wrapped the towel around my waist and removed everything else, replacing my shirt with my raincoat. I sat on a folding chair and studied the guidebook while the machines churned and hummed.

An hour later I returned to a disaster. Before I could open the door I had to cross a moat. The AC unit in the window was dripping steadily into one of Lemmy's boots directly beneath it. The boot was soaked, but clean; all of its mud was now in the moat. When I opened the door, a wall of steam blasted me.

The air conditioner was no longer cooling the room. It had given up the battle for temperature and was now trying desperately to suck the moisture out of the air and dump it into Lemmy's boot outside. The cloud of mist overwhelming the poor air conditioner poured forth from the bathroom door like orcs from Mordor. Lemmy was inside splashing in the tub while singing the theme to a Japanese cartoon playing on his phone.

His bed was completely covered with gear, food and clothes. The only chair in the room was lying on its side and there were wet towels everywhere. My bed remained untouched. The sheets and covers were still pulled tight. In the center of the bed were my pack and my hat. Everything beyond the invisible line was dripping chaos. "Is that you, Green Giant?"

"If it was anyone else we'd be in a lot of trouble." I waved away the mist.

"Will you do me a favor?"

"Maybe."

"Can you get us some more towels?"

"How did you—" I didn't want to know.

The hotel office was down by the laundry room, and I was slowing down. I still hadn't eaten after walking 19 miles (the candy bar in the laundry room had long since worn off), it was getting dark, the barbecue place was far away, and my feet hurt. Nevertheless I met the clerk with a smile when I requested more towels. "A lot more," I said. "My roommate is insane."

On the way back to the room I called Katie. I asked if she'd heard anything from Megan but she hadn't. Dingo said hi though. I walked a few laps around the pool to get more time with her and less in the steamy jungle. When I got there, Lemmy was trying to dry off the television with a moist shirt. I was ready to call it a night. "Fuck the barbecue, Lemmy. My feet and I are ordering pizza."

He dropped the shirt on the floor and accepted a towel. He thanked me and put a soggy wad of bills in my hand. "What's this for?" I asked.

"My half of the room."

I kicked the wet shirt to its side of the invisible line. "Your half of the room. Thank you."

"You're welcome." He resumed wiping the TV.

I counted the money. "Lemmy, you gave me too much. This isn't half; you gave me the whole amount."

"No. It is right."

I did the math. "We're taking a zero day here tomorrow, so here is how much it costs."

"No. We are not taking a zero. We are taking a double zero! I already told the lady when she called you on the phone. I told her, 'Green Giant' and 'Me no English.' She put it on your card. That is your half."

"Lemmy, why do we need to sit here for two days?"

"Because I have a package at the outfitters and they are closed until Monday." He handed me the dusty, dripping towel and turned on the TV. I was glad he was back, but damned if I knew why.

．．．

Breakfast at the hotel included do-it-yourself waffles. Lemmy did it himself three times, and the stack on his plate nearly toppled on his way back to our table. He piled on strawberries, whipped cream, and powdered sugar. He had two large glasses of orange juice and was going through a pat of butter with every other bite.

"Lemmy, you look like you've lost some weight." I spooned berries on top of my pancakes and poured syrup on top of that. I stabbed a sausage patty with my fork, dunked it in the syrupy berry mess and shoved the entire thing in my mouth.

He said, "You look thinner, too."

After breakfast we checked out and hiked to the grocery store. Because the water sources had been scarce, and because I wanted to continue my tenting phase, I planned a few meals that weren't dehydrated. That would get me one or two nights of freedom. No water? No problem. I started with something I called "hiker pizza"—flour tortillas, a stick of pepperoni, a tube of tomato paste, and a block of the hardest cheese I could find. This was much tastier than bags of dry noodles, but it was also a few pounds heavier.

On our way back to the trail I asked Lemmy to wait for me outside the post office. "I'll only be a minute. I need to make up for this extra weight. I'm going to mail home my sleeping bag."

He asked me if I was crazy, but I reassured him. "This thing weighs two pounds. I needed it when there was hail in the Smokies, but for the last three nights it's been 70 degrees."

"That is cold."

"Now you're the one who's crazy." I still had my liner, a fist-sized bundle of cloth. It was only a few ounces and was meant to supplement my sleeping bag, but still it was enough to make me sweat sometimes in my tent with the rain fly up. I'd be fine. "What's the worst thing that can happen? I get a little chilly one night? I'm not going to die."

It was the same logic I'd used when I was nervous about ditching my glasses; by now I'd forgotten that I even wore glasses. I was the only customer in the post office, and when I came back out Lemmy still had his pack on.

"Remind me the next time we get to a place with a scale to weigh my pack."

"Are you trying to become ultralight? Like Bones?"

Bones, the handsome skeleton Lemmy introduced me to back in Damascus, had been a practicing ultralight backpacker. These maniacs carry tents that use trekking poles for support and weigh less than a pound. They carry no stove and no spare clothes, and definitely no Schnozzle bag. It's common practice to snap the handle off of one's toothbrush to prevent carrying unnecessary *grams*.

The payoff for all this obsession was the ability to hike 30 or more miles per day. I had been passed multiple times by a crew doing just that. They'd knock out a hundred miles in three days and then park in town for three or four, staying drunk and watching World Cup matches. We would see them in town, and three days later they would whiz by us on the trail, carrying only tarps and water. We invented the term "soccer blazing" just for these guys.

"I'm nowhere near that level of crazy, Lemmy. I'm just curious, that's all." I was trying to make things easier on my feet, too. Two days of rest had helped, but we had only been hiking for an hour and I already needed a couple more Advil.

The climb out of Daleville was gentle, but rocky. And hot. By midday I was almost out of water. We came upon a sign pointing to a shelter a tenth of a mile east of the AT. It was a short, steep climb, but there was a spring up there. Lemmy didn't need water so I went up without him.

I came back with two full bottles and a story. "I just met the two most interesting people. Her name was Sunshine, his was Mad Science, she was topless, he had blue hair, and they carried matching umbrellas."

I was just about to mention that they each had one purple fingernail when Lemmy interrupted me. "What is that sound?"

"I don't know. It sounds like a lawn sprinkler, but faster."

"Is it bees?" It was getting louder.

"Maybe cicadas? But it's too... Shit! Lemmy, stop."

It was a rattlesnake, a timber. I don't know how we missed it—this one was yellow. Lemmy showed no fear, only curiosity. "Don't touch it," I told him, concentrating to keep my voice calm. "He's just letting us know he's here. He's more afraid of us than we are of him."

The snake was a few feet to the right of the trail. Its buzzing tail stood at the center of its coiled body while his arrow of a head watched us, occasionally flicking a forked tongue our way.

"Just move slowly and keep your distance." The snake watched us pass.

■ ■ ■

Just north of Daleville the Appalachian Trail stays near the Blue Ridge Parkway, crossing the famous road in many places. To Lemmy this was just another road, so he was surprised when I explained that it's like the AT for cars, winding almost 500 miles through the mountains.

"Do the cars have to hitchhike to town for supplies?"

"I know you're joking, but yeah, they kind of do. It's two-lane blacktop with no stoplights or gas stations. Its only purpose is to be pretty. I wish there were more roads like it."

Just as our guidebooks were dotted with tiny camera symbols wherever there was a view, the parkway is punctuated with pulloffs. We reached the overlook for Taylor's Mountain around dinnertime. We had heard the occasional car or motorcycle as we approached from the woods, but none stopped. The overlook was all ours.

We were leaving the rolling hills and farms behind and starting into an eternity of long parallel ridges. The parkway was atop one, a ribbon of black with steep drops on either side. The view to the left was the same as the view to the right. No more random horizons, these mountains were like the wrinkles in a bunched-up tablecloth. The shadows between them deepened as the sun slid west.

"What do you say, buddy? Not a bad place to spend the night, eh?"

"What about the cars?"

"No one drives up here at night. The whole point is the view. It's all ours."

I put my tent beside a copse of trees just in case there were any headlights later. We had nearly half an acre of flat space to work with, and Lemmy pitched his tent two feet from mine. Once our camp was made, we crossed the road and ate dinner while sitting on the hefty wooden guardrail overlooking the valley. Distant clouds were stacking.

"This guard rail, that sign," I said, "it all reminds me of home. I can see this road from my front porch. If we turned south tomorrow and walked 300 miles, I'd be home."

Instead, we awoke the next morning and kept walking north.

Throughout the day the big clouds we had seen the night before seemed to chase us, riding a cool breeze that followed us as the sky darkened. It was supposed to be another big day, making 22 miles to take us up and over 2,500 feet and past Thunder Ridge shelter. As we climbed higher, the mountain gave us a better view of the approaching storm. The breeze turned into a steady gale, and fat drops began falling. As soon as we saw the shelter we broke into a full run. I almost slipped at the entrance, while Lemmy dove onto the boards, sliding across on his stomach. I shook off my raincoat and the two ladies already inside greeted us.

Garnet was first to introduce herself. She was slender, athletic, and had long gray hair. Her friend sported a platinum blond haircut reminiscent of early '80s Madonna. She had ten purple fingernails and ten purple toenails. Her name: Purple. "It's short for 'Purple Paint Pimp,'" she told us. "But that takes too long to say."

I asked if she had anything to do with all the purple fingernails I'd been seeing lately. "I confess. Everyone who camps with me gets painted. There are a lot more up ahead than there are behind though." A flash of lightning was immediately followed by a crack of thunder. My arm hairs stood up. "Looks like you're next." She smiled.

"It looks like this shelter is going to live up to its name, too," Garnet said. We huddled against the inside wall while the wind threw moist spray at us. Turning our backs on each other for privacy, we changed into dry clothes, then moved to a corner where Purple painted one of Lemmy's fingernails and then one of mine.

I examined my fingernail at arm's length. "Nice work. This doesn't mean we're going steady or anything, does it?"

The rain and wind persisted and soon it became obvious that we weren't going to walk any further that day. Not without changing back into wet clothes, at least. I asked if anyone would mind if I boiled some noodles. Given the weather, we all breached shelter etiquette and cooked inside. While we ate, Lemmy produced his sketchbook. "Are you going to draw us in the rain?" I asked.

"No. I have some questions for you. Can you tell me what some words mean? I wrote them down."

Purple and Garnet were both eager to help. "Sure, Lemmy," I told him. "Go ahead."

"Okay. This first one I don't know how to say. Pro... pro..." The word was *procrastinate*. We told him what it meant and helped him say it. "Pro... crass... This one is hard," he said. "I will do it later."

Purple looked at me and whispered, "Is he serious?"

"I can never tell. What's the next word?"

"Okay, this one should be easy. It is *taint*."

The ladies looked at me and frowned. I shrugged. "Ah, it's like when something spoils, like when meat goes bad. We say it is tainted."

"This does not make sense," he said. "A guy at the last shelter said to his friend, 'I am going to punch you in the taint.' What body part is this?"

Garnet retreated to the other side of the shelter and started rummaging through her pack. Purple crossed her arms and glared at Lemmy and then at me. "Okay, Lemmy," I said. "I think we can practice new words later."

"I have one more. What is *blumpkin*?"

I stood. "All right! I need water. Who wants to come with me? Lemmy? You need water. Come on."

"I don't—"

"Come on."

I walked into the storm and Lemmy followed. We stood by the spring without our water bottles. "Lemmy, do you know the word *appropriate*?" I didn't wait for his reply. "You might want to take a minute and get to know who you're talking to first before you start throwing around words like those."

Why was I having this conversation? Why did I need to be Lemmy's keeper? Was it because he always put his tent so close to mine?

He shrugged. "Why should I care? I will never see these people again."

"You don't know that. Remember when you thought you'd never see me again?"

He said nothing. After a few seconds he batted his eyelashes at me.

"I don't know what that's supposed to be, but it's not going to work." I wiped rain from my face. "And don't try that 'Me no English' crap either. I'm on to you. You called me 'fragrant' the other day."

"Well, it is true." He did the eyelashes thing again. How could I possibly stay mad?

The storm that night brought a cold front with it. The temperature dropped nearly 30 degrees in an hour, and I'd just soaked my only dry clothes so I could stand in the rain and yell at my only friend. My down sleeping bag was most likely in a box on my porch back home, doing me no good at all. In the morning my muscles were sore from shivering. I had secretly hoped to wake with Lemmy's arm around me, but instead I learned another important trail lesson: Pack light, freeze at night.

■ ■ ■

Lemmy apologized, which was good because we shared a shelter with Purple and Garnet for the next two nights. I temporarily became a full-time tent dweller until the cold front passed. While I might not have had a sleeping bag anymore, if I wore all my clothes inside the tent I was at least protected from the wind, unlike in the shelter.

On our third morning together we all began the day by wishing each other a happy Fourth. It was Independence Day. I had been hiking for two months. Lemmy and the ladies left and I lingered. I was punchy from lack of sleep; each night had been spent shivering.

Who cares, I thought. There's no one to complain to, so pack up and get walking. One thing before I left, though: a note in the log for Megan, Forager, and Fiddlin' Jim. I still had no idea if they were right behind me, days away, or gone all together. Nevertheless, I described my plans in detail. *Green Giant and Lemmy—Headed into Glasgow for fireworks and food.* I drew my bearded smiley and closed the book.

I almost managed to zone out and just hike, but was constantly distracted by a high-pitched buzzing. My first thought as I scanned the ferns around me was that I was being stalked by a swarm of unseen bees. The buzzing continued while I walked and seemed to come from all around. Definitely not a rattlesnake, I thought. Unless snakes swarm.

Was it coming from above? I looked up and saw only trees. Now that the sound had my full attention, I focused intensely on finding the source. I cupped my ears and faced every direction. Still no clue, although I briefly detected a high-pitched whine behind it.

I snapped my head upward again when I clearly heard something knock against a high branch. My eyes caught the movement easily, but my brain was not quite ready to accept what they reported. A white plastic square hung in the air 40 feet above. It had four spinning rotors, one flashing red light, and a camera. I was being followed by a drone.

I waved at it, and a second later the rotors dipped left, then right, as the pilot acknowledged that he'd been spotted. The craft whizzed ahead, moving north along the trail. It stopped at the edge of a clearing just ahead and the rotors dipped again, front then back.

Each time I got within ten feet of the device, it would wave at me and recede again, until at last it soared 50 more feet straight up and retreated behind a distant pile of rocks to the left of the trail. The whining buzz rose in pitch, steadied, and then dropped as the thing landed behind the pile.

Two silhouettes scrambled to the top of the pile and waved. I gave a thumbs up and continued north.

■   ■   ■

The Appalachian Trail is rich with tradition. For instance, some people carry a pebble from one end to the other. The trail name is a tradition. One of the most popular is to jump into the James River, a dizzying leap from the longest footbridge on the entire AT. Lemmy said he'd wait for me at the bridge, where we planned to dive in, swim to the parking lot along the opposite shore, and stick our thumbs out. That is, after first stashing our packs and dry clothes along the far bank.

I saw the bridge but I didn't see Lemmy. I also saw a man with a badge and a gun. He smiled broadly and greeted me. Then he warned me that he was ticketing jumpers today and wished me a happy Fourth. I wished him the same and began the long walk across the bridge.

About halfway across I stopped. I leaned across the railing and looked down at the water. Good lord, I thought, I'm glad that officer was there—this looks damn scary. While I stared into the abyss, a horn started honking. I tried to ignore the sound, but it was backed up by a voice, one I recognized. "Green Giant! Run! Hurry!" I shielded my eyes and squinted.

Lemmy was waving frantically from the passenger seat of a beat-up red pickup. The front bumper was rusted and hung askew. The tailpipe popped rhythmically, a timer counting down to departure. "Run!"

I ran, and suddenly, as my feet pounded on the boards, white hot bolts of pain shot up from the soles of my feet through my shins and into my knees. What the fuck? I winced and slowed to a quick walk, gritting my teeth against each quick step, and soon I was in the grass. Much better.

There was already someone in the cab between Lemmy and the driver. "Get in back, Green Giant!"

The driver tapped the horn and waved. "Hop on in the back there. Just throw your pack in the canoe." A single canvas strap, worn to threads, barely held the boat in place. Surely the additional weight of my pack would cause it and all of my belongings to go bouncing down the road at some point. Nevertheless I obeyed. I wedged myself between the wheel well and the canoe, grabbed something, and held on. Tires spun, gravel sprayed, and we bounced out onto the winding blacktop.

I took off my hat and sat on it while the wind whipped around me. The world raced away in reverse. I heard a knock on the window from inside the cab. Through my own reflection I could just make out one meaty forearm showing a thumbs-up held just so to perfectly convey, "Everything alright back there?" I responded in kind with my own thumb and the truck bounced along.

A few sharp turns later and there was another knock on the window. This time the glass slid open, and the same big hairy arm handed me half a beer. It was cold. I happily grabbed the bottle and shouted my thanks over the wind and added, "YEAH!"

The glass slid shut. "Man, he's so excited," someone said amid muffled yukking from inside. The truck swayed left and right as we climbed higher. Center lines were merely a suggestion. As the trees rushed by, the sun strobed on my face. I tightened my grip on the canoe and downed the last of the beer in two long gulps. "Happy birthday, America!" I thought as a piece of garbage flew out of the truck.

. . .

If I stood on my toes and stretched my neck, I could almost kiss the brontosaurus on the mouth. "Take a few steps back, Lemmy, and squat down. That should make me look taller."

There's a lot to like about Glasgow, Va. Start with the one road through the center of town which you never have to look both ways before crossing because no one is ever on it. The guidebook told us of a free "hiker pavilion" at the edge of town, essentially a slightly larger version of a shelter but with running water, electricity, and a huge stack of seasoned oak from the trees that were felled to clear the land and build the box. We were on our way to the pavilion when we came upon a life-sized fiberglass dinosaur in the vacant lot next to the grocery store. A fiberglass caveman wielding a club was mounted on its back.

"Does it look like I'm kissing it?"

Lemmy sat in the grass and aimed his camera. "You look bigger than a dinosaur, Green Giant! Hold that pose." Click. "Epic!"

Purple and Garnet were already at the pavilion, joined by a good-sized crew of section hikers. Technically the pavilion was for thru-hikers, but there was plenty of bunks and firewood to spare. While I set up my tent, everyone started talking about fireworks.

As dusk fell, fast whistles and pops echoed from backyards and through the hills surrounding the town. Kids waved sparklers and occasionally something big and bright enough to certainly be illegal would rise up from one of the farms at the edge of the valley.

We made our way to a softball field behind the gas station, where the aluminum bleachers made a perfect viewing stand. There was no official display; everything was being launched from yards and cow pastures. The gas station lady abandoned her post and watched too, enjoying a beer and a smoke out at the picnic table behind the old place. We had already visited with her on our way to the park. While we paid for our ice cream sandwiches she gave us the town gossip. The guy at the old Bryson place was up to something. Rumor had it he might plant corn.

We ate and drank while the sky turned black. Two farms on opposite ends of town were taking turns one-upping each other. A barn to the west lit up with a flash, followed by a resonating *THUFF!* A rocket of silent sparks punched through wispy clouds, vanishing at its apex into a bloom of dazzling orange trails. A second later came the boom and sizzle. Cheers and applause came from various locations. Someone far off hooted and whistled.

The farm to the east answered the call. Three bright flashes illuminated the house, barn, and half the town's cows. *FOOF! FOOF! FOOF!* Three brilliant orbs shot straight up, each dragging a spiral column of fire and smoke behind: one red, one white, and one blinding blue. A second-stage booster exploded in each, sending the flames even higher and faster, finally bursting into impossibly tall flowers of light. The shock wave thumped my chest when the booms arrived.

A third farm joined the fray, and in no time everyone was shooting everything they had. Bright flashes revealed smoke trails hanging in the air like giant weeping willows, each a ghost of the light that made them. When it was over we all smelled like beer and gunpowder.

Sporadic fast whistles and pops still issued from backyards as we returned to the pavilion. There were no more sparklers; the kids were all in bed. As we sat around the fire, the farmers found their duds and misfires. We still heard occasional explosions, but the time between them was growing. The beer was almost gone and we were starting to repeat stories. The crickets had relieved the fireflies and someone mentioned bed.

Then Bones arrived. No one heard him before he stepped into the firelight. He simply appeared, like a ghost entering the parlor. The ghost of a skeleton. His stride was less than the length of his own foot, and he wasn't so much walking as perpetually falling forward, a few aching inches at a time. His cheeks were wet and when he stopped, he leaned on his poles. He was weeping.

Garnet and one of the section hikers jumped up and hurried to him. "What is it?" she asked. He held up a hand and made no answer.

Someone took his pack. Someone else offered him a stump for a seat. He collapsed onto it, nearly falling into the fire. Lemmy gave him water and everyone listened closely while he whispered what was wrong. It was shin splints. The pain was horrible. "But that's not what's worst," he said. Snot dripped into his beard and he sniffed. "It's the thought that I might have to quit."

I sat on my stump, stunned. Sure, I'd heard about various people leaving the trail. I had even known a few of them. But I'd never been there to see it happen.

*Never say goodbye on the trail.* I knew Bones. I liked Bones. If he dropped out, I might have to break one of the first rules I learned out here. And if that happened, all bets were off.

# 15

# EVERYDAY

HOLY SHIT, I'm still in Virginia.
I finally know what to say when someone asks me about my typical day. Everything I do is about economy of motion. Maintaining momentum. Every action has a method that has been rehearsed a thousand times. Every action has been trimmed to the minimum necessary steps.

I'm usually fully awake around 3 a.m. This surprised me initially, but it makes sense. I'm usually asleep by 9 p.m. Hard. No dreams, no memories. And when I wake up at 3, I feel great—at least mentally. Sometimes it's just because I feel the need to turn over, but more often I'm awake because my legs have cramped. A few minutes of stretching always helps, but it's impossible to do so in the confines of my sleeping bag, so I soon find myself standing, and since I'm up I might as well pee. Good lord, I'm turning into my grandfather.

If I'm in a shelter, I've already placed a small bottle of Advil and some water near my head. If I'm in my tent, they're tossed into the corner. I keep a wad of tissue in the bottle to prevent rattling. I never need light for this, and soon I'm asleep again.

Time no longer matters, but it's probably 5:30 when the birds start chirping. Unless it's raining, in which case I wake up because my body is done sleeping. I don't like to get to camp late, so I start early. My personal motto: If you don't want to hike in the dark, don't sleep in the light.

Most mornings, whether I'm alone or in a group, I try to move without sound. Stillness has become one of the most important parts of the morning, and it feels wrong for me to disturb it. Anything I might need upon rising, such as shoes or pants, has already been placed within reach.

If it's raining, I'll change out of my dry clothes and into my wet clothes from yesterday. I always have wet clothes from yesterday. Sometimes rain, sometimes sweat. No matter what, my shirts are always wet. Cold, wet underpants are no fun either.

If I spent the night in a shelter, I'll grab my bathroom bag and walk to the privy. I have learned how to brush my teeth with little or no water.

If there are bear cables, I won't retrieve my food until I've done everything else because the metal always squeaks. Usually by that time, a few others are up or I'm about to leave anyway, so I don't feel as bad.

My food is split between two bags. Breakfasts and dinners are in one bag, snacks in another. I also hang my stove because it smells like food. Some people, myself included, have begun using the mouse-hangs right there in the shelter. The idea is that they not only keep the mice away (tuna cans or pie plates mid-rope make impossible barriers for tiny climbers) but the very fact that they're in the shelter keeps the bears away. Bears don't like enclosed areas, especially ones that are occupied.

After silently verifying that my supplies survived the night, it's time to eat. Breakfast is almost always the following: one pack of Pop-Tarts, cold. That's a quick 500 calories. If I can find Honey Buns, they are even better at nearly 700. It only takes two minutes to boil water, so I also have a cup of strong instant coffee, to which I usually add a pouch of chocolate or vanilla Carnation Instant Breakfast. This not only adds a hundred calories plus vitamins, it helps to mask any tuna flavor left over from dinner. The small titanium pot I boil water with also serves as my dinner plate, soup bowl, and coffee mug.

If I have not already done so, I can break down my tent and my entire sleeping system while having breakfast. If I'm at a shelter, I carry my things to the table or some place away from sleeping hikers before I shove crinkly things into crinkly bags. I've done this so many times I never need my headlamp. Besides, the sun is almost up anyway.

Once that's done, I review the guidebook and my plan for the day. I'll check the shelter spacing, circle the water stops, and note the tent sites. Then I'll add 20 to whatever mile number I'm standing at and pick a stopping point, trying to stay within 20-25 total for the day. Once I know where I'm going, it's almost time to head out.

Systems. Economy of effort. I have numbered my toes. Starting from my left pinky toe and working right they are One through Ten. Three is beginning to succumb to hammertoe, curling under with every step. This is very distracting, so to prevent this I have begun taping it to its neighbor, Two. This acts like a splint and mitigates the curling effect, but the non-sticky side of the tape is abrasive and has worn a bleeding gouge into its neighbor, One, so I also wrap it individually to protect it.

The nail on Four has turned from bright red to deep purple and will probably fall off soon, just like Six did. The nail on Ten is turning dark red too. None of them hurt, and I wonder which one will go next. Once my toes are taped and my shoes are on, there is only one more thing left to do before stepping off.

I try to maintain an average speed for the day, including stops, of 2 to 2.5 miles per hour. Back at the beginning, I had to stop and unpack every time I got hungry. It didn't take long to realize that this was going to happen many times each day, so I needed to find a way to speed it up.

Now, before I leave each day, the last thing I do is stash snacks. I put Clif bars and beef jerky in the zipper pouches on my pack's hip straps. This way I can reach food and water bottles without having to stop and remove my pack. The other zipper pouch holds the bottle of Advil—again, so I don't ever have to stop for long.

Then I leave. I might share my plans with the other hikers and they might share theirs with me, but no one makes any decisions based on anyone else's plans anymore. When we do share our plans we don't even bother with the names of places. Only miles. No smiles. Today I woke up at 884. I want to get to at least 906 by dark. If we don't meet up at the next stop, we probably will at the one after that, or the one after that. Or not again. We are now officially in Hike Your Own Hike territory.

When I set off, I try to pick a landmark from the guidebook that will be easy to recognize when I get to it, for instance a peak or footbridge. I try to select one that will be about two hours away, and I tell myself I won't stop until I get there. Of course there's always something interesting or beautiful before my arbitrary checkpoint, and I never can resist a good sitting spot. That same stillness I enjoyed in the morning calls to me all day. Sometimes I'll just stop because there's a log. I don't need a view or a stream. The green tunnel is infinitely interesting. It's my Vortex.

The first half hour is slow going. The bottoms of my feet are very tender, although I can see no surface damage on the soles. The discomfort fades to numbness as I walk, and eventually I can get into a groove. But any time I stop for more than a few minutes, the numbness wears off and I have to deal with it all over again. So I try not to stop.

Almost everything I could possibly need while on the move can be reached without breaking stride. Snacks and Advil are in my pack pouches. Left pants pocket has my phone in a Ziploc bag. Left cargo pocket has my earbuds and the next few days' pages torn from the guidebook, already folded so the relevant section is on top and right-side up when I pull it out. My right front pocket has some sweet candies, and the right cargo pocket is full of the day's trash and wrappers.

Back at the beginning of the hike, I used to stop around the middle of the day and prepare a hot lunch. I would sometimes boil water and make a packet of ramen. I could remember being so hungry that I felt real pain in my abdomen, and how satisfying it was to have warm noodles fill my insides. Now I tear open the pack without stopping. I might sprinkle in the flavor packet, or I might save it for later. Then I'll bite off chunks of the dry noodle brick, chewing it and drinking water while I walk. The dry ramen brushes your teeth while you eat. Calories in, miles out.

I've developed a system for getting water. I can easily make a liter of water last for five miles, sometimes eight. My goal is to never be completely empty when I get to a source and it hasn't happened yet. I carry a squeeze filter, and I can produce a liter of drinkable water in about three minutes. Of course that's three minutes after filling the bag. The streams haven't been very wide lately, and some springs are nothing more than a wet rock, which makes it hard to fill the bag or any container. To deal with this, I have learned to use a rhododendron leaf and improvise a spout.

Once I have a full liter, I drink it. Too fast causes cramping, so I take my time. I'll sip it while I fill the other bottle, or maybe I'll just sit and drink. I love water sources. This is another opportunity to be still.

After I've filled my stomach and my bottles with water, I resume hiking. If there's a big climb ahead, I'll have second breakfast or second lunch, without stopping, of course.

When I do stop along the trail, I'll first plant my poles. I'll look around for a soft spot, and jam them down forcefully. The points stick, and if I've done it right, I can let go of them and they'll stand. At least long enough for me to pee, or do whatever it is I stopped for.

Almost every afternoon it rains. I usually welcome it; the gentle drizzle brings much needed cool air near the end of the day. Often the rain is so light that most of the drops get caught in the canopy, and the only thing that makes it down here is the humidity.

There comes a point while hiking in the rain that no one gives a shit anymore. Everyone takes careful measures to ensure that the important things stay dry: sleeping bags and at least one set of clothes. Mine are in the Schnozzle bag deep in my pack, which is also covered. Knowing that these things are dry means that rain really doesn't matter.

The first few drops always make me feel a bit hopeful. Maybe this won't last. It'll just cool me off, and soon I'll feel the sun on my face. Then the drops come harder. It's a bit uncomfortable, and then I have to decide—quickly—whether to put on my rain jacket. Usually the answer is no, but I do need to put on my pack cover at this point.

I'll stop, and plant my poles. I can take off my pack, find the pack cover and secure it, put the pack back on, and resume walking, all in under 30 seconds. My shirt is wet and my pants are wet. It doesn't matter; they were going to be wet from sweat anyway. Rain is cleaner than sweat. People pay extra for rain-scented laundry detergent. I'm the real deal.

I wear Gore-Tex shoes. Gore-Tex, like every piece of gear, comes with a tradeoff. The shoe is excellent at keeping water out. As long as the water is less than ankle deep, I'm golden. If it's deeper, the shoe is excellent at keeping water in.

So even if it's been raining for an hour, I still try my best to avoid the big puddles. But once my feet are finally soaked, I no longer care. Once I'm 100 percent wet, it's impossible to get any wetter. It's freeing. I can step in anything. Rustle any branch and let the splash fall where it may. My hat channels most of the water away from my eyes, and sometimes I lean forward and watch it spill over the brim.

Somewhere around the middle of the afternoon, I start to play games with the distance. In another two miles I'll be halfway to the next resting point. In another mile I can have some water. In half a mile I get to go downhill for a while. If I can get to that tree, I'll rest, but only for a minute. Never mind, to that rock. Fuck it. Now.

Momentum is hard to maintain for that long. Even thought it's mostly flat, the constant motion requires so much energy. My pockets are empty by the time I get to my camp.

Sometimes I'll find a stream with a flat spot near it. I can drop my pack and have a tent and a fire in 15 minutes. I no longer bother sitting on logs or rocks. Dirt is just fine.

If I'm at a shelter, the first thing I do is see who's there. Lemmy and I have been leapfrogging lately. Sometimes he's ahead at the end of the day, sometimes I am. Sometimes we're together. Dingo and Hungry Horse are days ahead. Still no word from Megan, Forager, or Fiddlin' Jim. I feel like Lemmy and I are slower than everyone, but no one is passing us. This concerns me.

There isn't any partying at the shelters anymore either. I can't say for sure what's happening way ahead, up in The Bubble, but back here everyone's too tired at the end of the day. Either that or the party people exhausted themselves and their funds a few hundred miles ago.

For me, making and eating dinner is party enough—party in a pouch. Almost every night it's the same thing. Knorr Pasta Sides. The recipe calls for milk or butter, neither of which pack well, so water will have to do. I've been adding a few ounces of tuna since Damascus and the extra protein seems to have finally eliminated the ammonia smell I had. Plus it tastes good. I also add half a bag of instant mashed potatoes. All of this goes into the titanium pot. When it cools, it thickens into a mushy gruel. Sometimes I have envelopes of salt or pepper from the last buffet, but usually I resort to the flavor packet left over from my afternoon ramen brick.

According to the various packets I've dumped into my pot, I'm having the caloric equivalent of dinner for three. Still not enough. I carry tortillas because they hold up to smashing better than bread. My preference is whole wheat, not because it's healthier, but because each one has ten more calories than plain. Another personal motto: No calorie left behind.

Plain tortillas are dry, so I keep fatty spreads in my food bag. At every restaurant and fast food joint I fill my pockets with packets of mustard, ketchup, barbecue sauce, and the ultimate—mayonnaise. Mayonnaise packets trade on the trail like cigarettes in prison. Single servings of Philadelphia Cream Cheese are the Lost Ark of trail cuisine. People will do anything to get their hands on one, and when you open it their heads explode.

I usually try to save half the tortilla for after I've eaten my gruel. My long metal spoon can only get so much of the gunk out of my cooking pot, so I use the tortilla as an edible sponge, eating as I clean. For the very last bit, I'll pour some clean water into the pot, swish it around, and drink it. It's disgusting but it's calories.

That's still not enough. I carry dried pineapple chunks or banana chips so I can have at least some fruit-like substance. Usually I have to force myself to close the bag and hang everything before I start eating tomorrow's supplies. I have no extras—I'm down to zero margin for error when it comes to food. On many occasions I've walked into town with a lone snack left in my pack. Exactly as planned, all according to my calculation.

If I'm at a shelter, someone else almost always makes the fire. Now personally, I enjoy the process of finding wood and building the fire. Creating a thing that maintains its own structural integrity while consuming itself from within fascinates me. But someone else always wants to do it, so I let them. Less work for me. Economy of motion and all that.

Now that there's hot gruel in my belly, I start to get sleepy. But there are a few things I must do first, like get things ready for tomorrow. Everything I could possibly want in the night has to be staged. Advil and water go by my head, pants for morning and Crocs for 3 a.m. privy walks go by my feet. All of this happens within a 12-inch glowing cone of red light beaming from my forehead. Now I'm done. Click. It's dark.

It's incredible, really, the way the dark enfolds you when you're in a shelter. The only light you have is your headlamp, and if you're lucky, the moon. Most of the hikers I encounter use a red headlamp in shelters as a courtesy to others, but it also results in not being able to see very well. It doesn't matter. Everything is always in the same place. I can always find everything by feel alone. I don't even know why I bother replacing the batteries in this thing.

I lie on my back in the dark and stare into infinity. My pupils dilate and shapes emerge. My brain has been dumping endorphins all day, and now my 14-hour runner's high is wearing off. I fade out, my last thought: *I forgot to stretch. Again.*

I'm usually fully awake around 3 a.m. It makes sense. I fell asleep around 9 p.m. Hard. No dreams, no memories. And when I wake up at

3, I feel great—at least mentally. Sometimes it's just because I feel the need to turn over, but more often I'm awake because my legs have cramped. A few minutes of stretching always helps, but it's impossible to do so in the confines of my sleeping bag, so I soon find myself standing, and since I'm up I might as well pee.

Holy shit, I'm still in Virginia.

# 16

# THROWN

"Green Giant, I am worried about you."
"Why?" I already knew what Lemmy was going to say.
"You are taking so many pills. Even in the night. What is this for?"
I sighed. "It's my feet."
"You shouldn't take so many of this. It is bad for your stomach."
"I know, but not taking them is bad for the rest of me." Bad wasn't the right word. By the end of the day my feet were almost completely numb. There was only enough sensation left for me to maintain my balance. The numbness wore off while I rested each day, and each night I would sit up in the dark thinking something bit me.

I could remember when it just felt like the tingling after your foot has fallen asleep and starts waking up. It tickled, and I squirmed. I would massage my toes for a few minutes and be okay for a while. But lately it was like being stabbed in the toes by burning hot needles. Massaging them felt like I was crushing the bones inside. But leaving them alone was maddening. So I ate Advil. A lot.

"I'll be fine."

Lemmy's expression said, "I don't believe you," so I turned my back and started packing.

Our camp was in a grassy meadow, two tents under a lone tree. The sunrise that morning was rose-colored and accompanied by a multitude of towhees. I needed a distraction while I waited for the pills to kick in. "Lemmy, are you ready to learn some more bird sounds?"

He was almost finished packing too. A warm breeze blew and the tall grass waved all around us. "I am, Green Giant. Which one is this?"

"This one is called the eastern towhee, but Katie and I call him 'Rufus.'"

"Why?"

"We learned it from an old book, before they changed his name. It used to be the rufous-sided towhee—it's a color, like brown. I just like that name better. Hear the song? It sounds like he's saying, 'Drink your tea.'"

We were awakened that morning by hundreds of them. Now a dozen at most were still singing. They were joined by wrens, nuthatches, and a few song sparrows. But the towhees made the most music that morning. Lemmy was about to put on his pack when he stopped. "Oh! I forgot to tell you, Green Giant. I saw a robin yesterday. It was so cool! I have never seen a bright red bird like that!"

"Bright red? I don't think that's a robin. How big was it?" He showed me with his hands and I corrected him. "That was a cardinal, Lemmy."

He shook his head. "No. It had to be a robin. He was wearing a black mask. Like Batman's little friend."

We were in the Shenandoahs, a national park less than 100 miles west of Washington, D.C. The Blue Ridge Parkway had turned into Skyline Drive and both the trail and the road wound through the park. At least three times each day we would cross the road, and I had started to hike with headphones and music to drown out the constant sound of RVs and motorcycles. We seemed to pass pay campgrounds with electricity and plumbing every ten miles, and each day featured multiple opportunities to have a sit-down meal at one of the park's many "waysides"—combination burger joint/gas station/gift shops.

Initially I was bothered by their frequency; the sense of wilderness adventure had been shattered. I relaxed my opinion after devouring a hot cheeseburger and a black raspberry milkshake for second breakfast on our first day in the park. I was still carrying three days' worth of the four day resupply that I picked up five days earlier. I used to be able to sense that a town was coming up solely by the diminishing weight of my food bag, but now I had no idea.

We were supposed to have lunch together at one of the waysides that day, but I was late by at least an hour. I'd left camp early as usual, but Lemmy had passed me much sooner than either of us expected. I ate my burger and shake alone while reading my guidebook. After lunch, I visited the gift shop.

The only two things I'd run out of since the last resupply was chocolate and Advil. They didn't have any ibuprofen, but there was aspirin behind the register, an acceptable substitute. The cashier greeted me. "Southbounder?"

"Excuse me?"

"You're a hiker, right?" I confirmed that I was. "Wow! You're our first southbounder of the year. You guys just keep starting earlier and earlier."

I added some postcards to my pile of purchases. "Not me, I'm going north."

He added the postcards to the total. "Ah, a section hiker then."

"No, I'm going north all the way."

He laughed and shook his head. "I don't think so. You're way behind schedule for a northbounder."

This guy clearly had no idea what he was talking about and I was getting tired of correcting him. "No, I'm not. I—"

He cut me off. "Let me guess. You've done the math. You have to average 15 miles a day. Yeah, I hear that a lot." He added the aspirin to the pile. His smile didn't quite reach his eyes.

I *had* done the math. I didn't need 15 miles a day to succeed; it was only 14.5. Not to split hairs, but I couldn't let it go either. "I bet you do hear that a lot. But I've been hitting more than 20—"

He cut me off again. "20 or more miles a day. Yep. Hear that a lot, too. Do you know what the rule is?"

Fuck your rules. "What?"

"They say if you're not at Harpers Ferry by the Fourth of July, you should definitely plan to flip-flop. You'll never make it to Katahdin before the snow."

"You don't say."

He flashed that same vacant smile again. "I do. So does everyone else."

"Never?" I grunted. My hands shook and I shoved them into my pockets to hide them. "Well, shit. Is there a pay phone around here that I can use?"

He looked confused. "Sir, the cell phone reception here should—"

I cut him off. "Yeah, you see, I really need to call my wife right now and tell her to come get me." I pretended to dial and put my phone by my ear. "Hi, honey? Yeah, come get me. I'm done. No, really.

Yeah. Why? Hang on." I covered the mouthpiece and said, "What's your trail name?"

"Excuse me?" His nametag said Chad.

"Your trail name. You know, the name they gave you when you hiked the trail."

His face flattened.

"I thought so." I returned to my imaginary conversation. I almost dropped my phone I was shaking so hard. "Yeah, I'm back. No really. Come get me. Some gift shop cashier who's never hiked farther than the length of his own driveway just convinced me that I'm wasting my time."

I locked eyes with him.

"What? Where should you pick me up?" I said to my phone. "Mount Katahdin, exactly as planned. Okay. Bye." I pretended to hang up and shoved the phone in my pocket. I threw a wad of sweaty bills on the counter, scooped up my pills and candy and stormed out, allowing the squeaky spring to slam the screen door for me.

It was the angriest I'd been since deciding to live outside, and unfortunately not the last time I would feel this way.

■ ■ ■

"Show me what you got there, buddy."

Lemmy didn't hear me. He was concentrating on the word balloons in his latest cartoon. Though his spoken English was quick and clever, he still struggled to spell certain words. Many of his stories took place in a "sheltar," for example.

This one took place on a road. The last panel featured an attractive young lady with a ponytail and exposed bellybutton, seemingly indifferent to the cars lining the road beside her, honking and waving, offering rides and beer. Beneath his signature, Lemmy wrote: *Dedicated to the girl with the hitchhike pants.*

"I like that one. You haven't drawn one in a while."

"We never have time. It's always miles, miles, miles." He hoisted his pack and brought me my poles. "I'm glad we stopped early yesterday."

I was glad we were starting late. I didn't want to start at all. Simply walking around the shelter was almost unbearable. The bottoms of my feet were on fire. Whatever was happening was both painful and unnerving, because the closest visual examination still revealed nothing. No blisters, redness, irritation, fungus…nothing. And the weird bunched-up sock feeling had now graduated to pebbles. There were imaginary rocks in my socks. When I was barefoot it felt like they were under my skin.

We had only been walking 30 seconds and Lemmy was already 50 feet ahead of me. He stopped and turned around.

"Don't wait for me," I said. "I'll catch up. I think it takes a while longer for aspirin to kick in than the 'Vitamin I' does."

I'd run out of ibuprofen and switched last night, and was beginning to think it wasn't going to kick in at all so I took two more. "Seriously, go. Look how heavy your pack is today. You know I'll catch you. What the hell do you have in there, anyway?" He was already on the move and I didn't hear his reply.

The green tunnel in the Shenandoahs was particularly lush. In the height of summer, tall trees were separated by carpets of grass and ferns that shone emerald everywhere the sunlight touched. A surprising number of rocks on the trail only served to further aggravate my feet.

Around second breakfast, I caught up. He was sitting and sweating at a place the guidebook identified as "Rock with view." There was a rock. There was a view. A damn good one, at that.

The ridges in the Shenandoahs must look like feathers when seen from space. One long spine runs 80 to 100 miles in a perfectly straight line, with smaller green ridges fanning out like barbs. The ridges usually provide access to the long spine, where we now stood. The valley below was a vast, flat expanse.

Lemmy stood, laid his memory sticks on the ground near the rock, and jumped up on it, greatly improving his view. "Green Giant! Come see this!" I climbed up with him and we stood there, taking it in. Then he held his camera at arm's length and took a selfie of us with the view in the background.

"Okay, one more," he said, and shuffled back a step to adjust the picture. Suddenly he slipped off the rock, and his boot landed dead center of one of his memory sticks, snapping it in two.

He dropped to his knees, crushed. I covered my mouth. "Oh, Lemmy. Oh no." He picked up the broken pieces and pushed them together, as if they would fuse by magic or sheer will. He tried two more times, then dropped them forlornly. "Fuck," he said, and wiped his eyes on his sleeve.

. . .

Eastern towhees invite you to tea twice each day: first during the hour immediately after sunrise and again just before sunset. Those hours were usually when we were in camp eating breakfast or dinner, so "drink your tea" became a Pavlovian dinner bell making us ravenous.

We were behind schedule again, and it was my fault. We should have stopped at the last shelter a few miles ago, but it had been early in the day and I thought my feet could take a little more abuse. I was wrong. We were halfway to where we wanted to be and it was getting dark. Lemmy could have easily been there by now, but instead he stayed a few steps ahead, entertaining me to keep my mind off the pain.

"I am hungry enough to eat you, Rufus!" Lemmy shook his fist at the birds and mimicked them. "Drink your...*tea?*" he said. Then he mimed breaking a tiny neck, made a cracking sound, and growled, "I DRINK YOUR BLOOD!"

He was hiking with one big stick now, wizard-style. The pieces of the other one were tied in an X on the outside of his pack.

I called for a break. "How much water do you have?"

He stopped and turned around. "I have enough. Why?"

"I think we should stealth tonight." There is a subtle difference between tenting and stealth camping. The former means spending the night at a place with an existing fire ring and clear evidence of recent tent placement, usually marked with a tiny tent symbol in the guidebook. The latter refers to spending the night where no established site exists. The key word is stealth; you're supposed to avoid making a fire, or keep it small if you must, scattering the ashes and rocks in the morning. Leave no trace.

"This will be the first time I did this!"

"You're kidding. Really? How long have we been out here, and you've never stealthed?"

He started walking again. "It's true. The only time I stayed at a tent site is with you."

"Well then, this should be fun! Keep your eyes open for a spot." The trail had been surprisingly rocky. We'd spent most of the day ridge walking, and despite being surrounded by trees, the ground was like slabs of broken sidewalk. Every surface was flat but nothing was level. Finding a place to pitch a tent was tricky, but I thought I saw promise to our left just before we reached the top of the ridge.

The best stealth spots are far from the trail, as this one certainly was. We also had a field of boulders between our flat spot and any passersby, unlikely though they were. I saw room for both our tents. Perfect, I thought. Just enough rocks between us that our tents won't touch for once. I yelled back to Lemmy that it was good, and soon I could hear his big stick clunking on the rocks.

The wind was picking up, though it carried no hint of rain. The sunset was so colorless it escaped my notice, and it was just suddenly dark.

"These boulders should do a good job of blocking the wind so we can get a fire going. I'll find wood if you'll throw the rope. You'd better get to it while we can still see a little."

I gave Lemmy the coiled cord I carried for this, 50 feet of blue nylon. He tied a rock to one end, chose a high branch, and threw the rock like a baseball. His aim was too good; the rock hit the branch and bounced back toward him. He hopped aside as it thudded at his feet.

I knelt and arranged some stones in a small circle. "That's one." We had a rule: The rope-thrower gets three tries, then someone else gets a turn.

His second throw was too hard and sailed high above the branch. The nylon rope escaped his grip and followed up and over, tracing the same graceful arc as the rock. It landed in a tangle on the other side.

I made a teepee of dry twigs in the stone circle. "Come on, Lemmy, you've got this." He untangled the blue coil from the bushes and wound up for his third throw. This time it was perfect. The rock cleared the branch at just the right height and at just the right spot. Unfortunately, Lemmy's grip on the rope was too strong, and when the slack pulled tight the rock shot free of the cord, which dropped back down and piled onto his head and shoulders.

I used my lighter to start the twigs and added bigger sticks until the small fire could sustain itself. "Okay, my turn." It hurt to stand.

Lemmy handed me the blue mess, not bothering to untangle it. "I don't understand how a cowboy can catch a cow with this thing." *Fing.* "I can't even catch a rock."

It took me three tries, so some of Lemmy's dignity was salvaged. We ate by our small fire, then walked back to the trail. I leaned on my trekking poles, feeling every sharp rock and pebble through my thin camp shoes. Through an opening in the trees we could see the neighboring ridge that paralleled ours. Tiny lights winked at the top, and we wondered if they were the headlamps of other hikers, and if they could see ours.

Way back at the beginning I had envisioned ridge walking by the light of a full moon. This was supposed to be my opportunity to make big miles. These were supposed to be flat, easy days followed by night hikes. Now I only wanted to sit.

I squinted across to the other ridge. The tiny lights had definitely moved. The moon was rising behind them, and I wondered how long before they stopped and turned around to stare in awe at the same blood red orb I saw.

■ ■ ■

In the morning we scattered the ashes from our fire and kicked the rocks around. Even if we'd had leftover water, there was no need to pour it on the coals. There had been about two hours of thunder and lightning during the night. As soon as the sun touched the rocks the trail began steaming around us.

I wanted to get an early start because our two consecutive early finishes had added up to one full day wasted. No big deal here in the land of waysides and day hikers, but if my feet had cost me unplanned time back in the Smokies—or worse, up in the 100 Mile Wilderness—it would mean rationing food. I needed to get my shit together.

But I didn't get an early start because I was exhausted. The storm had come in the middle of the night and really thrown me off my schedule. I usually sleep through rain, but this thing shook my tent hard. At one point I thought it was Lemmy, until I heard him yell from his own tent, asking me to stop shaking his.

After the rain I lay awake, reflecting. I thought about Mark and how it rained on us that very first day. I'd kept thinking, *I live outside now.* I thought again about what it meant to be in tune with nature. I kept forgetting that I still owned a phone. I could smell water, and birdsong made me hungry. This was exactly what I had been looking for when I started. My mind reeled at the potential for how much more in tune I could possibly get.

Now if only my feet would let met get there. I thought about Mark again. On every long hike we'd ever done together, his heels and toes would be mangled by the end of Day One. Part of his normal camp routine was wringing the blood from his socks. "Gary, you don't have feet—you have hooves," he'd say. I'd never had a significant blister— never in the Marines, not even on this hike.

Yet my feet were slowing me down. And not just me. I was starting to feel like a burden to Lemmy, although he never said or did anything to make me think so. But there on my back, in the dark somewhere between awake and asleep, I began sliding down a slippery slope. I was dragging someone else down with me and it was all my fault. I was angry at my feet and then I immediately felt sorry for them. I was, after all, the one abusing them.

I suddenly didn't feel very in tune with anything. After another long hour of tossing and turning under my thin blanket, I finally slept.

It seemed for a while as if the rain and wind had started again, but this time it really was Lemmy shaking my tent. He was never up before me. It took way too long for me to put my shoes on after we ate, which is why we had started our hike so late. Now, once again, I was why we were stopped.

Every time my feet touched the ground it was hell. I might as well not have been wearing shoes, because it felt like I was walking barefoot on hot rocks, with no padding left to the bottoms of my feet. It was as if all the soft tissue was gone and everything from the ankles down was a skeleton wrapped in skin, about to tear through with every step.

I leaned on my poles. "Where the hell are we, Lemmy?" I didn't look up; I was panting.

"We are less than a mile from a picnic spot." The Pinnacles. I remembered seeing that in the guidebook the last time we stopped. There was a bathroom symbol which meant the possibility of running water.

"It says in the book, 'No camping,'" Lemmy added. It was like he was reading my mind.

"Let's go there and have an early dinner while I rest my feet. Then we can get to the shelter and go straight to sleep. Okay?"

"Okay."

It was less than a mile, but it took me almost an hour. With every footfall came searing pain. Lifting each foot brought some relief, but I could only lift one at a time, and I did that slowly at best.

The picnic area was empty. Then sun was almost down. There were no birds, only wind. I staggered into the clearing where Lemmy was waiting, looking worried. "Green Giant, are you going to make it to the next shelter?"

I was worried too. "I don't know. Where's the next shelter?"

"It's only two more miles."

I don't know why I even asked. Two more miles meant two more hours, and I couldn't even do two more seconds. My chest began thumping harder, and suddenly I was disconnected from everything, watching myself from above as I dropped to my knees, reached back and pulled off one shoe.

"No." I pulled off the other and looked up at Lemmy, who was frowning.

"Green Giant, if I stop here I will run out of food. Maybe if we—" I didn't let him finish. "You don't stop here."

He looked to the north end of the clearing. There was a white blaze on a post beside a rocky path leading up what looked like a 500-foot climb. There was no way I would make it even in two hours.

"It's almost dark, Lemmy. Don't let me slow you down."

"When will you catch me?" We both knew the answer.

"You said it's only two more miles, right? You get a late start tomorrow and I'll start early. I'll be in your camp before you even get your socks on." We both knew that wasn't going to happen.

He was still frowning at me. "Are you sure about this?"

I wasn't. "Yes."

Before he left, Lemmy made me pull out my guidebook. Every 20 miles or so he drew a circle around the places he thought he might stop. My pack was off, and when we hugged he slapped my back. I didn't watch him hike out the north end of the clearing. Instead, I wandered in the opposite direction looking for a spot to pitch my tent. I headed deep into the trees and ferns until I could no longer see the tables and restrooms. I wasn't allowed to be there. The place was empty, but I didn't know if rangers would drive through in the night, so I moved a little further into the trees, limping gingerly as I went.

■ ■ ■

The bathroom was 300 feet away, but it took me almost five minutes to reach it. I did most of my packing on my knees. This was not going to be a good day.

Thankfully my pack was light. Unfortunately, that was because I was almost out of food. I was about to exit the park, so there were no more waysides. I stood by the blaze at the north end of the clearing, drew a breath, and began.

Every step was agony. I placed each foot as slowly as possible, but that required putting all my weight on the other foot. Hot coals every time. Involuntary gasps and low moans interrupted my normal breathing and soon everything began to sparkle. I was hyperventilating. I stopped.

"Deep breaths, Green Giant," I said aloud. Deep, slow breaths move blood and oxygen to the brain, which I needed to remain conscious. This also triggers the release of endorphins, which reduce pain and induce runner's high. I could only do it while stopped, though. As soon as I began walking again, my breathing would cycle out of control and I'd find myself lightheaded, afraid of passing out.

I clenched my teeth and bore down. I forced air through my nostrils and growled. The growling turned to swearing and again I had to stop. Pain melted into anger at my frustrating lack of progress. I felt a sting on the top of one foot. The pins and needles were back. First time I've felt that during the day, I thought. Then another hot bolt struck my ankle, and then my shin. It was bees.

I had unknowingly kicked aside a small rock uncovering a yellow jacket nest, and they were attacking. I ran, frantically slapping at my shins and ankles.

Adrenaline is far more powerful than endorphins, and I felt nothing until I was a safe distance away and clear of bees. I dropped to my ass and began rubbing and scratching my legs as soon as the pain came back. "Fuck, shit, fuck!" I was on the edge of going insane.

I remembered the anti-inflammatory cream Megan had given me and tore into my pack, dumping and scattering everything until I found what I needed. The relief was instant. I counted seven stings while applying the cream. Maybe I had an hour before it wore off and they acted up again.

I lay on my back beside the trail, surrounded by all of my things. My feet throbbed from the short sprint. I need a minute, I thought. I'm just going to rest my eyes for a minute.

All right, I thought. I'm ready to try this again.

I repacked, steeled myself, and started walking. I don't know why I thought something different would happen this time, but in mere minutes I was swearing again through clenched teeth. This called for medical attention. But help was somewhere up ahead, and it wasn't coming to me. I had to walk.

The swearing turned back into moaning as I shambled down the rocky slope, crying real tears, gulping and gasping from the pain. When I reached the bottom, I stopped. The trail was near a four-lane highway. A big green sign told me Luray, Va. was nine miles away. I lurched to the guardrail and sat on it. Then, doing my best to look happy and friendly, I put out my thumb and waited.

■  ■  ■

My phone had no signal to call a cab. I considered throwing myself on the ground and waiting for an ambulance, or more likely a police car. But my salvation presented itself in the form of a silver Cadillac. The man who stepped out of the driver's seat was well-dressed and had neat white hair. He held out a strong, tan hand and I shook it. "I'm Gary."

"Chuck." He popped the trunk and let me put my pack beside two small pink Disney princess suitcases. "My granddaughters are in the back seat. You can ride up front."

Everything was so clean that I was immediately self-conscious. I must look and smell horrible. I caught my reflection; my face was streaked with dirt.

"Girls, this is Gary. He's hiking the Appalachian Trail. Girls, say hello." Their tiny eyes met mine with silence. "We're going to take him someplace where he can get a hot meal and get cleaned up." I felt like the object of pity I was. "Gary, are you going to Luray?"

"I hope so."

"We can get you there." Why were these incredibly clean people being so nice to me? I was a wretch. "Gary, may we say a prayer for you before we go?" That explained it.

"Please, by all means." Chuck asked Jesus to look after me, which I appreciated but thought odd; from my perspective, Jesus had already assigned that task to Chuck.

The nine miles to town passed quickly, and when I offered Chuck gas money he predictably refused. "We were going this way anyway. Good luck and God bless!" One of the little girls pressed her face against the window and stared at me as the big car rolled away.

I was standing in front of the Budget Inn. There was a vacancy and free wifi. Plus I only had to walk ten feet to get there. I hobbled in and ordered a room. "How many nights will you be with us, sir?"

"I don't know. Can we leave it open?" We could. I gave the man my card and shuffled to my room. I dumped everything on the floor and plopped onto the bed. It was time to call Katie.

She answered on the third ring. "Hey! Hold on a second." She covered the phone and I heard muffled voices. There were footsteps and she came back. "Hi! How are you? Everyone misses you!"

"Where are you?" I asked.

"I'm in Ohio. We're at dinner. But I don't care. How are you?" I'd forgotten, she was visiting her parents. "Hello? Are you still there?"

"I'm still here."

"Is everything okay?" I told her about my feet, about how I forced myself to get this far, how the torment drove me to near hallucinatory madness. On top of the tortuous pain, I felt the guilt of the torturer; I was inflicting this upon myself. I told her about how I cried, reliving past mistakes and moments of shame. The trail had become my punishment, each rock an atonement for past sins. My entire universe had become pure anguish.

"Oh, Gary. I'm so sorry."

I said nothing.

"I can come get you if you want. It's okay."

"Can you, really?"

"I can," she said. "I don't have to be back to work for a few more days. Do you want me to take you home?"

I closed my eyes and saw Col. Butcher, his pack still bearing the Triple Crown trail patches. *Things are going to get tough for you out there. They always do.*

"I do want you to come get me," I answered.

"Are you sure?"

*Just remember one word.*

"I'm sure."

*Perseverance. You keep that one word in your head and nothing can stop you.*

"I do want you to come get me. But we're not going home."

## 17

## LODE

HARPERS FERRY is another one of those special trail towns. The AT goes through it, and the headquarters of the Appalachian Trail Conservancy is right in the heart of the historic district. For that reason, hundreds of flip-floppers and section hikers start or end their journeys here, sometimes both.

The ATC asks hikers to voluntarily sign a register and be counted at the headquarters, where they will also take your picture and put your face in a giant binder. Flipping through that book offered a more precise way to track how far ahead my fellow hikers were. For example, I was number 1,205 to pass through. Dingo and Hungry Horse had lower numbers because they passed so many hikers since I'd last seen them. Johnny Oak was even further ahead. Big Ups had been here a month ago.

I didn't see Lemmy or Voldemort, nor did I expect to. I also did not expect to see Forager and Fiddlin' Jim, but there they were. Not in the book; in the flesh. Neither of them saw me. They were stopped at a bench near the river along the northern edge of the tiny city. Forager was sprawled in the grass and looked up at the sound of my approach. "Holy shit, it's Green Giant!"

I beamed at my friends. "This must be where all the cool people hang out."

Forager still sported his mirrored sunglasses, but he had stopped shaving, and with his beard I almost didn't recognize him. Fiddlin' Jim still kept his hair short and chin clean. He slapped my shoulder. "Look at you there, Green Giant. You got a little fuzz on your face too!"

"Man, it's good to see you guys. When did you get into town?"

"We just got here," Forager said. "We're doing the Four State Challenge."

The Four State Challenge is a trail tradition typically attempted by young, ultralight crazy people. The idea is to hike through four states—42 miles—in a single day. None of us could remember the last time we crossed a state line, and suddenly there were four states in one day: Virginia, West Virginia, Maryland and Pennsylvania.

Forager and his dad had started hiking before 4 a.m. and were almost done with state number two. I quickly declined their invitation to join them, and politely informed them that they were crazy.

"So what's up with you these days?" Jim asked, motioning for me to sit beside him on the bench. "Geez, we haven't seen each other since when?"

"Somewhere in Virginia."

Forager sat up and reached for his toes, stretching out his hamstrings. "We were worried about you, man. Pops and I read about your feet in the log books and then we stopped seeing your name."

His dad put an arm around me. "Yeah, we're real glad to see you're still on the trail."

"Thanks, guys. I'm really lucky to still be here."

"You got time to tell us about it?" Jim asked.

"You got time to listen?"

■   ■   ■

I told them about my painful climb down into Luray, and my phone call with Katie. I explained the first part of my plan. The AT had been less than 50 miles away from I-81 for hundreds of miles. She would have to drive that very interstate on her return trip from Ohio to North Carolina. Luray wasn't that far out of the way either. While I waited for Katie, I went to see a doctor.

Jim's interest was piqued. "What did the doc say, Green Giant?"

"Pay attention, man," I told Forager. "This is your future right here. Couple of old guys sitting on a bench going into detail about their medical problems."

"Bring it on."

"Okay. So I told the doctor my symptoms. I only got through half the things on my list before he stopped me to say I had something called Morton's neuroma. Ever heard of it?"

"Don't ladies get that from wearing high heels?" Jim asked.

"Man, I hope there was a burn unit in that hospital," Forager laughed, clapping his dad on the knee.

"Actually, your dad's right. The doc asks me what size shoe I wear. I say ten. He says not anymore. My foot has gone up a size, maybe more. My shoes were too tight."

"That's it?"

"No. That's just the start. Because my foot was being compressed all day and pounded thousands of times, the main nerves have been damaged."

"Uh-oh."

"Uh-oh is right. Taking a couple of zeros helps a little, but the damage is done, and it takes a year, sometimes more, for nerves to grow back. If they ever do."

I held up my foot to show off my new, bigger shoes, with special arch supports to bear more of my weight and relieve the balls of my feet where it hurt the most. I described the padded inserts under my toes, then realized from their expressions that this level of footwear detail was possibly not as compelling as I might have first thought.

"Okay, we get it. Did you get any good drugs?"

"I did. All that ibuprofen I was taking made me numb to what was going on down there. So the doctor gave me some Vicodin. They still let you feel the pain a bit, but they make you so happy you don't give a shit."

"Yeah, and speaking of shit, they stop you up too," Jim said. "Be careful with those."

"Oh I know. I haven't had any yet. I'm saving them for when I really need them."

Forager stood up and stretched. Fiddlin' Jim passed him his pack and then reached for his own. "So then what? Katie shows up the next day, and brings you up here?"

"Not quite. We had one more stop to make."

I told them about Lemmy's circles in my guidebook. I was 99 percent sure he would stop in Front Royal for a zero. He had been in love with the name for some reason, and kept repeating it for days, really rolling the R's. It was circled on the same day that Katie would arrive. I told her about my diagnosis while she drove me there from Luray, about 30 minutes up the road by car.

Front Royal isn't very big and hikers are easy to find, especially one like Lemmy. We bought a pizza and sat down on a bench that had line of sight to both the hostel and the laundromat. We had set the bait in a hiker trap and caught more than we bargained for. The pizza disappeared quickly into the bellies of messengers sworn to fetch our friend. We bought more pizza, and moments later Lemmy appeared, amazed. "Green Giant! The last time I saw you, you were crying at a picnic table. And here you are, with the pizza and the girl!"

He made it sound so simple, but in reality I had agonized over the decision. I was hobbled and without Katie's help, I was destined to shuffle along desperately playing catchup or watching everyone pass me by. After much deliberation, I chose smiles over miles.

After I had explained my modified plan to Lemmy, Katie had brought me the rest of the way to Harpers Ferry to park for a couple zero days and recover. Today would be my first day back on the trail, and I would start off easy, aiming for five miles, maybe seven if my feet held up. By the time Lemmy caught up, I hoped to be back up to his pace of 20-mile days. It was like merging onto a freeway.

"You need to ramp up faster," Forager said. "We passed Lemmy yesterday."

"What?"

Fiddlin' Jim confirmed. "Yep, him and Voldemort."

"What?!"

Forager nodded.

"I was going to ask when I first saw you guys," I said. "But I didn't know if things were awkward with you two, or…"

"Nah, it's cool. Things just didn't work out."

"We read your note and we ditched the girl!" Jim said. He snickered and elbowed his son in the ribs.

Forager laughed along and I relaxed a little. "Anyway, it's no big deal," he said. "She'll probably tell you all about that and more when you see her. She seemed like she could really use your company."

"What does that mean?"

"You know, man. She just…" He closed his eyes and made a hand puppet by his ear, rapidly opening and closing its mouth.

"Yeah, I know." I couldn't wait.

■   ■   ■

The trail out of Harpers Ferry into Maryland was different than what I'd grown used to in Virginia. The first four miles were perfectly flat and level along the Potomac River, and put me at the lowest elevation so far, less than 300 feet above sea level.

The first climb was short, only a thousand feet, but it was rockier than anything I'd seen so far. The geology of my surroundings was changing; the rocks were a darker gray and had sharper edges. I couldn't kick them aside either. They were like icebergs, with most of their bulk buried below the surface. Stubbing a toe against these things was like kicking a curb.

I sat on one of the big rocks and tried to find a comfortable position that wouldn't jab me in the ass. Two hikers approached as I wiggled and squirmed. The first to arrive, at a fast clip, was a man in his mid-twenties with skin the color of coffee with cream. He had dark, curly hair and beard to match. "Great day, eh?" he said with a pronounced Canadian accent. He introduced himself as Two Pack, and before I could ask the story behind his name, his equally speedy friend arrived.

I knew he had to be Ninja Mike. His loose pants were shredded at mid-calf. His shoulder-length blond hair hung from a tattered silk scarf, and he wore a sharp goatee with a big curly mustache that reached his eyes when he smiled. He gave me a fist bump when I guessed his identity, then glanced at my hat and returned serve. "You must be Green Giant."

Two Pack was already a hundred feet up the trail and Ninja Mike was bouncing on his toes, ready to follow. "We're doing the Four State Challenge."

"Good luck, guys. See you up the trail."

"Right on, brother," he said, then danced up the trail, arms waving and fingers pointing in time to a rhythm only he could hear. He then ran past Two Pack, who sped after him, kicking up dust as he went. When the cloud settled, they were gone.

I was not doing the Four State Challenge. In fact, I had allowed two whole days just to get through Maryland.

Big rocks weren't the only thing different about the trail from what I'd known down south. I found myself following white blazes through more densely populated areas. It started with a few state parks, now increasingly marked with monuments and stone ruins of old fortresses. Most of these parks were accessible via two-lane blacktop roads, which were usually busy. The trail went through residential neighborhoods too. One suburb was at the top of a steep embankment, overlooking Interstate 70, a six-lane highway packed with rush hour traffic. I followed the white blazes down a street filled with parked cars and barking dogs. A white arrow told me to turn right and walk along someone's driveway. I could see the family inside watching TV. I knew which toothpaste they used because their trash can was tipped over.

I'd almost gotten used to the Harleys and RVs back on Skyline Drive, but this was ridiculous. I zigzagged down the switchbacked trail to a footbridge over the interstate. The roar from the busy highway almost drowned out the beeping construction vehicles and barking dogs. The bridge was a long concrete walkway, a covered bridge with walls and a roof made of chain link fence. I assumed it was there to prevent hikers from hurling themselves into the traffic below—I know I wanted to.

My mood improved greatly when I reached the other side of the bridge. During my climb up the opposite embankment, I found ripe raspberries growing along another chain link fence that paralleled the highway. I watched cars and ate berries in the sun until I'd picked all of the easiest ones to reach. At the top of the embankment it looked like I was going to leave the din behind me, at least for a few miles.

My feet were still tender, and I was walking slowly. The new foot gear was helping, but all the damn rocks were not. The big granite icebergs were everywhere, and I must have stubbed my toes a dozen times before I reached the aptly named Rocky Run shelter. I was tempted to stay, especially since it had been recently remodeled. The two-story structure still smelled like fresh lumber, and the upper loft faced a large bay window made of sturdy plastic.

According to the guidebook, in less than two miles I would find the Dahlgren backpack campground, Maryland's gift to hikers. There is a tenting area the size of a football field, with a picnic table on each site. There is also a real indoor bathroom in a concrete building with lights and working power outlets and showers with hot water. Besides all this are the two words that make it so special: no fee. I believe this is Maryland's way of apologizing for making us walk through the first half of the state.

When I got there, it looked exactly as I'd expected. A few of the tent sites were occupied, and their owners were gathered at one central table quietly playing cards and drinking beer. A few waved and one held up a bottle and nodded a silent "cheers."

I took the first tent site, the one farthest from the bathrooms, where several hikers were filling their water bottles at the hose outside. I wanted to sleep as far from the high traffic area as I could. And I also took the first tent site because I was tired.

Unusually so, I thought. After four consecutive zeros, a pair of five-mile days should have been trivial. But the fact was I almost needed a nap in the middle of that day's walk. But my legs and lungs felt great, and the climbs around here had been small. I blamed my fatigue on loss of momentum.

A hot shower should wake me up, I thought. There were three shower stalls in the bathroom. I sang in the hot steam while I lathered my hair and beard. Some kind soul had left a full bottle of shampoo and conditioner.

After finishing with a blast of cool water, I toweled off, put on clean dry shorts, and started to put a shirt on. The screen door squealed, squeaked, and slammed. I popped through the stall curtain, still putting my arms through the shirt sleeves, to find a young man standing by the sinks, looking at me and smiling. He looked familiar—like Droid, only with a beard.

"Is there anyone else in here besides us?" he asked.

It was Droid. "Uh, no. Why?"

He turned and shouted, "All clear! He's decent!"

The door flew open, nearly snapping the spring. Voldemort charged past Droid, almost knocking him into a stall, and screamed, "GREEN GIANT!" I still didn't have my shirt on yet, so my arms were pinned to my ribs as she wrapped me in a bear hug and lifted me off the floor.

. . .

"You're so *light!*" She put me down. "And look at your beard! Oh my god!" She gently pawed the damp fluff on my neck. "We knew you were in here when we saw your hat outside."

"This is great!" I dried my face. "You I was expecting. But Droid! What the hell are you doing here? I thought you were way ahead of all of us."

He tried to answer but I interrupted. "Hang on. Let's get her out of the men's room." I picked up my things and followed them back out through the door. There was a bench by the wall outside and I immediately sat. All this excitement is wearing me out, I thought. I'm pooped. "Sit down, guys. Catch me up. Droid, how are you here?"

He tried to answer but Megan interrupted. "Ooh, wait! How long has it been?"

Droid frowned and checked his watch, "Since I called? Twenty minutes. You're right, I should go. It's that way, right?"

"Yes, just past the bathrooms."

"What are you two talking about?" I asked.

"Droid ordered pizza."

I shouldn't have been surprised. I could hear a road just beyond the trees at the north end of the campground. Anyone with a brick oven and a working car would do well around here. "Wow! Do you need help carrying anything?"

He stood to go. "No, I'll get it. You guys catch up and I'll tell you my story when I get back." He disappeared through the trees. I told Megan about my feet, hitching into Luray, and what the doctor said. Then I recounted my difficult decision to pick smiles over miles. I explained how we surprised Lemmy on our way to Harpers Ferry, and that I ran into Forager and Fiddlin' Jim on my way out of town.

"Ugh. Yeah, Forager. That whole thing."

"You don't have to talk about it."

"No, it's fine. It was great, actually. We just wanted different things. One of us wanted something long-term and the other one didn't."

"Ah. Do I dare ask which was which?"

"We both kept changing our minds, just never at the same time."

Droid came back with three big, steamy boxes, handed them to us, and turned around again to go get the drinks. Voldemort and I relocated to the picnic table near my tent. Just as we put the boxes on the table, Lemmy entered the clearing. He saw us and yelled. "Hey! Buddy!" He ran to the table, his pack bouncing the whole way. But after sitting down beside me and wiping his face with a bandanna, he leveled his voice and eyed me seriously. "Green Giant."

"What is it, Lemmy?"

"Every time I see you now, you have a pizza and some girl. I want to hike with you forever."

Droid showed up with an armload of sodas and plastic cups. We opened the boxes and everyone grabbed slices. We laughed and talked around big mouthfuls of dough, meat, and cheese. Droid explained that his huge lead on everyone disappeared when he was forced to take seven consecutive zero days.

"Good lord!" I said. "Seven? Why?"

"Giardia." This was met with a collective, cringing "ooh." Giardia is a waterborne parasite that wreaks havoc on the human digestive system. Everything you eat is liquefied and quickly ejected. Since we were eating he spared us the details, suffice to say that no one deserved seven days of it.

"I started on antibiotics two days ago, so this is only my second 20-mile day this week," he said. This is why they called him Droid—he was a machine.

It was good to have the gang together again, but I was getting sleepy, so I climbed into my tent while they sat at the table, still eating and laughing. The last thing I heard was them setting up their tents in the dark.

■ ■ ■

I slept straight through the night, not moving, not dreaming. When I awoke, my neck and shoulders ached as much as my bladder. I crawled out of my tent and into my shoes. First one up. I was pleased, considering it the first step back to recovering momentum.

On the way to the bathroom, I passed the bear pole. That's it, I thought. That's why my neck hurts. I rubbed my shoulders and looked up.

Here in Maryland I had encountered my first bear pole, a 15-foot metal post with a fan of hooks at the top, each one loaded with food bags. The only way to put them up there or get them back down was with the big steel reaching-stick, which was eight feet of solid steel with a tiny hook on one end. The other end of it was chained to the bear pole, because in Maryland people will steal a 50-pound, 8-foot metal pole unless it's chained to something.

A hiker who is six feet tall, if he holds the reaching-stick over his head, can just barely hang his food bags on the bear pole's big hooks. As the only hiker over six feet tall, it had been my job to do all the heavy lifting. That must have been why my muscles were so sore.

The four of us entered Pennsylvania that morning. Just like the good old days, we moved at different speeds on our own, bunching up at water stops and lookouts. I caught up with all three of them at a brook around lunchtime and asked what they thought about resupply. Everyone was out of sync. I was almost out of food, while Voldemort still had five days' worth. Lemmy had no opinion on the matter until Droid mentioned the all-you-can-eat buffet in town.

I did some math. "Guys, we can do it if we hurry." Megan declined and offered to have the fire ready for us that evening when we got to camp. At the next road crossing, Droid called for a shuttle to take us to town.

The driver was friendly and wanted to tell us stories about every building we passed. Lemmy stared out the window while Droid explained our time constraints. We still had 12 miles to go after lunch, so we'd be in and out pretty fast. While we took a table, our driver sat at the counter, flirting with a waitress. "Go on, eat. Come get me when you're ready."

Lemmy and Droid piled their plates to maximum capacity. I walked up and down the salad bar, eyeballing the greens but not really wanting any. Broccoli was usually good, but I wasn't interested today. Pie? No. I settled on some fried chicken and mashed potatoes, and added some green beans, mostly for color.

When I joined them at the table, their plates were almost empty. I sat beside Lemmy and shivered. "Hey, if you guys see a waitress before I do, ask her to cut the AC a bit. It's freezing in here." Hugging my ribs with arms covered with goosebumps, I scooted closer to the table.

Lemmy kept chewing and looked right through me, a bead of sweat tracing the ridge of his nose. The family at the next table were fanning themselves with napkins and sucking ice water through dewy plastic straws. "There's no air conditioning in this place," Droid said. "It's a furnace."

My shirt was soaked. I ate a bite of chicken and pushed my potatoes around. The waitress finally took our drink order. "That's three Cokes. You want limes in those?" My friends declined, but I joked that I should have a slice in case I was coming down with scurvy. Droid suggested I might have the flu. Maybe I had caught something when I was at the doctor's office. Those places are worse than hot tubs.

The caffeine and sugar helped perk me up for a while, and I ate some beans, but after half a plate I just wasn't hungry anymore. "Guys, I think I'm going to go sit in the sun. Don't hurry just for me, but, uh,"—I didn't wear a watch, so I pointed to my wrist—"time's ticking away."

"Are you sure you don't want dessert?" Droid asked. "The driver raved about the key lime pie. What about scurvy?"

I put a few bills on the table and pointed at the slice in my drink. "I'm already covered. I'll be outside. Don't hurry."

Droid nodded and checked his watch. "Tick tick."

∙ ∙ ∙

I sprawled on my back in the grass beside the van, letting the sun warm me until I was no longer shivering. Maybe my lack of appetite was because all this rest and low-mileage days meant I was no longer burning calories. I touched my throat and squeezed—neither swollen nor sore. Maybe a summer cold?

I rode shotgun on the way back to the trail and laughed along with our driver's terrible jokes. We paid and tipped him at the trailhead, and when he drove away I felt full of energy and ready to tackle rocks of any size. Droid took the lead and after a few minutes was out of sight. Watching him disappear so quickly behind the piles of boulders reminded me of how slow I was really moving.

"Lemmy, I think I might take a while to get there tonight. Don't hang back here just for me."

"Are you sure?"

"Yeah, don't worry. If it gets late, I have fresh batteries in my headlamp." I was only partly joking. He allowed himself to hike at his normal pace, and minutes later he was gone beyond the boulders too.

The worst thing about the rocks wasn't how sharp they were, it was the crazy angles. There was never any place I could put my foot that was both flat and level. My ankles were constantly bent left, right, and backwards. My legs worked hard to maintain balance, and my arms worked even harder, hacking with my trekking poles to keep from slipping and falling. After an hour my forearms and triceps burned and my shoulders felt like someone had spent an hour punching them.

Sitting down on a rock, with my head buried in my hands, I wondered, What the hell is wrong with me? I could go to sleep right here. My map said I had nine more miles to go. Shit. It was only two more miles to Tumbling Run shelters. Maybe the gang got tired too, and I'd find them there. Probably not, but I should stay there anyway. I'd get an early start tomorrow and—I didn't want to think about it. Right now all I could think about was sleep.

By the time I arrived at the shelters, I felt fine again. I was talking to myself out loud, marveling at the speed of my mysterious mood swings, when I walked upon the twin log structures. They sat side by side atop a small rocky hill, beside a pounding stream. They were distinguished with a pair of signs: SNORING and NO SNORING. Both were empty.

The area between the shelters had a picnic table and some clotheslines. I had just finished eating and was hanging my laundry when dusk began to settle. Someone wearing a headlamp was approaching from the south. When the light shined in my direction I waved and called out.

The man wearing the headlamp waved back and climbed the boulder pile up to the shelter with ease. He leaned on one big walking stick and wore a small day pack. He was huge.

I shielded my eyes and said, "Hi, I'm Green Giant."

"Oh shit! My light! Sorry!" He clicked off his lamp and the moon showed me his face. A camouflage ballcap covered his large head and two bright eyes shined from the shadow of its bill. Broad white teeth smiled through his thick black beard. He held out a hand and I shook it—solid, like a statue come to life. "I'm Lode."

"L-O-D-E, right? Like the video game?"

He crushed my hand and showed me more of his big teeth. "Yes! Holy shit, we are going to get along, I can tell right away. I've never met anyone else who's heard of Lode Runner. That is what you meant, right? The old Apple game from the '80s?"

I rubbed my hand and nodded. "That's the one."

"Ho-lee shit! That is crazy. You know, as soon as I saw you I thought, this guy looks about the same age as me, and as soon as you made that video game reference I knew. I knew it! How old are you?"

I told him.

"Okay, close enough. Wow, what are the odds? Two hikers out here in the middle of nowhere, and both of us are geeks. What are the odds?" He put his pack on the table and sat. The bench creaked under his weight. "You're thru-hiking, right?"

"All the way."

Lode pounded the table. "Ho-lee shit! That is great!" He stood up, raising his voice. "You guys are really something," he yelled, still smiling. "Man, I wish I could hike the whole trail!" He crossed both hands over his mouth and his eyes widened. He looked left, then right, then back to me. He dropped to a whisper and uncovered his mouth. "Shit. Is anyone sleeping in there?"

I said no and he instantly returned to his former volume. "Whew! Thank goodness. I wouldn't want to bother anyone, right?" He pounded the table again and laughed. "So what do you like? What's your favorite candy?"

I thought a second too long and Lode asked again. "What kind?"

Slow down, man. I'm not ready for this kind of pressure. "Reese's peanut butter cups."

Lode said, "Easy!" He reached into his bag and slapped four packages onto the table. "Since you're the only one here, they're all yours. What else? Something to drink?"

"Coke. Regular, not diet."

"You guys are so predictable. Watch this: BOOM!" He slammed a can onto the table. "Hang on, you probably want this one instead." He traded it for one that hadn't been shaken. It was ice cold.

"How—"

"Ice packs. Pretty rad, huh?"

I had to agree. "You're a damn fine trail angel, Lode."

He wagged a finger at me. "Oh no. I'm no angel. Angels perform miracles, and these aren't miracles, they're simple illusions! I'm a trail magician!" He looked over both shoulders. "Do you smoke weed?"

I was about to say yes when he started up again. "I mean if you don't that's cool, but seriously—" He stood up. "Seriously, who has ever met a hiker that doesn't smoke, right? I mean, if you don't, that's cool. But I'm going to! Ha!" He smiled and laughed and packed a bowl without ever hearing my reply, then lit the pipe, took a toke, and handed it to me. He blew smoke and said, "This stuff is what keeps me so calm."

If this guy ever met Megan, we might solve the world's energy needs.

I thanked him for the pipe, puffed, and passed it back. "So what do you do for real, Lode?"

"I just told you, I'm a trail magician."

"Really? That's it?"

He stood up again. "I just told you! I'm a trail magician!" If he hadn't been smiling I might have felt menaced. He was genuinely excited about helping hikers, he explained. The idea "tickled" him. He took another puff. "I've got a place on a few acres right by the trail. Every few days I fill up my pack and visit the shelters and pass out candy and rides. Get a pen." It wasn't a question.

I took my journal from my pocket and handed him the pen.

"Not for me. You. Write this down. It's my number. If you're anywhere on the AT in Pennsylvania and you need anything, this is your get-out-of-jail-free card." He sat back down.

"Really?"

He stood back up. "Really! For real, Green Giant! Anywhere in the state. But as soon as you're in New Jersey you're someone else's problem. Fuck those guys." He sat back down. "And don't give that to anyone else. I'm not running a hostel. It's more like a *hostile*, as in a *hostile environment!* Get it? Ha!"

"Don't give your number to anyone else. Got it."

"I'm serious. This offer is good for cool people only. And you're cool. I can tell. Boy I'm glad I met you."

I closed my notebook and put it on the table. "Thanks, Lode. I'm glad I met you too. I guess by your small pack that you're not staying?"

"Not unless I pull a double bed with box springs and a mattress out of this thing. I'd be a hell of a magician if I did that, right? Ha! Oh shit. I have to get back home or my wife is going to kill me. Hey, you were paying attention when I came up here. Which way did I come from?"

I pointed him south and thanked him again. He crushed my hand again and let me know he was glad we met one more time before bounding off into the night.

I was more relaxed than I had been all day. My neck and shoulders had stopped hurting and my appetite was back. I tore open one of the candy bars and put my notebook back into my pocket. I'd better hang on to this number, I thought. I have a feeling it might come in handy.

## 18

## A HOSTILE ENVIRONMENT

PENNSYLVANIA HAS THE MOST exceptionally well-maintained shelters on all the trail. The one I was now entering had a picket fence at the entrance to the clearing. Its freshly painted gate swung shut behind me, pulled tight by a silent spring. A carved duck, painted bright yellow, held a sign that said WELCOME.

A tiny natural spring flowed somewhere in the bushes to my right and splashed into a small pool. That fed a man-made channel of flat rocks, just a few inches wide, that cascaded down a series of steps and continued its journey behind a concrete bench near a sundial. All of this was the work of a loosely organized base of volunteers, mostly retirees and lunatics like Lode.

The big three-sided sleeping box was decorated with hanging plants, and its shelves were full of board games. I marveled at how clean the place was, kicking off my shoes before entering. It had probably taken a lot of work to get this place to look so nice. Hikers seemed to respect the effort: the walls were clear of carvings and graffiti.

The log book was in a mailbox the same bright yellow as the welcome duck. Lemmy's note was brief—no time for a cartoon, only words. They were at the next "sheltar," five miles ahead.

Five miles was nothing in the big picture. I had another thousand over which to make up a two-hour lag. In the little picture, here on the rocks, five miles might as well be a thousand. Anyway, it wasn't happening tonight. I closed the book and put it in the yellow box when I realized that I'd had company all along.

"Hey man, you done with that?" For a moment I thought it was Big Ups, but the hair was too long.

"Oh hey, sure. Sorry, I didn't hear you." I handed him the book and introduced myself.

He smiled and thanked me. "Nice to meet you, Green Giant. I'm Dude."

"No 'The?'"

"Nope. Just Dude."

His gear was smaller and lighter than anyone's I'd seen, even Bones. I asked him if he was thru-hiking and I was intrigued by his answer. "Depends on who you ask," he said. "There are some really cool side trails that I took this time, so maybe. Unless you're a purist. Then no." He shrugged.

"'This time?'"

"Yeah, I did the traditional Bubble hike a few years ago. I dicked around too much and drank a lot. Took like seven months to do it. Then I did the PCT last year with some guys who introduced me to speed hiking. So now I'm trying to do the AT in 90 days."

"Wow! How's that going for you?"

"Oh, good. I need to average a mile per hour. Overall, that is. Twenty-four miles every day. So not too many zeros." He closed the book and gave it back to me. "I started on June 9th."

I had a full month's head start, and here he was passing me in Pennsylvania. "You don't see a lot of people twice, do you?"

Dude closed one eye and tilted his head. "I never thought of it, but no. Huh."

*I'm still not saying goodbye.* "Do me a favor, would you Dude? Tonight or tomorrow, you're going to meet Lemmy and Voldemort. You'll know them when you see them. Just tell them I said hi, okay?"

He laughed, adding that his trail name should have been Mailman. My request to deliver a message was his third today. I thanked him again as he set off down the trail.

After a hot dinner I rolled out the new sleeping bag Katie had helped me pick out in Harpers Ferry. The one I mailed home had never arrived, but it was starting to smell anyway. I was more dejected that the memory card full of photos I'd sent with the bag was also missing.

I turned onto my side and wondered if Dude had delivered my message yet. He'd probably take a short sleep break and then knock out 24 miles or more, passing more hikers every day. I wondered how far he'd get before he stopped passing people. Probably all the way to Katahdin. Well, if he could pass me after a full month's head start, I would close the gap on my knuckleheads in no time.

I was still lying on the same side when I woke up. The hot sun baked my face. My shoulder was totally numb and my fingers were swollen. I hadn't moved. Sitting up wasn't easy. My arm refused every command and my head ached. Getting out of the bag and my tent was worse. I lost my balance and stubbed my bare toe on a rock. I cursed and hissed. What the hell time is it? I have to catch Lemmy.

It was half past ten.

■   ■   ■

The same people who told me Virginia was repetitive also said Pennsylvania was rocky. Either they were downplaying things as a cruel joke on those who hadn't hiked yet, or they were still too tired from barely surviving the ordeal to go into any detail. The rocks start at the north end of Virginia and get worse, becoming sharp granite icebergs that get bigger and harder to maneuver around. Immovable, jagged triangles crowd the trail until there is no more trail. Every painful step becomes a balancing act—will the next step tip you left or right? This lasts all day, with no break, for about 60 miles.

Then it's more rocks, only now they're not triangles, they're circles—imperfect, lumpy balls of rough stone ranging in size from softballs to pumpkins. Somehow trees grow among them, but you'll never see any dirt. You'll roll and wobble over 100 miles, feeling like an ant on a gravel driveway, as they keep getting bigger. The ones on the trail are shoulder-high, but going around isn't an option because the ones to the left and right are even taller. This goes on for days. Sometimes there are no trees, and as the sun heats the rocks, the rattlesnakes come out.

Long stretches of tumbled boulders are occasionally separated by miles of sharp slate. Vertical black slabs surround your feet like shark fins. Every wrong step robs your sole of precious material and wears down your patience.

It was hard enough to keep my balance, and now I was having dizzy spells. Whatever version of a summer cold I had must have been a nuclear one. Near Harrisburg I got word from my brother, who lives in the state and wanted to drive out to visit me, along with his 10-year-old son. Despite being thrilled to see them, I was extra grumpy. I complained most of the night, then sullenly did my laundry. My nephew hid in the basement of the hostel. All he knew was that his dad was taking him to a haunted mansion to visit his weird uncle who smelled funny and lived in the woods. I'd hide too.

The next day my blisters started. All of the extra insoles and padding designed to help the bottoms of my feet also changed the way my shoes fit, and now they were rubbing. Thin red welts across the tops of my toes filled with fluid. When they popped, my socks were soaked. By the next morning, my toes looked and felt like they had been worked over with a branding iron.

Another half day of sliding, wobbling, and kicking shark fins and I was spent. I hadn't taken a zero since Harpers Ferry, and decided it was time for another one. I needed some magic. I needed a magician. It was time to call Lode.

■ ■ ■

He answered on the first ring. "Hey! Green Giant!"

I needed a second. "Hi! Yeah, it's me. How did you know?"

"You said you were from North Carolina, so when I saw the area code I knew right away it had to be you. I don't give my number to just anyone. How are you doing, pal?"

I was relieved that he not only remembered me, but was in a good mood. This would make the next part easier. "Oh, you know. I'm actually kind of under the weather and my feet are banged up. If you were serious about your offer—"

"Say no more! Tell me where you are and I can come get you by the end of the day." I heard him pick up car keys.

"No need," I said. "I'm roughly five miles outside of Boiling Springs. That is where you said you were from, right?"

This delighted him. "That's great! You're probably past the Deer Run Campground. Have you done 'Rock Maze' yet? Be careful in there, pal. That place is a breeding ground for rattlesnakes! And I like you, buddy, but I don't know you well enough to suck the poison out for you yet! Ha!" He burst into laughter that trailed off into wheezing and then coughing. When he came back to the phone he was catching his breath, and I could hear his smile. "I'll start walking and I'll meet you when I meet you."

He hung up before I could thank him. I had barely gone a mile when I heard two big boots and one big stick pounding the rocks ahead. He handed me a comically oversize travel mug filled with ice water, the cubes jostling and sloshing inside. I took a gulp and squeezed my eyes shut as my throat went numb. My ears rang and I thanked him.

He took the cup and ordered me to remove my pack. "No offense, but you look like shit! Hey, don't take it personally, buddy, I can just tell you're really beat down. I'll carry your stuff. You look like you could use a break. Come on, drop it."

I wanted to shed the weight, and I could tell he really wanted to help, but we had only just met, and for all I knew he could have been the Bad-Feet Backpacker Bandit and run off with all my things. So I feigned being a hardcore purist about carrying my own load. "Tough guy, huh?" He smiled and gave me the mug again. "No problem, I'll let you set the speed. I brought my headlamp just in case! Ha!"

Lode led the way and stayed a few steps ahead without ever looking back to check. As I described my condition, he offered to let me crash at his place for as long as I needed. Both his volume and enthusiasm rose in crescendo as he insisted. "I've got a pretty sweet trailer, I'll take great care of you! You can stay as long as you need to. Two days, three… Whatever you need, pal! I mean, if you're still around in October, we might have to work out some kind of deal for RENT AND UTILITIES! HA!" He laughed himself into a coughing fit again, and when he recovered he repeated himself. "Anything you need, pal!"

When I heard "trailer" I immediately thought of the single-wide from my childhood. Maybe I was lucky and Lode's was a double-wide. The single would be tight quarters for a pair of giants, one of whom might be just a tad off his rocker. One? Who am I kidding? I'm not exactly the picture of stability these days either.

When we arrived, I understood that by "trailer" he meant "camper," the kind that gets towed behind a large pickup truck. The large pickup truck was parked at the entrance to what appeared to be a small airplane hangar. Next to that was a cozy blue house with several partially completed additions. The wraparound porch almost wrapped around. Beside the unfinished end, a pile of lumber was neatly stacked beneath a clear plastic tarp.

"Here we are, pal! The Lode Land Hostile Hostel for Banged-up Hikers! That's a lot to say. Let's just call it Lode Land!" He opened the door to the trailer. "This is the guest house, and it's all yours for as long as you need it. The wifi reaches out here and the password is on a sticky note inside. TV works, and I started the air conditioner right before I left to come get you. Drop your stuff here and I'll give you the tour."

I did as I was told, and followed him up the driveway. The airplane hangar turned out to be Lode's garage. Twin bay doors 20 feet high opened onto a well-lit space that looked bigger on the inside than the outside allowed. Every wall was full: tools hung from pegs next to shelves full of jars full of screws. In addition to the big diesel parked out front, there was a smaller pickup inside. Also a snowmobile, a pair of ATVs, a quiver of kayaks leaned against one wall, a weight bench (with a lot of weight on it), an array of amplifiers taller than me, a computer with three flatscreen monitors, and a disco ball.

"Welcome to the Garage Mahal!" Lode beamed with pride.

He took me into the main house through the side door. The lemony sweet smell of pot was strong and immediate. "Whew!" I waved my hand in front of my face. "Do you just keep plates of the stuff on tables like potpourri?"

This was the funniest thing he'd heard all day. "That's great! Ha! You know what? I do, actually. Come look. Follow me." He took me to his living room, and there on the desk next to more monitors and speakers was a cereal bowl full of buds. "I told you, pal, that's what keeps me calm. You want some now, or after your shower? Oh, who am I kidding—both! Right? Ha!"

Lode sat at his desk and packed a pipe. "You know, a lot of people tell me that I smoke too much, and I tell them they're crazy! I tell them HEY! I say HEY! I ONLY SMOKE WHEN I'M AWAKE! HA!" He lit the pipe, took a few puffs and handed it to me. "Here, hit this and go get a shower. You really need it."

I did as I was told, and about 15 minutes later, standing in the steam, I let my chin fall to my chest. The hot water ran down my scalp and over my neck, giving me goosebumps. For the first time in days, I didn't feel like shit.

• • •

I stepped out of the shower and Lode called to me from the living room. "Good news, buddy! I just got off the horn with Mrs. Lode and she's bringing home a rotisserie chicken! I told her we had a hiker in the house so she picked up two more! Isn't that great?"

"That's fantastic, man." I tried to match his enthusiasm, but the hot water made me sleepy. "Do I have time to go unpack first?"

"Sure, man! Anything you need." He had his own ridiculous travel mug, this one filled with iced coffee. It held at least half a pot. He took a sip, put it down, and began typing. He was quickly lost in his thoughts, smiling and laughing softly by the monitor's glow.

The inside of my trailer was cool and cramped. It was comfortable, but I had to stoop. When I fell into the big bed, the trailer rocked, and for a moment I felt like I was below decks in some tiny ship, seasick on land. I plugged my phone into an outlet by the bed and called Katie.

"Hey! Are you in Boiling Springs?" Damn, she was good. "Where did you end up staying?"

"You're never going to believe this." I told her I had an entire shelter all to myself; one with electricity, wifi, air conditioning, and wheels. I described Lode next.

"He sounds like a big, friendly dog!"

"Yeah, the kind that drools all over you." The kind that might bite.

"So, how's your flu?"

"It comes and goes. Like right now, I feel fine. I'm supposed to zero here tomorrow. Lode's going to take me on a tour of the city, and if I still feel like crap, I'll go to the doctor."

"Promise?"

"Promise."

This satisfied her, and she cheered up even more. "Want to hear some good news? Megan texted me. She and Lemmy aren't that far ahead of you."

That was good news. I was almost keeping pace, and I'd catch up within a resupply or two, no problem. Right after this zero.

We were just about to say how much we missed each other for the fourth time when a car pulled into the driveway. "That would be Mrs. Lode," I said. We hung up and I looked in the mirror. Starting to get a little shaggy, I thought. I'd be pretty reluctant to let someone like me stay at my house. I had to be on my best behavior.

I ran out of the trailer and to the car, offering to help carry chickens. When Mrs. Lode opened her door, I was a little surprised that she was normal-sized and not as big as Lode. The only normal person here right now, I thought as I caught my reflection in her window.

She also moved at a normal pace and spoke in a normal volume. At dinner, I watched her talk Lode down from his near manic shouting with barely a word, just touching his arm and whispering something. He smiled, then picked up where he left off, with the same fevered gestures but at a lower volume. This was a routine they'd clearly rehearsed. She looked a little tired.

After dinner we retired to the Garage Mahal. Lode showed me framed medals he had arranged along the walls, belonging to his father, his grandfather, and Mrs. Lode's family too. The disco ball and amplifiers were from when he used to be a wedding DJ. He suggested that we take a couple of the kayaks and paddle the big lake in the middle of town, and maybe after that we could go out to a shooting range and hit some targets. I reminded him that I might need a doctor instead.

"Oh shit, man. Well, maybe we can do some of those things after. I'll get you taken care of, don't worry, pal. I'm best friends with one of the best doctors in town. We grew up together. He'll take care of you."

"I'm not worried, Lode. I trust you." I thanked him and Mrs. Lode hugged me. He took a sip of his coffee and pointed at the moon. "You'd better get to your trailer and get some sleep. You have a big day tomorrow."

• • •

That night I cracked the windows in the trailer and turned off the air conditioner so I could hear the far-off trains. The whistle and rumble combined with the crickets into the perfect lullaby. When I awoke, there was a message on my phone: *Coffee's ready.*

Mrs. Lode's car was gone, and when I opened the door the house was hazy, the air full of weed and coffee. I poured myself a cup in the kitchen, then went to join Lode in the living room, where his monitor shined through the fog, lighting up his Cheshire Cat smile with a hazy glow. "Are you ready to tour the city?"

Lode's other best friend was the guy who curated the museum archives for the county historical society. Which meant that our first stop on the tour was an hour of trying on silly hats in the basement of a gorgeous old building downtown. Our next stop was another one of Lode's best friends, who had a batch of strawberries for him. When Lode told him about my feet, he gave me a bundle of leaves that looked like spinach, a folk remedy called comfrey leaves. "Boil these and stick 'em in your socks before you go to sleep."

Next up on the tour was lunch at a restaurant managed by someone Lode grew up with who really was one of the best friends a guy could ever hope for, really. We ordered and I excused myself to wash my hands. While I was drying them, I noticed a faint pink blotch on my right forearm and two on my left arm that looked like old bee stings. None of them itched. I think I've seen this before, I thought. Better get a second opinion.

When I got back to the table, I showed Lode my arm.

He frowned. "Oh, shit. Have you been sleeping in the shelters?"

"Of course I have."

"That's ringworm, man. That is not great. I know—I used to coach wrestling, and we used to get it all the time from the mats."

"That's was I was afraid of." I'd had it once before, back in the military. Our gym on base was filthy despite regular scrubbings. A little ointment, and I'd be good as new. Maybe I'd even get something to treat this cold.

Now that kayaking and the rifle range were off the table, Lode took me to the doctor's office. His best friend the doctor was busy, but I was happy to see his assistant, a young lady with short blond curls. She asked the reason for my visit, and I confidently explained I had the flu and ringworm.

"Show me this ringworm," she said. I showed her the marks on my arms. She inspected them, frowning, then let my hand fall back to my lap. "You have Lyme disease."

"No I don't."

"Do your muscles ache? Have you had the chills? Fatigue? Mood swings?" *Do you live in the woods?*

She pointed to my leg, just above the knee, where I had somehow missed the classic bullseye pattern. "That's where he got you. Do you check for ticks?"

"Every day. I've flicked a few crawlers, but I've never had one latch. Don't they have to latch for 24 hours to transmit Lyme disease?"

"That's a myth. All it has to do is latch on for an hour. It could have happened in your sleep."

I should have been horrified, but actually I was ecstatic. There was a *reason* for my malaise. I wasn't losing my edge; I wasn't the problem. And there was a solution.

"I'm going to write you a script for doxycycline. You're going to become extra sensitive to sunlight and lose your appetite."

"But those are the only two things I do: eat and be outside!"

"Well, you guys are mostly under the trees anyhow. But you are going to be queasy and unable to eat when you take this. Also, you have to take it with food. And it's going to make you irritable at first, but you only have to take it for a month."

"This sounds an awful lot like the problem I already have. What if I don't take it?"

She placed her clipboard in her lap. "You'll continue to feel like crap. And in a year you'll get misdiagnosed as clinically depressed. A year after that, one side of your face may stop working. Permanently."

I happily accepted the prescription. When I returned to the waiting room, Lode was still at the window trying to get the receptionist to deliver a message to his busy doctor friend. I squeezed myself between them to pay and check out.

On the way to his truck, I asked if our next stop could be the pharmacy. And maybe after that, some trailer time for a nap. "I have good news and bad news, and they're both the same thing: I have Lyme disease."

"Whatever you need, pal. How long does it take for the meds to work?"

"The doctor said it would take two or three days."

"That wasn't a doctor—that was his assistant! I can't believe he couldn't make five minutes for us! I mean, come on, man!" He laughed. "We grew up together! He couldn't even come out into the waiting room to say hello TO HIS BEST FRIEND?"

"The *assistant* said it would take two to three days before I felt normal again. But that I should keep taking them."

"Well, it looks like you're squatting at Lode Land for a few days! You take your pills and just hang out in the trailer. I'll get more leaves for your feet and the wife will bring you soup. Unless you want something else?" He opened the passenger door for me.

"I don't want to be a bother."

"Nonsense!"

"Can I at least give you guys some money?"

"I told you before. Don't bring it up again. It's not like I'm using the trailer for anything else right now, right? It's yours for as long as you need it."

He climbed into his side and shut the door. "You're like family. We're practically best friends!"

. . .

I swallowed my first pill, sat on the bed, and called Katie. "I think I'm going to live," I told her. "You'd be proud of me. I finally went to the doctor today." I told her about my mystery spots and the diagnosis, and said I had decided I needed some more zeros while the meds kicked in.

"Three days, huh? You just took four."

"Yeah, back in West Virginia!" My voice was a little too sharp.

"No, it's okay," she said in a soothing tone. "I was only looking at a calendar." I had already begun doing the same in my head. "You know you're cutting it close now, right?"

Based on my present location and pace, before this new delay, I had been on track to finish with only a few days to spare. Just because Baxter State Park promises to close Mount Katahdin on a certain day does not mean winter will obey their rules too. Maine is a wild and unpredictable place; in the past, heaps of snow have buried that mountain as early as mid-September. Tomorrow it would be August.

"Have you thought about what to do? You know, if you have to stop again?"

"I have."

Earlier that morning I'd spent a few minutes reading my notebook. I had turned to my last entry before I had to hitch into Luray with my shoulders slumped and my head hung low. It was the night I had watched Lemmy hike away, then sat on a picnic bench and cried.

*"You can make yourself do anything for a day, even a week,"* I had written. *"With the right amount of mental trickery, you can make yourself do something for years. But when you're doing something you love, nothing can make you stop."*

I was on my back in a trailer with my feet elevated and wrapped in leaves. My arms and legs were covered with spots, I could barely keep my eyes open, and I wanted to vomit—and all I could think was, What do I have to do to keep going? I don't want this to end.

"I'm going to rest a few days, and then ask Lode to drop me off just ahead of Lemmy and Megan so I can ramp up again and do the traffic merge thing. I have to keep going."

"Right..."

"But if one more thing happens—not like a broken leg, but like one more three-day or four-day recovery thing—then I'll just do as much I can."

She agreed. "Would you hitch up to the Whites? Or still do Katahdin?"

"Let's just think about Pennsylvania for now."

"So where will Lode put you back on the trail?"

"I don't know. We'll work it out." I shook the pill bottle. "This stuff's supposed to work pretty quickly. Maybe I'll do a practice hike tomorrow or the next day and see how I feel."

"I miss you."

"I miss you too," I said. "I wish it was you taking me back to the trail." The next time I saw her, wherever that was, she would take me home.

After dinner that night, Lode's friend from the museum showed up for a surprise visit. He brought his wife and little girl and a tray of brownies for the banged-up hiker. We retired to the Garage Mahal, and soon Lode's friend who gave me the comfrey leaves arrived. He brought his wife and little girl too, and a tray of Jell-O shots. Even the doctor showed up.

Lode repositioned himself at his bank of monitors and turned on the wall of amplifiers. He dimmed the lights and powered up the disco ball and got the music started. Mrs. Lode and the other wives took off their shoes and held hands in a circle while the little girls danced barefoot in the middle. The men drank beer and told me stories while the girls spun, and Lode held one headphone up to his ear while dancing in his chair.

■  ■  ■

As Lode predicted, for the next two days I spent a lot of time in the trailer on my back with leaves wrapped around my feet. I got caught up on a lot of reading and talking to Katie. I ate a lot. On the third day, my test hike went well. The sun hurt my skin and eyes, but I was only a little nauseous, and the urge to nap had finally left me. I wasn't grumpy at all, and after three miles I was ready to crush mountains and make more miles.

Figuring that Lemmy and Voldemort were probably still making 20 miles per day, and allowing for a zero for them, our best guess was to drop me off at a place called Wind Gap.

"I sure am glad I met you, Green Giant!" Lode said as I pulled my pack out of the truck bed. "I knew right away that we'd be friends, and I was right. Ha!" He crushed my hand and pulled me in for a hug, and when he slapped my back I coughed a little. "You're still in my jurisdiction, so you can still call me if you fall out again. But remember, once you're in New Jersey—"

"Someone else's problem, got it. Thanks again!"

He climbed back into his truck. Just before he turned onto the road, he stuck his head out the window. "Look in your pack! Bye!"

The window closed and he drove away. I put my pack on the

stone steps that led to my first climb and opened it. There on top was a 35 mm film canister. I popped the lid and it smelled like Lode's living room. A note mixed in with the buds said: *This will help with your appetite!*

I suppose it will, I thought, and shoved it deeper into my pack. A buckle had broken, so I was tying a knot in my makeshift drawstring when I realized I had company. It was Dude. I lifted my pack and greeted him with a smile.

"Hey, it's you—Green Giant!" He offered a fist bump. "I didn't think I'd see you again. Or anyone again really. How's it going, man?"

When I told him I had Lyme disease, he recalled that I had looked "a little rough" the night we met. Then he told me about meeting my friends. "Lemmy's a riot, man. And that chick is crazy. She kept up with me for like a day and a half. They're pretty far back, though. Those rocks messed a lot of people up."

I told him about Lode and the Garage Mahal, and the spontaneous dance party, and how the two of us kayaked across the lake in the middle of town, right by the white blazes of the AT. "I guess that makes me an aqua blazer now too, among other things."

Dude ran his fingers through his hair. "See, man—you're doing it right. You aren't missing anything on this hike. You're doing it all."

"I don't know about that, Dude. I just spent an hour in a car to get here. I must have missed something."

He looked at his shoes, which were in tatters. "Nope. Whole mess of rocks, and a lot of places to get drunk."

"Really?"

"Really."

# 19

# A FRIENDLY EXCHANGE

I CHECKED MY SHOES for mud purely out of habit. My feet hadn't touched dirt in a week. The trail had been nothing but rocks, and my shoes were dry as bone, but I kicked them anyway and stepped through the screen door into the church basement.

The drop ceiling was low, maybe a foot above my head. Two rotating fans pushed the thick air around the windowless room where a group of hikers was seated, scattered and leaning in various stages of exhaustion. They watched me enter as if they had been staring at the door, hoping for something interesting to happen.

"This must be the right place," I said. When no one replied, I asked about a sign-in sheet or someone to check in with. One of them finally perked up and pointed me to the bunks, the shower, and the donation box. It was a simple slot in the wall—more or less the same as the bunks, which were human-sized plywood shelves lining the cinderblock walls of what used to be a storage room.

"At least they're carpeted," I said as I lifted my pack onto a top bunk. After showering and starting a load of laundry, I returned to the common area and took the empty seat at the far end of an oversize leather sofa.

I was happy to just sit and listen to the group chat, sinking into that big, soft couch. Everyone had just met, and they were all tired from a hot day of scrambling on the same rocks I had, but more of them; it had taken me all day to go a mere seven miles, while they had probably done triple that.

The pill I'd taken before showering was beginning to make me queasy, and I closed my eyes and leaned my head back. Just then the screen door opened, and my couchmate stood. "Hello, Reverend," he said, and extended a hand.

The reverend was a stocky woman in her mid-fifties with a square blonde head and smart makeup. It felt strange introducing myself to someone with such a clean, professional bearing while I was clad in full laundry-day regalia: long johns and a raincoat with no shirt. My beard was still dripping from the shower.

She greeted each of us and insisted that we sit back down. Then she began with the hiker to my left. "I assume you're all northbound?" He nodded and the rest of us joined him. "One thing I really enjoy is hearing the stories from all you hikers. Tell me, what motivated you to take on such a challenge?"

He squirmed in his seat. "This probably isn't the answer you want, but it's honest: I was bored."

"Oh, come now. Surely there must be more to it than just that. There's so much to explore, to learn about oneself."

He leaned forward, more confident this time. "No, actually, that's about it. I'm in my twenties and I have no real responsibilities. For a lot of us, this is just something fun to do for the summer." He finished with a shrug. I'd heard this line countless times and was surprised that she hadn't.

She addressed the group again. "You're pretty far along, so you've probably had plenty of time to think about this. Regardless of why you're hiking, by this point you've changed in some way." Next she looked to me. "What about you? You're a bit older than the rest. You must have some pretty special reason for hiking the trail. Why are you doing this?"

My stomach gurgled, mostly from the pill. All I could think of was that I loved hiking. Naive thoughts from the early days came back: *I live outside now. Whatever the weather throws at me...bring it on!* Did I love swearing and kicking rocks all day? Did I love having my will sapped from the bite of crawling parasites that might bite me again?

Actually, I did. I was in the Vortex, and I loved it. Not the one that sucks you into a town and holds you there, but another kind, the spin cycle of life. To outsiders, things may have seemed out of control; from here inside my head, everything reduced to a single simple directive:

*Keep going.* The white blazes, hand painted and unique as snowflakes, were the only consistent and stable thing in a mad, swirling chaos. Everything I needed to survive—in the most real sense of that word—was on my back. My footfalls had become my mantra. I had found Zen.

Or it had found me. However the hell Zen works.

More than the Vortex was spinning now. I was nauseous, and my head felt like it was on sideways. The reverend was still looking at me as I dripped sweat. I still hadn't answered her question. Hikers were waiting to be interrogated. "I wanted a challenge," I said. Weak. Come on, Green Giant, I thought. What kind of bullshit answer was that?

She narrowed her eyes and nodded. "And what have you discovered about yourself?"

I learned that I get pissy when someone wants to conduct a full-scale investigation into my life story when the only place to eat in town closes in half an hour. "I surprised myself by how much I can withstand physically."

Still not enough. Okay, how about this? "I think I have a better understanding of what it might be like to be homeless."

She straightened in her chair. "Oh! So you sold or gave away all your possessions before undertaking this journey?"

I peeled my forearm from the leather armrest. "No, I still have a house and a couch and all that stuff. I just haven't been there in a while."

"Well, that's not exactly the same thing," she said, folding her arms.

My stomach was in my throat. "No, but I did just shower in a church basement. And I have no idea where I'll be tomorrow or the next day, or the day after that." I closed my eyes and breathed through my mouth, trying to minimize my headache.

She took this as a signal that I was done and addressed the young lady to my right. "How about you, dear? It must be so much harder to hike the trail as a woman. Is it?"

The girl covered her face and nodded. She was crying.

"There, there, honey," the reverend said. "Why the tears?"

From behind perfectly manicured hands, she answered, "Because my hike is over tomorrow." She looked up, uncovering red puffy eyes. "I'm going home."

"Why, dear?"

"Because it really *is* harder for a girl!" Her hands fell into her lap and she continued. "I'm just so sick of it always being bro time!"

"Bro time? What does that mean?" the reverend asked.

She had everyone's attention now. She looked around the room. "I'm sorry, but boys suck. All they ever want to do is talk about poop. They swear constantly, and everything is a joke."

"So it's beyond just a physical challenge?"

"It is," she said, dropping her shoulders even more. She sniffed. "All I want is just once to have someone I can open up to and share my feelings with. But no—it's just nonstop poop jokes and poop talk. And I'm so sick of being gross all the time!"

"Oh honey, I know."

I had been pressing my fingers into my temples while she talked. I let go of my head and looked at the girl, thinking, If Voldemort were here right now, she would pop a blister and then blow a snot rocket at you. "I'm sorry," I said. "I'm not feeling well." I excused myself to the laundry and gathered my clothes from the dryer.

. . .

I was in the bunk room putting on warm shorts when the guy from the couch grabbed some things from his bunk. He introduced himself as Thespian. "I'm going to go outside to smoke a pipe before dinner," he said. "Would you care to join me?"

We walked to a bench behind the church, where he produced an elegant briar pipe with a leather tobacco pouch and a stainless steel cleaning kit. "This is a select blend I picked up in the last town, mostly Turkish. What are you smoking this evening?"

I pulled Lode's film canister from my pocket. "Any objections? I'm happy to share." He said no to both and we sat on the bench and smoked.

"I suppose," I said, "that one of us needs to make a poop joke now."

"Yeah, I know, right?"

"I almost said something to her. 'Boys suck' is just as bad as me saying women are weak. Sure, some of us do, and some of them are, but not all." My nausea was already starting to subside, either from the pot or the righteous indignation.

He blew a smoke ring. "She looked like she was having a pretty rough time. She's a 22-year-old girl. Give her a break."

"No," I said. "She doesn't get a break just for that. If there's more to it, then yes. I'm sorry, but one of my hiking partners is a 22-year-old girl who could kick her ass, and probably mine and yours too. Poop jokes? Good lord, give me a break. You know who makes poop jokes? Hikers do. Not just bros or dudes—hikers." I jerked my thumb toward the church. "She's dropping out not because she isn't a dude, but because she isn't a hiker."

The irony of my accusation was not lost on me. After all, I had just yellow blazed 150 miles. But I had made those compromises ultimately so that I could stay on the trail. I wanted the poop jokes and the muddy fingernails. She just needed a pedicure.

"I'm sure that having to leave the trail is hard, regardless of why. I get that. I just don't want her to carry the idea for the rest of her life that my entire gender was responsible for her having a bad time because she made a poor decision on how to spend her summer."

"That's pretty harsh, man."

"Well, I am a little upset, but I really feel that way. Thanks for being someone I could 'open up to and share my feelings with.'"

He smiled and tamped his pipe, and took a puff. "So, who's this girl you hike with," he said. "Is her trail name Voldemort, perchance?"

"It is! I take it you passed her not too long ago? How's she doing?"

He put away his pipe and stood. "I did pass her. She had to slow down for a day or so. She had an infected blister on her heel. She showed it to me but I'd rather not describe it."

I remembered that blister. If it was the one I was thinking of, she'd gotten it back in North Carolina, and if that was still bothering her, and infected...I didn't want to think about it. "Did you meet Lemmy?"

"Ah yes, that fellow." Thespian smiled and stroked his beard. "He's an interesting one."

I checked the time. "Want to talk about him over some food?"

∙ ∙ ∙

Thespian was good company, and food also improved my mood. After dinner we walked back to the church. It was 8:30, nearly hiker midnight, and I was brushing my teeth when one final hiker arrived for the night. He entered quietly and put his pack on the floor beside the big leather sofa. He and I were the last ones awake.

I whispered, "Hey, I'm Green Giant." He introduced himself as Kodiak. He was short and stocky, built like a wrestler. When he told me he was a speed hiker, I said, "Oh, cool! You're not too far behind Dude. Do you know him?"

"Yeah, I passed him this morning."

I was confused. "No, he's ahead of us, unless you mean a different Dude."

Kodiak pursed his lips. "I'm SOBO." The word rhymes with hobo, and it means southbound. Everyone I knew so far was NOBO.

"You're the first one I've seen!"

He nodded.

"How was Katahdin?"

"Amazing."

"And Maine in general? What about the White Mountains?"

"Beautiful."

"Are they are hard as everyone says they are?"

"Yep."

"Oh, man, I can't wait! You must be tired. I haven't seen any southbounders yet. I wonder what it must be like."

"You know those three questions you just asked me?"

Oh no. "Yeah."

"You're the thousandth person to ask me those three questions in that exact order. Everyone said, 'Go southbound for the solitude.' Right. I keep thinking I've met the last NOBO, and you guys just keep coming."

Now I felt bad for bothering him. He had a legitimate gripe, and I was one more raindrop in the flood. "I'm sorry, man."

"Nah, it's cool. You guys are all excited. I get it."

"So how far behind The Bubble am I?"

He sighed. "And there's question number four."

"Dammit. I should go to bed. Good night."

"Good night, Green Giant."

The next morning I woke up at 5:30 to use the bathroom and he was already packed and gone.

■   ■   ■

The New Jersey state line sits at the bottom of a great descent. Not great as in size—it's actually quite small—but as in scenery. The last three miles of Pennsylvania offer exciting views of the ascent awaiting on the other side. I've never seen another mountain like it: a huge twisted mound with alternating bands of trees and exposed rock spiraling to the top. It looked like pulled taffy turned to granite.

To reach its base, and New Jersey, I had to first cross the Delaware River. The white blazes took me to a pedestrian walkway on the same bridge that carries Interstate 80 for more than a mile over the river. The trail then goes up that same weirdly-shaped mountain. Immediately before the ascent is a brown sign bearing the National Park Service logo, with bold text proclaiming NO SWIMMING! NO GRILLING! NO FIRES! NO CAMPING! At least they had shelters. At least New Jersey was short.

The first ascent in the new state was already less rocky than Pennsylvania. Along the way I passed the remains of several campsites. Circles of ash and coals could be seen among the scattered rocks of old fire rings, kicked apart by rangers weekly, judging by their look. The trees bore official looking plaques reminding passersby of the rules, and warning that the area was patrolled. One sign lay in a fire ring, partially roasted. Aside from these historic mini-battlegrounds where campers fought authority, the climb was pretty. A gurgling stream paralleled the trail, shrinking as I climbed to the source, a mere spring near the top.

I had a quiet night at a shelter, and in the morning I felt great for the first time in a long time. Really great. I had been on the antibiotics long enough to completely kill the bacteria responsible for Lyme disease. My mood and appetite were back to normal and my foot problems had been scaled back to the former imaginary bunched-up socks, which I still didn't enjoy but could tolerate. It was time to try for 20 again. The last time had been Virginia, so long ago.

I was nearing a water stop when I thought I heard familiar voices up ahead. Hiking with a partner or a group is something like talking on the phone, since you can't see the person you're talking to. You almost always walk single file, so you spend a great deal of time looking at the backpack of the person you're talking to. Voices and backpacks become as easy to identify as faces. So I had plenty of time before catching up to them to settle down from the initial excitement of seeing Dingo and Hungry Horse again.

They couldn't hear me over the running water. So they jumped when I called out, "Hey guys! What's it been, about 500 miles?"

Dingo stood up and offered a fist bump. His beard was amazing; it had doubled in size since I last saw him and was now a gray mane that exploded in all directions, obscuring his neck and almost reaching his shoulders. Hungry Horse still wore his hat and glasses. His red beard was noticeably longer too, but had not undergone the dramatic growth spurt Dingo's had.

Pennsylvania's rocks had slowed them down too. "That whole state is just a big old rock tumbler. No crew makes it out intact. We even lost Johnny Oak—I mean, he lost us. He's way ahead now. At least we think so. Nobody knows where anybody is anymore. So how the heck did you catch us?"

I told them about my feet, Lyme disease, and how I was a no-good goddamn dirty yellow blazer now. Hungry Horse laughed. "We're just glad you're still out here, dude!"

My mood was still good by the end of the day, but my feet hurt. Nowhere near emergency levels, but enough that I was excited about taking my shoes off and rubbing my toes at the end of the day. That excitement was replaced by curiosity the moment we arrived at the Brink Road shelter. The box was new, with a covered porch, but that's not what held our attention.

There was a large, green, metal tube lying on its side about a hundred feet in front of the shelter. It was the size of a Volkswagen and had strong metal braces preventing it from rolling. A square frame six feet high suspended a flat metal plate, guillotine-style, above the open end of the tube. Large white letters were painted on the plate. *DANGER! BEAR TRAP — KEEP AWAY!*

"Good thing bears can't read," Hungry Horse said.

The warning was painted on the sides and back too, plus a phone number to alert rangers should a hiker find it occupied. This one was not. Bagels and orange peels littered the ground around the opening. A bag of bait hung from a triggering mechanism deep inside, but some raccoons or other small vermin had ripped into it and eaten their fill before waddling off to nap somewhere.

We had dinner in the shelter and watched the green metal tube from a safe distance. Nothing happened. The only sounds that night were the three of us slapping at mosquitoes. We awoke tired and said little while eating our breakfast. We were staring at the green metal tube in silence when Dingo tapped my arm and pointed. Hungry Horse was already looking.

The black bear was as big as a small horse. If we hadn't already been facing in its direction, we never would have known it was there. It never broke a twig or kicked a single rock. Four hundred pounds of muscle and fur sailed across the clearing in seconds, then slowed, finally pausing at the scraps at the door to the tube.

No one said a word. The bear nosed a bagel and swallowed it whole. Its massive head sniffed the circumference of the entrance and licked it once. Then the beast backed away and found another bagel, then pawed at an orange peel before slowly retreating to the trees.

Hungry Horse looked at us and whispered, "Holy shit, did you see that!? I mean, I know you did, but wow!"

I was about to reply when Dingo tapped my arm again and pointed. It was coming back, but slower this time. There were still a few bagels left in the bait bag deep inside, and the bear could smell them. It crept to the front again, sniffed and licked again, and then stepped inside. The back half of the bear was still visible when it stopped, paused and backed out. It had a bagel in its mouth. The bagel fell, but the bear snatched it with a paw before it hit the ground. Again, the bagel disappeared in one bite.

Nobody moved. The bear looked inside. It had seen these green tubes before. It couldn't remember what, but something bad was about to happen. It backed up a step, and then the wind changed. The smell of food was too much to resist, and the bear marched confidently into the trap. When the spring released, the heavy steel gate slammed shut with a clang. It sounded like a car hit a dumpster. The bear immediately panicked.

The tube rocked and the heavy braces seemed about to snap as the bear threw itself against the walls. Frantic claws scratched at steel while it snorted and bounced inside. There wasn't enough space for it to turn around. Safe but confused in this temporary metal coffin, it gradually calmed. After one more slam from within, it settled down to the occasional snort or scratch.

Dingo ran full speed to the trap, Hungry Horse followed, and I yelled, "Holy shit!"

"What are you going to do?" Hungry Horse asked him. "Call the rangers?"

Dingo was already dialing. He was jumping and pointing while they transferred him to the correct department. After telling the story three times, he finally reached someone who understood. Fifteen minutes later, a small pickup from the New Jersey State Park Police came up the dirt road and a uniformed officer stepped out and greeted us. "What ya got there, fellas?"

"We got ourselves a bear in a can, sir!" Hungry Horse replied.

The officer circled the silent green tube. "You sure? Not one of your buddies in there, is it?" He rapped on the outside. Were it not for the side braces, the whole thing would have rolled over him from the force within, as the bear responded by slamming all of its weight sideways.

We all jumped back. Two more slams were followed by more snorting and scratching. I noticed the officer's hand was on the butt of his gun. He took a breath and relaxed his arm, then glanced back at his pickup. "I don't know why they sent *me* out here." He keyed the mic on his shoulder and requested backup. Metal boomed as the bear shouldered the tube. The officer keyed the mic again. "We're going to need a bigger truck."

While we packed up, he told us to our surprise that New Jersey has the densest population of black bears on the trail. They'd been trying to catch this particular bear for weeks. It had become used to humans and developed a reputation for aggressive behavior, even coming into the shelter one night.

"What's going to happen to it?" Dingo asked.

"We have been relocating them, but we're running out of places to put them. I've lost count personally, but I think we've already moved 30 this year."

This wasn't so surprising when I thought about it. Up north, the trail no longer felt so isolated. Hardly a day passed that I didn't detect distant traffic or airplanes. Even on clear nights we couldn't see the stars, because the sky was orange from nearby cities and industry. If I lived in those woods, I'd become aggressive too.

"So how are you boys liking New Jersey so far?" the officer asked. "If you guys are looking for things to do in town, I can recommend a good strip club that's open for lunch."

We looked at each other, and my memory snapped back to our pants-free day in the Virginia sun, "No thanks. We've had enough nudity for one hike."

■   ■   ■

Eighty miles—that's all New Jersey is. This far into the hike we were high rollers, ignoring the last two digits on mile markers and dealing strictly in hundreds. This place was small change. Mountains now disappeared behind us like years as we age—the farther along we were, the faster they seem to go. Not seeing someone for two days had been cause for alarm back in Georgia. Up here, two weeks ago felt like yesterday.

Eighty miles takes less time than the average work week. For a hiker, it's one small resupply and a lot of walking. If not for the sudden change in terrain, the bear trap may have been the only highlight from our brief tour of the Garden State.

Short, flowery climbs were separated by miles of swampy boardwalk. Hundreds of narrow wood platforms 10 feet long were placed end to end, sometimes shored up by large rocks or concrete pillars. Every tenth one or so had a white blaze. The boardwalks twisted and curved through wet marshy grass, tall reeds, and cattails. Patches of purple flowers six feet tall sprung up all around. The sun blasted my face and arms until I was coated with a fine slime of sweat mixed with dead gnats. A mile later, I'd be a thousand feet higher and in the green tunnel enjoying a cool breeze. Then back to the swamps.

New York wasn't far ahead, and that was only 100 miles. There it was again: *Only a hundred miles.* I could do that in less time than it takes the average person to wait for the next episode of their favorite TV show.

Judging by the pulsing line in the guidebook, I could expect more brief climbs separated by more busy road crossings each day. New York is often referred to as the Deli Run. Hikers going both directions stop carrying food altogether for that whole week. With little or no planning, it's possible to eat three hot meals a day at greasy diners and family-owned sandwich shops. The average hiker gains seven pounds in New York.

I still had one more stop before the state line though, a little deli on the New Jersey side. Outside was a bench and a sign telling hikers to leave their packs. Most places aren't worried about items mysteriously vanishing into them. It's more a problem of bulk—they tend to knock into things. Plus, they smell. I put mine on the bench and walked in.

A bell jingled and the man behind the counter eyed me silently. He returned to the grill where he was cooking something for two men at the register. A small fan blew smoke from the grill while a radio yelled angry political opinions.

Thinking it might be a while before he got to me, I plugged my phone into the power strip by the door and went to the freezer. I took out an ice cream sandwich, met the owner's eyes and pointed to it, then to the register and nodded. *I'm not stealing this.* He returned my nod before finishing the other customers' lunches.

I ate the ice cream and looked for a garbage can. There was none, so I shoved the wrapper into my pocket. It was my turn. "What'll ya have?"

"I'd like a number three, please. And I'll take one more ice cream sandwich, so that's two total. Thanks."

He said nothing and started my sandwich, a simple grilled ham and cheese. My mouth watered when the meat sizzled. My stomach growled when he wrapped it up and I paid him. My eyes widened when he handed me my change and said, "Now get the fuck out of my store."

I was speechless.

"You heard me. Go." He pointed at the door.

"I'm sorry, did I do some—"

"You plugged in your phone without asking. What do you think, you own the place? I don't allow it."

He was still pointing.

"Okay, okay, I'm going. This takes a second." I folded my charging cable while he watched and pointed. "Maybe hang a sign? Or don't have a power strip right by the—"

"Get out."

I held the cable in my teeth, put my sandwich in one hand and used the other to open the freezer. I took my ice cream, and backed out of the deli, pushing open the door with my butt. I dumped everything into a pile on the bench and seethed. Then I got an idea.

From the change, I selected a single penny. I stomped around the corner and back in through the front door. Before he could say anything, I held the penny at eye level and crossed the room. I slapped it onto the counter and slid it across under my index finger.

He looked down. "What's this for?"

"This is for the electricity."

I raised my finger and he calmly took the penny. He pressed "No Sale," the drawer slid open, and he dropped the penny in with the others and closed the drawer. He smiled and said, "Thank you."

I returned his smile. "You're welcome."

He pointed at the door. "Now get the fuck out of my store!"

This guy might just have come up with the next New Jersey state motto, I thought. "I don't suppose you have a restroom I could use?"

He threw his arms up and yelled. "Get out, and go fuck yourself!"

"Fine!" I shouted back. "I will!" *Damn it, I think I just lost that round.* I pushed through the door and stepped back out into the sunshine.

My ice cream was melting, which meant I had to eat it first. I laughed, wondering if this was simply the local vernacular and that from the shopkeeper's perspective we had just shared a pleasant exchange. All that shouting had been exhilarating, and I kind of wanted to hold on to it. But it's hard to be mad while you're eating ice cream.

# 20

## PINKY SWEAR

LIKE MANY TRAIL TOWNS, the village of Unionville, N.Y. is at the bottom of a descent. But this one is only 50 feet of elevation loss while walking along a mile of paved road. The white blazes are on the telephone poles as the road winds through wooded and grassy areas, passing close by an old Victorian mansion by a pond. Driveways and mailboxes belonging to more practical homes became more frequent as I neared a sign welcoming me to UNIONVILLE, POPULATION: 612.

According to the guidebook, behind the village office they let hikers pitch a tent free of charge. If you got there while the office was open, you might even meet the mayor.

The town was pretty deserted. Through the windows of a small storefront, I could see a young man mopping the floor. COMMUNITY CENTER was painted on the glass, so I assumed someone inside might be able to point me to the right place and went in. When the door closed behind me, the young man dropped his mop and spun around to look at me. He didn't have a neck. His eyes were too close together and he wore a big, permanent smile. He clapped excitedly and announced, "We have a friend! A friend is here!"

Through the door behind him, a set of curious eyes appeared behind thick, round glasses. The rest of her followed—a short, muscular girl with a pixie haircut, holding a spray bottle and a rag. "We don't know if he's a friend yet. We have to ask him." She turned to me and raised her voice as though she were hailing me from across a moat. "HELLO! ARE YOU FRIEND OR FOE?!"

"Friend, of course," I said, and bowed, removing my hat. "Green Giant at your service."

They both laughed and clapped. She added, "If we're friends, you have to pinky swear!" She held out a fist like a hiker offering a bump, but with her pinky extended and slightly curled. I gladly agreed, and when our pinkies linked her smile brightened. When she squeezed, for a second I thought my finger would come off. She let go and then moved in for a hug, and her friend soon joined the circle.

Two more of their friends entered the room, everyone maintaining expressions of wonder and joy as they surrounded me. I was someone new and this was the best thing that had happened all day. The shortest, stockiest young man stood inches away from me and puffed his chest. "I like your feather," he told me.

His taller friend clicked his heels and stood at attention. "This is how you salute," he said, as his right hand popped like lightning and stopped with fingers barely touching his brow, arm at a perfect forty-five degree angle, with more enthusiasm and heart than many salutes I'd seen in years of military service. I returned his courtesy as best I could, and he shook my hand. "Hey! That was a good salute!"

Forget meeting the mayor, I thought. Can I stay here? These guys are the best.

Footsteps from above came down the stairs, and a tall woman in jeans and a polo shirt entered the room and welcomed me. "Okay guys," she said. "Let's not crowd our friend. Finish your duties now. Good job, guys." I introduced myself and asked about the village office, and she told me I was close, just across the street and up another block. I thanked her and returned to the sunshine. The girl with the thick glasses pressed her face against the window and watched me cross.

The mayor was out, but that was okay. I already felt plenty welcome. The clerk had me fill out a simple slip of paper with my names (real and trail) and the date, then directed me to an area past the playground and basketball courts with plenty of flat, grassy space. I put my tent under a tree in the back corner, far from sight. Even though I was allowed to be there, I still felt like I was technically a drifter, and was sure some residents might also assume as much.

Out of sight as I stripped to my shorts and trimmed my remaining toenails, I decided that if I really needed a self-esteem boost, I could always go back over to the Community Center and get some free hugs. Then I remembered Dingo had mentioned meeting one of his old college buddies at the tavern here, and I decided to try for free beers instead.

． ． ．

I awoke to the sound of church bells and a rooster calling from someone's yard. About a mile down the road was a grocery store, where I restocked. I was almost finished arranging things in my pack when my phone vibrated. It was Katie.

"Hello! Wow! No one ever calls me!"

"I wasn't expecting you to answer," she laughed. "Shouldn't you be hiking?"

"I was just about to, and I will be soon. I mean, take your time! How are you?"

"Great. I'm at work. I just thought you might like to hear something interesting. I just got off the phone with Megan. She's in New York."

"Wait a minute, I thought she was behind me, and I just got here. Where is she?"

The city she named was nowhere near the trail, but it sounded familiar.

"It's where my sister Priscilla lives," Katie explained. Megan had texted Katie that she had blisters so bad that she couldn't walk anymore and needed help.

"So you gave her to your sister? They're both crazy. I'd watch that show."

"Priscilla's getting back into walking again too, so they'll have something to do together," Katie said. When Megan had heard the story, back at Clingmans Dome, of my sister-in-law's slow rehabilitation from a near-fatal car crash, she had said she wanted to meet Priscilla. Looks like she was getting her wish.

I thought about Lode, and yesterday's free hugs, and shook my head. Some random girl I met at a mosquito-infested shelter a thousand miles ago was now convalescing on my sister-in-law's couch in New York. It was beginning to feel as if all this magic wasn't coming from the angels and magicians, but from the trail itself.

"What's she going to do about getting back on? Jump up to wherever Lemmy and I are?"

Katie laughed. "Nope. She's going to go right back to where she got off and make up the miles. She said she's going to start cranking out twenty-fives."

"She's bonkers."

Katie agreed.

"Remember the day you came up with her trail name? You told me to take care of my own problems. Now Voldemort has both you and your sister working for her."

That night I pitched my tent by a wide, shallow stream. The sky was clear and winds were calm, so I left my rain fly bunched up deep inside my pack. Nearby was a sturdy footbridge and the remains of an old rock wall. I sat on the wall while I ate my dinner and listened to the water.

Now that I was a bit farther away from it, I could hear a quieter background noise that I had missed earlier. Hundreds of baby toads no bigger than my thumbnail were bouncing and hopping all around me, landing in the dry leaves with a tiny crunch. As far as I could see, the ground was covered with them, all hopping in the same direction, uphill and away from the water. Once the little stampede passed, I walked back to my tent, carefully placing each foot so as not to crunch any toads.

The sky remained clear, but as I slept the wind picked up, knocking acorns out of the oaks overhead. When the first one bounced off my tent I sat up with a start, convinced that the toads were back. Minutes later when the second one landed near my tent, I convinced myself to ignore the sound. After a few more impacts, the plunks faded into the background along with the white noise of the wide stream whooshing and the gentle patter of rain drops.

When one of the bigger drops splashed onto my sleeping face, I sat up startled again. My rain fly. Shit.

I fumbled for my headlamp, then emptied my pack. The mesh above me was not designed to stop water, so everything was damp. When I found the fly, I unzipped the mesh and stood, holding the fly over my head like a poncho. There was no time to find a rock to pound the stakes in, so I slipped my foot into a shoe to stomp them. My bare toes found a wet slimy mess inside. It was full of slugs.

They were everywhere—on the trees, on my tent, in my shoes. One was already crawling up my leg. I had avoided being trampled so far by cows, ponies, other hikers, and even an army of tiny toads, and now I was being run over by a slug stampede.

I worked frantically in the rain, flicking slugs off of my tent and legs. I emptied my shoes, stomped the stakes, tightened the fly, and then crawled, exhausted, back into my tent and toweled off. The rain stopped almost as soon as I got zipped up and comfortable. It took about an hour for me to fall asleep, and an hour after that the birds started.

■ ■ ■

New York wasn't all hugs and slugs. The state offered plenty of ups and downs, and as promised, delis galore. I climbed dozens of miniature mountains every day, fueled by ham and eggs, Italian subs, Reubens, ice cream sandwiches, and paper-thin wedges of pizza bigger than my head. I ate a deep-fried turkey leg from a food truck parked beside a crowded manmade lake.

The trail even goes through a real zoo at one point, the lowest on the entire trail, both in elevation and in mood. Just before crossing the Hudson River up near West Point, less than ten steps past the sign proudly announcing the AT's literal rock bottom (it's in a tunnel beneath a busy road), a black bear languishes in a steel cage no bigger than the average bathroom. He has a dish of water, a log to climb on, and a hollow wooden cube where he usually hides from the cameras and shouting tourists. One of the zoo's hot dog vendors told me I looked like Amish Robin Hood. I smiled and ate my hot dogs while he and his friend pointed and laughed at my hat.

One of my final camping spots in New York was a place called Nuclear Lake. The lake is so named because it was once the home of a nuclear research facility. In 1972 an explosion threw plutonium powder into the surrounding area. The government spent millions cleaning it up, and the labs have been razed. We know that the area is perfectly safe now, because the government has been testing it for decades and they said so. But just in case, there are signs all around warning against drinking the water, and forbidding camping altogether.

My eyes and nose were full of mosquitoes, which had been swarming and biting me all day. I had misjudged how long it would take to eat that second funnel cake earlier, and was behind schedule.

Now the sun would be down soon, and my only other option would be to keep walking past the lake at dusk, eventually nighthiking through a swamp.

I was done. I walked far enough into the trees so that I could no longer see the NO CAMPING signs or the trail, and then I walked some more just to be sure. As soon as I was secure in the safety of my mesh,

I devoured my dinner, a two-pound to-go container of bowtie pasta and meatballs left over from lunch, and passed out shortly after.

. . .

Crossing state lines always provides a morale boost, and getting so many of them in rapid succession compounded the effect. Another thing intensifying my sense of gaining momentum was the increasing number of SOBOs I encountered. The day I crossed into Connecticut I met six of them. They were easy to spot: They were thinner and smelled worse than day hikers, but not nearly famished or worn out enough to be mistaken for a NOBO. That, and they were usually headed south.

I wanted to be friendly and conversational while avoiding the dreaded questions Kodiak had warned me against. "Going all the way?" I would ask, and was surprised by how often the reply was "I'm going to try," or "We'll see how far I get." It had been a while since I'd heard that. Back at the start, plenty of NOBOs said they would try to go the whole way. But by now, anyone who'd said "maybe" had either changed their answer or dropped out.

Connecticut would take a seasoned hiker two days, and I desperately needed to do laundry; rainwater and streams no longer do the trick after a week or so. The guidebook had a lot of good things to say about a place called Bearded Woods One-of-a-Kind Bunk & Dine. I called the number and arranged for pickup in Kent, only a mile from the trail.

When my ride appeared, the driver introduced himself as Hudson. His dark hair was neatly combed and matched his trimmed beard, and he had the wiry, muscular build of a woodsman. Hikers climbed out of his backseat and thanked him, and I pointed them to the trail. Hudson offered to wait while I bought supplies from the small store in Kent, and when I returned, the van was full of new hikers, with one space left for me and my gear.

As we drove he explained the rules. He and his wife Lu ran the Bunk & Dine, and they didn't call themselves a hostel because they were, as their name implied, one of a kind. The flat fee included a shuttle to and from their house in the mountains, unlimited hot showers, laundry service, a real bed, plus a restaurant-quality dinner and breakfast together at a long table on their covered porch.

"The way other places do it," Hudson explained, "they nickel and dime you to death for every little thing. And then what happens? You get people who don't want to pay for breakfast, because they have some in their pack. They wind up out in the yard boiling water while their friends eat eggs. That's sad. At our place, everyone gets the same thing."

Hudson was humble about his house, letting Lu explain to us that he built everything there. The walls, floors, and stairs were all beautifully handcrafted and polished hardwood. The floor of the entryway before the stairs was inlaid with a 5-foot AT logo. The walls along the stairs down to our sleeping area were lined with shelves of animal skulls, arranged by size from the tiniest mouse to something with a football-sized head and pointy horns. They were all perfectly bleached, well preserved, and mounted, a collection both grim and beautiful. "These were all given to me, found on my land, or killed for food," Hudson said, "so I don't want you to think I'm some weirdo who collects skulls."

The common area was also Hudson's work, and it announced that his skills were not limited to carpentry. One entire wall was covered by a blown up, high quality photo he took of Knife Edge, a famous rocky ridge near the top of Mount Katahdin. The shelves beside the TV were full of books and DVDs, with a whole row of AT movies. I picked one called "Flip Flop Flippin'." Hudson said, "That's a good one! I know the guy who made it. His name is Squatch. He just came through here not too long ago, making another one."

There was also a row of books dedicated to Hudson's previous section hikes on the AT. He had done the entire trail piece by piece over a decade, he said, and this year he was doing the trail again, thru-hiking it all at once.

"How is that possible?" I asked. "Unless you're already finished?"

Hudson and Lu, his wife, business partner, and trail boss, tag-teamed telling the story of his hike while we ate dinner—big plates of pasta, salad, corn on the cob, and homemade bread, all cooked by Lu. He had started in February, one of only three people on the trail at that time. The ground then was almost always covered with snow and ice, and never any dry wood to build fires. The Southeast had experienced several of the heaviest snowfalls on record that winter, yet Hudson persevered, cranking out 20-mile days. He was well into Virginia when the weather finally warmed up, and had walked past his house all the way to Vermont *by Memorial Day*.

Lu brought him home and they opened the Bunk & Dine for the season the following week. They were about to close with Labor Day approaching, at which point Hudson would pick up right where he left off. "Hey," he said. "Maybe we'll finish together!"

"Yeah, more like you'll fly by me at an unbelievable pace."

"No," he countered. "We'll be starting the Whites around the same time. The Whites slow everybody down. Take whatever miles you're doing now and divide it by three."

I'd heard this around the campfire often, usually by southbounders. We NOBOs were skeptical, and sometimes would even correct the SOBOs that they must surely mean subtract a third, not divide by three. The southbounders would reiterate that they had just been in the Whites, and the northbounders would quietly assume their slowdown to be a sign that the SOBOs simply didn't have their trail legs yet. Hudson was about to do it for the second time, so I suspected he might know what he was talking about. Still, I thought, he'll be starting cold, no momentum. It'll slow me down by half, tops.

. . .

After a delicious and abundant breakfast, I was loading my gear into Hudson's car when I saw something for the first time on the trail—frost on the high trees. My breath was visible too on this crisp morning. Katie wasn't supposed to send my cold weather gear for another few weeks. But I shrugged off weather concerns, figuring I'd managed for half the summer with no sleeping bag at all.

My final climb in the tiny state of Connecticut was Bear Mountain. It looked small on the map and it was, but it was also the first of its kind that I had encountered so far. The tall pines to the left and right of the trail were beautiful, and would have been the perfect backdrop for six or seven lazy switchbacks to carry a hiker to the top.

But I was in the North now. Yankee trails, much like their speech patterns, were a window into the Yankee mindset: straight and to the point. The summit was less than a thousand feet up, but there were no turns and it was all rock. It looked like a giant had taken the worst of Pennsylvania and tilted it 45 degrees.

It was less than a mile, but it took me nearly an hour. I needed to strap my poles to my pack and use my hands in at least three places. I thought about throwing the poles ahead, but if I missed, they would tumble past me, and then I'd have to go back down to get them. My arms were almost exhausted when just in time, the mountain stopped going up.

I wasn't quite at the top yet, but I could make out the silhouette of someone resting at the summit. He had a strange head—a black cylinder that made him look like an old 1950s movie robot. As I got closer, I could see that his sleeves were buttoned at the wrist and his pants were tucked into his socks. The thing on his head was a bug net. I had one in my pack, but I didn't like to wear it in the sun; it was hot under there.

"I like your hat," I said.

"Holy shit, it's Green Giant!" The robot hiker ran toward me. "Oh shit, you can't see me. Ha! It's Bones!"

We hugged, and I could tell he was still alarmingly thin. I thought back to the Fourth of July campfire in Virginia when I'd last seen him, breaking down in sobs at the campfire at the thought of being forced to leave the trail. He had zeroed there four days until he was able to walk again.

Now we were meeting again, almost a thousand miles later at the edge of Massachusetts. We hiked down the other side of Bear Mountain where the trail was far less dramatic, allowing us to catch up on stories while we walked.

In order to achieve what Bones admitted was an eccentric personal goal to hike the whole trail "naturally," he hadn't taken any medicine, not even an aspirin, to relive his shin splints. Eventually, he conceded, he had to make an exception when he caught both Giardia and Lyme disease at the same time.

"That was eight days of me just lying in a hotel bed, crying and running to the bathroom. Those were the worst days of my life," he said. "They're also why I have this stupid thing on my head. I'm not taking any chances on any bug touching any part of my skin for the rest of this hike."

Over the thousand miles between here and where I had last seen him, Bones had suffered every problem a hiker could expect. But through it all, Bones had hiked as close to the center of the trail as he possibly could, and never missed a single white blaze. Never. Unlike the other hiker now with him on the same mountain.

Let's see how this goes, I thought. I told him about my woes, my decision to yellow blaze, and how I had tried my best to catch my friends. And how terrible my aim seemed to be.

To my relief, Bones was genuinely happy to see me, and otherwise had no opinion on the matter. "I made these rules for me," he said. He was the true embodiment of the old hiker motto: Hike your own hike.

I asked him if he had any news from the rear. Voldemort was either still at my sister-in-law's or just getting back on, so he would have missed her, but Bones had passed Lemmy yesterday. That was good news. I knew I couldn't keep up with Bones, and wondered if Lemmy and I were still at the same pace. Guess we would find out.

Near the bottom we found ourselves in a tight gorge following a tiny, gurgling stream. We hopped across and found a small wooden sign covered in moss, welcoming us to Massachusetts. Just behind it was a wall of mosquitoes.

Bones pointed to his net. "Maybe you should put yours on."

• • •

For the next 10 miles, the mosquitoes were relentless. One persistent straggler buzzed incessantly by my ear no matter how fast I walked. I was wearing my bug net now too, which at least prevented him from biting. He must have known this, and refused to land. I swatted with my right arm until it was too tired to continue, then swung my trekking pole back and forth past my ear like a metronome. This seemed to work for brief periods, after which he would switch to the other ear.

Spider webs near the trail excited me, since I could walk very close by and let them clear me of my whining burden. Often it worked, but moments later another bloodsucker would take the last one's place. The word must have gone out through the mosquito news network that fresh meat was on the trail. I was the top story on Mosquito Net. It was all the buzz.

Finally Bones and I reached a pair of shelters, the Hemlocks and Glen Brook. The former is ancient by trail standards, a rickety wooden box that holds four to six hikers if they don't mind spooning. The latter is only a few years old, and was fully occupied by a large group of college students on a freshman orientation trip. Many of them had never camped before, and they were quite curious to meet bearded freaks such as Bones and myself.

We answered questions for about an hour by their fire before retiring to the smaller shelter just up the hill. Bones pitched his tent among some trees behind the shelter. While the site he picked featured a nice cool breeze, the bugs were bad there, so I decided to breach hiker etiquette and pitch my tent in the shelter, planning to move outside if anyone got in late. In my tent, finally safe from the swarming marauders, I relaxed for the first time that day and was asleep immediately.

The sound of my trekking poles sliding down the wall and tipping over jolted me awake. Scurrying footsteps followed, the sound of claws on wood, with more weight than a mouse. I pounded the floor. "GRRRRRR! YAAAAAA!" I knew it wasn't a bear, but whatever it was didn't belong inside with me. "Humans only!" I yelled, and roared again.

At the start of my hike, nighttime animal encounters filled me with adrenaline that lasted hours. But I'd had so many by this point that I was back asleep in no time.

The next noise that startled me awake was the sound of something being dragged. Something heavy.

I sat up and fumbled for my headlamp, feeling the floor vibrate with each scrape. By the time I found my light, I had fully emerged from the fog of sleep. That's not dragging, it's chewing. Something is gnawing on the shelter.

I flicked my light and pointed it toward the sound. Most of the glare reflected off the tent's mesh, and the only thing I could make out was a brown shape the size of a watermelon. It quickly waddled into the dark. It looked way too big to be a beaver, and we were up high, where there were no bodies of water to dam.

I was almost asleep again when the thing came back and started gnawing on the shelter again. This time I was quicker. I unzipped the tent, reached out my light and turned it on.

It shone on an enormous porcupine. I turned off the light, pulled my arm inside, and zipped the tent all in one second. It continued gnawing.

I had a hamster as a kid, and I remembered that it needed hard blocks of wood to chew on, otherwise its teeth would grow freakishly long. Porcupines are rodents. Maybe that's what it was doing. I was sleeping in a porcupine's chew toy.

Well, he was here first, I thought. While the gnawing continued, I thought about the bear in the cage, and the bear in the trap. They were here first too. I was getting in tune with nature. If that meant letting a porcupine eat my sleeping quarters, then so be it. He wasn't hurting me. I rolled onto my side.

For as long as I remember being awake that night, the porcupine chewed the floor. The rhythmic scraping made a soothing sound, and after a while I didn't even mind how it shook the boards. My last thought as I drifted off was how Fiddlin' Jim's snoring used to do the same thing.

. . .

For the next ten miles the mosquitoes were relentless. The trail took me through some lower elevations, and when it did, there they were, much worse than the previous day. Now, instead of a lone wingman I had dozens. And these ones bit.

My head and face were protected by the net, but my arms and legs were host to legions of flying parasites. When the attacks first began, I was able to smack them. My arm hair glistened red. My blood or his, it didn't matter—in 95-degree heat, the sweat quickly washed it away. Hadn't there been frost a few days ago?

In time, the mosquitos began arriving in pairs, then in threes. Soon I was covered. I considered doing nothing, but each landing site soon swelled into an itchy red welt. Instead of smacking I tried rubbing them away, but that just created a thick smear of blood, bug parts, and sweat which seemed to anger the swarm, drawing more winged attackers.

I tried to run, but ahead lay only more mosquitoes. They were everywhere.

I threw my pack at the base of a tree and rummaged through my laundry. I zipped the legs onto my shorts and tucked them into my socks. I put my long sleeve shirt over my short sleeve shirt, since the bugs could bite through a single layer.

Ten minutes later I had to stop again because the swarms had found the only exposed flesh for miles: my hands.

Again, I threw my pack down and rummaged. I didn't have gloves, but I found my spare socks. As I was putting them on my hands, I realized I was now wearing every article of clothing I possessed besides my raincoat. If I put that on I really would die—I was soaked with sweat.

It was hard to close my pack and buckle everything with socks on my hands, but I did it. For the next half mile, the bugs tried their best to eat me, landing on my sleeves and biting me through my shirt. Every few steps I was slapping myself silly. I would walk some more and then run. Then stop. Then slap. I was going mad and I couldn't stop itching.

My mouth was dry and I had stopped sweating. Dizziness started to hit me, and I realized I hadn't been drinking or eating, just running and swatting. Lifting my water bottle to the edge of the bug net, I carefully pulled at the elastic around my neck and lifted just enough to get my lips on the lid.

Mosquitoes assaulted my chin and neck, bit my ears, crawled up inside and landed on my forehead, but I didn't care because I was so thirsty. I was so thirsty and I drank with one hand while punching myself in the head with the other, trying to kill everything inside the net that was biting me. My face turned pink and swelled. I gasped, then burped. I threw the empty water bottle to the ground and smashed the net against my skin, destroying every bug inside, grinding them into a pulp, smearing my cheeks.

I felt a hot sting on the top of my foot and looked down. One of them was biting me through my shoe. "DIE, YOU FUCKERS!" I cackled and fell to the ground writhing, scratching every part of me I could reach.

That's when Lemmy showed up.

"Green Giant! There is a shelter right there! Run!" He grabbed my wrist and dragged me to my feet. A bandanna masked the bottom half of his face, while the top half...well, the top half looked like a bear. A koala, specifically.

This might be it, I thought. I've gone mad. Either that, or Lemmy now wears a hat that looks like a koala and is saving me from mosquitoes.

Oh shit. It's both.

The shelter was at the top of a small pile of rocks and exposed to the wind, which helped keep the bugs away. For now. I left my net on, and Lemmy kept his bandanna. Only his eyes showed.

"It really is you," I panted.

Lemmy's eyebrows were full of sweat. "These bugs. This is hell." He shook his fist at the sky and yelled. "Damn it, nature! Why?"

I laughed, and he looked at me with serious eyes. "Green Giant, I am so tired."

"I know, buddy. Me too."

He swatted at his face and blinked. "This makes me want to be done so bad. I keep going, and I keep going, and I ask myself why am I doing this thing? I think about Katahdin, Green Giant, and do you know what I think?"

"What do you think, Lemmy?"

"I think it is going to be just one more mountain. I think I am just going to get there and say, 'Okay, now what?' There might be some champagne or something, but it will just be one more hard day. I just want it to be special for real, do you know? Different. I want someone to *care*."

"I care, Lemmy."

He let me continue.

"I care, Lemmy. I really do. Let's do this together. Let's go all the way."

"How can you say it, Green Giant? That would be epic, but you see this." He pointed left and right. "One day you are ahead. One day I am ahead. How can you know? We can't."

"Yes we can," I said. I used my teeth to remove the sock from my hand and held out a fist. I extended one pinky and curled it. "I will if you will."

He looked at my finger and scrunched his eyebrows. Sweat dripped. "What does this mean?"

"Pinky swear. It means we have to do whatever we say." I held it out further.

Lemmy curled his pinky finger and linked it with mine. "Are we married now?"

"Yes. Now listen. Whoever gets to Mount Katahdin first waits for the other one."

"What if it is like six months?"

I sighed. "Okay, two day limit. How's that sound? I'll camp out and wait for you if I get there first, and you do the same. Deal?"

The koala nodded. "Deal."

"Pinky swear?"

"Pinky swear."

It was done. No matter what, Lemmy and I were going to climb Mount Katahdin together.

I lost him at the next water stop, and when I woke up the next day I had no idea where he was.

## 21

## ENTER THE NINJA

For the next 60 miles, Lemmy and I went back to leapfrogging each other, but trading places for days now instead of hours. The little ups and downs were still getting bigger, and many of the climbs had taken on the rocky, straight-to-the-top approach I saw back at Bear Mountain. The lowlands in between were marshy and plagued by mosquitoes, especially at the wide, slow streams the color of weak tea.

About halfway through Massachusetts, the AT passes through the center of Dalton. All of the marshes had ruined my socks, and my pants had collected enough mud that when they baked in the sun, they turned into something like pottery shin guards. According to the guidebook, a gentleman named Tom Levardi allowed hikers to spend the night on his porch or in his yard as long as they checked with him first before showing up.

As soon as I got near town I called him, and Tom said he had plenty of room. Then I called Katie, who told me her sister had just dropped off Megan near Nuclear Lake.

After descending a steep muddy slope, the white blazes took me down a tree-lined street where immaculate lawns grew between tiny houses with steep roofs. After a few blocks I arrived at a house with lots of tents in the yard, and climbed the steps to the porch, where I met a young man with glasses and shaggy curls named Breakfast Club. "This must be where all the cool people hang out," I said, introducing myself.

As we chatted, it turned out Breakfast Club had hiked with Lemmy and Voldemort while I was recovering in Lode Land three states ago. He smiled when I told him Lemmy was nearby and would probably arrive soon, then sighed with relief to hear that Voldemort was several days behind. "Don't get me wrong, I like her. But she's like ice cream. It's great, but too much of it makes your head hurt."

I pitched my tent in the yard behind the house and Breakfast Club showed me a garage full of bicycles that hikers could borrow. Choosing the tallest three-speed I could find, I rode it to town with a sack of laundry on my back. On my way to the laundromat I passed Bones, on his way back to the trail after a night at Tom's.

Once my clothes were clean and my belly full of pizza and donuts from the neighboring restaurant, I took a small sightseeing detour. It had been years since I rode a bike, and my newfound leg muscles made it enjoyable as well as effortless. Eventually I found myself a little lost, looking at a map in the parking lot of the local VFW.

A Mercedes with a Marine Corps bumper sticker pulled into the spot nearest the door. When a tall man with white hair stepped out, I greeted him with "Semper fi!"

"You a devil dog?" he asked.

I confirmed. "A long time ago."

"What the hell are you doing out here in the parking lot? Get in there. Have a beer."

This sounded an awful lot like an order, so I followed. The man never told me his name, but he put me on a barstool and ordered me a glassful while we both stared ahead in silence at the TV above the bar, showing golf.

Eventually my host ordered another round and squinted at my beard and hair, now almost long enough to keep the bugs out of my ears. I was clearly not up to inspection standards.

"What do you do now?" he asked as our drinks arrived.

"I walk," I said. "I'm hiking from Georgia to Maine."

"Didn't you get enough marching in the Marines, son? Why the hell would you want to do that?"

"Who the hell knows?" I said, and took a deep pull.

. . .

On the way back to Tom's I passed Two Pack. I steadied the bike and leaned on the curb. "You going to Tom's?"

"I was thinking about it. I might keep hiking and camp north of town."

He and Ninja Mike had sped by while I was sulking on a rock outside of Harpers Ferry. Now Ninja Mike was a day or two ahead, Two Pack said.

"You should at least stop by. Lemmy will be there." That sealed it for Two Pack; it seems everyone had met Lemmy by now. "I'd offer you a ride, but…"

Lemmy was there, and as usual, his tent was set up inches from mine. Breakfast Club was already asleep on the porch, so Lemmy stage-whispered from the yard. "Green Giant, we have to zero here tomorrow!"

"What? We're running out of time, Lemmy." Some of the leaves at higher elevations had been turning bright yellow.

"It is for something epic!"

"It better be. What is it?"

Lemmy reached into his pocket and pulled out a crumpled flier with a staple hanging from one corner, something he'd obviously torn from a bulletin board. The 9th Annual Western Massachusetts Craft Beer Festival at the local fairground promised over 150 beers from 50 brewers, plus food and live music. Tickets were cheap.

Two Pack joined us just as I finished reading. I handed him the flier. "Do you see what we're doing tomorrow?"

The fairground was two miles up the road from Tom's house, and could also be reached by several miles of trail that wound through the hills around town. Technically we wouldn't be zeroing. We would leave everything but snacks and water at Tom's, hike to the festival in the afternoon, and then take the road back to our tents and be asleep before dark.

When we were ready to leave, Breakfast Club was still in his sleeping bag on the porch. He told us to go ahead and enjoy ourselves, but he was feeling too ill for a beer festival.

Lemmy practically sprinted the whole way. Hours later, when Two Pack and I arrived and were in the line for wristbands, he ran to greet us. "You guys! This is epic! I knew it would be!" His face was dripping sweat and he had clearly taken advantage of his extra time at the booths.

Once we were through the line, Lemmy gave us a tour. "Take a plastic cup, both of you. Now watch this." We entered a long canvas tent, 50 feet wide and triple that in length. The sides were lined with display tables bearing signs, posters, and cardboard cutouts naming famous and obscure beers from all over the country. Lemmy picked one at random and handed the man his sample cup. "One beer, please!"

The man poured, explaining the recipe and history of the brew. Lemmy nodded in all the right places, but kept looking back at us and smiling. When the cup was full he drank just enough to prevent spilling and ran back to us. "Did you see this? They just give you a beer!"

Two Pack grinned. "You did pay to get in, right?"

"Of course. But I am going to try all 150, which makes them cost one penny each!" His math was off, but it was clear that correcting him would be futile.

"That's a great idea," Two Pack said. "Let's get our money's worth. Green Giant, we have some catching up to do."

"You people are insane! There's no way I'm drinking 150 beers and hiking tomorrow. Or even living for that matter."

Lemmy showed me his sample cup. "Look how small it is. You can do it!"

"No, thanks. I'll watch."

We started at the entrance and worked our way clockwise. Each time Lemmy and Two Pack asked for only half a sample cup, but at about two ounces per beer, by the time we reached the far end of the tent they'd both had the equivalent of a six-pack each. I was already lightheaded from a single cup, and marveled at their stamina until I remembered they were both in their twenties. They were only getting warmed up.

Two Pack pointed back to the place we came in. "Let's see if we can make it back around the other side in half the time. Speed round! Go!"

Lemmy dashed to the nearest booth. There was a line, so he jumped ahead to a display with no visitors, something pumpkin-flavored. I filled my cup once more and observed from a safe distance. It was like watching bees pollinate a flower garden. Following no clear pattern, they fluttered from one bright display to the next, drunk on sweet nectar, sometimes bumping into one another during landings and takeoffs.

Their goal was 15 minutes. They did it in 10. I snatched a complimentary water bottle from a bin of ice and handed a pair to my friends. Lemmy drained his, burped, then smiled and swayed. Two

Pack drank slowly and pointed. "There are still two more tents."

Lemmy wobbled. "We should…" He burped again. "Hurry."

I put a hand on his shoulder. "We should eat."

We found an empty picnic table in the crowded field between the beer tents and loaded up on fair food. I ordered a big, greasy sausage sandwich with mustard and grilled peppers and onions and a large, sickeningly sweet lemonade. When I got back to the table, Lemmy was giggling at his plate.

"I know there's no dog in this hot dog. But why do they call it this?"

I ignored him. "There sure are a lot of people here. I mean, not just here, but even back at Tom's. His yard looked like we were at a music festival."

Two Pack nodded and finished his bite. "Dude, we are right behind The Bubble. Ninja Mike thinks the center of it is up in Rutland right now."

Lemmy leaned in between us and whispered, "It was the cows!" He leaned back and began eating.

"I wonder if we'll catch them," I said to Two Pack.

"Probably. They'll slow down in the Whites and we'll speed up in Rutland." He scooped meat and cheese onto a corn chip and filled his mouth. I asked how we'd speed up, and he held up a finger and chewed.

Lemmy leaned across the table. "Get along, little doggies!" He giggled and fell back into his seat.

Two Pack swallowed. "Ninja Mike and I are going to try to find work-for-stay in town and then slackpack for a few days, really make some big miles. You could join us."

Lemmy waved the remaining half of his hot dog in the space between us. "This! This is a little doggy!" He shoved the rest into his mouth and chewed furiously.

Once we made it to Vermont, the trail would continue due north for 100 miles, then take a sharp right turn to head east for almost another 50, where it would enter the penultimate state, New Hampshire. That sharp right turn happens at Rutland, making it a strategic center for shuttles to and from the trail. Some call it Slackpacker Central.

"Yeah, man, I'd love to try."

Lemmy lifted his second hot dog. "This thing is made of cows. Little hot doggies."

"Good, Lemmy. We get it!"

Lemmy burped. "How many more tents?"

"Two."

He stood up. "I can do it."

"That's the spirit," Two Pack said, heading for a trash bin with our empty paper plates.

"I want to see a bear," Lemmy told me.

"I don't think we'll see one here," I informed him.

"I want to catch one. I want to catch a bear and ride it to the top of Mount Katahdin." He leaned on me. "I am serious, Green Giant."

Two Pack returned and pulled Lemmy up straight. "Are you going to make it, buddy?"

Lemmy burped. "Yes."

I joined them for one more cup and then walked back to Tom's. Lemmy pleaded for me to stay and then called me a little girl when I insisted that I was tired. Then he told me I was pretty.

It was hiker midnight when they returned. I was almost asleep when I felt my tent shake, as Lemmy tripped over my stakes while he fumbled with his door. He heard me stir and unzipped my tent without knocking. "We did it!"

I blinked twice and pushed his face away from mine. "That's great, Lemmy. A hundred and fifty beers? Is there a prize? What did you get?"

From three tents away, Two Pack answered. "Kicked out."

Lemmy palmed a rock from the yard and put it in my tent. "Green Giant, look at this!"

"No. Get that out of my—"

"Do you know how old this thing is?" *Dis fing?*

"Lemmy, go to—"

"Green Giant, it is as old as the Earth!" *Erf.*

"Lemmy—"

"A dinosaur could have stepped on this!"

I waited.

"I am going to keep this. This is my dinosaur rock."

Two Pack had been trying not to laugh, but this broke him. He sprayed spit and snickered. Someone in another tent grumbled and turned over.

"Lemmy. Good night."

He took his rock and zipped my tent. "Good night, Green Giant."

. . .

Lemmy and Two Pack were already packed and eating breakfast on the porch when I emerged from my tent. Lemmy offered me a donut. "Damn you twentysomethings and your stupid metabolism," I said, taking it. "Don't get too used to it. Did Breakfast Club leave already?"

"No," replied Two Pack. "Tom took him to the hospital. All he did yesterday was sleep on the porch and not eat. That's all we know."

"Damn. That sucks."

"Yeah." Two Pack had been hiking with Breakfast Club on and off since Georgia. There wasn't anything else we could say or do, so we changed the subject.

We were eager to climb Mount Greylock, the tallest peak in Massachusetts, which would mark our first day above 3,000 feet since Virginia. After the rolling hills of Virginia, the cornfields of Pennsylvania, and the last two weeks of swamps, we wanted to see a "real" mountain again.

It was two days north, and on our way there we refined our plan for Vermont. At one rocky outcropping on the way, with the mountain in view on the horizon, Lemmy carved the shape of a foamy beer stein into his memory stick while Two Pack pored over his guidebook. "I think I know how we're going to do this," he said, pointing at the big bend in the trail. "Day after tomorrow we'll be 50 miles south of Rutland. If we can get someone to shuttle us in, we can easily slackpack 25 miles a day, especially if we're eating town food every night. We could do the whole state in four days and three nights."

"Insane," I said. "Where can we stay for three nights, eat, and get shuttled to and from the trail each day, without breaking the bank?"

"What about the Yellow Deli?"

Lemmy looked over his shoulder, shook his head, and returned to his carving.

The guidebook didn't mention anything out of the ordinary about the Hikers Hostel at the Yellow Deli. But the shelter logs had a mix of praise and warnings. We'd seen entries like, *Beware of the Yellow Deli* and, *I think I just spent the night with a cult* next to, *Hell yeah Yellow Deli* and *Best maté on the trail.*

Even if they were a cult, it wouldn't be the weirdest thing that happened on this hike. "Let's do it," I said.

The next afternoon we reached the peak. A tall monument at the summit of Mount Greylock commemorates the state's fallen soldiers from World War I. There is also homemade ice cream in the gift shop. I ate two pints and began my descent.

Lemmy and Two Pack stopped short that day, so I had the Wilbur Clearing shelter all to myself.

My first order of business was water. There was a small stream about a tenth of a mile from the shelter, so I carried two empty bottles and my filter down the small hill and sat on a rock. I filled the small pouch and screwed it into the filter, then lined up the nozzle and squeezed.

A jet of cold water sprayed from a tiny pinhole leak near the bottom. I tried to cover it with my finger, but as soon as I touched it, it erupted into a split three inches long, and water splashed out onto my leg and shoe. I stared at the useless bag. It was my third, and final spare.

I would have to boil my water. I filled both bottles and carried them, plus the remains of my filter, back to the empty shelter. When I took out my Jetboil and shook the fuel canister, I was dejected to discover that it only had enough left for about one, maybe two more boils—barely enough to fill one of the water bottles.

I put everything on the picnic table and folded my arms. I paced. The next town was Rutland and that was a long day plus a hitchhike away. I only had one dinner left: dehydrated pasta. If I used the fuel to make drinking water, I could eat the noodles raw. It would taste awful but I wouldn't starve.

I sat on a log by the fire ring and thought some more. But if I got one bottle of water out of the Jetboil, and a dinner of crunchy noodles, I'd still need to drink tomorrow.

Bad Dinner had boasted that he never used a filter. "The closer you get to the source, the less chance of piss or shit in your water," he said. I closed my eyes and visualized the tiny water source I just left. Had it been a spring or a stream? I couldn't remember—they were all starting to blur together. Mindlessly, while I pondered over this new puzzle, I picked up some twigs that the previous occupants had stacked by the circle of rocks, and started snapping them and tossing them into the ring. And then it hit me.

I'm such an idiot. I can make fire.

It was the one remaining thing distinguishing me from an animal right now. I broke more sticks and moved some of the rocks into a tighter circle to concentrate the heat, then started my fire. Once I had coals, I stripped the insulation from the pot and put it on my little stone stove, leaving an opening between two rocks so I could push twigs in from the bottom, sustaining the heat. It took 10 minutes to boil enough to fill one bottle.

With socks on my hands, I quickly pulled the steaming pot off of the flames. Getting the water into the bottle was going to require precision, so I needed to wait for it to cool. While I waited, I thought about how much of a pain in the ass this was going to be in the middle of the afternoon next to some random stream, with no fire ring or stacked twigs handy. Maybe Bad Dinner was onto something.

It was getting dark as I was filling the second bottle when I heard voices. Someone was trying to find the shelter. I stood up and called, "Over here!" Four hikers stomped their way through the bushes and into the clearing, two young men and two young women. The men had short beards, definitely less than a thousand mile's worth of whiskers. Southbounders for sure.

One of the girls asked why I was boiling so much water, and when I explained my situation she smiled. "I have just the thing for you!" She opened her pack and handed me two eyedroppers full of chemical water purifier.

"Are you sure? Thank you so much! But what will you use?"

She explained that between them they still had three more filters. That only works if you manage to stay together, I thought. I wanted to warn her that they were barely 500 miles into this. Two weeks from now, she might be the one hunched over an ashy pit, trying not to blow soot into her water. Instead I thanked her again.

As the five of us ate dinner together, I told them about my encounter with Kodiak, the first SOBO, and his reaction to the dreaded four questions. They all laughed. "We aren't jaded yet," said the taller of the two men. "We're still riding high from the Whites, which are just as amazing as you've heard. Vermont's not bad either."

His buddy sat up straight. "But dude. Maine." All four of them leaned back and sighed in unison, exchanging smiles and glances, silently reminiscing. "The place is just...magical. I mean, I know there's mountains down south. But up there are *mountains!* And the flat stuff between them is like some kind of mystical fairyland from a coloring book or something. There are caves and waterfalls. And lakes!"

The taller hiker picked up the story. "Moose. Bears. I saw a fucking *eagle*, man. And it was summertime, so the weather was perfect almost every day. Those two skinny dipped every chance they got." The girls giggled.

He went on for another five minutes, describing in great detail the hostels and the people and the animals. The more he spoke about the beauty, the more I could hear genuine longing in his voice. I had already been excited about what lay ahead. Now I actually felt chills when he halted, choked up, barely able to speak. His buddy patted him on the shoulder and the girls slid in closer.

"I'm sorry," he said. "It's just that I miss it so much. My heart actually hurts from how much I miss Maine."

. . .

Three interesting things happened at the Vermont border. The first was the border itself. After climbing a thousand feet, the trail plateaus for the final mile of Massachusetts. Then right at the state line, the entire forest becomes a split-level, like a cliff in miniature. Everything on the Vermont side of a nearly straight line looks like it's been pushed up exactly three feet. Either that or Massachusetts is slowly sinking.

The second interesting thing was that the mosquitoes stopped. Vermont still had a few, but they were neither as numerous nor as aggressive. The angry swarm stayed on their side of the line, hovering there, mocking me. Their northern cousins circled my head lazily, rarely landing and never biting.

The third interesting thing was the tall lacquered sign welcoming me to Vermont, and informing me that I was now also on the Long Trail, the oldest long-distance trail in the United States, spanning 273 miles from the Massachusetts line to the Canadian border. The AT and the Long Trail would share the same path for the next 105 miles, diverging where the AT makes that hard right near Rutland.

We still had a day or two until we were within reasonable shuttle range, and we took our time. With another state came yet another change in terrain. Everything here looked landscaped, almost too good to be true. The streams were so clear they appeared empty. Flowers grew beside ponds encircled by perfect pines, and everything smelled clean.

The ups and downs that separated all these lovely scenes had become more severe, and the marshes were muddier by far. The pitch of our climbs was such that stopping to rest often required hanging onto something, and the low muddy stretches were shin deep. Our feet made gurgling, sucking sounds with each labored step. Two Pack and I had to help Lemmy find his boot twice by the end of our second day.

We spent that night at a shelter just below 3,000 feet. The sky was clear, which gave us a spectacular view of the stars, but the absence of cloud cover made for one of the coldest nights so far. I was still tired when I woke up, and the shelter mice had chewed holes through my pants because I'd left an empty Clif bar wrapper in one pocket when I hung them to dry overnight.

I was shivering in my shorts and repairing my pants with tape when Two Pack came into the shelter with his phone in one hand and guidebook in the other. "I have good news and more good news," he announced.

I looked up. "Tell me the good news first."

"Breakfast Club is back on the trail. I got a short text from him and he'll tell us what happened when we see him in Rutland. He's hitching up there today."

"Sweet. So what's the good news?"

"They're picking us up tomorrow."

"Who is?"

"Yellow Deli."

Lemmy, who had been drawing in the log book, stopped and looked up. "No, they are not."

"Sure they are," Two Pack said. "I just talked to them. End of day tomorrow."

"They are picking you up. I am not going. They scare me." He went back to his drawing and would say no more on the topic.

I put on my pants. "Well, I for one am looking forward to it. I need some real food and I need to do laundry. Oh, and I also need a new fuel canister. And new shoes. And new trekking poles—look at the tips on these!"

"You need new pants, too."

"No, just more tape."

After 1,600 miles, nothing was operating at 100 percent. Not a piece of my gear was anywhere close to its original condition. One of my trekking poles was bent and both pointy metal tips had been eroded to mere nubs. One of the main buckles on my pack had snapped off long ago, forcing me to learn some new knots. My shoes would just barely make it to Rutland.

My body was in the same condition as my gear. As soon as one part healed, another malady, twist, or sprain replaced it. My feet still hurt every day. Long ago I had resigned myself to the idea that something was always going to hurt, and eventually I accepted a certain level of pain as the new baseline. I could continue like this for another 500 miles, I thought, as long as nothing else major went wrong.

The next day we climbed up and over Stratton Mountain. We had to hustle because our ride would be waiting for us 10 miles after the big climb. Lucky for us, we hit the peak early, and it was a long easy downhill from there. The spacing between ups and downs was no longer regular, and judging by the guidebook, it appeared that this section was followed by hundreds of miles of erratic climbs and descents. This would be the perfect time for us to lighten our loads for a few days.

Lemmy stopped at a shelter a few miles before our road crossing. We'd be covering a lot of the same ground over the next few days, so we agreed to use the log books to stay close. When Two Pack and I reached the road crossing, a white van was parked at the trailhead. The driver's door opened the second we were in sight and a slender man in round glasses got out and smiled broadly. His hair was tied back in a short ponytail and his beard was trimmed short. His clothes were homemade, handstitched and loose-fitting.

"You must be Green Giant and Two Pack! I can guess which is which. Please, let me take your packs. You must be tired. I'm Jon!" He pronounced the J as a Y—Yon. Noticing our curious looks, or maybe just accustomed to explaining, he continued. "It's my Old Testament name. Kind of like your trail names! Hee hee!"

His strange laugh made us smile, and we gladly gave Jon our packs. "Please," he said, "get in."

He never stopped smiling. I rode in the passenger seat, and Two Pack sat behind me. Jon started the engine and turned onto the empty road. "I can tell why they call you Green Giant, but why do they call you Two Pack? I only counted one! Hee hee!"

When Jon laughed, Two Pack grinned. "When I started my hike, my mom wanted to walk with me for the first couple days. But when we got to the first big climb she had a hard time with it, so I carried her pack. When I got to the top someone saw me, and well, that was it."

I twisted in my seat. "It wasn't an old guy with a Triple Crown patch by chance, was it?" Two Pack shook his head.

Jon asked Two Pack what he did back in the real world. When he said, mechanical engineer, Jon laughed his weird laugh again. "Wow! That's really neat! I've never met a mechanical engineer hiker before! Wow!"

"Jon, I'm going to blow your mind, buddy," I said. "I'm a computer engineer." *Used to be.*

"No way! This is really neat! Two engineer hikers! Wow!"

If his smile gets any wider, I thought, the top half of his head is going to come off.

The rest of the drive consisted of Jon asking us more questions and being consistently amazed by our answers. "Wow! I've never met anyone from Canada before! Hee hee!"

When we arrived in Rutland I was surprised by its size. I was expecting another lazy trail town, but Rutland is the third-largest city in Vermont, with traffic lights and crosswalks, things I had almost forgotten existed. The Yellow Deli was in the heart of the historic district. Beside the entrance there was another door for the hostel.

We took off our packs, opened the door, and climbed the narrow stairway. The walls were lined with postcards from previous hikers. The stairs were covered by thick strips of leather, each one its own unique deep shade: burgundy, coffee, oxblood, and olive. A single white blaze was painted on the first step. "It's not real," Jon said, giggling again. "The trail is miles away!"

The bunk room had a tall, ornate wardrobe near the entrance. Jon opened it, revealing hangers and shelves packed with homemade shirts and pants similar to his. "You can wear these while you do laundry." The washing machine was coin-operated, and on a small shelf above it was a hand carved walnut bowl full of quarters. The machines were free, our host explained, and if we ran out of quarters he would refill the bowl. "You're in my house now, brothers. Here you pay for nothing."

The long hall branched and turned, and I was almost lost when we reached the back of the building. "This is your lounge," he said. It was a well-appointed living room furnished with leather couches and small tables. There was no TV, but there were books, games, and musical instruments. "I'll let you get settled. I hope you can join us for dinner tonight."

The back wall of our lounge had a sliding glass door opening onto a large wooden deck that overlooked the courtyard between our building and the next. Down below, six hikers were trying to balance on one foot with their eyes closed and arms raised. A yoga class was in session.

Breakfast Club was one of the students, and Ninja Mike was the teacher. He was wearing homemade clothes and headphones. His face was upturned, and he was steady as a tree. He lowered his hands to Prayer and switched feet, and the class followed his example, or tried—Breakfast Club and another guy had to lean on their neighbor for a second.

Before he continued, Ninja Mike opened his eyes briefly to check on the students. Two Pack caught his attention up on the deck, and Ninja Mike nodded and closed his eyes again. He inhaled and the class inhaled. He raised his arms and the class raised theirs.

I whispered, "He doesn't talk when he does this?"

"No, it breaks his focus."

"What's he listening to?"

"I forget how to pronounce it."

"Ah. Some kind of Eastern flute music or something?"

Two Pack snorted. "You would think. No, when Ninja Mike does yoga, he listens to Norwegian death metal."

## 22

## ONE OF US

I WAS RELIEVED when I saw Ninja Mike dressed like a pirate again. His clothes had been in the dryer, so after yoga he looked like himself again. I was worried he'd become *one of them*.

Not that there was anything wrong with that. Jon may have been a little giddy, but he and everyone else who lived there seemed friendly and genuinely excited to help people in need, especially hikers.

Two Pack and I had joined Breakfast Club downstairs in the deli when Ninja Mike came down after his post-yoga shower. Our table was made from thick blocks of hand-cut wood, deeply stained and highly polished. Dimly lit walls were of hand-stacked stone or brick, ornamented with paintings depicting wildlife and nature, planets, and rainbows. One bright mural covering an entire wall outlined the history of the group who ran the Yellow Deli.

They called themselves the Twelve Tribes...

Members of the Twelve Tribes tried to live their lives as simply as possible, practicing mercy and kindness and giving. They believed in charity and helping others as often as they could, giving until it hurt and then giving more. They lived in communes, every member an equal.

Breakfast Club finished reading the painting and folded his hands. "Okay, so that's a little weird."

Then he told us what happened to him on the porch back in Dalton. It was acute pancreatitis, and he'd brought it on himself, he admitted sheepishly, from too much alcohol.

"Good thing you didn't go to the festival with us."

Ninja Mike took the seat beside me. A hot shower had left his hair as fine as corn silk, hanging past his shoulders. The purple headscarf was now embellished with a thin gold chain. His goatee had doubled in length since Harpers Ferry and the curly tips of his mustache almost covered his eyes when he smiled. "I bet you have some stories," he told me.

"I bet you do too," I replied.

"Well then, let's climb a bunch of fucking mountains and tell them to each other!"

A middle-aged man in homemade clothes and a neat beard, short ponytail, and round metal glasses matching Jon's approached our table. He introduced himself as Aish. "Have you eaten? Won't you please join us for celebration downstairs? It's already started, but we don't mind. Please. Come!" And now we were already walking down the cellar stairs, Aish's one hand on my shoulder the other pointing the way. I didn't remember standing or pushing my chair in.

Bible study was just wrapping up. A young man who also looked and dressed like Aish had just finished reading a passage to a large circle of Tribesmen who looked and dressed like each other. The only variety I could discern was that some wore glasses while others did not. Women and children sat among them, listening silently, with their hands folded in their laps.

The four of us stood against the wall observing. When the man leading the study finished explaining his interpretation, he told everyone to prepare for the announcement. "Our tradition is to have one of the children announce dinner," Aish whispered to me. "In German."

A young boy, maybe six or seven years old, walked into the center of the circle and yelled something in German, something that he had clearly rehearsed and was only slightly nervous about. When he finished yelling, all of the adults clapped and cheered. They leapt to their feet and the room exploded into a flurry of activity. People stacked and carried chairs away to make room for two dozen tables that appeared from nowhere, then the same chairs were unstacked and placed around them. Knives, forks, and napkins materialized, along with trays full of water glasses tinkling with ice. Plates of steaming bread and piles of whipped butter appeared. Aish tapped my shoulder, and before I knew it, the five of us occupied our own table with seats to spare.

All of that activity, the well-practiced and perfectly timed restaurant-style hustle, was carried out by the women and children while the men sat. Salads came, and more bread. There was corn on the cob and a spicy chicken noodle soup. Aish insisted that we eat, that there was no reason to wait. All of the men were eating, so we did too.

The food was amazing. It was better than any restaurant I could recall. The greens were as crisp and fresh as the ones Katie and I grow in our garden. The bread was warm and slightly crisp on the outside, the inside a steamy fluff. Aish explained that the Tribe members grew and produced everything we were eating. The vegetables, the bread, even the chickens.

Breakfast Club was impressed. "You guys do it all, huh?"

Aish smiled proudly. "Oh, we do a little bit of everything."

• • •

Aish kept us fed, and someone else named Jon sat with us in the lounge after dinner and again before breakfast. Apparently, Jon the First was assigned as our driver, because any time we needed to go anywhere more than 10 minutes from the deli, he was there with keys in hand. When he dropped us off at the trail next day, he bid us farewell with his signature giggle. "See you fellows tonight! Hee hee!"

Two Pack and Breakfast Club took off immediately, while Ninja Mike and I took time leaning against a tree to stretch. "Those dudes are some spiritual motherfuckers," he said.

On any other day I would have balked at our plan: 26 miles, including multiple 1,000-foot climbs and descents. But this day all of our heaviest things—tents, sleeping bags, several days' worth of food—were all safely tucked away in our bunks, awaiting our return.

Ninja Mike was a few steps behind me. "Hey Green Giant, what was in your welcome basket?"

When we had returned to our bunks after celebration, each of us found a small handmade wicker basket on our pillow. Mine had a bag of popcorn, I told him, plus an apple, two cookies, and some maté.

He laughed. "Of course." It was all they drank.

"Oh, and a card. Mine had a picture of a bunny." Each basket was decorated with a ribbon and a welcome card, drawn and written by a child. "It said, *We are happy to help.*"

"Dude, mine had a bird! It was so fucking sweet. I got a little choked up, I don't mind saying."

I mentioned that I was surprised by how crowded the bunk room was. "Oh, dude," he replied. "The Bubble is right there." He pointed to the horizon.

"How do you know?"

"Two Pack and I have been in it a couple times now. Miss Janet is there."

Miss Janet is an AT legend, the ultimate trail angel. No one knows for sure how many hikers Miss Janet has helped. She ran a hostel in Erwin, Tenn. for decades before taking her show on the road, but now, for as long as there has been a Bubble, Miss Janet has been in it. She lives in her 15-passenger van and slowly migrates up the East Coast, shuttling hikers from the trail to town, and occasionally hospitals, airports, and train stations. She is the queen at the center of the swarm.

We caught up with Breakfast Club and Two Pack, and when Ninja Mike passed them he said, "We were talking about The Bubble."

"It's like a constantly moving summer camp," Breakfast Club said, "with no counselors and nothing but activities."

The three biggest climbs of the day were tough, but they would have been tougher had we been carrying full loads. There were low-lying clouds that day, and each peak put us into them, denying us any views. The miles passed quickly, and when we reached the road crossing, Jon was there with keys in hand, as giddy as ever. "Hee hee!"

Celebration was only for the Sabbath. Tonight was just like any other night, so we ate in the deli. Aish sat with us, but instead of eating, he talked, encouraging us to tell stories while he listened. He was glad to tell us stories as well. When Two Pack asked where they kept the chickens, Aish replied, "We have farms. Oh yes, we can see where the world is heading, so we strive to be self-sustaining. All this masonry, the wiring, even my glasses are all crafted by brothers." He smiled and gestured toward the kitchen. "Matthias was a plumber before he joined us. He helped build our deli in Gorham."

I pointed at his glasses. "You have some skilled brothers."

"We also practice many lost arts."

Breakfast Club looked alarmed, but Aish reassured him. "I'm referring to essential skills lost on most. Spinning yarn or churning butter, for instance."

After dinner we went to the lounge, but it was occupied and we only stayed for about five minutes. It seemed the only place that wasn't under the watchful eye of at least one Tribesman was our bunks, or the woods.

The next morning Jon dropped us off again, and again with lighter packs we dashed toward the pine-covered hills. Two Pack and I looked up nervously at the clouds, but Ninja Mike had a different opinion. He leaned back, cupped his hands to his mouth, and hollered. "WOOOOOOOO-WEE!" He waited for his echo and nodded approval. "I am grateful for today." He sped up the trail, and we followed.

I wasn't able to keep up with them, but I was close. While they practically ran, I merely speedwalked, sometimes stopping to force the air out of my lungs and stomp like a horse. I caught up with them eating at the Cooper Lodge shelter near Killington Peak, just short of 4,000 feet. The clouds Ninja Mike had cheered at earlier now surrounded us in a whiteout. With the high winds, we were grateful to be in one of the few AT shelters with four walls and a door we could close.

By the end of the day we were back in the land of little ups and downs, with sap on our hands and thick mud on our boots. "You fellows get right in," Jon said when he met us. "Don't worry about your boots. I need to wash this thing tomorrow anyway!" He giggled and sniffed the pine on his hand after high-fiving Ninja Mike.

That night while Ninja Mike, Two Pack, and Breakfast Club ate with Aish, I sat in a bar across the street, glad to be alone for an hour. I was gnawing on a chicken wing when my phone vibrated. I licked two fingers and used them to extract my phone from my pocket and read the text.

*Guess where I am. lol*

*First tell me who you are,* I typed back, then reached for another wing while I waited.

A minute later my phone vibrated again. *Oh sry. Katie gave me your number. lol*

That narrowed it down to someone on Earth who wasn't Katie or me. Who did I know that would be so difficult?

Megan.

My phone vibrated again, and this time it was a photo of someone pulling a night crawler out of the dirt. Or maybe it was a closeup of a frog being dissected. The text came next. *Just pulled this out of blister on heel. At Hudsons. Going to Dr tomorrow.* I turned my phone off and tried to finish my hot wings and beer.

When I climbed into my bunk, Breakfast Club was still awake in the bunk below mine. "Hey Green Giant," he whispered. "I set my alarm a little early. We're going with full packs tomorrow."

"Oh. Okay. How come?"

"I feel like we're getting spoiled, you know? Soft."

He made sense. The Whites had been on everyone's mind. Every southbounder praised the beauty while warning us of the difficulty, and as Vermont kept getting taller and steeper, we were starting to believe them. They had just been there, and they were calling the mountains we had dropped our packs to get over "a nice, easy relief."

Additionally, we all planned to pick up our cold weather gear in Hanover, near the state line. That would add pounds to our packs immediately before the most challenging climbs along the entire AT. Instead of building our endurance, we had been acting like day hikers for a week. In retrospect, this was a terrible idea.

"Yeah." I turned onto my side. "I do know." Terrible idea or not, it had been nice.

■ ■ ■

Aish said he was sad to see us go. He had really enjoyed helping and serving us. We offered a collective donation that barely covered their expenses, and Aish accepted it gladly. The money in his palm made him giddy, almost as much as Jon when he dropped us off for the final time.

"You guys sure do have heavy packs." He swung mine by the strap as he hoisted it from the van. "Whee!"

During our short trip back to the trail, Jon spoke excitedly about other Yellow Delis. They were everywhere, he said: Brazil (that's where the maté comes from), Australia, Peru, Europe. Everywhere.

This intrigued me. I love to travel. These guys had really treated us right, and it was a cheap place to stay, too. When Jon handed me my pack, after thanking him I asked if he had a card or something listing all their locations.

His face was pure joy. "I do! Hee hee! It's in the van. I'll go get it!" He ran to the passenger door and returned with a pamphlet for each of us. The back cover was full of city names.

We thanked him one more time and said goodbye, and Jon drove off. The others handed me their pamphlets and headed straight for the trail. "Use these for kindling, dude," Breakfast Club said. "Or toilet paper. Just don't read them." He pointed to the woods. "Get in there. Hurry."

"That was some next-level shit right there, man," Two Pack said.

"What are you talking about?"

"Dude, you just gave money to a cult and then *asked them for a pamphlet.*"

"Sweet baby Buddha, those fuckers were spooky!" Ninja Mike hooted.

I laughed. "You're being dramatic. They're nice people. Their religion is based on helping others. I want to help them get to heaven, that's all."

"Turn that thing over."

The pamphlet was titled "Like a Beehive." Inside was a simple drawing of figures that looked more like aliens than humans. They were stacking hexagonal blocks. "Every one of us an equal," the caption read.

"When someone joins," Breakfast Club explained, "they give everything they own to the community."

"Aish gave us the pitch last night while you were at the bar," Two Pack said.

"They've had some heavy hitters join," Breakfast Club continued. "Like CEOs and shit. They're building their own hydroelectric plant somewhere up north. They're not just off the grid—they're making their own grid."

Two Pack nodded. "Next fucking level, bro."

Ninja Mike started up the trail. "Let's go boys! Goddamn, it's good to be back in the woods!"

I folded the pamphlet and shoved it into my pocket. Breakfast Club held his arms out like Frankenstein's monster and lurched toward me. "One of us, one of us." Two Pack added a pretty accurate "Hee hee!" We chased after Ninja Mike, who once again was grateful for the day.

The remaining fifty or so miles of Vermont did not go quickly, and while the climbs were small, there were many of them. The views were worth the work. These mountains felt like home, with the familiar rounded edges I knew from the Smokies, but covered with pines, lichens, and moss. Squirrels chattered, hurrying to bury nuts and acorns. The green tunnel was starting to turn yellow.

Our last day in Vermont was a series of small climbs finishing with a long, steady descent into Hanover, N.H. Hanover pulls double duty as a trail town and a college town: Dartmouth is there. So was our cold weather gear, at the post office. For me that meant a fleece hat and a puffy, down-filled jacket.

By the time we finished at the post office and walked across town, it was dusk. Behind the school soccer field was a "tent city" for hikers, but we were surprised to find it mostly deserted. The Bubble was nowhere to be seen.

Instead of a tent, Two Pack strung a hammock between two trees, and Breakfast Club did the same. Ninja Mike just put a plastic tarp down, then wrapped himself in an old wool army blanket. "G'night, boys."

"That's it? What do you do if it rains?"

"He wraps the tarp around himself," Two Pack explained from his hammock. "We call that the Ninja Mike burrito."

I turned back to Ninja Mike. "Really?"

He was already asleep.

. . .

He wasn't asleep for long. None of us were. The reason tent city was abandoned was because the bars were still open. At 2 a.m. the woods behind the soccer field turned into a circus.

Someone grabbed my tent and shook it. "HEY! DO I KNOW YOU? DO YOU HAVE ANY BOOZE IN THERE?"

Someone else was flashing a light. "You don't know who that is! Leave them alone!"

"Shut up! All these tents look the same."

For the next hour, stakes were hammered and flies were unfurled as people laughed and tripped over each other in the dark. It was almost 3 before the chaos subsided.

Because we were up all night and in the shade the next morning, no one stirred until well past second breakfast. Ninja Mike was grumpy and begrudgingly thanked the universe for another day while Breakfast Club roasted a bagel over our small fire. Two Pack made coffee using his bandanna as a filter. I asked him how much of his sweat was in each cup, but he swore that the cloth had no other use, and when I accepted a cup it was delicious.

The Bubble emerged from their tents like a brood of cicadas: Their noise was incredible and they left nothing behind. That's actually a compliment; they did an excellent job of cleaning up, especially considering their number. There must have been 50 tents around us when the ruckus began. Within an hour, Tent City was ours and ours alone.

The soccer field, however, was overrun. There were girls with hula hoops and men flying kites. Someone was playing fetch with a small dog that kept getting confused by the nearby game of frisbee. Someone yelled, "Miss Janet is here!" and the herd migrated toward the white van parked at the other end of the field. We crammed the last of our things into our packs and bolted across the field.

Surrounded by hikers, Miss Janet exuded an air of motherly love and hard authority. He face shone like the sun and her voice rang with deep Southern charm. Her hands fluttered as she greeted and hugged adoring hikers from the mob surrounding her. "Now y'all, I have one more run to make before I take y'alls things to Mr. Ackerly's. If two or three of y'all want to sit with the gear till I get back, the rest of y'all can start hiking."

I wiggled my way through the crowd. "Miss Janet, so nice to finally meet you. I'm Green Giant."

She looked me up and down. "Yes you are!"

I blushed, feeling like the new kid at school. She gave us permission to add our gear to the growing pile, and just like that, we were slackpacking to Mr. Ackerly's with The Bubble.

Bill Ackerly was known as the Ice Cream Man. His house was less than 100 yards from the trail and was a famous respite for hikers because of his hospitality. He didn't run a hostel; much like our friend Tom in Dalton, Bill Ackerly is retired and offers the use of his yard as a courtesy to thru-hikers. He holds croquet matches for them, and keeps a stocked freezer on his back porch filled with ice cream.

Before I knew it, the four of us had been swept away along with the herd. The biggest group I had hiked with had been five, with maybe the occasional sixth for an hour or so. Counting this group was futile. I thought there were 15 of us, but eight or nine more greeted us at the first water stop. They made reference to the other six ahead, and that's when I stopped trying.

Over the course of the next 17 beautiful miles, I introduced myself to as many of them as possible. These were the same people that Mark and I had read about in the log book on our first day back at Springer Mountain. First was Color Bandit, the guy who had been filling in all the monochrome sketches others had drawn. A huge muscular dude who wore a championship wrestling belt was Chosen, part of the Shrimp Gang, along with Papa Shrimp and Shrimpette. There was Hufflepuff, Barticus, Grampa Walker (who couldn't have been a day over 25), Yukon, Man Bear, K-Bar and Smoove-D. There was even a guy named Gerp. He wore a hunters cap and kept a cat named Henry, who would come when he whistled and sometimes hid in his pack.

Working my way through The Bubble as we marched at full speed toward ice cream, I passed a surprising number of strangely outfitted and bizarre characters. Yogi looked like a Spartan king and hiked barefoot. His pal Gadget was a rail-thin goofball who hiked in a bathrobe and carried a purple ukulele. He told me he had met up with Fiddlin' Jim, and their jam session that night was allegedly epic.

As I maneuvered to what I thought was the front of the parade, I kept my eyes open for anyone wearing a koala hat. Rumor was that Lemmy was a day or two ahead of us now. He had passed us while we were at the Yellow Deli, but hadn't signed the log books like we agreed.

It was dark long before we arrived. At a high cliff named Holts Ledge, which the guidebook described as "precipitous dropoff, views," we gazed at the full moon rising above the ridge across the valley, illuminating the rocks where we stood. The tiny lights below were our goal.

After an hour of fumbling over rocks by headlamp, we found Mr. Ackerly's house. Unlike Tom's place in Dalton, Bill has no neighbors for miles. At least 20 more Bubble people were on Bill's long covered porch, drinking, smoking, and listening to music. When they saw our headlamps they cheered. Breakfast Club found the freezer and returned with four fudgsicles. He passed them out, and that was dinner.

The party on the porch sounded like it was just getting started. Knowing how many people were still behind us, I made no attempt to sleep. As the other hikers arrived, the party became an uproar. Jokes were met with unnecessarily riotous laughter. People were falling over. Four different songs were playing simultaneously.

I leaned close to the young lady sitting beside me. "I don't want to be that guy, but isn't Mr. Ackerly trying to sleep?"

She pointed her thumb toward the house. "He told us he takes out his hearing aids before bed. We could set off fireworks right now and he'd never know."

"Then I guess I'll let my hair down and get a little crazy tonight too," I said. "Breakfast Club! Another round of fudgsicles, my good man."

For the second consecutive night we stayed up late and slept past sunrise. Somehow the majority of the porch crew was already packed and gone by the time the four of us stumbled onto the back deck, squinting and rubbing our heads. Ninja Mike was still wrapped in his wool blanket, and he wore a crown of wildflowers one of the girls made for him. He winked at me. "I am grateful for this day, for sure!

How you doing, brother?"

"I was just thinking that the only reason we didn't join a cult back there is because we might already be in one."

Bill made pancakes for us, and after our late breakfast he and I talked on the porch. I was curious about his birdfeeders, which led us to a discussion of wildlife and eventually to the two of us poring over an old field guide, trying to identify a small creature I'd seen days before. It was a mink.

Once again we found ourselves swept away with the herd and drawing ever closer to Mount Moosilauke, which marked the beginning of the Whites. The whole day felt like Sunday, when it's hard to enjoy the day off because you know what's coming. Plus it rained all day, hard.

When the four of us arrived at Hikers Welcome Hostel near the base of the mountain, once again it was dark. This was our last chance for laundry for at least a week, and with a single dryer it took hours before everyone was warm and happy again.

Someone in the kitchen told me there was a 12-pack in the fridge with my name on it, left for "Green Giant" by someone named Joe. That was Forager's real name, but why would he use that? And Forager was more of a liquor guy. Weird. "I'll take two. You guys split the rest."

The bunkhouse was full, so the caretakers set up a large canvas tent in the yard and filled it with cots and mattresses. I collapsed onto mine and was asleep in seconds. I dreamed about Mount Moosilauke. It is the tallest and steepest mountain for hundreds of miles, and immediately following it is a never-ending series of mountains just as tall and just as steep. It is the beginning of the end.

For the first time in days, I was awake before dawn. I hadn't slept long, but I slept hard. The Bubble was preparing for the big climb, nearly 4,000 feet of continuous uphill. Some people packed, while others sat on their cots, quietly staring at their guidebooks, psyching themselves up.

There was a koala hat on the cot in the corner. Lemmy was here.

And he was wearing a dress.

• • •

The elevation profile for Mount Moosilauke resembles the first drop of a big roller coaster. There is a long, steady rise that lifts you higher than you're really comfortable being, and then it throws you over a sudden decline so steep you're practically in free fall. It fills you with adrenaline, and for years, one of the ways hikers have coped with that specific flavor of fear is by wearing dresses.

It's something like Hike Naked Day, but regional. Depending on whom you ask, the tradition is either on its way out or in a resurgence. About half the men in the room were dressed like fancy ladies and princess fairies with big feet and hairy legs. All of the women were simply dressed like hikers.

Lemmy's curly hair was wild, and he wore a simple green gown with rainbow-striped socks. "Your beard really makes that outfit work," I told him. He wasn't ready to go, but with a limited number of places to stay on the other side of the mountain, I knew we'd meet again that night. I told him he looked pretty and carried my pack outside, and Two Pack and I set out.

Less than a mile past the hostel was a wide brook. The water was barely ankle deep, and had we been climbing any other mountain I would have splashed through without a care. But with a 4,000-foot elevation change comes unpredictable weather. Down here it was supposed to be sunny and in the 60s, but nearly a mile up, it might be freezing. I took off my shoes and waded across. Two Pack opted to get wet and splashed through. He was at least half a mile ahead by the time I dried my toes and put my shoes and socks back on.

The first 1,000 feet of elevation came gradually, stretched out over a mile and a half, with meadows, a few narrow brooks, and even a small pond. After crossing one final paved road, the trail became steeper, but with plenty of switchbacks so the grade was steady and predictable for a few more miles.

The switchbacks carried me past smaller streams, more mossy rocks, and lichen-covered pines. The air was becoming cooler and since this was probably the last water I would see until the other side, I filled both bottles and ate a Clif bar while I waited for my chemical drops to kill any microbes.

The next hour of hiking was even steeper and rockier. The trail was a thin line of exposed rock, barely visible through the encroaching tuckamore, as the stunted alpine trees are called. Multiple times I needed to haul myself up by a root or branch. And then suddenly there were no more trees.

The last mile to the summit was bare rock, fully exposed. The wind shoved me backward with every other step and made my ears ring and hurt, so I stopped to put on my rain jacket as a windbreaker and swapped my feathered hat for a Buff. Wiping my watering eyes and squinting at the view, I saw something I hadn't seen in a thousand miles: wave upon wave of mountains reaching to the horizon and beyond.

These mountains, however, did not have the familiar rounded peaks and balds I remembered from down south. The Whites were pushed up during the millions of years it took for the North American continent to drift over a volcanic hot spot after Pangaea shattered. Millions of years of erosion have softened some of the peaks, but the vast majority are sheer, spiky cliffs. And the scale—I'd come nearly 2,000 miles and felt like I was seeing real mountains for the first time. I had no idea places like this existed in the eastern United States.

Shoulder-high manmade rock piles called cairns marked the way to the summit. I leaned into the wind and plodded to the top, fighting the gale as much as gravity. Every few steps I stopped to wipe my eyes and take in the view. The top was marked by an orange square sign with simple hand-painted black letters: *MT. MOOSILAUKE– 4,802 FT.*

Standing at the sign, my view was now a full 360 degrees. A few feet behind the sign was a natural rock wall that would block the brutal wind, but the panorama held me in place.

Among the hikers huddled behind the rocks, one in particular stood out. He wore a red windbreaker and had a dark handlebar mustache. I was trying to enjoy the view, but the man with the mustache was staring at me. I must be going crazy, I thought. That's a fake mustache.

For a second I thought I recognized him from work, but the context made no sense and my brain rejected the idea. Then he waved. "Get down here behind these rocks!" There was no mistaking the strong Boston accent. *Heah. Rahks.* It was Joe, my friend from work.

I jumped down the few steps and crouched beside him. "Dude. What the fuck!"

. . .

Katie and Joe had been conspiring for weeks to make this happen. He was one of my best friends from the software company I had worked for before my hike. For the past five days, Katie had been emailing and texting him in Boston, where he lived, passing along my location, which in many cases was at best a guess. He had the gear and skills to pull off surprises like this, which was one of the reasons we got along. The fake mustache was meant as a silly dig at my shaggy appearance.

Joe fished a small sack from his pack. "I was going to hike south from the hostel and intercept you yesterday, but that rain—forget that! Sorry for the cheap beer, too. It was all I could find."

"Never apologize for giving someone beer, Joe."

The sack he handed me was full of gifts. Joe dried his own beef jerky, and this vacuum-sealed batch was made from brisket. There was a variety of crunchy snacks as well as some dried fruit, chocolates, and a tiny bottle of what appeared to be very expensive gin. "This looks pricey—I mean delicious. Thanks!"

"It is. Don't worry about it." Joe shielded his eyes and looked up. A military helicopter with Red Cross insignia was circling while we talked.

"There's no way he's landing in this wind," I said.

"I don't think he's trying to," Joe replied. "He's been circling for an hour. They're either training or looking for someone. And unless we want a ride in that thing, we should get going while there's still light. The climb down is no joke—I came up it. My truck is at the bottom."

Despite the quickening wind, we enjoyed a flat half mile above the trees before the roller coaster dropoff. Joe cut straight to the interesting questions as we walked. "Have you had any brilliant revelations now that you're no longer one of the jet-setters?"

"When I used to make a regular hop up to Boston, I remember looking at the map and thinking it'd be two, three hours tops." I held my fingers an inch apart. "Nothing to it, right?

Now that I've walked that distance, the world feels huge again. Bigger than I can imagine."

Then Joe stopped so suddenly I almost knocked him over. Two hikers were seated on rocks near the trail. "Trail's blocked," one said, not looking up. "Hiker down."

We were at a bend in the trail and couldn't see around it. But from up ahead I could hear someone making the horsey sound Colonel Butcher taught me. Perseverance. But we were about to go down, not up. "What's going on?" They continued to stare at their shoes.

Another raspberry sound, then a loud voice from up the trail. "He's with us." The pair looked up and the voice called out, "Let them through, he's one of us." As Joe and I cleared the bend, I recognized the man behind the voice. His stern eyes and square jaw contrasted his kind nature. It was Yukon. We'd met at Bill Ackerly's house.

"What's going on?" I could hear the horsey sound again from up ahead, a long slow exhale with flapping lips, but still couldn't see beyond another bend in the trail.

Yukon frowned. "We've got a runner collapsed on the trail. He's unresponsive."

Yukon and quite a few other hikers were veterans. Some were combat medics, and there were even a couple actual EMTs in The Bubble. "They've been doing chest compressions for..." He looked at his watch. "For way too long now."

He cupped his ear and turned toward the bend. The wind stopped. There were no more horsey sounds. A quiet voice from up the trail said, "We're calling it." Yukon looked back to us and shook his head.

I wobbled and put a hand on Joe's shoulder. "I need to sit down." I closed my eyes at the top of Mount Moosilauke and felt the free fall.

# 23

# LAUNCH

JOE LOOKED OVER the edge. "I don't know how they're going to do it."

The rescue operation had already been underway for an hour when Joe and I arrived. They were now referring to it as a recovery, and they were calling for volunteers to help move the body down the mountain. First responders were in contact with crews on the ground, who were still three hours away.

We stood at the top of a narrow waterfall, the wet rock beneath our feet shiny and slick. About 20 feet below us was a white blaze. Holding onto the root of a sapling, I lowered myself over the edge and strained to reach my footing, a piece of railroad tie supported by two steel spikes hammered into the rock.

Once I was settled on the tiny ledge, I could see the next one. And so on. The bottom step had rotted away and only the rebar supports remained. I looked back up to Joe. "This is where you would tie a rope and lower the stretcher, right?"

The idea seemed mad, but that is exactly what the recovery crew would have to do. And it would be dark by the time they started. With one headlamp to share and only enough thin cord to hang a food bag, we would have been ill-equipped for such an endeavor.

"Are we terrible people for not staying?" I asked.

"No, not at all," he said. "It's going to be hard enough to get ourselves down."

Fortunately, nearly a hundred volunteers were on their way, ready to position themselves in a human chain stretching from the road at the base all the way to the summit 3,000 feet up.

The small pool at the bottom of the waterfall gave us about 10 feet of flat earth before another wet rocky scramble. I let Joe go down first. According to the guidebook, we weren't even at the steep part yet. The day was full of obstacles, not the least of which was now half a mile behind us: the dead man we had to step over to get here.

The trail had been extremely narrow and we had no choice. The recovery crew was still hours out, and anyone not assisting was in the way. While we waited for the go-ahead to descend, we learned the identity of the fallen man.

He was Chad Denning. He was 39 and in the best shape of his life. In fact, he was in better shape than most people alive today. Chad was an accomplished trail and ultramarathon runner. He didn't just win races, he organized them. He also led hiking clubs and running groups all over New England and directed national programs to promote health and outdoor education for young people. Friends and colleagues referred to him as "Superman" because of his incredible athletic condition.

Chad and two friends had hiked up Mount Moosilauke that day and stopped to enjoy the view. He was smiling, about to say something. A second later he was on the ground. The official cause of death was later found to be sarcoidosis, a rare heart condition.

We were at the bottom of another difficult scramble when Joe and I encountered the first members of the recovery team, two volunteer firemen lugging heavy coils of rope. "Are we close?" They were already drenched in sweat and looked exhausted.

"It took us about an hour to get down this far, so maybe?"

Not too long after them, we met the guys with the stretcher. Then two more behind them carrying more rope. As Joe and I climbed down the mountain, the grim parade pulled themselves past us to the top.

Hours later, when Joe and I finally reached the bottom, the trailhead parking lot was clogged with emergency vehicles and the cars and trucks of all the local volunteers hauling rope, water, and other provisions to the top. The human chain would be there for many hours, and they needed to eat and drink too. The logistics were staggering.

Before Joe surprised me, I had thought I would spend the night in the Eliza Brook shelter, eight miles beyond the trailhead. There was no way I could make it before dark even if we hadn't been held up at the summit. Miss Janet had already taken The Bubble to the nearby town of Lincoln, where a friend of hers offered floor space for hikers.

We took Joe's truck. On our way to Lincoln, he and I talked about how beautiful and treacherous the hike down had been. But what was really on our minds was Chad. I had never met him, but I felt like I had. How could I miss someone I never knew?

In Lincoln, we pulled over when we spotted Ninja Mike walking beside the road without his pack. He jogged to the truck and smiled when he recognized me. He had already claimed space on the floor back at the house and was on his way to a burger joint. He was happy to ride in back, and as we sped up, Ninja Mike closed his eyes and let his hair fly in the wind.

Two Pack and Breakfast Club were seated at the bar with a half-full beer and an empty shot glass each. Breakfast Club waved. "Did you hear?"

I nodded and pointed to a table. He shook his head and pointed at the TV. I sat at the table while Joe used the men's room and Ninja Mike went to the bar to order our first round. It occurred to me that my sorrow for Chad had transformed into respect, with a tiny hint of jealousy. His last conscious thought had to have been one of joy. *He was smiling, about to say something.*

I took a breath and meditated upon the last few years of my own life, sifting through random memories. Quite a few involved mountaintops or waterfalls, but the majority took place in gray, windowless conference rooms, featuring men in neckties arguing over ones and zeros.

Based on what little I knew of Chad, it seemed that if you chose a random sample from his life, there was a strong probability that he was on a trail or atop a mountain, doing something that he loved—most likely *with* someone he loved.

That was where the hint of jealousy came from. The respect came from realizing that he had increased that likelihood on purpose. Chad Denning engineered a life that kept him surrounded by everything he loved most. And in doing so, he not only followed bliss, but became a source of it.

*A second later, he was on the ground.*

When would my moment come? And where? Right here, at this table? What about a year from now, in some nice but inoffensive cubicle? If I haunted the break room, would I be a happy ghost?

Probably not. The idea of haunting a mountaintop had much more appeal than the copier room on the sixth floor downtown. Hell, I'd prefer a water source, or even a privy, as the setting for my final breath.

Ninja Mike came back with three beers. Joe was still in the bathroom. "Fucking crazy day, brother." He put a beer in front of me and I thanked him.

He sat and put a beer in front of Joe's chair. "Your buddy seems pretty cool."

"Yeah, he's one of the good ones."

Ninja Mike sipped his beer and opened a menu. "You guys used to work together back in the real world, right? Think you'll go back?"

"I don't know, man. I still have some time before I need to decide. But I do know this..."

Joe was back. "What's that?"

I raised my glass. "I am grateful for today."

Ninja Mike raised his glass. "Right on, brother."

The three of us clinked our glasses and drank to life.

. . .

Ninja Mike put his phone on the ground and stepped back. From its tiny speaker came a soft flute crescendo accompanied by some discordant twanging, followed by a low somber tone. Ninja Mike breathed deeply and assumed a battle stance, raising a trekking pole like a sword above his head. Suddenly he leapt into the air, spun around, and slashed an invisible foe. His left foot flew into the face of another. The flute dropped an octave and Ninja Mike performed a one-handed cartwheel, using his pole to hack at yet another foe's Achilles heel. He stuck the landing, spun again, and bowed.

Miss Janet clapped and cheered. According to a longstanding rule, anyone who forgets something in her van must do a dance to get it back. During yesterday's chaos, Ninja Mike had left his poles behind. "That was terrific, honey. Now get in the van y'all, hurry up. Everybody's waiting."

She dropped us off at the trailhead to a scene much quieter than the day before. Her van and two other cars were the only vehicles in sight. The sun was just hitting the exposed rock cliffs on the north face of Mount Moosilauke and there were neither crowds nor flashing lights.

The very first thing the trail had lined up for us was a 1,000-foot climb as steep as the descent from Mount Moosilauke. After that, we could expect a few more little ups and downs, then one big climb, Kinsman Mountain.

Breakfast Club pointed at the guidebook map to a stream on the other side of Kinsman. "This looks flat. If we stealth there, it's a 15-mile day. That'll get us mostly caught back up." Two Pack and Ninja Mike agreed.

I told them they were crazy. "Have you guys not heard a single word any of the SOBOs told us? Even Miss Janet said the Whites would cut our mileage to a third. Not *by* a third, *to* a third."

Two Pack presented his case. "We were cranking out 20s with ease back in Vermont. Okay, sure we were slackpacking, but it didn't make that much difference, right? Look at the map. This is only a little steeper. It's early; I'm positive we can make 15 miles." He scoffed. "Those are beginner numbers!"

Ninja Mike was way ahead of us. He disappeared over the first rock pile and Breakfast Club shrugged and followed.

I let them go ahead. "Eleven. That's what I predict. There's a shelter right on the other side of Kinsman that puts us at 11 miles for the day. If you guys make it past there, I'll give you a dollar. But you'll have to backtrack to collect, because I'm only doing 11."

It took us the entire day to go seven miles. The Eliza Brook shelter was supposed to be our lunch stop, but when I arrived it was almost dark. Ninja Mike was already rolled up in his blanket and Two Pack and Breakfast Club were tossing sticks into a fire.

"Boy, am I glad to see you guys here," I said. "I was starting to think I was alone."

Two Pack looked up from the fire. "That was an ass-kicker. What the hell just happened?"

The Whites just happened, that's what. Each of what looked like little ups and downs turned out to require as much handwork as footwork. We had to lash our trekking poles to our packs and pull ourselves up and down 50-foot rock walls all day. This shelter was the last stop before a 2,000-foot climb. Two thousand feet would have been a warm-up back in the Smokies, I thought. But right now I didn't even have the strength to brush my teeth.

"Guys, we averaged one mile per hour today," Breakfast Club announced.

Two Pack shook his head. "Nope. Not even."

In addition to misjudging our speed, we also had misjudged our appetites. Switching from legs-only to a full-body workout required twice the calories, and we needed a resupply before tackling the rest of these mountains. If we could get to the next road crossing, which was nine miles north, by lunchtime the following day, we could hitchhike back into Lincoln, get food, and be halfway up our next monster climb before dark. We'd still be one day behind schedule, but at least we'd have food.

It was almost dark when I got to the road. Ninja Mike was already in Miss Janet's van, and Two Pack and Breakfast Club were tossing their packs into the back. "Boy, am I glad to see you guys here."

We found supplies and some cheap floor space back in Lincoln. It was well past hiker midnight by the time we had dinner, and I collapsed soon after. Morning came too soon, and after another hitchhike back to the trail, we found ourselves once again at the bottom of something beautiful and intimidating.

Mount Lafayette is among the tallest and most iconic mountains not just on the AT, but in the eastern United States. Its peak is well over 5,000 feet, and can only be reached by traversing Franconia Ridge, a 3-mile knife edge of moss-covered rock, all above the tree line, towering over steeply angled drops on both sides. On a clear day the view can stretch over 100 miles.

At the campsite near the halfway point, Breakfast Club reminded us that we were now a day and a half behind our original schedule. Two Pack suggested that we throw out the schedule.

We could hear the wind about 300 feet before we emerged from the tree line. Stepping out onto the exposed rock, we felt the strong but warm breeze.

Walking along Franconia Ridge was like hiking in the sky. Craggy drops on either side of the worn rock path fell hundreds of feet into lesser waves of peaks and valleys. Haze obscured the horizon, and big clouds approached. Not far above, rays of sunlight broke through to cast spotlights on the shadowy sea of pines below.

For an hour we walked the winding granite tightrope through the clouds amid yellow beams of light. Some of the lower clouds piled up along the ridge below, building in height and mass until they rolled over us in slow motion waves of gray, crashing on the rocks, leaving blue sky and golden streaks in their wake.

Dumbstruck, we climbed higher. At the summit the clouds were too thick to take in the view, but after three miles of continuous sweeping panorama we had no complaints. The next four miles were a slippery struggle in near whiteout conditions.

Not only are the shelters in the Whites well maintained and beautiful, but they often have a caretaker. At Garfield shelter, ours told us to hunker down before she retreated to her tiny shack. She had radioed the weather station at the base and the forecast was grim: high winds and freezing rain. The good news was that our shelter was unusual in its design. It still had one open wall, but instead of the classic box, this one had an L-shaped floorplan that allowed us to keep out of direct wind.

I thought back to hail in the Smokies, and climbing Roan Mountain at night. That time I slept in a shitter. These things did nothing to prepare me for the torrent that was unleashed on us that night.

Garfield shelter is almost as big as my house, and I was afraid the whole structure would blow away. Large pines bent nearly over, and three times something slammed against the wall in the dark outside. The L-shape did keep out the direct wind, but it also acted as a funnel, so there was a permanent cyclone of cool mist swirling in one corner.

The storm only intensified at sunrise. Breakfast Club volunteered to brave the quarter-mile descent to our water source and collect for all of us. We were just beginning to worry when he finally returned. His raincoat was torn and his hair was soaked. Two of the water bottles were missing.

"Guys, we're not going anywhere today," he informed us as we helped him in. The trail was a whiteout; he'd fallen twice, and the wind had knocked him over two more times. On his way back to the shelter, he'd met the caretaker. News from down low was that this thing was turning into a full-blown squall. "They're saying 50 to 60 miles an hour, sustained."

I started boiling water for coffee. "So what do we do? Zero here at the shelter?"

"What else can we do?"

We spent the entire day sitting in the L-shaped box, watching the trees bend over and telling stories. By lunchtime, everyone needed a nap. We were tired from not doing anything. When we woke up at 3, the weather was still treacherous. Bored, we'd eaten an entire day's rations, huddled together in a tiny rumbling box. I smiled at Breakfast Club.

"What are you looking at?"

"You ever see one of those old cartoons where two people are stranded on a desert island, and one of the guys starts to see his buddy turn into a hot dog or a steak with arms and legs?"

"Yeah."

"I was just thinking that you look like a Snickers bar right now."

Ninja Mike laughed. "You look like a joint."

"Sorry, can't help you there," I said, reaching for my pack. "But I do have this gin from Joe." It wasn't much to split four ways, but it warmed us up and helped us sleep.

Overnight the storm broke, and the next day we finally climbed down from Mount Garfield, slipping and falling multiple times on the wet rocks. My palms were scraped and bloody from grabbing at branches to stop a long uncontrolled skid. Ninja Mike had a large purple bruise on his right butt cheek from an earlier fall. He was proud of it and gave us daily reports on its changing size and shape.

I was about to suggest second breakfast when we saw a sign for Galehead Hut. The Whites are not only spectacular and challenging, they are also popular. To help ensure safety and comfort for those who visit, the Appalachian Mountain Club (the same group who provides caretakers and maintains the shelters) runs a number of lodges at some of the range's most scenic locations. These lodges—or huts, as they are officially known—must be what the man with the ridiculously heavy pack back in the Smokies thought all shelters on the AT would be like.

Some of the huts had room for 100 guests or more, with stacked bunks, running water, flushing toilets, and a full-sized kitchen operated by a crew who served meals to the guests in a real dining room—with dishes! The huts were big-time.

When we got there, they still had leftover pancakes and hot chocolate from breakfast. While Ninja Mike and the others finished eating, I stepped outside and checked my phone on a whim. One bar came and went. I took a chance and called Katie. She answered on the first ring.

"Hi, Green Giant! I missed you!" Every other word was a crackle.

"I missed you too. It's been a while."

*Crackle.* "—bet you've been busy—" *Static.* "How were the Whites?"

I laughed and told her I was still in them.

"Oh. Everything okay?"

Our miles had been single digit every day, I explained, and the last 15 had taken us almost three days. The terrain was exactly as rugged as we'd been warned, no exaggerations. Each of us already needed to replace gear. Luckily, the hut had some things we needed for sale, such as hats and gloves.

I heard her say something about Voldemort. The only other words I could make out were "Hudson" and "Hanover."

"I don't know if you can hear me, but we're shooting for Mount Washington day after tomorrow. I'll call you if I can." I looked at the screen. The call had already dropped.

Ninja Mike joined me outside. The sky was clear and blue again, glistening rocks the only visible sign that the weather had not always been this idyllic. "You ready, brother?" he asked me.

If things got so crazy with no warning here, what the hell was happening further north? How insane is Katahdin right now? What's it going to be like in two weeks when it's almost October?

I put on my pack and tightened the straps. Ninja Mike was waiting for a reply, so I looked him in the eyes and told him the truth. "Nope."

■ ■ ■

That night I enjoyed a rare opportunity to stealth camp in the Whites. I found a little flat spot near a small waterfall and a footbridge, simply too lovely to pass up. The rest of the gang were at a shelter two miles ahead. Around midnight I thought it was raining, but the sound was really just the leaves falling onto my tent.

When I climbed out in the morning, the ground was bright yellow. After packing up, I kicked and rustled my way to the shelter, where Two Pack and Breakfast Club were still milling about.

"Hey, Green Giant. We wondered what happened to you. Did you stealth?"

"Yeah, about two miles back. Pass me the log book?" There was no note from Lemmy. At this point, I had no idea if he was ahead or behind. Just in case he was behind, I signed my name and drew the Green Giant smiley, then passed the book to Two Pack. "Where's Ninja Mike?"

"He just left. Want to talk about Mount Washington?"

I did. Mount Washington is known for regularly recording the highest wind speeds on Earth. The world record was set there in 1934, when the observatory at the summit withstood a blast of 231 miles per hour. It is the highest peak in the Northeast, and the AT goes right over the summit.

We wanted to reach the top today, but the only shelter beyond the peak was five miles further. Having finally learned to manage our expectations, we settled for the hut right before the top, Lakes of the Clouds Hut. The name itself made me want to stay there.

The huts cost money, but they also offer what's known as work-for-stay, which is exactly what it sounds like. A few thru-hikers get the opportunity to work in the kitchen or clean the building in exchange for a very nice place to stay for the night. They had a limited number of work-for-stay slots each day at Lakes of the Clouds, so we would have to time our arrival just right.

We descended into Crawford Notch, just over 1,000 feet above sea level, enjoying jaw-dropping views the entire time. Across the notch we could see towering rocky cliffs that we knew were the first in a series of false summits which eventually led to Mount Washington, which was just over the horizon. At the bottom of the notch we realized that those cliffs were the AT: Webster Cliffs, according to the guidebook, had a half-mile exposed traverse with many views. Excited, we charged toward the climb.

Again we found ourselves strapping poles to packs and hoisting ourselves up by roots and rocky handholds. The green tunnel was occasionally so tight that we practically wriggled through it, eventually bursting through the tree line and onto boulder-filled outcroppings like rock stars taking the stage.

At each successive stage we felt more like aging rock stars, and for the fourth time in as many days we reached our planned lunch stop long after lunch.

It was 3 p.m. when we entered the clearing at Mitzpah Spring Hut. The sky was silver, and the big round thermometer by the door read 58 degrees. When the wind blew, the pines sprayed us with mist. Ninja Mike waved from inside and opened the door. "Guys, you're just in time. He's taking work-for-stays and we're the only ones here! Come on, I think they need four, hurry up!"

We met the guy in charge, a lanky fellow in an apron with a shaved head and a neat, long beard that hung past his chest. "Sit tight, guys. I'll go see what the crew needs in the kitchen to prep for dinner."

The four of us put our packs and coats on hooks by the door and sat on a bench. The guy with the long beard appeared at the kitchen door a moment later and waved us over. "Fellas, I feel like a real jerk for having to do this, but I screwed up. It's only 3 o'clock; we pick work-for-stays at 4. I forgot what time it is. I'm sorry, my fault."

"No worries, man," Ninja Mike replied. "Can we just come back in an hour?"

"Sorry, you're not allowed to wait. It's a weird rule, but we're supposed to take whoever shows up at 4, not who's already here."

It *was* a weird rule. But his confident, well-rehearsed delivery suggested that he'd also heard every rebuttal, and that resistance was futile.

"How much would it cost for us to stay?" Breakfast Club asked.

"One twenty-five."

He winced. "You mean total, right?"

"Nope. Each."

"Ow! Never mind."

We regrouped by the door and tried to come up with a plan. The mist had become drizzle. I took out my map. "Lakes of the Clouds is six more miles. If we leave immediately, we can get there before dark."

Two Pack said, "Five of those six miles are above tree line. Exposed."

"I know. That's why we have to leave now." We'd already wasted half an hour. It was September, so the days of 14 hours of sunlight were long gone. It would be dark in a few hours and we were standing still.

Ninja Mike had another plan. "It's getting pretty sketchy out there. I'm going to stay outside till 4 and hope he forgets me, and try again."

"What are you going to do if he turns you away?"

"What are *you* going to do if Lakes of the Clouds turns *you* away?"

He had a good point. What were any of us going to do, really? There were cliffs behind us, cliffs ahead of us, and no flat spots, only huts. The drizzle was picking up.

"I'm going to do what I always do," I told him. "I'm going forward. I'm tired of constantly falling short of my goal for the day, and I think if I leave now I can get above this mist."

Lakes of the Clouds Hut was above 5,000 feet, where camping is forbidden, so I was banking on arriving at dusk and relying on the caretaker's mercy. It would be dark and cold, and if it came down to it, I'd throw down the credit card.

I told the guys I'd see them up there for second breakfast and stepped out. While I was tightening my pack, I checked the thermometer again: 54. The temperature had dropped four degrees since we arrived.

■ ■ ■

The trail resumed at the other side of the clearing, and I walked into the tight tunnel of thick small pines. Rocky and too narrow for switchbacks, it went straight to the top. The rocks were mostly granite, light gray slabs that sparkled from the drizzle. Hiking through the pine boughs was like going through a car wash; my rain coat was saturated and my legs were soaked.

Thanks to all the effort I was exerting, at least I was warming up from the inside. Whenever I came to a brief break in the trees, my hood would slap my face on the windward side. A few times the white blazes were difficult to locate, often at the top of vertical scrambles.

The higher I climbed, the stronger the wind. I left the tree line for good somewhere near the peak called Mount Eisenhower. According to a sign, the actual summit was at the end of a loop trail. But I couldn't tell which way, because the wind had knocked the sign free of the pile of rocks that served as its base.

The gusts were coming from behind, so I had to lean backward while I walked forward. My poles kept slipping on the wet rocks and were only useful when they kept me from falling. I leaned back more and held them in front of me, scurrying along like some giant praying mantis.

Then the trail switched back and the wind was in my face, blowing back my hood and filling my eyes and nose with water. I turned my head and my ear filled too. I crouched, and tightened my hood. Then I squinted and leaned into the wind. Four more miles and another 1,000 feet up. This was insane. It was already getting dark.

Suddenly someone—or something—tackled me. That was the first explanation my brain could conjure when confronted with the question, "Why am I lying on my stomach and sliding toward that ledge?"

I rolled onto my back, and my pack snagged momentarily on a withered stump, slowing my slide somewhat. I grabbed another stump and stopped completely. I turned back to the trail, and again my hood flew back and my face was splashed by spray. Crouching again, I turned just in time to see my pack cover sail off into the abyss, a flapping green sacrifice. But not offered by me. Something the storm had just taken.

It's going to take me next, I thought. This is beyond insane—this is stupid. I have to get down, not up.

I crawled back to the trail and turned back the way I thought I'd come, hunching and crouching and clutching at my hood for half a mile before realizing I was still going up. Dejected but determined, I turned back again, for real this time. This time when I reached the point where I'd fallen, I was braced for the crosswind. Even so, it still almost took me.

Despite my steady exertion, I was no longer warming up from the inside. Even walking as fast as I could without slipping on the wet rocks, I was still shivering. The tree line brought moderate relief, but I knew I would have to repeat the steepest part of the day, only in reverse this time. Hand over hand in a freezing, sideways rain.

I did it.

When I stumbled back in through the front door of the Mitzpah Spring Hut, the guy in charge with his long beard and bald head was there to greet me. "Wow! You're lucky to be here. Lakes of the Clouds just radioed down: They've got 70 mile per hour winds up there! You're not heading north, are you?"

He didn't recognize me. Of course he didn't. He saw dozens of hikers every day, and I hadn't looked like a drowned rat the first time we met.

"I am."

"Well, you're in luck," he said. "We have room for exactly one more work-for-stay. You should probably go put on dry clothes and eat some turkey first." He led me to the kitchen. "Here, eat this." He handed me some hot meat and a cup of tea.

I took it and thanked him as I stood dripping all over the kitchen floor. In a blink, Breakfast Club was on it with a mop. The guy in charge asked me my name and I told him. He introduced me: "Guys, this is Green Giant."

Two Pack was washing dishes with his back to us. He didn't turn around. "Never heard of him."

Ninja Mike handed me a towel. "You look like hell, brother."

I was left in their custody, and after I found a place to change into dry clothes, I put on an apron and joined the guys in the kitchen.

We served dinner to the paying guests, mostly couples my age and their children. The women all wore nail polish and the men sported perfect haircuts and a day or two of stubble. Their parkas were spotless and the crowd smelled like soap. One man still had a price tag on his pants.

After we fed them, the four of us sat at a table and ate our own huge plates of turkey, beans, mashed potatoes, and bread. We had three bowls of soup each, and I ate two salads. Dessert was apple cobbler.

We spent the next hour washing dishes while watching the storm rage outside. All of the bunks were full, so the guy in charge put the four of us upstairs in a small library, a single room with shelves full of games and books. We put our sleeping bags in the corners and took turns playing chess while planning the next day.

The weather forecast for tomorrow was perfect. The top of Mount Washington would be cold but clear, with visibility predicted at 120 miles. You could almost see the curvature of the earth. But we needed supplies again, beyond what the huts could offer. We had to go down.

In the morning, we took an easy supply trail from the hut down to Pinkham Notch. After a resupply there at the bottom, we switched trails and started back up towards Mount Washington through Tuckerman Ravine. The first two miles took us up a relatively gentle slope, with a nearly vertical rock wall looming in the distance. Halfway up, the pines abruptly stopped in a neat horizontal row, and the trail drew us into a steep fold carved out by a waterfall. Since we could see the falls from here, I thought, it had to be hundreds of feet high.

Ninja Mike pointed at the falls. "Let's go! Straight up!" He ran. Two Pack followed.

Breakfast Club shrugged. "I'm not running, but holy shit, I can't wait to get up there." He took off at a brisk pace and I followed.

We spent the next hour scrambling up rocks, looking back over an ever-increasing spread of pines and smaller mountains. The roar of the falls increased as the trail zigzagged closer to it. At one tight bend in the notch, the trail disappeared behind the falls, allowing us to view the valley through a veil of mist and rainbows.

Ninja Mike proposed that we skip the rest of the AT and just set up camp here. "Right here, man. Let's just live in the Whites until it gets too cold. There's no fucking way that it gets better than this!"

He cupped his hands and leaned back. "WHOOOOO-WHEEE!" He waited for his echo but it never came; the chasm was too vast. He cheered anyway and bounded up the rocks, faster than any of us.

The summit comes abruptly. You cannot see it or hear it until you are standing in the parking lot. There is a visitor center at the top of the world, and finding it there was so alarming that we couldn't help but pine for the relative peace of the rocks and the wind again. We stayed long enough to eat a slice of pizza and to appreciate the view.

I did my best to estimate north and looked toward the horizon. So that's what 120 miles looks like, I thought. I walk from here to the horizon two more times and we're almost there.

Ninja Mike was ready. "All right, boys. It's time to take off."

## ORBIT

THE AT NORTH OF Mount Washington makes a great clockwise circle, and for many miles we hiked due south while somehow still making progress toward Katahdin. A day and a half later, we actually found ourselves back in Pinkham Notch again, at the same visitor center where we had resupplied days before, looking up at Mount Washington from the bottom of Tuckerman's Ravine.

"We were just here," Breakfast Club lamented. "Why does the AT hate us?"

The northern part of New Hampshire is made of mountains and places with fantastic names like Thunderstorm Junction, Parapet Trail, and Crater Mountain. A 20-mile section goes through the Wildcats, a range that consists of only ridiculous climbs and descents. From the tops we could see forever, but everything between was a mystery; we could barely find our way from blaze to blaze.

The Wildcats began with a 1,000-foot climb so steep it looked like a printer's error in the guidebook. The exit was a bit more forgiving, but our knees and shoulders ached as we approached the White Mountains Lodge and Hostel near Gorham, the last little town before crossing our final state line. I shivered, partially from emotion, but also because flurries that morning had left any place still in the shadows dusted white.

We arrived at the hostel just in time to meet a group of hikers headed back to the trail. Much to my surprise, among them was my old friend Bones. Most of the biting insects were long gone, so he no longer wore his head net. He was still thin as a twig, and his big round beard atop his stick-like frame made him look like a lollipop.

My first thought was that he must have been sick or hurt again for me to have caught up to him. But he was just another ultralight speed hiker humbled by the Whites, exactly like the rest of us.

When our groups met, we all stepped further away from the road and exchanged updates. This was the hiker grapevine in action. People were buzzing about crossing in to Maine and locating friends. There was one bit of news in particular that everyone was talking about. Bones was the first to share it with me. "Green Giant, this should interest you. It's about a friend of yours."

"Who's that?" I said.

"Your old pal Voldemort almost ended her hike in Hanover."

"Whoa, really? What happened? Is she okay?"

"She's fine, but she lost all her gear."

"What! How?"

To say she lost her gear was inaccurate; her pack had been stolen. Megan had almost caught up with us. She was at the grocery store in Hanover, resupplying to start the Whites when it happened. She left her pack outside the store, as hikers do in every trail town, and when she returned, it was gone. For Megan, this was the equivalent of losing her home. Tent, sleeping bag, clothes, all of it gone. Even her poles.

Word spread fast. Miss Janet and The Bubble weren't too far ahead, and soon people were sending donations: extra gear, things abandoned in the van, cash, even a pack that belonged to someone who had been forced to quit because of a broken ankle. Hanover is a hiker-friendly town, and more than one resident offered up a spare room in their homes while she re-equipped, but the ordeal set Voldemort back almost five full days. She should have been barreling down the Wildcats, hot on our tails. Instead, she was probably just now starting the Whites.

I wondered whether all the never saying goodbye business really only applied at the start. We had assumed any deficit could be overcome back when the trail seemed infinite. But now we were running out of trail. I could count the number of remaining resupplies on one hand.

The following day as we headed back to the trail, our group met another arriving at the hostel, and much to my surprise, among them was Lemmy. He had picked up his cold-weather gear and was wearing all of it: thick pants, gloves, a parka over a sweater, and a scarf that covered everything but his eyes. He leaned on his memory stick with each step, and his hat made him look like a puffy, lumbering bear, ready to hibernate.

"You should be careful dressed like that around here, Lemmy. Someone's going to shoot you and make a rug out of you."

He tugged the scarf enough to uncover his mouth. "If it gets me next to a fireplace, I will pull the trigger for him."

. . .

The first climb out of Gorham ended at the top of a rocky bald named Mount Hayes. The wide, exposed top was a maze walled in by knee-high blueberry bushes. Occasional tufts of grass were surrounded by piles of moss and pillows of spindly lichen. The sky was gray and it was beginning to rain, but Ninja Mike and I dropped our packs.

"What are you doing?" Two Pack asked.

I knelt and examined the lichen, which looked like shrunken coral up close. "Are you kidding? This place is amazing! Look at it!" Ninja Mike was already standing on a rock pile with his arms outstretched. "See? He gets it."

Breakfast Club was on Two Pack's side. "My guess is that this rain picks up and you guys have a miserable time."

Ninja Mike opened one eye and looked over his shoulder. "The rain is part of what makes this place so beautiful."

Two Pack laughed. "When you two hippies are done picking a name for your cult, Breakfast Club and I will be somewhere down that way. We'll be the two dry guys eating warm rice."

Ninja Mike and I stayed at the top for another hour, munching on blueberries and examining the various mosses and fungi. Neither of us knew what we were looking at, but their diversity and assortment of colors were mesmerizing. While we were distracted by the little things, the rain stopped and we failed to notice.

I stood up. Through a break in the pines, I could see a dark gray pyramid substantially taller than the one we were on. "Hey, look! Is that Mount Success?"

"I think so. You know what's on the other side of that, right?" Ninja Mike asked.

"Success?"

He smirked. "Maybe. Hopefully." The real answer was Maine. The state line was on the far side of Mount Success, a mere two miles beyond the summit. We could almost see it from here.

I sat back down and we watched black and gray clouds swirl slowly over the top of the mountain. Ninja Mike asked me if I had ever heard of Pamola.

"Is that what we're going to name our cult?"

"We could. Pamola was the name of the god of thunder for the people who were here before us. The dude had the wings of an eagle and the head of a moose. Guess where he lived."

"Katahdin?"

He nodded. "Katahdin. Home of the storm god. That's why they said it always has a dark cloud over it." He touched a pile of moss to check if it was dry and then used it as a pillow. It was dusk and bright stars were appearing between the clouds. "I like to think of Katahdin as the final boss fight in a video game. The difficulty just keeps ramping up and up until there's this giant epic bastard at the end, you know?"

"I like your analogy, Ninja Mike. But for me, I like to think of all this as something I've already done."

"What do you mean?" he said, propping up on his elbows.

"It's a trick I did in boot camp to pass the time. That place was constantly miserable, so I pretended it was already over and that everything happening around me in the present was actually just me remembering it. I'm not miserable here—at least not too often—but I do the same thing when I zone out on the trail sometimes. On those days when it feels like Katahdin is a million miles away, I time travel into a future where the goal is already complete, and I pretend that all this is me simply looking back on how I got there."

"That almost makes sense, brother." He sank back into the moss.

As the air cooled, the clouds thinned and eventually vanished, revealing a multitude of stars. We marveled at the view, and mulled over the idea of our universe being a single electron in some massive atom. Staring into the Milky Way from the top of a mountain will do that to you. As the temperature dropped and dew began to collect on the moss, we gathered our packs by starlight and slowly climbed down into the dark, carefully placing our feet and poles on the slanted rocks.

After about a mile Ninja Mike pointed to a shimmering red glow at the top of a distant ridge. "That has to be them. Holy shit, did they make a bonfire?"

I put my head next to his and squinted. "I don't know—that's a lot of light."

We continued walking and the light continued to grow. Sometimes it was difficult to see directly because of the thick trees, but after a few minutes there was no mistaking it. The glow was getting redder and bigger. "It looks like they're trying to signal the aliens," Ninja Mike said.

My heart raced. I took a breath. "What if that's not them? What if that's a wildfire?"

The far off light flickered through the thick branches, now orange and much larger. Almost half of the sky was glowing from that direction.

He took a step back. "Oh fuck, dude. That's a fucking fire! Run!"

We turned and sprinted back the way we had come. It didn't look like the blaze was directly on the trail, so I hoped Two Pack and Breakfast Club were okay. They were probably already fleeing north.

When I made it back to the top, under the stars again, I fell wheezing into the moss. Ninja Mike had beaten me there, and he was doubled over.

Laughing.

I caught my breath. "What?" I pushed up to my knees and repeated myself. "What!?"

He pointed. I felt like an idiot.

The top half of the rising full moon had crested the horizon behind us, blood red and casting long, crimson streaks among the shadows of the thick black pines. When the boughs waved in the breeze, pumpkin-colored moonlight and triangular black shadows flickered like flames, while bright orange flashes danced across the surface of a pond in the valley below.

"My god, Ninja Mike. Were we just afraid of *the moon?*"

He wiped his eyes. "Oh, dude. We just went full-fucking Neanderthal." He pointed at the moon and grunted. "Sky fire! Scary! Ahhh!" He fell back into the moss and howled.

Now that our flight had put us back in prime stargazing territory, we stayed up on Mount Hayes past hiker midnight and even actual midnight, until the moonlight defeated all but the brightest stars. When we eventually found Two Pack and Breakfast Club sleeping beside the trail, we woke them up as we guffawed and grunted like cavemen at the glowing remains of their puny fire.

■ ■ ■

The next morning, Two Pack and Breakfast Club were the ones laughing as Ninja Mike and I grumbled beside our own puny fire. "I think six more hours of sleep would be perfect," I groaned. "I'm exhausted."

Two Pack was already tying his shoes. "Sounds like you forgot to take your Triactin."

"What's Triactin?"

"Try actin' like a man!"

Breakfast Club spat coffee and Ninja Mike snorted.

Today was the day we'd get to Maine. We gathered around Two Pack's map to see what lay ahead. All we had to do was get up and over Mount Success. Since we were likely to split up along the way, we agreed to wait at the sign for Maine and all step over the line together. The Whites were behind us now, which meant we should be able to get back to our big mileage. It was eight miles to the summit and two more to Maine. "Hell, we could probably be there by lunchtime," said Two Pack.

Breakfast Club pushed his finger east of the state line. "These climbs are steep, but look how small they are. We could even be at the start of Mahoosuc Notch by the end of the day."

"The start of?" Ninja Mike scoffed. "Let's get *through* that fucker!"

Mahoosuc Notch is notoriously the most difficult mile of the entire Appalachian Trail, though that same mile also is frequently described as the most fun. The Notch is a mile-long jumbled boulder pit, with rocks as big as cars and houses, and the only way through is to scale them or squirm under them. A few years before, a moose had wandered in and fallen into one of the many deep crevasses. It broke a leg and lay there bellowing for days until some kind soul with a hunting knife finally showed the only mercy possible by climbing down and slitting the poor thing's jugular.

"Let's get to Maine first, guys," I said. "Then we'll see how it goes. I don't want to find my way through The Notch by headlamp."

Even I had been too optimistic, surprised to end the day still in New Hampshire. When I finally reached the top of Mount Success, Ninja Mike was on his back in the moss, wearily twirling a trekking pole, Two Pack was trying (and failing) to find firewood, and Breakfast Club was filtering rainwater collected from a dip in the exposed rock.

I dropped my pack and squatted. "How many times, guys?"

"How many times what?" asked Ninja Mike from his bed of moss.

"How many times did you think you were at the top of this thing before you finally got here?"

"I stopped counting at 12," yelled Breakfast Club from our puddle.

"I guess if we're going to fail," said Two Pack from over by the empty fire ring, "here would be the best place to do it."

The sky was mostly clear, and they had already rolled out their bags on the rocks. They invited me to stay, but with my light summer bag, I relied on my thin tent to retain at least some heat while I slept. Instead, I raced down the backside of Mount Success, desperately searching for any flat spot big enough to make camp. For at least a mile past the summit, the greatest distance between two pines could be measured in inches. Even if I wanted to collapse onto the ground, I couldn't. There never was any ground.

It was almost dark when I finally found my home for the night. Someone in a similar predicament must have become frustrated and chopped down just enough trees to clear just enough room for a single small tent. This was not some cute little campsite with a tiny fire ring and rock chairs; it was a flat patch of dirt so minuscule that I was genuinely concerned about someone tripping over me in the night. After I pitched my tent and wriggled in, I could easily reach out and touch the trail.

I awoke to the sound of gentle rain. The trees were collecting mist from the clouds and dripping onto my tent. The wind far above howled, and I wondered how Ninja Mike and the gang were doing. I was about to take my first sip of hot coffee when I heard them coming. Ninja Mike was at the front of their soggy parade, testily repeating his mantra.

"I am grateful for today, I am grateful for today, I am— There he is. Fuck you, Green Giant!"

My tent was already packed up, so we crowded into the flat spot like four men in an elevator. I raised my cup and took another sip. "How was your night?"

"Night was fine. But I didn't get to do any yoga before hauling ass down here. I was just snoring, then dreaming, then *BAM!* Eyes open. Fuck! Run! We beat the worst of it, though."

"Notch today?"

"Notch today!" We high-fived.

Of course, we didn't make The Notch that day. Full Goose shelter, five miles into Maine, was as far as our excitement from crossing the state line could carry us. There was still plenty of time and sunlight left to get through Mahoosuc Notch if we really wanted to. There was even a campsite with water at the other side. But no one said a word; we all started unpacking as soon as we arrived. Ninja Mike gathered wood and started a fire, even though it was only three in the afternoon. We sat around it and watched the coals.

We had crossed into Maine almost first thing after coffee. There was a simple white sign with simple black letters and a whole lot of trees. We tried to celebrate as best we could, but energy was scarce. The trail rambled through piles of moss-coated dead trees that leaned in every direction. Much of the moss was thick enough that ferns and other large plants grew among it. In many places, new trees sprouted right atop the dead logs and boulders. Everything was wet and smelled ancient.

The vertical rock walls started almost immediately upon entering Maine. Rebar ladders and boulder scrambles took us up the sides of unnamed mountains taller than skyscrapers where we could see for miles, while in the valleys between we could barely find each other. Maine was a beautiful obstacle course, and we were bruised and bleeding after only five miles.

Two Pack made us each some of his famous bandanna coffee, and my cup was cool before I had drunk even half. We huddled and shivered at the shelter while more hikers filed in. By dark, the place was packed, and rumor had it that still more were coming. The box was full, and almost every tent site was taken.

I pitched my tent behind the shelter and rejoined the growing crowd by the fire. There must have been 30 people shoulder to shoulder around the flames, and only one person was speaking. Someone I didn't recognize said nervously, "I told everyone back home that I was hiking from Georgia to Maine. If I go home tomorrow, I guess technically that means I met my goal. Right?" No one answered, but a few nodded.

We were all bushed, and that was just as contagious as the misguided enthusiasm we had shared at the start of the day. I quarantined myself in my tent and shivered all night, despite wearing every article of clothing I had.

It was good that we stopped early, because Mahoosuc Notch was every bit as demanding as we feared. Two nearly vertical rock walls have been crumbling into the vast pit in between for millennia. For two hours, I balanced, climbed, leapt, and pulled my way across, around, and under mammoth rocks of every shape. In many places I hung by my fingers, unsure where to go. Once, I spied a white arrow pointing the way into an impossibly small gap. I trusted the paint, took off my pack and dropped it, then lowered myself into the blackness. I could see light at the other end, but had to feel my way to it, alternately pushing or dragging my pack through several tight squeezes. Unseen water gurgled somewhere in the cold below, and I couldn't help imagining my fate should I slip and fall into it.

The Notch was intense, but brief, and soon I was back on normal trail, or at least what passes for normal in Maine. Somewhere among the boulders I lost track of everyone, so I climbed up and over the next mountain solo. Old Speck is a 3,000-foot monster that drops into Grafton Notch on the north side, where there is a small parking lot and a two-lane blacktop road. A few cars were there, and one hiker: Lemmy.

I jogged toward him, calling from across the lot. "Hey, buddy! I thought you were behind me. Maine is a strange place, huh?"

He nodded. "Two Pack and Breakfast Club just left. They are hitching to Andover for supplies."

"What about Ninja Mike? Did he go with them, or is he up ahead?" I indicated the next big climb, just across the road.

"No," Lemmy said. "He is gone."

"What do you mean, gone? I didn't pass him. Where is he?"

"I mean he is done. Ninja Mike said goodbye."

. . .

Ninja Mike hadn't been injured, at least not as far as Lemmy could tell. He had last seen Ninja Mike smiling and waving from the back of a truck mysteriously headed *away* from the nearest town. Maybe Two Pack or Breakfast Club could fill in the blanks. Assuming I ever saw them again.

The next day was warmer, but still gray. Lemmy and I climbed over the Baldpates, a close pair of high, exposed rocky balds with a grassy saddle between them. High winds forced us to cut short our stay at the top. On the way down, I found an overlook with cell phone coverage and used the opportunity to arrange a shuttle to a hostel called The Cabin in Andover.

The Cabin is run by a charming retired couple known as Honey and Bear. I talked to Honey on the phone and she told me where we'd meet, so I was surprised when a younger man greeted us at the road crossing. He was closer to my age than to retirement, so I assumed he wasn't Bear. He wore an old beat-up cowboy hat and a vest with many pockets, and he looked familiar.

I waved. "Hi, I'm Green Giant. This is Lemmy."

He returned my wave and opened the trunk. "Hi guys. Honey usually drives, but The Bubble is here, so I'm helping out. I'm Squatch."

"Squatch? I saw one of your movies not too long ago. Back at Hudson's place."

He removed his hat and bowed deeply. "Guilty as charged, and at your service. How did you like it? Careful how you answer, I have all of your belongings." He shut the trunk and smiled.

I tried to count the people at The Cabin, but every time I got to 30, I started double-counting as they moved from room to room. Two Pack and Breakfast Club were nowhere to be seen, and the log book showed that they had departed that morning—probably trying to get ahead of The Bubble. There were so many hikers in town that Honey and Bear had to augment their generous bunkhouse with a squadron of trailers *à la Lode,* and even those needed to be double- and triple-booked.

Somehow I scored a bottom bunk inside the main house. The bunk's top occupant was about to leave for the day when Lemmy threw his own gear among the neat stacks of food bags and clean laundry. "I will sleep here tonight. This is the best spot."

Miss Janet was in town, and so was her friend and ally, Baltimore Jack. He knows the trail like the tops of his boots, having walked the whole thing nine times and authored the very spreadsheet Katie and I found online during our preliminary research. Baltimore Jack is also the culinary counterpart to Miss Janet's shuttle, and being an excellent cook has made Baltimore Jack huge, both in reputation and in girth. When I met him, he was mostly yellow blazing from town to town, leveraging his kitchen skills for bunk time wherever possible.

Baltimore Jack and Miss Janet helped our hosts drive everyone into town that night for resupply and an all-you-can-eat pizza buffet. We filled the restaurant to capacity, yet there was little conversation. Everyone was tired of repeating themselves. We were all nervous about Katahdin and the 100 Mile Wilderness. Our guidebooks were down to the last few pages, and we each had them memorized. Every campsite, shelter, water source, and bunk house between here and Katahdin had been evaluated, analyzed, and appraised ad nauseum.

At breakfast, I ate pancakes at the table with Miss Janet while Baltimore Jack fried bacon and talked at length about music and the weather. I tried not to look starstruck when Squatch asked me for the syrup. When it was time to go we loaded up every vehicle possible, and I corralled hikers into the van and tried to keep count while Miss Janet strapped packs to the roof.

"Okay, Miss Janet, we're almost ready. As soon as Lemmy gets in… Has anyone seen Lemmy?" Of course no one had.

I ran back into the house and Lemmy's pack was still open and on his bunk. The shower was running and I could hear him singing. I'm not even going to try, I thought, and jogged back to the van.

If I had been so naive as to continue trusting the elevation profile, I would have expected an easy day leaving Andover. A bird's-eye view reveals the truth: In southern Maine, the trail twists like a snake. In order to travel five miles north, you must first walk a quarter mile west. You might have to go up and over two 500-foot mountains along the way, but don't worry—for some reason you'll go around the third one. At the bog, you'll make a sharp right and then walk two miles northeast, through chest-deep brackish water populated by swarms of weird bugs and the weird plants that eat them. Moss-covered, partially rotted balance beams will help you get across most of the mess. Then you'll make another hard right and ascend a rocky bald, turn left and climb down the ladder, wade through more bogs, turn left at the moose, and keep going until you're on the other side of Westanuthin Pond. If the trail in southern Maine were a piece of string, and you could pick up a mile of it, pulled tight it would be at least three times as long.

And every bit of it is almost too lovely to believe. The mud is coal black and smells like a freshly opened bag of potting soil. Twisted pines are coated with green velvety lichen, and motes of dust hover in shafts of sun. I was beginning to understand what that southbounder meant about his heart hurting because he missed this place so much.

Which reminded me, the water purification drops his friend had given me were almost used up. With only two or three more towns left, I'd have to remember to add those to my list. At the end of the day I found myself camped at the base of Sawyer Notch, a steep V running parallel to the sun's path, keeping the deepest part in shadow all day. From the small brook at the bottom I could see long icicles hanging along the rock walls that were the next morning's climb.

Silver mist rolled over the mountains. Amid the yellowing trees I'd grown used to were now occasional streaks of rust, and the trail became surprisingly gentle, at least compared to the prior section. Over the next few days, I walked mostly under the cover of trees or beside large ponds. I saw my first moose track near a place called Unnamed Gap, but no moose.

When I reached the road crossing nearest Rangeley, the rust-colored leaves had bloomed into bold red. The oaks were as bright as fresh oranges, and some of the maples were purple. With the blue sky and espresso-colored mud, every primary color was represented. I stuck out my thumb and waited.

■ ■ ■

I didn't have to wait long. The first driver to stop was Stacey from the Farmhouse Inn. They had just opened down the road in Rangeley, and weren't listed in the guidebook yet. She was dropping off and picking up, so I climbed in back and thanked her for the lift.

The Farmhouse Inn is a beautiful old hotel and restaurant that sits atop rolling green acres overlooking Rangeley Lake. The bunk rooms were all renovated, and it also had plenty of bathrooms, hidden staircases, twisting hallways, and private rooms with wood burning stoves. The small store had been cleaned out by The Bubble, but a young man with a neat beard and a small pig under one arm had the solution to my problem.

"Hi, I'm Nuke," he said, offering me his non-hog hand to shake. "This little guy doesn't have a name yet." He put the pig on the floor and it ran up the nearest flight of stairs.

"Is his room up there?"

"It is. He's almost housebroken. Follow me." Nuke turned a corner, opened a screen door onto the back deck, and stepped down into the yard.

"Down there? I'm already housebroken."

We walked to the garage, where Nuke proudly showed me a row of bicycles in various states of repair before choosing one that seemed my size. "Go empty your pack and bring it back while I give this thing a little air."

When I came back, the bike was dusted off and ready, with three working gears and the seat raised to maximum height for me. Nuke gave me directions to the best pizza in town, then explained his strongly recommended gameplan. Though there were two more towns between here and Baxter State Park, the home of Mount Katahdin, neither were useful for resupply, he said. I was advised to fill my pack today at the local grocery store with everything I would need between here and the end. I should keep enough food to get me from here to Monson, at the start of the 100 Mile Wilderness, Nuke instructed. The rest, I should mail to myself at the post office in Monson.

I leaned on the handlebars and adjusted my pack. "Why am I doing all this? Surely there is some kind of general store, or gas station, or something in Monson. It's the town immediately before a place called the 100 Mile Wilderness."

He laughed. "That's exactly why there *isn't* anything there."

"But with all that foot traffic, why haven't these places grown and turned into trail towns? Like Hot Springs or Damascus?"

Nuke shook his head. "We don't even have billboards in Maine."

"What about my water drops? Is there a place that sells filters?"

"It's *wilderness*, Green Giant. After the grocery store here, the only thing you'll find for sale is fish hooks and hand warmers. Welcome to Maine." He looked at the sun. "Better hurry. Post office closes soon."

Before I pedaled off, he leaned close and whispered. "Also, uh, this might be a little embarrassing, but you need to hear it. You kind of smell like cat pee. Do you know what that means?"

"Yeah. Unfortunately I do."

. . .

I sat in front of the grocery store and tried to calculate the number of days I'd need, but there were too many unknowns. There were still a handful of medium-size climbs left, and though the majority of the Wilderness looked flat, I'd learned that looks were deceiving.

I did my best with the math and bought more just in case. When I hauled my booty out to the bike, I was faced with yet another puzzle. Even unpackaged, my haul amounted to more than my pack could hold. I tied bags to the outside straps, gripped a bag at each handlebar, and wobbled to the post office. A half dozen other hikers were double-checking each other's math as they packed food into boxes.

After a hot shower back at the inn, I tried to call Katie but couldn't get a signal. There was wifi though, so I emailed her an update. In the morning, I had a reply. She had reserved a lean-to shelter for the two of us at Katahdin Stream campground, along the AT just before Mount Katahdin.

She'd get there a few days early to take a mini-vacation in the mountains. And she would be bringing food.

I lumbered out of Rangeley with an overloaded pack, but I was ultimately glad that I listened to Nuke. The first climb out is a legend among Vortexes. The shelter at the base of Saddleback Mountain has a two-seater privy with a cribbage board between thrones. Welcome to Maine, indeed.

The three miles which follow twist and turn and rise and fall so drastically that I only realized I was going backwards when I saw the two-seater privy a second time. For nearly two hours I had passed streams and big obvious rocks that seemed familiar, figuring I had become delirious from hunger. I even had to step aside for Mecca, a hiker I had just seen in Rangeley, coming the opposite way. He gave me a confused look.

Apparently a lack of protein doesn't merely make you smell like pee—it makes you stupid too. I chewed a melted protein bar while I tried to put myself back on course. As I realized the magnitude of my error, I ate a second one and then a third. They didn't make me smarter, but it made me feel better about my mistake.

My blunder cost me time and supplies; the shameful fists of chocolate that followed the protein bars meant that I had to eat less over the next few days. That was unfortunate, because the medium-size climbs weren't so medium after all. I had to scale back on my dwindling water drops too. The recommended dose was probably set by the government, I rationalized, and was no doubt twice the amount truly required. Erring on the safe side, I settled somewhere in the middle. There was little choice.

A day and a half later, I was on my way down the north side of Avery Peak, the last high point before a hundred miles of lowland. From the summit, the smaller hills below looked like endless mounds of gold and copper coins shining in the sun. Clusters of plum-colored maples formed chunks of garnet tossed in among the treasure.

Nightwalker crashed through the brush and into the clearing so noisily that I genuinely thought a bear was charging. The last time I had seen him was in the Smokies. In the cage. "Nightwalker!"

"Holy shit! Is that—now wait...Jolly Green Giant?"

"Close enough." We shook hands. "I guess you're flip-flopping after all."

"You know it, man. And I need to hustle too. It's getting cold up there! Hey, whatever happened to that crazy girl you were hiking with?"

"Good question. She's somewhere back there." I pointed behind me, the way he was headed. "When you see her, tell her I said hi."

We both hiked on.

At the bottom of the mountain, the trail flattened out and followed the shoreline of East Flagstaff Lake. At the far end of the lake, I found a large campsite alongside a flat pebble beach. Long hunks of driftwood had been arranged into a comfortable seating area surrounding a large stone fire pit, already stacked full with dry branches. The fire lit easily and I had no need for my tent.

As the sun set, I stripped to my shorts and waded into the lake to feel the cool water splash on my shins. The rocks were all perfectly smooth disks, and walking on them barefoot in the gentle waves was like getting a foot massage.

The sky darkened and I stayed in the water, watching the red mountains slowly dim to dark shadows, massive black humps backlit by a tapestry of stars. The Milky Way blazed overhead, a golden streak against a perfect charcoal sky. Yellow light bounced off the water, and I had to squint against it while I rechecked my math.

If I eat the last tortilla tonight, and put the mayonnaise packet on it, that leaves me one Clif bar for tomorrow. And for the day after that? A raisin. I had eaten my last pinch of homemade granola for second breakfast earlier that morning, and when I reached the bottom of the bag, I spared the last raisin, just in case. This was that case.

I closed my eyes, took a breath, and fell back into the water. When I came up, I opened my eyes and floated on my back under the galaxy, smiling. I had the stars, and a raisin. What more did I need? I took another breath and said it aloud. "I am grateful for today."

# 25 LANDING

WAY BACK AT THE START, I made an assumption about hunger. That assumption was that I knew what the word meant. I thought I knew what hunger was the time I sprinted to the bottom of a hill for a slice of pizza offered by a stranger. I thought it was getting to the top of a mountain and needing to save part of the beef jerky for later.

I've never been out of food in my life. Even as a bachelor, when the fridge was "empty" it still had eggs or old mustard packets to suck on for calories if it came down to it. Or I could just walk to the store, like a person. Even during the hardest parts of my childhood we could run across the street and share a plate of watery spaghetti with grandma.

Real hunger makes you hallucinate. It interrupts every thought, every action. If necessity is the mother of invention, hunger is its weird uncle who sleeps in the woods, dreaming up ways to trap and eat squirrels.

It was a long way from my magnificent pebble beach to Monson, but at least the terrain and the weather were on my side. First, I was finished climbing mountains, at least until Katahdin, the god of thunder. A few tall spots and rocky balds, but no more knee breakers. It would be mostly rivers and ponds, with warm days and cool clear nights.

I split the last Clif bar in two, and the evening that I feasted on the second half, my stomach grumbled all night at Pleasant Pond shelter. I dreamed that I had discovered a previously forgotten protein bar in the depths of my pack. I awoke and drank a full bottle of water to trick myself into thinking my belly was full, but the plan backfired when I had to pee it all out an hour later.

Then I remembered that I still had my raisin. I dug it out of my pack and looked at it.

If I eat this raisin, I have nothing, I thought. Reluctantly, I closed the bag and put it away. The loons and I watched the sun rise, and then I hiked on toward Monson, and the post office with my food.

That afternoon, I was the grateful recipient of real trail magic. There were no angels or magicians involved; this magic came directly from the trail itself in the form of blueberries.

At the top of Moxie Bald, just a few feet from the trail, there they were. It was a small bush, and they were impossibly late in the season, but I wasn't hallucinating. I took off my pack and crawled into the bushes, picking blueberries and eating them one by one, completely lost in the ecstasy of eating again. When I stopped munching I was pretty far from the trail, though I could still see my pack. I licked and sucked my fingers, savoring every bit of sugary juice, wanting to stay there forever. But every minute I picked berries left me a minute further from the mailbox many miles ahead with all the *real* food in it. I filled my pockets with berries and was walking back towards my pack when something else blue caught my eye.

Snagged on a low branch near the trail was a filthy but familiar bandanna. I bent over and sniffed the brown stains: coffee. Two Pack was here not too long ago.

I now had a mission. I tied the bandanna to my pack and vowed to return it to its rightful owner. This would give me something other than food to focus on while I marched.

The diversion worked. When I made my camp a few miles south of Monson, I had actually forgotten the berries in my pockets. They were a real surprise for the second time. I turned my pockets inside out to pick out the remaining pulp, sucking at the purple stains like a baby at a nipple.

• • •

I still had my raisin when I saw the cabins at the outfitters two miles from Monson. All of the doors and windows were wide open for cleaning, and the man out front was about to set fire to a good-sized brush pile.

"Wow, am I glad to see you!" I said, hurrying toward him. "Are you guys open?"

He took off his gloves and put them in a pocket. "Just closed for the season yesterday."

"Is there anything left in the store? I'll gladly pay for anything edible. I'll even eat gum."

"Sorry, we're all cleaned out. You can check the hiker lounge though. Might be some old ramen or something in the donation box. You're welcome to it if you can find anything."

I barely heard him finish and was already halfway to the cabin he indicated. The donation box was empty, but there was a half-eaten bag of unsalted peanuts on the table next to a warm, unopened can of Mountain Dew. I popped the lid and chugged, and sweet life-giving bubbles fizzled on my tongue and in my throat with every greedy gulp. My eyes watered and my sinuses stung. I fell to my knees and released a long, satisfying burp.

The guy outside laughed. I wiped my eyes and caught my breath. "Do these nuts belong to anyone?"

"Nope. Have at 'em."

Carrying the bag and cracking shells with one hand, I walked to town.

Nuke was right: Monson consisted of two hostels, one open restaurant, and the post office. When the clerk passed my boxes across the counter I could smell the meat and chocolate inside. I drooled a little as I paid, and tore off the tape before I made it to the door.

At a hostel named Shaw's, an old woman chain smoking Benson & Hedges took my cash, pointed to my room with a shaky yellow finger, and returned to her romance novel. The young woman working inside was much happier to see me, and welcomed me with cookies and clean sheets.

I unpacked in the bunkroom alone. Two couples were staying overnight in the private rooms. The five of us sat together and conducted a mini hiker grapevine at dinner, where I learned that The Bubble had split. Half of them were a day or two ahead, the other half a day behind. According to the folks at Shaw's, we were the only ones in the middle.

Everyone was still nervous about the 100 Mile Wilderness, and we all wanted to get through it as quickly as possible. The finish line was in sight, and the last month of hiking had felt like driving a sports car through a series of red lights.

"How many days are you going to do it in? I'm trying for four."

"I heard that this one guy, he did it in three."

"No way!"

"Really. I could see it, though. Like, your adrenaline would get going and you can't sleep, so you night hike. I could totally see it."

"Yeah. How about you, Green Giant? How many days are you doing it in?"

I closed one eye, did some math, chewed a forkful of dinner and swallowed. "Seven? Maybe eight. We'll see."

"Are you okay? Are you like, sick or something? Or hurt?"

"No, I just..." *I just don't want this to end.* "I just remembered they have the bucket service here. We should do that."

The operator of Shaw's is one of a handful of people with access to a private logging road that intersects the AT somewhere near the middle of the final vast woods. The road is terribly inconvenient to locate and is behind a locked gate, which means zero chance of hitchhiking on it. But for a reasonable fee, Shaw's will give you a five gallon plastic bucket which can easily hold enough food for the next 50 miles for several hikers. They will hang it in a bearproof location near the road crossing and paint your name on it. This is the only way to resupply in the 100 Mile Wilderness.

"It's like, *fifty dollars.* No way."

I looked at them like they were crazy. "That's only ten dollars each."

"Uh, no, we're couples. So it's twenty dollars each. We're not falling for that one."

I gave up. I had a full plate of mashed potatoes in front of me and one-fifth of a supply bucket ready to go on the back porch. "That's okay. I already paid anyway, so I'll be taking eight days." And not going hungry.

"You already did the bucket thing?"

"Yeah."

"Oh, cool! Hey, can we like, put some stuff in it?"

"No way."

. . .

The sign that the Maine Appalachian Trail Club has posted at the southern end of the 100 Mile Wilderness says: THERE ARE NO PLACES TO OBTAIN SUPPLIES OR GET HELP UNTIL ABOL BRIDGE 100 MILES NORTH. DO NOT

*ATTEMPT THIS SECTION UNLESS YOU HAVE A MINIMUM OF 10 DAYS SUPPLIES AND ARE FULLY EQUIPPED. THIS IS THE LONGEST WILDERNESS SECTION OF THE ENTIRE A.T. AND ITS DIFFICULTY SHOULD NOT BE UNDERESTIMATED.*

It ends with, *GOOD HIKING!*

We were the only carload of hikers to be dropped off at the trail that day. The couples took pictures by the sign, and after they headed north, I lingered until I couldn't hear them anymore. I waited a few more minutes just to be sure I was alone.

Seven miles into the Wilderness, I arrived at Little Wilson Falls. A narrow stream flowed over a wide bed of smooth slate, funneling into a tight notch at the top of a 75-foot drop into a box canyon. Trees of every color surrounded massive rock columns. The sun filtered through the leaves and shone on the rocks like the light through a stained glass window.

Just above the roaring falls I found an easy rock hop to a footpath on the other side. It led to a hidden campsite just far enough upstream to soften the roar down to a soothing whisper. It was the middle of the day, I'd only traveled seven miles, and my hands were setting up my tent as if they had a mind of their own. Well, I thought, looks like I live here now.

I spent the afternoon climbing around on the slate columns, basking in the sun. At night I built a fire on the rocks near the water. No one could possibly hear me, so I stood at the top of the falls and howled at the stars.

The next morning, I dunked my feet in the cool water beside my fire and ate generously. The package I mailed myself from Rangeley had extra protein bars, and they appeared to be working. Either that or I was losing my sense of smell completely.

With nowhere to buy refills, I had finally run out of water purification drops, and was now just filtering stream water through the blue bandanna, and that was it. Sometimes I'd miss a twig or small stone, but as Bad Dinner claimed, that's what a mustache is for.

My next stop was the shelter at Cloud Pond. I pitched my tent three feet from the still water and learned in the morning why the place was called Cloud Pond. Despite the previous night's clear sky, I woke up in a perfect whiteout. My headlamp was useless, and I found my way up to the shelter by feeling the ground. I wrote in the log book: *Lemmy, I am going slow on purpose.*

I stopped writing. Should I have included Voldemort in the note? Was that even remotely possible at this point? I wished, but I also knew better. I simply added my signature smiley, closed the book, and crawled back to my tent in the fog.

While I was packing I heard a tremendous splash, followed by a heavy thud and a loud *PLOONK!* My first thought was that a small car had somehow crashed into the pond. A second splash was followed by something that sounded like a moo, and then more splashing. Peering through the fog, I discerned the hazy forms of two moose, a bull and a cow. The bull was shaking the water from its huge rack, and I concluded that getting smacked by an antler that big would be fatal. Fortunately the creatures were on the far shore and posed no danger. I watched them laze about in the muck and silently gathered my tent.

My resupply cache had been delivered without a hitch. I opened the plastic tub and knelt beside it in the leaves, tearing open a protein bar with my teeth. The only sound besides the wind rustling in the treetops was me grunting and smacking my lips as I hunched like a predator over the guts of my plastic prey. I wiped my hands on my pants and briefly considered taking the bucket. If things got bad again, I could use it to trap a squirrel.

That night, necessity unexpectedly went into labor. Around 2 a.m. I felt water on my face—a lot of it. As I sat up, chilly water ran down my hair into my shirt and down my back. The rain fly was flapping uselessly in the wind, and rain was spattering down from the screened opening at the top of the tent and blowing in sideways through my door.

I pushed everything into the foot of my tent, as far from the opening as I could, and checked my shoes for slugs. Finding none, I put them on and donned my raincoat, then stepped into the rain and flicked on my headlamp.

The zipper on my rain fly had broken, and when the flap fell open, the entire night's catch had dumped onto my face. I had no sewing kit, and tape wouldn't hold. The nearest shelter was a day away. Eventually, I hung my raincoat over the opening like an umbrella. I only had to wake up and fix it twice, and in the morning it didn't matter because the rain had stopped.

Just to be safe, I spent the next night in a shelter. I left Lemmy another note, and it rained again. I dreamed that I was still in my tent and that my raincoat had fallen onto my face. Then I realized a mouse was burrowing into my beard, looking for warmth, nesting material, or crumbs. I panicked, pulling out some whiskers along with the stowaway, and threw him across the shelter. He squeaked on impact with the wall, followed by a second little thunk an instant later, and then the sound of tiny scurrying feet.

Luck shone on me one final time, my final night in the 100 Mile Wilderness. I didn't need a shelter, and I didn't need my rain fly. I found a campsite on flat, soft ground, surrounded by tall pines and rainbow-colored softwoods. The forest was lit like the inside of a cathedral, and I knew as I moved through it that Katie was near. If she had stuck to her plan—as she always does—then she had been in Maine for two days already.

I wondered if she had explored this far, and expected her at every turn. It wasn't realistic; I was still 20 miles from the base camp she would have just set up for us after driving for two days. She wasn't hiking this far. I was still alone. But it was fun to imagine, and the idea propelled me forward.

My food bag was nearly empty again, but this time it no longer mattered. There were no more resupplies. I binged on pasta, following it up with nearly a pound of hard salami and a block of cheese. For dessert there was a special treat: some dark chocolate with a hint of hot pepper. I washed the whole bar down with a cold bottle of honest-to-goodness crystal clear Maine spring water. They charge you for this in the grocery store, I thought, and chugged another.

The rushing of a nearby river began lulling me to sleep by my small fire. I didn't need my tent, but climbed in anyway. The trail had, after all, been full of surprises. The night was cold and clear, and the moon woke me up three times. My adrenaline was responsible for the other two times, and the final reveille was due to a combination of sunshine and my full bladder.

Light was hitting the mist from the river at just the right angle to produce tiny rainbows. The little splashes of pee at the base of the poor tree I chose did the same. I must have stood up too quickly when getting out of my tent because I briefly saw spots. Steadying against the tree and taking a deep breath, I felt dinner gurgle and settle in my gut, followed by an urge to fart. Only what happened next wasn't a fart.

I let go of the tree and yanked my shorts to my knees with a split second to spare, barely avoiding the powerful jet of soupy brown goo that sprayed from my ass. I wobbled forward and pulled my shorts further down just in time to miss the second stream as it exploded into a grotesque pile between my feet.

The volume was surprising and it came with no sense of relief; its origin a mystery. Crouching there frozen in place, unsure whether there would be more, I waddled away from the mess and did my best to clean myself off with leaves. My bathroom bag was in my tent, and I was *not* going in there without at least a cursory wipe-down.

Once I was satisfied that my body was properly sanitized, I disposed of my waste. Fortunately, I had walked far enough from the campsite and the river that I didn't have to worry about moving it. I dug a hole beside the pile deep enough to create a miniature cave-in, a shit sinkhole. When it collapsed, I filled it in and covered it with the heaviest rock I could move without hurting myself. No one ever needs to find this, I thought.

Surprisingly, I felt pretty good after what I'd just been through, including the digging and heavy lifting, the lack of rest, the horrible diet, and so on. My adrenaline had been coursing for days, and I couldn't sleep. I didn't night hike, but I certainly could have. Things were coming to a head. I was burning up on reentry, that was all. With stress comes a little rumble-gut. I gave it no more thought as I folded up my little portable home for the last time on the AT.

. . .

Abol Bridge has a tiny campsite and general store at the northern edge of the 100 Mile Wilderness. There is also a bridge, from which one can usually see Mount Katahdin. The bridge was foggy that day, but the general store was open, and I rushed in, eager to buy something hot to eat. I found a ham and cheese sandwich to microwave while I chatted with the clerk.

"You're the first one today," he said.

"No kidding? How were the last few days?" I asked, moving to the ice cream counter.

"Busy, then slow. We had some weirdos yesterday. About 50 the day before. That's why there's not much left, sorry." The ice cream was gone.

I got my sandwich, thanked him and paid, and stepped back outside, where a young man with a tattered pack and a clean-shaven face recognized me. He ran across the parking lot. "Hey, Green Giant! You're a hot commodity, did you know that?"

I held up a finger and wondered why everyone felt compelled to ask me questions while I was eating. Perhaps because hikers are always eating. "I'm so sorry. I don't recognize people with naked faces," I said, drawing an imaginary circle around my bearded chin.

He re-introduced himself as Red Foot. We'd met only briefly a thousand miles ago, and he'd had a beard then.

"Well, thanks for remembering me at least. I'm flattered. And what do you mean by 'hot commodity?'"

"There are some people back there pretty excited to catch up with you," he said, pointing a thumb over his shoulder.

*Some?* "Is one of them Lemmy? Is that how you knew who I was?"

"Yep. And Voldemort talks about you a lot too."

I was dumbstruck. Lemmy I expected; I'd been leaving him notes and had even slowed down for him. I knew where he was. But Voldemort? Megan?

Red Foot laughed. "Yeah. She said you'd be surprised. She also said that if she catches you coming down Katahdin, she'll slit your throat. Or something like that, there were a few variations. I stopped paying attention."

"How far back are they?"

"Oh, you'll see them today."

I gaped while Red Foot put his pack and poles by the door and walked into the store. Lemmy and Voldemort were probably ten miles back. I finished my sandwich, leaned forward, and hiked as fast as I could. I didn't want it to be over. I wanted another hundred miles. Katie was ten miles ahead, which gave me an unexpected burst of energy. I crawled over rocks and logs and clawed through moss. I balanced on planks and crossed rivers in my shoes and socks, not caring.

When I turned the last corner and saw the row of shelters at the base of Katahdin, I stumbled to a halt. My car was parked beside one, and I could hear a familiar voice humming from inside. Cupping my hands around my mouth, I leaned back and shouted. "WHOOOOOOO-HOOOO!"

Katie's head appeared from behind the shelter wall, and the instant she saw me she ran at me smiling. We collided and wrapped our arms around each other right there beside our little base camp. Noticing that her arms reached much farther around me than usual, she gave me a quizzical look, then tugged me back to her. We kissed, and I felt her wet cheek through my beard.

She leaned back again and wiped her eyes. She laughed and smiled and we kissed again.

Finally pushing me back, she sniffed. "You look...so thin. Oh my god. Wow, I missed you." I hugged her again and she whispered in my ear. "Oh, and happy birthday!"

It had indeed taken me eight days to traverse the 100 Mile Wilderness. I went in on October 1 and came out on October 8, my 45th birthday.

I threw my pack into the car. I didn't need it any more. Katie brought me clean clothes straight from my dresser at home. They smelled like our dryer. She also brought food. It reminded me of Clingmans Dome: vegetables, fruit, hot dogs, chips, drinks...and a cake. With candles.

Just as I was opening my mouth to complement her on the cake, someone tackled us. I was briefly reminded of nearly being flung from Mount Washington, but this time I landed safely on the floor of the shelter in a tangle of arms. Katie and I sat up and Voldemort, our assailant, shouted, "GREEN GIANT! KATIE! OH MY GOD WE MADE IT! WE'RE HERE!"

She grabbed Katie by the hands, let go and bounced in place beside our car.

"Megan, you look amazing! Damn, look at you!"

She rolled up her sleeve and flexed. "Aw, yeah. What do you think about that!?" She raised her other arm. "Boom!"

I was about to complement her as well when I was blinded by an approaching headlamp. "You know what they say—"

"Lemmy!" Katie interrupted, hugging him and kissing his koala hat on the nose.

He blushed. "Mmm! You are warm!"

I was dizzy with joy. "Hey, buddy!"

Megan, now finished flexing, asked Lemmy what he had been about to say.

"They say that the women on the AT all turn into Greek goddesses, and the men turn into trolls," he said. "And look, it is true. This girl belongs on a gold coin." He shook his head at me, already with mustard smeared on my new pants and leaves in my hair from being tackled. "You belong under a bridge."

Megan's family had come to meet her and reserved a small shelter too. Katie lit the candles on the cake and everyone sang to me. While we were eating, a ranger joined us. "Whose birthday is it?"

Everyone quieted. "Mine, sir. Sorry if we were being too loud."

"Not at all! I came over to say happy birthday to whoever it was." He shined a light into the hatchback. "Cokes? It's his birthday. You guys should be having beer to celebrate."

"I thought there was no alcohol allowed in the park," Katie said.

"Well, that's what they say," he smiled. "But as long as no one's causing a problem, no one really cares."

Megan had a bottle of champagne ready for the summit tomorrow. "What about this?"

"Don't drop it, bring it back down, and be smart."

Katie seemed surprised, but Voldemort and I weren't. We'd heard the same talk countless times the whole way. Common sense really meant something out here.

We thanked him and he congratulated us. We ate more cake and I huddled between Katie and Lemmy, sleeping in a shelter for the last time on the AT.

. . .

Standing at the base of Mount Katahdin, you would never guess that you were anywhere near the tallest mountain in Maine. The summit is five miles away and almost a vertical mile up. From the ground, any tall pile of rocks or grove of pines is enough to obscure the true scale of the behemoth.

It starts like any other trail. There is a gentle approach through moss and conifers as it rises along a wide, clear stream with plenty of falls and crossings. Surrounded by trees, this first part could be anywhere in Maine.

While we were loading our day packs, Lemmy told us how they caught up. Megan had lucked out with only sunny, clear days in the Whites, making it through them in half the time it had taken me. She caught Lemmy halfway through the 100 Mile Wilderness and reminded him about our epic night hike up Roan Mountain while she goaded him into a *50-mile day.*

"She was like the Terminator, Green Giant! She would stop for nothing!"

They hiked continuously for a day and a half, reading my notes and sleeping only once, for 20 minutes. Lemmy seemed to have forgiven her, because he kept chasing after her for the first mile that day.

Then we literally hit a wall. A towering rock monolith was studded with steel rebar pounded in to form rungs and handholds. Were it not for these, we definitely would have needed ropes. At the top of the wall, we zigged and zagged through more towers, each 20 to 30 vertical feet, separated by narrow flat places with only enough room for one person to stand. Trekking poles were of no use here.

As we climbed, the trees thinned, and when they were gone the wind picked up. We had just stopped to put on extra layers when we noticed a hiker with a long white beard resting nearby. He waved when we passed, and we noticed with shock that his beard wasn't actually white—it was covered with ice.

"Holy shit, dude! Is it really that bad up there? I mean, congratulations! But is that ice?"

"It is," he said. "Once you get up to the Tableland, everything is covered. It's probably low 20s, maybe upper teens up there. Look at this." He snatched a water bottle from his pack, unscrewed the lid, and turned it upside down. Nothing came out. "Frozen solid. And I was only up there for about half an hour. Once you get up to the Tableland, the wind is insane."

Lemmy frowned. "This sounds like hell to me." Voldemort, spurred on by impending mortal danger, was already 100 yards up the trail, charging toward it.

The Tableland marks the beginning of the third and final phase of the climb. After several miles of near vertical boulder scrambles, we ultimately pulled ourselves up to a massive plateau that resembled the set of a vintage science fiction movie, an otherworldly expanse with basketball-sized rocks and stunted alpine brush forming a vast frozen hump.

The trail was marked by thin ropes and low cairns drawing us ever upward toward the horizon, toward Baxter Peak and the famous wooden sign. Rime ice covered every surface.

The god of thunder must have been about, because the summit was shrouded in gray freezing mist. Megan and Lemmy succumbed to their adrenaline and sprinted up the rugged incline all the way to the top, vanishing into the clouds.

Katie and I were almost to the summit when we saw Lemmy walking back down toward us. "What the hell is he doing?" Katie shouted over the wind. When he reached us I asked him the same question.

"I have to go back down," he answered. "I am going to die up there."

I made a hook with my right pinky finger and shook it at him. Then I pointed back to the summit.

"It's so cold!" he protested. "I am freezing!"

"If I give you extra layers to wear, will you go back up?" I shouted, pulling him close. "We have to do this together! This isn't just any other mountain—we pinky swore!"

Rooting through my pack, I pulled out my down jacket and the wind pants that Katie had brought me. They weren't going to fit over his own bulky pants, so I cut the waist band with my knife. "You'll have to use your pack strap to hold them up!"

While the three of us put on the last of our layers, the wind pushed the remaining clouds away, and as we crested the last rise, we could see Megan at the summit surrounded by bright blue sky. Ornamenting the sign were balloons and a happy birthday banner Lemmy had given her to unfurl while he came back down and stalled me. A lump formed in my throat.

"I am a day late, Green Giant, but happy birthday!" He hugged me, then hugged Katie, and we took the last few steps together.

There were no more hand-over-hand scrambles, no more switchbacks. There was only one more pile of rocks, crusted with needles of ice. There was only one more white blaze and it was on the sign, straight ahead.

The 100 Mile Wilderness stretched out dizzyingly behind the sign, and Megan, and the balloons. The gold and copper treasure of autumn had expanded, and the forest below exploded with color as far as the haziest notch in the farthest horizon.

The trail stopped going up, because there was no more trail.

I shut my eyes and was transported back to Springer Mountain with Katie and Mark. I took another step and felt my feet pounding on all those jagged rocks. A swirling vision of hundreds of instant pasta sides flashed behind my closed eyelids. The wind on my face was the pelting storm that pinned us down in the Whites. All the bug bites, blisters, bruises, and blood were for this. All that pain, joy, shivering, and loneliness. All that beauty. The long, unnamed places between horizons and water stops. All those sunsets and sunrises. Multitudes of birdsong, howling coyotes, crickets, and frogs. The laughter of other hikers around a fire at the next shelter.

Feeling dizzy, I opened my eyes again. There was the sign. I moved closer in slow motion, drawn to it. I could see Megan holding balloons and Katie pulling her camera from its pouch. I leaned forward and kissed the sign.

"I am in hell. Can I go back down now?" Lemmy begged, snapping me out of my trance.

"As soon as we get a group picture, buddy." I pulled my friends in for a tight hug as tears froze on my cheek. Everything was finally right.

Megan bit off one of her gloves and fumbled with numb fingers to open the champagne. There was a loud *pop!* but no spray of bubbles. It was partly frozen, almost turned to slush. We were inside a freezer at the top of the world.

We were still happy to share the bottle. Katie took our picture and then asked Megan to get one of just the two of us by the sign. As Katie hugged me and kissed my frozen cheek, she whispered, "Congratulations. How do you feel?"

I closed my eyes again, and once more I was transported through time. As I exhaled, I recalled the wind on my face the morning I met Flat Feet, the day Green Giant came to be. The Triple Crowner had asked me the very same question.

"I feel fantastic."

I closed my eyes one last time, and for a moment I could almost hear the old man's voice. *Of course you do. You're just getting started.*

# EPILOGUE

THE HIKE DOESN'T END at Katahdin. It never does. Baxter Peak is five miles and change from the campsites below. It takes the average thru-hiker two or three hours to reach the top, and the rest of their lives to get back down.

Megan drove home with her folks and we left Lemmy in Miss Janet's care. Katie and I took our time getting home. We visited some of her relatives in Maine and spent a night in Boston with Joe, who did not wear a fake mustache this time. We even stayed with Lode in Pennsylvania, where Katie was amazed by the Garage Mahal, and Lode let us sleep in the house.

At each of these places, everyone was shocked by my appearance. They put heaps of food before me, but I couldn't eat. This loss of appetite, I reasoned, was because I had suddenly switched from walking to sitting all day. Burning zero calories in the passenger seat, I didn't need to consume any.

Or sometimes I felt too tired to eat. I woke up queasy each day, and continued to have frequent unpleasant bouts of diarrhea. I blamed that on switching back to real food. My gut was confused, that was all.

Katie finally convinced me to see a doctor after two weeks. I am 6'3" and I weighed 158 pounds the day I went in. The doctor drew blood and ran a bevy of other tests, and two days later he called me personally to explain I was carrying a crowd of unwanted guests in my belly, thanks to drinking unpurified water. "You have a *lot* of Giardia. And C. diff, too. I'll phone in a script for you."

Otherwise, he congratulated me on having the vitals of an athlete. Three days later, things began to settle down in my gastrointestinal tract. I have since added "backup water treatment" to every gear list.

The months immediately after the hike are hardest. After seasons of sun and wind on my face, still air and artificial light felt *wrong*. I opened every door and window in the house, even though it was November. Snapping out of trances, I would find myself standing on the porch, staring at nothing, having no recollection of going outside.

I kicked off the covers at night and pushed Katie away, thinking I was still in a shelter and that she was Lemmy, crowding my precious little personal space. In my dreams, I was asleep on the trail—not beside it, but actually on it, nestled safely in the deep groove worn down by thousands of boot-clad feet.

■　■　■

For me the sleeplessness began my very first night home, but for a reason I never could have predicted.

A relatively new and modern trail tradition, one only practical in recent years, is the "selfie" beard video. For as long as digital cameras have been around, hikers have been compiling picture-a-day beard animations, compressing six months of facial hair cultivation down to five *captivating* minutes of film.

I had no plans to start on mine just yet, but one shot in particular caught my attention. I was glowering at the camera from arm's length, sweaty, disheveled, and clearly pissed off. It must have been the day of the lone raisin.

For fun, I cropped the image and pasted it beside a shot I took from the plaque at Springer Mountain. My bare cheeks were round, I still wore glasses, and I didn't have burn marks or duct tape on any of my clothing. I added two more stills: before and after double-biceps in the hallway at home.

I grouped the shots into a single image and as a lark, posted it to Reddit, the self-proclaimed "front page of the internet." I told Katie I was going to bed early and brushed my teeth. I rinsed, spat, and checked my messages one more time. There were three, each regarding the picture.

One was a congratulatory note, and the next two were strangers asking questions about hiking the trail. It wasn't *too* late, so I responded, happy to help, and by the time I was finished, there were five more. Then twelve. Then a hundred.

Within an hour, over a thousand people had been exposed to a double-whammy of me in my underpants: pudgy on the left, near death on the right. Dizzy and exhausted from four days in a car (not to mention five months in the woods,) I collapsed into my bed, temporarily forgetting the brief burst of attention.

When I awoke, nearly three million people had seen the picture.

Every inbox I owned was flooded with questions and congratulations. Numerous "click-bait" websites had latched onto the image, and while I slept the social media breakfast crowd scrutinized my shorts. This persisted for weeks, and to be honest, I didn't mind. It gave me the chance to talk about the trail, and to share some stories. In a way it was the ultimate group therapy.

My 15 minutes were extended slightly when Mountain Xpress, an Asheville based magazine, interviewed me. Very rarely, someone on the street or in an elevator would look at me sideways and say, "Hey...aren't you that guy?" It still happens, and I confess: I don't mind.

"The trail has a way of staying with you," the retired couple back in Virginia had warned me. I had no idea.

A year later, Katie, Mark and I revisited the AT and hiked together for a week near NOC, Land of the Noonday Sun. We were over a hundred miles north of Springer Mountain when I encountered a SOBO nearing the end of his trek. While he and I talked, his face brightened as recognition dawned. He asked me if I was the underwear guy. I blushed. He had never even heard of the trail until seeing those pictures.

Not a day goes by.

• • •

While adjusting to the civilized world, I learned that Ninja Mike yellow blazed up to Katahdin, where he defeated the final boss in spectacular fashion. Lemmy is now back in Israel studying art, and Voldemort has a job at a hospital. Working with children. Ugh.

I am incredibly fortunate to live in a part of the country renowned for its natural beauty. My post-hike rehabilitation over the course of countless hours has consisted mainly of writing this book on a tiny computer while sitting by a waterfall or huddled in my tent.

A year after climbing Katahdin, my feet still hurt. If I walk barefoot on my hardwood floor for more than a few minutes, the invisible bunched-up socks come back. The doctor says the damage may be permanent, though if I'm lucky the nerves might grow back over the span of years. Strangely enough, the one thing that brings fast, temporary relief for my feet is to use them. Hiking seems to work best.

. . .

I eventually went back to work for a small software firm, similar to what I'd done before. The job allowed me to travel again, and provided me with much needed focus; besides, standing on my porch appreciating the wind wasn't paying the bills.

The work was the same as I'd remembered it, and I even teamed up with some old colleagues. But something was off. The lights hummed. The air never moved. The water coolers were haunted, and none of the ghosts were happy.

I kept thinking about the man who died on the mountain. His ghost was mid-smile, about to say something.

I started having the dream again, the one where I ran through cubicles, smashing plants and monitors with my trekking pole. It was cathartic, not quite a nightmare. I could have dealt with it, had it remained a nightmare, but I started having the dream during meetings. While I was presenting.

The fast pace of modern data was too much. I had spent the previous year downgrading my brain's operating system to a much older version, and jumping back into the deep end was like filling a tea cup with a fire hose. When there was no room left in my head for any more ones and zeros, I short-circuited. The dreams became full blown panic attacks, complete with sweaty palms and heart palpitations. I was starting to look like the guy in the "after" picture again.

When I resigned, I tried my best to explain what had happened that day in the clouds. A good friend and colleague did his best to understand and remarked, "The trail really changed you."

Actually, it was all those years on the corporate ladder that changed me. The trail simply put me back where I needed to be.

. . .

One of the most commonly asked questions was: *How did the trail change you?* It was so common that people started asking before we were done, even as early as Georgia.

Unless you already were one at the start, a hike of that duration makes you feel like a rock star, as though you can do anything. In retrospect, what we did was ridiculous, and few of us could even truly say why we tried.

For some reason, strangers were impressed. Day hikers had begun congratulating us weeks before the finish line. The collective adrenaline from the final hundred miles and the epic scale of the ultimate climb elevated everyone's self-confidence to all-time highs, trivializing formerly daunting goals, presumably for life.

Along the way we learned that everything *is* actually possible. All you have to do is decide. Be passionate about something. Choose a path, and go. Take a step. And then another. Keep chipping away until that thing, no matter how ridiculously impossible it seemed at first, really *is* a memory that you can look back on. And *then* you can skip the hard parts if you like.

All you have to do is take the first step.

I'm sorry that the last part of my epic journey contained so much poop. But when you're telling a true story, you don't always get to decide how it ends—only how you react to it.

And to be honest, I don't think this is the end at all. This hike was just one step in a much bigger plan to achieve more life goals. There's still much to do. There are so many trails and mountains out there.

And when I tackle those mountains, standing at the base feeling tiny and insignificant, I stomp my foot and whinny. I clear my lungs of bad air and remind myself to be grateful for the chance to take on the challenge at all, because as the colonel reminds me in my dreams, I really am just getting started.

# ACKNOWLEDGEMENTS

This book is already a clown car as it is. There is no way I could fit any more characters into it. I was only able to include a small fraction of the hundreds of amazing and inspirational people I met along the way, on and off the trail. If I were to include everyone and tell each person's story with the detail they truly deserve, you would be reading a five-volume epic with a thousand pages per book.

First and foremost, none of this would be possible without Katie Farrar. She is my trail boss, my favorite hiking partner and the one person I'm happiest to see when I finally stumble into the glow of the fire.

Thank you, Mark Calcagni, not only for the incredible cover art and illustrations, but also for inspiring Katie and me to push ourselves and to keep exploring.

I am especially grateful to have Mark Houser not only as an editor, but as a friend. We've been going on walks and telling stories since we were kids. Here's hoping the tradition lasts.

This project was made possible in part with help from Kickstarter. A big thank you to those supporters: Priscilla Farrar, Gary and Becky Farrar, Joe and Kirstin Melchionda, Sam and Lisa Hutcheson, Travis Michaels and Angelica Beck, Ed Breault, Rusty Manley, Tom Corzine, Doreen Hoover, Mark Houser, Dave and Marcy Nisbeth, Daniel Rubin, Kevin Beatty, Adam and Mary George, Dale Penn and Brian Hunt, and Chris Davis.

## ABOUT THE AUTHOR

Gary Sizer was born in New Castle, Pa. Years of military service and software consulting fed his passion for travel, which he now enjoys full time. He is an adventure writer and hiker currently residing in the hills near Asheville, N.C. After he walked the Appalachian Trail in 2014, his before and after pictures went viral, and since then 3 million people have seen him in his underpants.

## FOR MORE INFORMATION

Contact Gary Sizer at TheNextShelter@gmail.com

Visit WheresTheNextShelter.com
to see photos, Lemmy's cartoons, and the original blog posts

Read Gary Sizer's guest blog posts, stay up to date on AT news, follow current thru-hikers, and prepare for your own AT hike at AppalachianTrials.com

To get *The A.T. Guide* that Gary Sizer used on his hike (which is updated annually) visit TheATGuide.com

Learn more about and support the
Appalachian Trail at AppalachianTrail.org

Learn about Leave No Trace principles at LNT.org

Made in the USA
Middletown, DE
08 June 2025